Comprehensive Planning
for Safe Learning
Environments

School Based Practice in Action Series
Series Editors
Rosemary B. Mennuti, Ed.D., NCSP
and
Ray W. Christner, Psy.D., NCSP
Philadelphia College of Osteopathic Medicine

This series provides school-based practitioners with concise practical guidebooks that are designed to facilitate the implementation of evidence-based programs into school settings, putting the best practices in action.

Published Titles

Implementing Response-to-Intervention in Elementary and Secondary Schools: Procedures to Assure Scientific-Based Practices
Matthew K. Burns and Kimberly Gibbons

Assessment and Intervention for Executive Function Difficulties
George McCloskey, Lisa A. Perkins, and Bob Van Divner

Resilient Playgrounds
Beth Doll

Comprehensive Planning for Safe Learning Environments: A School Counselor's Guide to Integrating Physical and Psychological Safety; Prevention through Recovery
Melissa A. Reeves, Linda M. Kanan, Amy E. Plog

Forthcoming Titles

Behavioral Interventions in Schools: A Response-to-Intervention Guidebook
David Hulac, Joy Terrell, Odell Vining, and Joshua Bernstein

A Guide to Psychiatric Services in Schools: Understanding Roles, Treatment, and Collaboration
Shawna S. Brent

Serving the Gifted: Evidence-Based Clinical and Psycho-Educational Practice
Steven I. Pfeiffer

Ecobehavioral Consultation in Schools: Theory and Practice for School Psychologists, Special Educators, and School Counselors
Steven W. Lee

Comprehensive Planning for Safe Learning Environments

■ ■ ■ ■ ■ ■ ■ ■ ■ ■ ■ ■ ■ ■ ■

A School Professional's Guide to Integrating Physical and Psychological Safety – Prevention through Recovery

Melissa A. Reeves ■ Linda M. Kanan ■ Amy E. Plog

Routledge
Taylor & Francis Group
New York   London

Routledge
Taylor & Francis Group
270 Madison Avenue
New York, NY 10016

Routledge
Taylor & Francis Group
27 Church Road
Hove, East Sussex BN3 2FA

International Standard Book Number: 978-0-415-99834-5 (Hardback) 978-0-415-99835-2 (Paperback)

Library of Congress Cataloging-in-Publication Data

Reeves, Melissa A.
  Comprehensive planning for safe learning environments : a school professional's guide to integrating physical and psychological safety, prevention through recovery / Melissa A. Reeves, Linda M. Kanan, Amy E. Plog.
       p. cm.
  Includes bibliographical references and index.
  ISBN 978-0-415-99834-5 (hardcover : alk. paper) -- ISBN 978-0-415-99835-2 (pbk. : alk. paper)
  1. Schools--Safety measures. 2. School crisis management. 3. School violence--Prevention. I. Kanan, Linda M. II. Plog, Amy E. III. Title.

LB2864.5.R44 2009
363.11'9371--dc21   2009023373

Visit the Taylor & Francis Web site at
http://www.taylorandfrancis.com

and the Routledge Web site at
http://www.routledgementalhealth.com

Contents

List of Figures xv
List of Tables xvii
Series Foreword xxi
Preface xxv
Acknowledgments xxix
About the Authors xxxi

SECTION I Establishing a Comprehensive Safe Schools Climate

Chapter 1   Introduction and Overview to Establishing a
Safe School 3

What Is a Safe School? 5
Barriers to Establishing Safe Schools 7
What Is a Crisis? 8
Characteristics of a Crisis. 9
What Is Physical and Psychological Safety? 9
Physical Safety 9
Psychological Safety 10
Essential Elements to Comprehensive
Planning for Safe Learning Environments 11
Multi-*P*hase Elements (M-*P*HAT). 11
Multi-*H*azard Elements (M-P*H*AT). 15
Multi-*A*gency Elements (M-PH*A*T) 16
Multi-*T*iered Intervention Elements
(M-PHA*T*) 16
Why Do We Need to Establish Physical and
Psychological Safety? 20
Safety and Crime Statistics 20
Legislation 24
No Child Left Behind Act of 2001 24
Zero-Tolerance Policies 25
Family Educational Rights and Privacy
Act 26
Proposed Legislation 27

The Present Volume. 28

Chapter 2   System-Wide Considerations: Stakeholder
Support and Data-Driven Decision Making. . . . 33

The Importance of Stakeholders. 33
Who Are Key Stakeholders in School
Safety? 34
Barriers to Collaboration With Stakeholders . 35
Integration With Multi-Hazards Approach
to Prevention and Preparedness 36
Importance of Data in the Process 38
What Does the Data Gathering Look Like? . . 39
Physical Safety Audit 39
Psychological Safety Assessment 41
Comprehensive School Safety
Assessment: Real-World Example 61
District Example of Using Data to
Establish a Safe School Climate. 63
Physical Safety Data 63
Psychological Safety Data 64
Development of District-Level Safety Team. . . . 68
District-Level Safe Schools Design Team:
Real-World Example 72
Parallel Process at the School Level 75
Effective Collaboration With Community
Agencies. 75
Conclusion 77

SECTION II   Physical Safety: Multi-Hazard Prevention and Preparedness

Chapter 3   Integrating and Expanding a Multi-Hazards
Approach to Establish a Safe Learning
Environment 81

What Does It Mean to Use a Multi-Hazards
Approach for Safety Planning?. 81
How Is the Multi-Hazard Approach
Expanded or Modified for Schools? 83

The Importance of Multi-Agency
Collaboration for Multi-Hazard Preparedness
and Response Readiness. 84
School Multi-Hazard Preparedness and
Planning: Types of General and Specific Plans . . 86
   Building Control and General System
   Procedures. 86
      Crisis Go-Kits 93
      Accidents and Medical Emergencies. 93
      Weather and Other Natural Disasters 94
      Hazard-Specific Building Responses. 96
   Specific Psychological Safety Response
   Planning. 96
      Psychological Safety Preparedness and
      Response Training: Real-World Example. . 97
Conclusion. 97

Chapter 4   Establishing an Effective School Crisis Team
Using Incident Command System Principles . . 99

The National Incident Management System . . 101
   NIMS Training for School Personnel. 101
   Real-World Example 102
Incident Command System. 103
Command Structure 108
   Integrated or Unified Command. 108
   School Incident Command System Crisis
   Team Structure 108
      Real-World Example 111
Conclusion. 113

Chapter 5   Comprehensive Safe School and Crisis
Response Planning 123

Comprehensive Plans for Safe Schools 124
Crisis Response Plans 125
   School/Building-Level Crisis Response
   Plans. 125
   School Crisis Team Response Plan 132
   RESPONSE PLAN (i.e., School Crisis
   Team Response Plan) 133
   School Staff Crisis Response Plan 134
Types of Practice Exercises and Drills. 134
   School Staff Response Plan 135

Release and Reunification Planning 141
Working With the Media................. 143
Conclusion.............................. 144

SECTION III   Psychological Safety: Multi-Level Prevention, Intervention, and Recovery

Chapter 6   Universal Prevention Efforts in Schools 147

Mitigation and Physical Safety............. 148
Prevention and Psychological Safety........ 151
  School Policies and Management
  Strategies 152
  Social-Emotional Skill Building
  Instruction........................... 155
  Overall Climate and Culture 156
  Positive Youth Development............ 156
  Parent Involvement................... 159
Importance of Coordinated Efforts......... 159
  Real-World Example of Organizing a
  District-Wide Universal Prevention
  Program in Schools: The CARES Model ... 161
    Communities Are Connected, Inclusive,
    and Work to Prevent Bullying.......... 164
    Asset-Building Is Integrated in the
    School, Family, and Community....... 164
    Responsive Decision Making Is Based
    on Data............................ 165
    Expectations Are Clear to Students,
    Staff, and Parents 165
    Social-Emotional-Behavioral Skills Are
    Taught 166
Importance of Evidence-Based Interventions . 166
  Resources for Finding Evidence-Based
  Interventions 168
  Real-World Example: Examination of
  CARES Model Fit and Research Base for
  Programs in Use in a Large Suburban
  School District....................... 173
Conclusion.............................. 182

Chapter 7 Early and Targeted Interventions 189

Definition of Early and Targeted Interventions 190
Why Are Targeted Interventions Needed? 192
The Benefits of Providing Targeted
Interventions 194
   Academic Performance and Educational
   Outcomes. 195
   Helping Students Learn Well With Others. . 195
   Increasing Student Engagement. 195
   Decreasing Behaviors That Interfere With
   Learning. 196
Evidence-Based Interventions 196
Selecting Targeted Interventions 197
Considerations for Implementation of
Targeted Interventions 198
   Participant Selection. 198
   Staff Training 198
   Staff Resources 199
School Demand and Expectations Versus
Student Functioning 199
Types of Targeted Interventions 201
Academic Interventions 202
Alternatives to Suspension. 202
Social-Emotional Interventions 204
   Emotional Regulation 209
   Anger Management/Aggression Reduction . . 210
   Social Skills/Problem Solving 210
   Coping Skills Regarding Grief and Loss . . . 211
   Coping Skills Regarding Divorce 213
   Substance Abuse and Suicide 213
Awareness of Risk Factors and Early
Warning Signs for Early Intervention 214
   Risk Factors and Warning Signs 214
   Staff Awareness Training. 214
Breaking the Code of Silence: Methods of
Reporting Concerning Behaviors 216
Specific Reporting Guidelines for Tip Lines . . 217
   Real-World Example: One State's Tip Line . . 217
Summary 218

Chapter 8   Managing Risk Behaviors and Other
                Intensive Interventions 219

                Risk Behaviors and Threats to School Safety . . . 220
                Legal and Policy Issues 221
                Breaking the Code of Silence for High-Risk
                Behaviors 222
                    Reporting of Dangerous Student Behavior:
                    Real-World Example 224
                Suicide as a School Safety Issue 225
                    Best Practices for Suicide Intervention 227
                    Suicide Risk Documentation: Real-World
                    Example 233
                Other High-Risk Behaviors 233
                    Self-Injury 233
                    Victims of Child Abuse, Sexual Abuse,
                    and Sexual Assaults 234
                    Substance Abuse 234
                Threats of Harm to Others or the School 237
                    Interventions Equal to the Level of
                    Concern 243
                    Documenting Interventions After Threat
                    Assessment 244
                    Real-Life Example: Danger Assessment
                    and Intervention Plan 244
                Students With Significant Emotional and
                Behavioral Issues 245
                    Collaborating With Community Agencies
                    for Intervention 246
                        Wraparound Services 246
                    Functional Family Therapy 247
                    The Safe Schools/Healthy Students
                    Initiative 248
                Summary 248

Chapter 9   Recovery Efforts and Management of Crises
                in Schools 249

                Physical Recovery Efforts 250
                Psychological Recovery Efforts 251
                Assessment of Individual Physical Safety
                and Psychological Impact 251
                Trauma Assessment Variables 253
                    Crisis Exposure 253

Personal Vulnerability 253
Threat Perceptions 254
Crisis Reactions....................... 254
Common Reactions 256
Psychological Triage 260
Primary Level 260
Secondary Level 261
Tertiary Level 261
Psychological Recovery Interventions 262
Psychological First Aid................. 262
Reestablishing Social Support Systems.... 263
Classroom Meetings 265
Psychoeducation as Crisis Recovery
Intervention.......................... 266
Individual and Group Psychological Crisis
Interventions 268
Individual Crisis Interventions (ICI) 272
Group and Classroom-Based Crisis
Interventions (CCI) 274
Research Regarding Group Crisis
Interventions....................... 276
Listen, Protect, Connect—Model and
Teach 276
Psychotherapeutic Interventions 279
Care for the Caregivers 281
Guidelines for Dealing With a Death and
Memorials 282
Conclusion........................... 284

Concluding Comments............................. 285

Web Site Resources............................... 287
U.S. Department of Education Resources 287
National Incident Management System Web
Sites 287
Federal Agency Web Sites................. 288
Resource and Professional Organization Web
Sites 288

References 291

Index 331

CD Contents..................................... 339

List of Figures

Figure 1.1   Practical information on crisis planning. A guide for schools and communities. 12

Figure 1.2   Multi-Tiered Intervention Model. 17

Figure 1.3   Cherry Creek School District Comprehensive Safe Schools Plan (2008). 29

Figure 1.4   Comprehensive safe learning environment: The M-PHAT approach. 32

Figure 2.1   Percentage of students, parents, and staff who report that students are *not* safe or very safe at school. 56

Figure 2.2   Example of a Potential Data Summary Worksheet. . . 60

Figure 2.3   Cherry Creek School District Prevention and Intervention Planning Template. 66

Figure 2.4   Integration of safety and crisis team roles. 71

Figure 4.1   Basic Incident Command Flowchart. 107

Figure 4.2   Integrated/Unified Command Structure. 109

Figure 4.3   Example of how to modify the ICS to fit a larger school setting. 112

Figure 4.4   Example of how to modify the ICS to fit a smaller school setting. 113

Figure 5.1   Overview of district and schools plans for comprehensive safe schools. 124

Figure 5.2   School Crisis Team Response Plan. 133

Figure 5.3   Essential components to be included in a school staff response plan. 135

Figure 6.1   Examples of acronyms utilizing the PBS/PBIS structure to help facilitate universal school policies and management strategies. 153

Figure 6.2   Example of a positive reinforcement that can then be exchanged for other prizes/reinforcements. 154

Figure 6.3   Universal prevention and intervention model
for establishing a safe school learning environment. 161

Figure 7.1   Instructional gap between target performance
and current level of functioning. 200

Figure 8.1   Suicide Risk Intervention (SRI) steps. 229

Figure 9.1   Factors impacting the level of psychological
trauma to be considered when evaluating level of traumatic
impact. 255

Figure 9.2   Multi-tiered levels of crisis interventions. 264

List of Tables

Table 1.1 School Violence and Safety, 2005–2006 School Year: Percentage of Public Schools Experiencing at Least One Incident and Reporting at Least One Incident That Occurred to Police 22

Table 1.2 Physical and Psychological Safe School Measures Spanning a Comprehensive Framework for Creating and Sustaining a Safe Schools Climate 31

Table 2.1 School Safety Stakeholders 35

Table 2.2 Online Resources for Physical Safety Audits. 40

Table 2.3 Domains to Be Included in a Physical Safety Audit With a Brief Description of Desirable Features for That Domain 42

Table 2.4 FEMA/U.S. Department of Education Risk Index Worksheet to Be Used With Categories of Potential Hazards . . 54

Table 2.5 Domains to Be Included in a Psychological Safety Assessment 57

Table 2.6 Resources for Psychological Safety Assessment . . . 62

Table 2.7 Questions to Consider When Looking at the Student Survey Report 69

Table 3.1 10-Step Preparedness Plan for Schools 87

Table 3.2 Multi-Hazard Planning Needs for Schools— Types of General and Specific Plans 89

Table 3.3 Administrative Go-Kit Contents 94

Table 3.4 Classroom Go-Kits Contents 95

Table 4.1 Identification and Planning for Medical Triage and Support. 110

Table 4.2 School Crisis Teams Roles/Responsibilities Within the ICS 114

Table 4.3　Assigning School Crisis Team Roles for School
Incident Command System (ICS). 119

Table 5.1　Essential Components to Be Included in the
Multi-Phase Comprehensive Safe Schools Plan 126

Table 5.2　Essential Learning Objectives and Potential
Training Forum Involved in Each Type of Crisis Drill/
Exercise 136

Table 5.3　General Crisis Drill and Exercise Procedures 140

Table 5.4　Essential Elements to a Release and
Reunification Plan 142

Table 6.1　Prevention and Mitigation Efforts. 149

Table 6.2　Brief Summary of Research Pertaining to
Universal Prevention and Intervention Programs 157

Table 6.3　Key Universal Components to Psychological
Safety Prevention Efforts 160

Table 6.4　Models for Organizing Psychological Safety
Prevention Efforts. 162

Table 6.5　Online Web Sites Providing Reviews of
Evidence-Based Programs 170

Table 6.6　Overview of Universal Evidence-Based Social-
Emotional Programs and Interventions 174

Table 6.7　Research Base CARES Prevention Model. 183

Table 7.1　Alternatives to Suspension 203

Table 7.2　Overview of Specific Targeted Evidence-Based
Social-Emotional Programs and Interventions. 205

Table 7.3　Components of Effective Skills Training 212

Table 7.4　Potential Risk Factors. 215

Table 8.1　Warning Signs of Youth Suicide 226

Table 8.2　Sample Process for Response to Suicide Threat . . 228

Table 8.3　Sandoval and Zadeh's Five-Step Protocol for
Responding to Suicidal Behavior in Schools 230

Table 8.4　Nine Recommendations for Responding to Self-
Injury in Schools 235

Table 8.5   Ten Key Findings of the Safe School Initiative and Their Implications for Comprehensive Planning and Intensive Interventions. 238

Table 8.6   Steps in a Threat/Danger Assessment Process. . . . 241

Table 9.1   Common Reactions to Crises 257

Table 9.2   Developmental Reactions to Trauma 258

Table 9.3   General Structure of a Classroom Meeting 267

Table 9.4   General Process for Student Psychoeducation and Caregiver Psychoeducation Groups 269

Table 9.5   How Adults Can Help 270

Table 9.6   How Parents Can Help 271

Table 9.7   Key Phases and Components for Individual Crisis Intervention (ICI) 273

Table 9.8   Group and Classroom-Based Crisis Intervention Process (CCI) 275

Table 9.9   Types and Levels of School Psychological Crisis Interventions 277

Table 9.10   An Overview of the Listen, Protect, and Connect Model of Crisis Intervention 278

Table 9.11   Stress Reactions in Crisis Responders 281

Series Foreword

The School-Based Practice in Action series grew out of the coming together of our passion and commitment to the field of education and the needs of children and schools in today's world. We entered the process of developing and editing this series at two different points of our career, though both in phases of transition. One (RWC) moving from the opening act to the main scene, and the other (RBM) from main scene to the final act. Despite one of us entering the peak of action and the other leaving it, we both continue to be faced with the same challenges in and visions for education and serving children and families.

Significant transformations to the educational system, through legislation such as the No Child Left Behind Act and the reauthorization of Individual with Disabilities Education Act (IDEA 2004), have had broad sweeping changes for the practitioners in the educational setting, and these changes will likely continue. It is imperative that as school-based practitioners we maintain a strong knowledge base and adjust our service delivery. To accomplish this, there is a need to understand theory and research, but it is critical that we have resources to move our empirical knowledge into the process of practice. Thus, it is our goal that the books included in the School-Based Practice in Action series truly offer resources for readers to put directly "into action."

To accomplish this, each book in the series will offer information in a practice-friendly manner and will have a companion CD with reproducible and usable materials. Within the text, readers will find a specific icon that will cue them to documents available on the accompanying CD. These resources are designed to have a direct impact on transitioning research and knowledge into the day-to-day functions of school-based practitioners. We recognize that the implementation of programs and the changing of roles come with challenges and barriers, and as such, these may take on various forms depending on the context of the situation and the voice of the practitioner. To that end, the books of the School-Based Practice in Action

series may be used in their entirety and present form for a
number of practitioners; however, for others, these books will
help them find new ways to move toward effective action and
new possibilities. No matter which style fits your practice, we
hope that these books will influence your work and professional growth.

In developing the School-Based Practice in Action series,
the idea of having a book on crisis intervention and management continued to be at the top of our list. However, in reviewing the literature, there were a number of good books that
seemed to cover this topic. Yet, we continued to believe there
was a void in the literature that needed attention. We had the
pleasure of having a discussion with Dr. Melissa Reeves, who
presented the concept of developing a book that focused not
only on crisis management and response, but also on the planning effort for prevention, all of which leads to fostering a safe
learning environment.

The process of working with Dr. Melissa Reeves, Dr. Linda
Kanan, and Dr. Amy Plog on this book has been a great opportunity. They have developed a unique and needed resource
that blends their knowledge of research and the literature,
with key elements derived from their practical experience.
In Comprehensive Planning for Safe School Environment,
Reeves, Kanan, and Plog have laid out an all-inclusive and
well organized guidebook full of ideas from preventions
through recovery. The thoughtful approach of the authors
offers resources that can be used by school-based practitioners and administrators to enhance their current programs or
to make a shift in how their schools function with regard to
crisis management. We are grateful to have been part of the
process leading to this book, and we look forward to using it
in our own practice.

The continued growth and expansion of this book series
would not be possible without our relationship with Mr. Dana
Bliss and Routledge Publishing, who from the start have supported our vision. We are grateful for their belief in our idea
of having a book series focusing on "action" resources dedicated to enriching practice and service delivery within school
settings. Their dedication and belief in meeting the needs of
school-based practitioners made the School-Based Practice in
Action series a reality. We hope that you enjoy reading and
implementing the materials in this book and the rest of the

series as much as we have enjoyed working with the authors on developing these resources.

Rosemary B. Mennuti, EdD, NCSP
Ray W. Christner, PsyD, NCSP
Series Editors, School-Based Practice in Action Series

Preface

The purpose of this book is to provide school administrators, school-based mental health professionals, and other educational professionals with the framework and tools needed to establish a comprehensive safe learning environment. This book provides many examples of the "nuts and bolts" needed to identify and implement safety measures, while also showcasing specific examples of how these tasks work together to enhance academic achievement and align with other initiatives occurring in schools.

This book supports a relatively new concept in regard to safe learning environments and crisis planning in schools: the importance of the balance between *physical safety* and *psychological safety*, throughout all four phases of establishing a safe school. In addition, the authors emphasize the importance of offering programs and interventions to meet the needs of *all* students through a multi-tiered service delivery model. So many safe schools efforts focus on an increase in physical safety and security measures (locking doors, requiring staff and student ID badges, hiring more security officers, utilizing metal detectors, etc.). These concrete and visible measures provide only one aspect of safety and security in schools. Equally as important, but more time intensive and complex, is the notion of providing psychological safety. Students must *feel* safe, and their social and emotional needs, in addition to academic needs, must be met in order to ensure psychological safety. This is done by establishing a safe-schools climate through whole-school (universal) initiatives, while also providing more targeted and intensive support and interventions for students at risk. The importance of these types of climate and intervention efforts can be seen, for example, in cases where a student is planning to do harm to the school or other students. Students who are aware of these plans must feel comfortable enough to tell an adult, so adults can intervene. Students must trust that the adults will act upon their concerns; that a positive, respectful environment will be maintained; and that students can get emotional assistance when needed. This is not to say that the physical safety efforts mentioned above are not important, but rather that when establishing a comprehensive safe learning environment, physical safety without psychological safety (and vice versa) is not enough. Both are needed and must work together in today's and tomorrow's schools.

When people talk about "safe schools," it is often in the context of crisis response and preparing for a crisis. However, just as a focus on physical safety alone is not enough; establishing a safe schools climate is a much larger and broader task than just preparing for a crisis response. Specifically, *four* phases are involved to achieve a comprehensive safe school environment: prevention, preparedness, response, and recovery. Establishing a safe school encompasses the prevention of negative events from occurring in the first place by having universal safe school initiatives and prevention programs in place within each school. In addition, preparing for potential events that could take place and having plans for response to these potential events is needed. In the event of a crisis or identification of concerning behaviors, responding to the event or concern with a continuum of multi-tiered services is of necessity. Lastly, support within the recovery phase can help to mitigate the negative impact of the event/behavior and allow students to reengage in learning as quickly as possible. Therefore, good interventions and recovery measures help prevent further negative impact. It is critically important to remember that "prevention is intervention and intervention is prevention." This book expands on each of these phases, and provides guidance in integrating physical and psychological safety within a multi-tiered continuum of services to enhance the safe and productive learning environments for students, and the teaching and working environment for staff.

This book is divided into three sections that together encompass comprehensive planning for safe learning environments. Section I discusses the systemic factors for establishing a safe schools climate, and topics covered include obtaining support from key school and community stakeholders, important legal and governmental guidelines regarding school safety programs, relevant financial and risk management considerations, and specific examples of how one school district began addressing both physical and psychological safety issues. Section II addresses physical safety in schools focusing on establishing a safe and secure learning environment for students and staff though specific mitigation/prevention and preparedness efforts utilizing a multi-hazards approach to school safety, and preparing for crisis response in schools and with multi-agency community partners. Specific roles and responsibilities for safety teams and crisis teams that align with the federal government's National Incident Management System (NIMS), Incident Command System (ICS) are discussed, in addition to the essential components needed when developing a comprehensive safe school plan and a more specific crisis response plan. The final section of the book, Section III, focuses more specifically on psychological safety by providing information on universal and targeted prevention and intervention strategies, as well strategies for managing the risk behaviors of students through established suicide and threat assessment procedures. The book concludes with a discussion of multi-tiered crisis intervention services that schools should be prepared to provide in the event of a crisis, which can help mitigate the negative impact of an event so academic achievement can continue. Readers should note that while this book contains two sections distinguishing physical and psychological safety for the sake of better organizing the information being presented, many safety efforts will require overlap and integration of these two components.

We hope this book and the accompanying CD provide you with the tools needed to comprehensively plan for a safe and successful learning environment and a school that is responsive to needs of students and staff. The task will have long-term positive outcomes for your school, students, and staff.

Acknowledgments

The authors gratefully acknowledge their current and former colleagues, administrators, and members of the Safe Schools Design Team of the Cherry Creek School District in Colorado for their leadership and dedication to the physical and psychological safety of students. Our work for this district has served as the foundation for much of what has been included in this book. This district has always advocated for excellence in meeting not only the educational needs, but also the mental health needs of students. This has served as the true foundation for establishing and maintaining safe schools.

To Drs. Ray Christner and Rosemary Mennuti who sought us as authors due to our practical experiences and expertise they felt should be shared with other educational and mental health professionals. This journey allowed us to pull together all of our years of training and experience into a product of which we are proud.

This book is dedicated to all those educational and mental health professionals who continue to juggle many roles that contribute not only to the educational needs, but also to the safety and well-being of the youth they serve. The importance of the stability and encouragement that you provide to children may not always been seen immediately, but will definitely be evident in their futures. In these times of high-pressure academic achievement and standards, thank you for the work you do to balance the emotional needs with the academic; with this you help create safe schools.

About the Authors

Melissa A. Reeves, PhD, NCSP, is a school psychologist, licensed special education teacher, and licensed professional counselor. She received her doctorate in school psychology from the University of Denver and previously worked for the Cherry Creek School District. Currently, she is a lecturer for Winthrop University in South Carolina and trains professionals nationally and internationally in the areas of crisis prevention and intervention, threat and suicide assessment, the impact of trauma and PTSD on academic achievement, and establishing a positive behavioral support and response to intervention model. Dr. Reeves is co-author of the *PREPaRE Crisis Prevention and Intervention Curriculum,* and two books titled *Identifying, Assessing, and Treating PTSD at School* and *School Crisis Prevention and Intervention: The PREPaRE model.*

Linda M. Kanan, PhD, is the director of the Colorado School Safety Resource Center. She received her doctorate in school psychology from the University of Denver. She is a former teacher and school psychologist with more than 25 years of experience in public school settings. She was the intervention coordinator and Safe Schools Design Team facilitator in the Cherry Creek School District before her selection as the director of the Resource Center in 2008. Her expertise is in the area of prevention and intervention services for high-risk behaviors in youth. Dr. Kanan has trained nationally in school crisis response, PREPaRE, threat assessment, suicide intervention in schools, and best practices for response to self-injury. She is an adjunct professor teaching crisis prevention and intervention at the University of Denver and the University of Northern Colorado.

Amy Plog, PhD, received her doctorate in clinical psychology from the University of Houston. She has worked with the Cherry Creek School District since 1998 as the research and data coordinator for the district's Safe Schools Design Team and has directed several district-wide assessments of bullying, school climate, and perceptions of student safety. Dr. Plog is also the director of research for Creating Caring Communities, a nonprofit organization that oversees the Bully-Proofing Your School (BPYS) program.

I

ESTABLISHING A COMPREHENSIVE SAFE SCHOOLS CLIMATE

One

Introduction and Overview to Establishing a Safe School

School systems are not responsible for meeting every need of their students. ... But when the need directly affects learning, the school must meet the challenge.

—Carnegie Council Task Force (1989)

S chools today face many challenging factors such as bullying, assaultive and gang violence, drug and alcohol use, natural disasters, car accidents, suicide, and death of a student or faculty member that can directly affect learning. In the 2007–2008 school year, 75.7% of public schools reported at least one type of violent crime had occurred on campus with rates of violent incidences being higher at middle schools than primary or elementary schools (Neiman & DeVoe, 2009). Up to 25% of schools report illegal drug activity, student bullying, and/or gang activity as a daily or weekly problem, and 11% of students reported that someone at school had used hate-related words against them (Dinkes, Cataldi, & Lin-Kelly, 2007; Neiman & DeVoe, 2009). All of these incidences can lead to a serious disruption in teaching, learning, and school routine, in addition to emotional upset, disruptive behavior, and decreased attendance. Students who experience a traumatic crisis event have been shown to have lower grade point averages, more negative remarks in their cumulative records, increased absences, greater difficulties concentrating and learning, and a greater likelihood of engaging in reckless and/or aggressive behaviors (National Child Traumatic Stress Network, n.d. [c]). While these statistics may paint a dismal picture for some regarding the overall safety of schools, the number of violent deaths and rates of victimization for students ages 12–18 at school has declined between 1992 and 2005 (Dinkes et al., 2007). Schools are beginning to implement proactive educational models such as Positive Behavior Supports (PBS), also referred to as Positive Behavior Interventions and Supports (PBIS), Social-Emotional Learning (SEL), and/or violence prevention programs that have been shown to lead to improved student perceptions of school safety and an increased number of resiliency and protective factors (i.e., caring relationships, high expectations, opportunities for participation) and to have a positive correlation with academic performance (Collaborative for Academic, Social, and Emotional Learning [CASEL], 2008; Johns, Patrick, & Rutherford, 2008; McKevitt & Braaksma, 2008; Neiman & DeVoe, 2009; Office of Safe and Drug Free Schools [OSDFS], 2006). Prevention programs such as school-based drug and violence prevention programs have also been found to improve school climate and to directly and indirectly lead to improved academic performance (Centers for Disease Control and Prevention [CDC], 2008b; Mandell, Hill, Carter, & Brandon, 2002). In the unfortunate event of a crisis, an existing positive school climate fosters connectedness and feelings of safety. This in turn makes it easier for students and staff to successfully deal with and manage a crisis event and restore teaching and learning. As Del Elliott, director of the Center for the Study and Prevention of Violence, has argued, until kids feel safe and respected at school, there is "little reason to believe that changes in curriculum or instructional practices will have any significant impact on academic performance" (OSDFS, 2006, p. 2). In summary, a safe school is also a higher performing school.

This chapter begins by defining a "safe school" and highlights current statistics pertaining to a variety of events that can impact school safety. Two key concepts to this book will be introduced: balancing *physical* and *psychological* safety while maintaining focus on academic achievement, and utilizing a multi-phase, multi-hazard, multi-agency, and multi-tiered approach to establishing a comprehensive safe learning environment. In addition, the need for establishing physical and psychological safety, legal issues pertaining to school safety, and an overview of subsequent chapters will also be presented.

WHAT IS A SAFE SCHOOL?

The use of the words "safe school" resonates with all of us who work in the educational field. However, what does it really mean, and how does one determine that a school is really safe? Part of establishing a safe school is to prevent a crisis from happening in the first place or in those incidences where a crisis cannot be prevented (i.e., natural disasters), to be prepared to respond to the crisis in order to mitigate the negative impact. However, a safe school is more than one that is prepared to respond to a crisis; it is also one that establishes and maintains a positive school climate and implements good prevention and intervention programs.

In 1998, the U.S. Department of Education published *Early Warning, Timely Response: A Guide to Safe Schools* (Dwyer, Osher, & Warger, 1998) in which 13 research-based characteristics of a safe school were outlined. That guide emphasized that all members of the school community—staff, students, parents, and members of the larger community—play a role in the establishment of safe school environments. Such environments were described as having mutual respect and caring, early identification of troubled youth, and comprehensive response to the needs of students, all of which contribute to the goal of safety and security. Research was reviewed that supported the idea that well-functioning schools not only promote learning, but also attend to safety and teach socially appropriate behavior. The 13 characteristics were identified as being necessary in order for schools to best provide effective prevention, intervention, and crisis response strategies. Safe schools

- Focus on academic achievement
- Involve families in meaningful ways
- Develop links to the community
- Emphasize positive relationships among students and staff
- Discuss safety issues openly
- Treat students with equal respect
- Create ways for students to share their concerns
- Help children feel safe in expressing their feelings
- Have in place a system for referring children who are suspected of being abused or neglected
- Promote good citizenship and character
- Identify problems and assess progress toward solutions

- Support students in making the transition to adult life and the workplace

This thinking carries over to more current descriptions of safe schools. In 2006, the Office of Safe and Drug Free Schools defined safe schools as having the following characteristics:

- High academic standards
- Clear rules and policies that are fairly enforced
- High levels of parent involvement
- Effective community/school partnerships
- Extended-day and after school programs
- Good citizenship and character
- Well-prepared and practiced plans for crisis or emergency

Also, Sprague and Walker (2002) summarize a safe school as having

- Clearly defined goals in a school improvement plan and close monitoring and feedback regarding progress toward these goals
- High academic expectations for all students
- Clear and positive expectations for behavior
- High levels of student bonding and engagement with the schooling process
- Meaningful involvement of parents and the community

For well over a decade now, the literature has been identifying a safe school climate as one that entails more than just a good crisis plan; there are a multitude of other components needed in the comprehensive effort to prevent crises from happening. Therefore, determination of whether or not a school is "safe" is based on a multifaceted list of descriptors, many of which are more related to a positive school climate than to crisis and emergency planning. As authors of this book, we propose adding the following to the list of characteristics that are necessary for establishing a safe school, and these are all addressed further in subsequent chapters:

- A balance between physical and psychological safety to create and maintain a safe and positive environment
- A shared goal of helping students reach their full potential academically, socially, and emotionally

- Prevention of and preparedness for a crisis event balanced with best practices in response and recovery, when needed
- A continuum of academic and social-emotional interventions being available for all students, regardless of achievement level and education label (i.e., disability)

As new crisis events have occurred and threats to safety in school have broadened over time to include threats both internal to the school and threats from outside the school, the need for well-prepared and practiced plans for crisis and emergency, in addition to a safe school climate, have moved again to the forefront in many discussions.

Barriers to Establishing Safe Schools

There are many common barriers to establishing a safe school environment. These include the myth that taking preparedness steps implies a school is unsafe, and territorial issues regarding whose job it is to implement safe schools initiatives. In addition, many schools lack one or more of the following resources: equipment; curriculum; time for planning, training, and staff development; and personnel with the expertise in emergency planning and resource allocation. As a result, school safety planning and training often take a back seat to academics. A recent Government Accountability Office report (United States Government Accountability Office [U.S. GAO], 2007) found that schools are struggling to balance priorities for educating students with other administrative responsibilities focused on emergency management.

With violent events that occur in schools or in the community, there is often the erroneous belief that individuals "just snap." Quite the contrary, in over 90% of school violence incidents, there was evidence from the attacker's behavior of a plan or preparation to harm a target (Vossekuil, Reddy, Fein, Borum, & Modezelski, 2000, 2002). There are typically red flags and warning signs (see Chapters 7 and 8 for further discussion) coupled with an immediate stressor that leads to the negative act. This speaks to the importance of establishing safe schools where students and staff develop positive rapport, identify red flags and warning signs, and sustain a culture where the right thing to do is to report concerns and get help, instead of feeling afraid of being called a "snitch." Teachers and students are the "front lines" to establishing a safe school environment, and a mechanism for confidential reporting when a safe school culture is being compromised is a critical component to safe schools.

WHAT IS A CRISIS?

Establishing a safe school climate includes prevention efforts in addition to planning and preparing for a potential crisis or emergency utilizing a *m*ulti-*p*hase, multi-*h*azard, multi-*a*gency, and multi-*t*iered approach. As authors, we propose using the acronym, M-PHAT, in order to remember this comprehensive approach.

M = *M*ulti
  P = *P*hase
  H = *H*azard
  A = *A*gency
  T = *T*iered

As a precursor to using this approach, it is critical that schools understand and agree as to what constitutes a crisis. The Webster Dictionary (2008) defines crisis as the following:

1. A turning point for better or worse in an acute disease or fever
2. A paroxysmal attack of pain, distress, or disordered function
3. An emotionally significant event or radical change of status in a person's life
4. The decisive moment
5. An unstable or crucial time or state of affairs in which a decisive change is impending
6. A situation that has reached a critical phase

In a school crisis, all of the above definitions can apply and impact the stability of a safe school. A school crisis is a turning point and oftentimes pain, distress, or disordered functions are prevalent, whether it be psychological and/or physical. The event is emotionally significant and for those "in charge" at the time of the event, the crisis is a very decisive moment where their decisions can create more stability or less stability. However, good prevention, planning, preparation, and leadership decrease the potential for the situation to reach a critical phase and minimize the physical and emotional impact.

Characteristics of a Crisis

There are three characteristics to a crisis (Brock, 2002a, 2006a, 2006b) that may increase the need for a school crisis response: (a) extremely negative, (b) uncontrollable, and (c) unpredictable. The *perception* of the event being extremely negative is key (Carlson, 1997). Especially in working with children and adolescents, school professionals need to keep in mind that although the facts may not indicate that the event itself is extremely negative, if *perception* of the event is extremely negative, then the need for a school crisis response and/or more intensive interventions can be elevated. Likewise, the more uncontrollable (or the perception of uncontrollability, e.g., accidental death, random shootings) and unpredictable the event, the more likely the traumatic impact (Brock, 2006a, 2006b). In contrast, if the situation is more controllable and predictable (e.g., death following long-term terminal illness), there is time to make cognitive and emotional adjustments that can lower threat perceptions and negative impact.

WHAT IS PHYSICAL AND PSYCHOLOGICAL SAFETY?

One of the most important and unique concepts presented in this book is the distinction between and overlap of physical and psychological safety. These two concepts are interrelated and span all phases of crisis prevention, preparedness, response, and recovery. Both are critical to the success of establishing a safe schools climate.

Physical Safety

Physical safety is concerned with the physical vulnerability of the building and the measures the adults take to ensure that students are safe from bodily harm at school. Most often, physical safety is characterized by the following (Cherry Creek School District, 2008; Nickerson & Martens, 2008; Noguera, 1995; Pagliocca & Nickerson, 2001; Reeves, Nickerson, & Jimerson, 2006):

- Policies and procedures that address the physical design layout and vulnerability of the school
- Preparation, planning, and mitigation of physical hazards

- "Get tough" approaches that include zero tolerance policies (i.e., suspension, expulsion for violating school conduct policies)
- Restricting autonomy through use of punitive measures (i.e., time-out procedures, more restrictive placements)
- Policing functions such as hiring resource officers and security guards
- Integrating a multi-hazards approach to establishing a safe learning environment
- Establishing an effective school crisis plan and team, with support from a district or community crisis team, if needed
- Monitoring crisis planning and preparation through practice drills and exercises
- Reflective thinking and modifications to crisis plans after an event or drill occurs

Some specific examples of physical safety include having one main entrance and locking all other doors, video surveillance of entrances and hallways, and staff and visitor identification badges. Typically, physical safety is the primary focus of risk managers, school security specialists, and school resource officers, as physical security has been the foundation of their training background.

Psychological Safety

Less familiar is the concept of psychological safety. In contrast to physical safety, psychological safety is concerned with the climate and relationships within the building and measures that ensure that students *feel* safe at school and view it as a place where they can learn and are free from emotional or psychological harm. This is impacted by both physical security and fear or anxiety about being harmed by others (Rigby, 2007). It is important for staff to recognize that students' feelings of safety can be independent of adults' evaluations. Therefore, a psychologically safe school is one that provides for the emotional well-being and social development of students, and has a positive school climate that maximizes the likelihood that students are available for learning. When children are afraid in their environment, their academic performance can be impacted and they are not as likely to develop their cognitive or emotional potential (Ratner, Chiodo, Covington, Sokol, Ager, & Delaney-Black, 2006; Rigby 2007). Psychological safety encompasses the following (Cherry Creek School District, 2008; Noguera, 1995; Pagliocca & Nickerson, 2001):

- Resiliency and asset development
- Bullying prevention
- Positive behavior supports
- Awareness, early identification, and intervention for at-risk students
- Educational, psychological, and/or therapeutic interventions
- Parental engagement and involvement
- Teaching conflict resolution, problem solving, and anger management skills
- A continuum of mental health services

By nature, psychological safety needs must also be considered within the multi-phase safe schools planning, preparedness, response, and recovery stages. The emotional well-being of students, and in the event of a crisis, the maintenance or restoration of the positive school climate and learning is the goal. Research has shown that for students who do not feel safe at school and/or are threatened at school, there are many negative ramifications such as not reaching full academic potential, school avoidance and/or avoidance of specific places in school, and nonattendance (United States Department of Justice, 2003).

ESSENTIAL ELEMENTS TO COMPREHENSIVE PLANNING FOR SAFE LEARNING ENVIRONMENTS

In addition to recognizing the need for both physical and psychological components to safe learning environments, comprehensive planning for safe learning environments should include all elements of the M-PHAT approach.

Multi-Phase Elements (M-*PHAT*)

Multi-phase thinking ensures the plan addresses all phases of a potential crisis to include prevention and mitigation, preparedness, response, and recovery. This specific element of our model embeds the phases of crisis planning advocated for by the U.S. Department of Education (2007d). Each phase has established policies, procedures, and programming (Figure 1.1).

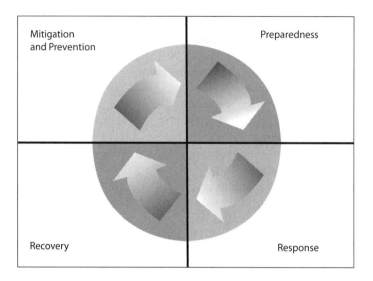

Figure 1.1   Practical information on crisis planning. A guide for schools and communities. The Office of Safe and Drug-Free Schools, U. S. Department of Education (2007). Washington, DC. In public domain.

Prevention-Mitigation

The goals of mitigation and prevention are multifaceted. Mitigation is any sustained action to reduce or eliminate long-term risk to life and property, and therefore decrease the need for response (OSDFS, 2007). A primary goal of mitigation is to take inventory of potential hazards or dangers and identify what to do and how to prevent or reduce injury or damage (OSDFS, 2007; Cherry Creek School District, 2008). In regards to psychological safety, schools must use data to assess and reflect upon the climate of their school and students' perception of safety and security. Another primary goal of mitigation is to increase response capacity in regards to physical and mental health response measures in the occurrence of an event. Mitigation is critical as schools can be vulnerable to a lawsuit for negligence if they do not take the necessary good faith actions to create safe schools. As one of the authors conveys to workshop participants, "You may never know if you prevented a crisis, but you will know if you didn't" (M. Reeves, personal communication March 29, 2006).

Prevention involves creating a safe and orderly school environment (Cherry Creek School District, 2008). Just as with mitigation, prevention strategies include physical safety measures and also psychological safety measures such as violence prevention programs, promoting positive character development and the learning of social-emotional skills, and establishing positive school climates that are free of harassment, threat, and bullying.

The Office of Safe and Drug Free Schools (2007) outlines specific strategies to successfully conduct mitigation and prevention, which are further discussed in following chapters:

1. Connect with community responders to identify local hazards
2. Review physical safety audit/assessment of school buildings and grounds
3. Identify a school staff member who will oversee violence prevention strategies
4. Encourage feedback from staff and key stakeholders during the planning process
5. Review incident and behavior data to identify major problems
6. Assess how the schools can address these problems and identify other resources that may be needed
7. Conduct an assessment to determine how problems may impact vulnerability

Prevention and mitigation are discussed further in Chapter 2 and also Chapters 6–10 as part of multi-tiered interventions offered to students that can prevent and reduce the negative impact of future actions.

Preparedness

Crisis preparedness ensures that a school and district are ready to respond to those crises that are not or cannot be prevented (Brock, Jimerson, & Hart, 2006). The first step in preparedness is to accept that a wide range of emergencies can happen anywhere and overcome the myth that "it can't happen here." Preparedness includes developing steps or actions to facilitate a coordinated, rapid, and effective response when a crisis occurs (OSDFS, 2007). Preparedness also includes pre-establishing command posts, evacuation sites, crisis teams and roles, acquiring necessary materials and equipment, and drill and practice with multi-agency partners. Consistent components of preparedness will help to support a multi-hazard plan and are further discussed in Chapter 3.

Response

Response involves steps taken during a crisis situation to minimize crisis damage and restore immediate coping by assessing the situation and choosing the appropriate responses (OSDFS, 2007). Good planning and preparation are critical to response implementation, and appropriate response is critical to decreasing the traumatic impact the event can have on students and staff. In a crisis, the plan must be followed (U. S. Department of Education, 2007d) and general procedures need to be implemented such as assessing the situation; responding within seconds; notifying appropriate emergency responders to include district administration, school and district crisis team; deciding on response protocol (e.g., secure perimeter, lockdown, or evacuation, etc.); triaging physical and psychological injuries and providing emergency first aid; and using student release and family reunification plan. No two crisis events are the same, so school personnel should generally "expect to be surprised." The crisis team and school staff should be reminded to trust leadership; project a calm, confident, and serious attitude; yield leadership to others, if appropriate, or form a unified command; utilize and keep supplies for quick access; allow for flexibility; and document actions (Cherry Creek School District, 2008). Response plans and protocols are further discussed in Chapter 5.

Recovery

During recovery, the goal is to restore the infrastructure and return to learning as quickly as possible (OSDFS, 2007). Recovery involves ensuring the school is both physically and psychologically safe and secure by taking additional security precautions and providing a caring and supportive school environment with multi-tiered interventions available. The purpose of care and recovery efforts is to determine the psychological impact of the event on students and staff, identify the response and intervention services needed, assist with coping and understanding reactions, supporting the emotional stabilization of students and staff to restore psychological safety, and restoring a safe and effective learning environment to help the school return to educating students as quickly as possible (Cherry Creek School District, 2008). To meet these goals, within the preparedness stage, a school needs to have a good recovery plan identified, to have already verified appropriate skills and certifications of those providing direct service, and to have provided staff development to ensure competency in delivering intervention and response services. The services to be provided in the aftermath of an event include reaffirming physical health, avoiding crisis scenes or images to minimize traumatic impact (Brock, 2006a), conducting psychological triage to identify crisis impact on individuals, providing ongoing assessment of the emotional needs of students and staff, and providing direct interventions (i.e., caregiver trainings, group crisis intervention; see Chapter 9).

Restoring psychological safety is just as important as restoring the physical structure of the school. Throughout the recovery phase, good communication is needed between the school, parents, and community as ongoing support and resources are identified. It is critical to provide suggestions for staff members, students, and parents regarding how to support one another and how to improve understanding of the various reactions. Appropriate memorial activities can also be helpful and anniversary dates need to be considered (see Chapter 9). Recovery can take days, months, or years so schools need to be flexible and able to sustain these efforts or seek other agency help if needed. Lastly, evaluating and reflecting upon care and recovery efforts by identifying what worked and what didn't helps to better prepare for the next crisis (Cherry Creek School District, 2008).

Multi-Hazard Elements (M-PHAT)

A multi-hazards (or all-hazards) plan refers to the universal, coordinated approach to dealing with any and all emergencies that integrates the consistent response structure of the National Incident Management System (NIMS) (Federal Emergency Management Agency [FEMA], 2004b; Minnesota Department of Education, 2008). In addition, common procedures are developed for responding to a variety of potential hazards that can compromise school safety to include fire, evacuation, flooding, bomb threat, severe weather (tornado, hurricanes, snowstorms), gas leaks, chemical spills, bioterrorism attack, and school closure due to crisis or pandemic. Hazard identification and risk assessment questionnaires and checklists have been developed to help schools identify which hazards should be addressed within a school or district crisis plan (see Chapters 2 and 3). Integrated into the multi-hazards approach is the need for a variety of drills, both tabletop and real-time practice, including such important responses as secured perimeter, lockdown, and shelter-in-place (see Chapter 5).

Multi-Agency Elements (M-PH<u>A</u>T)

Schools cannot always provide needed response to crises alone. Therefore, a multi-agency approach is also necessary to develop effective crisis plans. Collaboration with such agencies as police, fire, rescue, medical, local federal emergency management, social services/child protection and welfare, human services, and mental health agencies are critical, as they may serve as first responders or provide service in the recovery phase. This is not an all-exhaustive list, but schools need to identify key agencies whose help may be needed in the event that one of the potential crises occurs. Chapters 2 and 4 further discuss multi-agency collaboration.

Multi-Tiered Intervention Elements (M-PHA<u>T</u>)

A fundamental concept that has emerged since the No Child Left Behind (NCLB) Act of 2001 was passed is the multi-tiered service delivery model and multi-tiered interventions. The multi-tiered concept first began with a primary focus on academic interventions but now encompasses behavioral interventions as well. The premise of a multi-tiered service delivery system is that students have different strengths and needs and that interventions are provided on a continuum based on need (Osher, Sprague, Weissberg, Axelrod, Keenan, Kendziora, & Zins, 2008), not educational label. A multi-tiered system of interventions provides for the educational and psychological needs of students (psychological safety) while balancing physical safety to support a safe and caring learning environment. Below is a brief introduction to the multi-tiered intervention model and Figure 1.2 provides a visual overview of a multi-tiered model. Chapters 6, 7, and 8 will expand further on this framework.

Universal Level/Tier 1 Interventions

Interventions at this level prevent the likelihood of academic and/or behavioral problems by providing students with the knowledge, skills, and behavioral supports needed to meet the school's expectations. Likewise, school staff is thought to have the knowledge, skills, and structure to reinforce student behaviors positively (Osher et al., 2008) and provide quality academic instruction. Behavioral interventions at this level address the school climate and implement a framework that

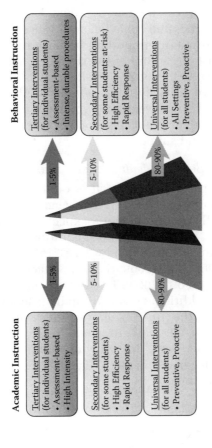

Figure 1.2   Multi-Tiered Intervention Model. *Source:* Office of Special Education Programs (2009). *Response to intervention and PBS.* Retrieved April 11, 2009, from http://www.pbis.org/rti/default.aspx. In public domain.

focuses on the entire student population by building assets and protective factors, teaching pro-social skills, and providing universal interventions that address potential risk factors through the use of positive behavioral supports, good classroom management strategies, clear expectations for behavior, positive staff-student connections, and engaging school activities (Osher et al., 2008). Academically, schools focus on implementing a researched-based curriculum for all students, and if students are not making academic progress, specific classroom-level interventions may be implemented such as class-wide peer tutoring (Burns & Gibbons, 2008). Universal instruction for both academics and behavior, and other safe school climate initiatives, are vitally important because they can positively impact at least 80%–90% of the student population (Burns & Gibbons, 2008; Office of Special Education Programs [OSEP], 2009). Effective universal interventions minimize the need for Tier 2 and Tier 3 interventions, which are more time and cost intensive to implement. Chapter 6 reviews specific universal interventions and supports.

Targeted/Selected/Tier 2 Interventions

There are approximately 5%–10% of students who will not respond adequately to the universal general education curriculum or overall school behavioral expectations. These students are deemed at risk and will need additional academic and/or behavioral support provided by Tier 2 interventions (Burns & Gibbons, 2008; OSEP, 2009; Stollar, Schaeffer, Skelton, Stine, Lateer-Huhn, & Poth, 2008). Tier 2 interventions are best delivered through additional small group instruction that supports (not replaces) the universal-level interventions. Examples include specialized small group reading or anger management instruction. In regards to behavior, a functional behavioral assessment may be conducted. Chapter 7 reviews specific targeted interventions.

Intensive/Indicated/Tier 3 Interventions

Despite best prevention and early intervention efforts, in some schools approximately 1%–5% of the student population may not respond successfully to Tier 1 and Tier 2 academic and/or behavioral interventions (Burns & Gibbons, 2008; OSEP, 2009; Stollar et al., 2008). These students are at a higher risk level than other students (e.g., multiple disciplinary referrals, multiple failing grades) and therefore require more intensive services. These interventions are individualized and typically focus on multiple domains such as family and school (Osher et al., 2008). Examples of intensive interventions are 1:1 academic instruction, mental health interventions focused on self-regulation of emotions and behavior, community-based mental health services, and possibly an alternative learning setting to better address intensive needs. Chapters 8 and 9 discuss a variety of Tier 3 intervention options.

Wade S. Brynelson of the California Department of Education summarized the relationship between academic performance and other contributing factors:

> Schools seeking to improve the academic performance of their students cannot ignore the role that health, school safety, caring relationships in the school, low rates of alcohol and drug use, nutrition, and exercise play in their overall efforts (OSDFS, 2006, p. 1).

Based on this relationship and the supporting research (Catalano, Mazza, Harachi, Abbott, Haggerty, & Fleming, 2003; CDC, 2008a, 2008b; Dunkle & Nash, 1991; Hanson, Austin, & Lee-Bayah, 2004; Mandell et al., 2002; WestEd, 2003), it is not surprising that many schools are focusing on more than just core academics in regards to student success. For example, some schools across the country are beginning to move towards the Comprehensive System of Learning Supports framework. This involves moving from a marginalized and fragmented system of student support services to one that is comprehensive, multifaceted, and cohesive, thus providing the resources, strategies, and practices that support the physical, social, emotional, and intellectual development of *all* students and providing each student with an equal opportunity for success at school. Internal and external barriers to learning are addressed, in addition to collaboration efforts between the school, home, and community. Comprehensive systems of learning supports address not only a multi-tiered continuum of social and emotional services as introduced in this chapter, but also include various aspects of developing and sustaining a safe schools climate that is addressed throughout this book. The Comprehensive System of Learning Supports framework is supported by the Council of Chief State School Officers who has hired their first director of Systems of Support for Student Learning (Center for Mental Health in Schools, 2008b). There is also the Coordinated School Health Program (CSHP) model from the Centers for Disease Control (2008a), which emphasizes that schools alone cannot—and should not—be expected to solve the nation's health and social problems. This model consists of eight interactive components and advocates for families, health care workers, the media, religious organizations, community organizations that serve youth, and young people themselves to all collaborate and work together to maintain the well-being of young people. The eight interactive components are as follows: health education; physical education; health services; nutrition services; counseling, psychological, and social services; healthy school environment; health promotion for staff; and family/community involvement. Both of these frameworks directly address the link between school climate, safety, and academic success for all students.

WHY DO WE NEED TO ESTABLISH PHYSICAL AND PSYCHOLOGICAL SAFETY?

Safety and crime statistics, in addition to legislative mandates, relate specifically to the need for a physically and psychologically safe school environment.

Safety and Crime Statistics

The Gallup Kappan poll surveys teachers and community members about their most prevalent concerns regarding public schools. In 16 of the past 38 years, the greatest concerns have been discipline, conduct, and control (Rose & Gallop, 2006; Sugai, Horner, & McIntosh, 2008). In regards to school violence and safety, the Institute of Education Sciences (2008) looked at the percentage of public schools during the 2005–2006 school year that experienced and reported at least one violent incident at school. Table 1.1 summarizes these statistics from which a common theme emerges. The number of incidents that actually occurred was greater than the number reported to police, and school administrators report far less school violence than students report (Coggeshall & Kingery, 2001). These results could be explained with multiple arguments: (a) not all incidents need to be reported to police; (b) teachers and school staff are hesitant to report incidents due to negative repercussions if the school is labeled "a persistently dangerous school" (see discussion of No Child Left Behind Act [2001] in subsequent section), and a large number of disciplinary infractions can impact a school's ability to meet Adequate Yearly Progress, which is a key component to meeting NCLB requirements; and (c) a teacher may be fearful of reporting incidents that could be negatively reflected on his/her job performance appraisals as the evaluator may conclude, "the teacher cannot handle these students." The authors have encountered all of these explanations in their professional experience of consulting and training school districts across the country. The latter explanations are of great concern, as schools cannot address problems that are not talked about. In addition, a recent survey (Neiman & DeVoe, 2009) of public schools reported major factors limiting schools' efforts to reduce or prevent crime "in a major way": (a) lack of or inadequate alternative placements or programming for disruptive students, (b) inadequate funds, (c) federal, state, or district policies on disciplining special education students. When a school is hesitant to discuss safety issues openly, or afraid to report negative incidents due to perceived consequences, or barriers limit their ability to reduce or prevent crime, *perceptions* (and even the reality) of physical and psychological safety and security at school can be negatively impacted. When students and staff *feel* or are less safe, school climate and academic achievement suffer.

The Gallup Kappan poll also found that the number of incidents experienced and reported increased significantly between the primary and middle school levels (Ma & Willms, 2004; Rose & Gallop, 2006) and overall, schools located in cities had a higher number of experienced incidents with the exception of theft. Furthermore, large schools and those schools with a larger percentage of special education students were found to be more likely to experience higher levels of school disruption and crime (Nickerson & Martens, 2008). Even so, it should be noted that incidents occurred in all types of school settings. In conclusion, school crime and disruption has no boundaries; therefore, all schools need to be prepared to deal with incidents that can negatively impact school safety.

Keep in mind, however, that schools also need to prepare for more than just crime or violent incidences. Natural disasters, car accidents, death of a student or faculty member, death by suicide, community violence, and communicable diseases/illnesses, to name a few, also impact the school climate and the perception of physical and psychological safety. As will be discussed further in Chapter 4, these events also provide an opportunity for school psychologists, school social workers, and school counselors to provide much needed leadership and broaden the role of school-based mental health service providers (Poland, 1994).

Table 1.1 School Violence and Safety, 2005–2006 School Year: Percentage of Public Schools Experiencing at Least One Incident and Reporting at Least One Incident That Occurred to Police

School Characteristic	Violent Incidents[a]		Serious Violence Incidents[b]		Theft[c]		Other[d]	
	Experienced	Reported	Experienced	Reported	Experienced	Reported	Experienced	Reported
Total	77.7	37.7	17.1	12.6	46.0	27.0	68.2	50.6
School level								
Primary	67.3	18.7	11.0	6.2	27.8	12.5	54.8	34.1
Middle	94.4	63.1	25.2	19.7	68.7	43.3	87.8	72.6
High	95.2	77.3	31.8	29.5	85.6	67.7	93.6	86.9
Combined	83.5	46.2	17.4	13.2	54.9	33.9	75.0	55.3
Locale								
City	82.5	39.9	23.2	17.4	47.2	30.3	73.1	54.6
Suburban	78.2	35.3	15.4	11.5	47.0	29.7	71.0	52.5

Town	81.7	41.8	16.6	12.1	51.0	32.3	70.1	56.4
Rural	71.9	35.9	14.4	10.0	42.1	22.1	61.5	44.1

[a] Violent incidents include the serious violent incidences (rape or attempted rape, sexual battery other than rape, physical attack or fight with a weapon, threat of physical attack with a weapon, and robbery with or without a weapon), physical attack or fight without a weapon, and threat of physical attack without a weapon.

[b] Serious violent incidences include rape or attempted rape, sexual battery other than rape, physical attack or fight with a weapon, threat of physical attack with a weapon, and robbery with or without a weapon.

[c] Theft/larceny (taking things worth over $10 without personal confrontation) was defined as the unlawful taking of another person's property without personal confrontation threat, violence, or bodily harm to include pocket picking, stealing a purse or backpack, theft from building or motor vehicle, bicycles, theft from vending machines, and other thefts.

[d] Other incidences include possession of a firearm or explosive device; possession of a knife or sharp object; distribution, possession, or use of illegal drugs or alcohol; vandalism.

Source: Adapted from Institute of Education Sciences, U.S. Department of Education—National Center for Education Statistics (2008). The condition of education: School violence and safety. http://nces.ed.gov/pubs2008/2008031_App1/pdf. To access full report http://nces.ed.gov/surveys/AnnualReports/.

Legislation

There are federal and state laws and initiatives that provide a foundation for establishing a safe school, many of which address disciplinary issues. The conflicts that typically occur around safety and discipline issues are often because laws are applied too broadly, disciplinary policies disregard specific circumstances, and/or students are kept out of school (National Conference of State Legislatures, 2000). This next section focuses on federal legislation that addresses school safety, school crisis planning, and disciplinary issues; however, readers are also encouraged to identify specific state legislation and initiatives within their own state that support building and maintaining a safe schools environment.

No Child Left Behind Act of 2001

The No Child Left Behind (NCLB) Act of 2001 has put tremendous pressure on administrators and other school personnel to increase academic achievement. However, if students do not feel physically and/or emotionally safe at school, little academic instruction and real learning can take place (Ratner et al., 2006; Rigby, 2007). Interventions and programming that promote a safe school climate while maintaining focus on academic achievement are of critical importance.

Although NCLB is primarily directed toward academic growth, Section 9532 (Part E—Subpart 2) of NCLB contains an Unsafe School Choice option, which states the following:

> (a) UNSAFE SCHOOL CHOICE POLICY—Each State receiving funds under this Act shall establish and implement a statewide policy requiring that a student attending a persistently dangerous public elementary school or secondary school, as determined by the State in consultation with a representative sample of local educational agencies, or who becomes a victim of a violent criminal offense, as determined by State law, while in or on the grounds of a public elementary school or secondary school that the student attends, be allowed to attend a safe public elementary school or secondary school within the local educational agency, including a public charter school.

While this section of NCLB is meant to protect students, it also has some educators fearful, and therefore potentially less likely to publicly report disciplinary infractions. Yet, at the same time, this section of NCLB has also grabbed the attention of school administrators to facilitate the open dialogue and initiative to address school safety in a more direct way. Ninety-two percent of states have passed school safety–related laws (School Health Policy and Programs Study [SHPPS], 2007) and NCLB also has a provision that requires districts or schools to have a crisis plan. However, many of these school safety laws lack specific best practice guidelines and definitions, which in turn results in great variability in how the laws are interpreted and implemented (U.S. GAO, 2007). Some school crisis plans are missing key components altogether, for example, addressing only the response phase and not the mitigation/prevention, preparedness, or recovery phases.

NCLB also includes a duty of care and supervision provision that protects teachers, principals, and other school personnel from frivolous litigation when they take reasonable actions to maintain order (U. S. Department of Education, 2007f). This provision also extends to suicide and threatening behavior. According to Bailey (2006), a school typically cannot be held liable for sudden, spontaneous acts of violence as long as adequate supervision of school grounds was in place. Therefore, Bailey recommends providing an overview of school safety plans in board meetings, school newsletters, and other outreach efforts to heighten awareness and knowledge of school security efforts.

Zero-Tolerance Policies
Zero-tolerance policies were intended to provide uniformity with punishment. However, the reality of implementing zero tolerance policies has placed many administrators in very difficult positions as a "one size fits all" approach does not allow for common sense to prevail and can lead to overreaction. In addition, such policies may lead to an unrealistic approach where teachers and administrators lose discretion to respond to specific situations (National Conference of State Legislatures, 2000). Most zero tolerance policies include expulsion for taking a gun to school. However, many also include suspension or expulsion for threats, possessing drugs, having a weapon, and/or disruption. Zero tolerance policies are also questioned when the developmental and cognitive age of the student and the seriousness and viability of the situation is not taken into consideration. For example, a first grader stating, "I'll kill you," is different from a high school student making a similar threat. Suspending or expelling a student for having aspirin, because it is considered a "drug," is not the

same as a student who possesses crack cocaine on campus. Contrary to the research and counterpoints regarding zero tolerance policies, these policies are still popular even though they are found to be ineffective in making schools safer (Skiba, 2004). Zero tolerance policies have created environments with unfair practices. Specifically, research has shown those students who have been suspended under these policies are more likely to be referred for disciplinary action in the future and these policies have led to a disproportionate number of males and children from low socioeconomic status (SES) and ethnic and minority backgrounds being referred for disciplinary actions (Skiba, 2000, 2004; Skiba, Peterson, & Williams, 1997; Tobin & Sugai, 1996). There is also concern, especially with bullying, that zero tolerance policies may actually discourage children and adults from reporting observed bullying due to the severe punishments (United States Department of Health & Human Services, n.d.). The exclusionary practices of suspension and expulsion may decrease undesired behavior at the time it occurs, but over time these practices do not usually result in long-lasting positive behavior change (Constenbader & Markson, 1998; Skiba & Peterson, 2000). Therefore, instead of exclusively using punitive measures, the student should also be provided with appropriate services to help change the undesired behavior. However, such appropriate counseling services and social skills–building curriculums (i.e., anger management training) are not available in many schools. When options are not available to help the student, but instead punishment is the only intervention available, the chance for the student to develop positive replacement behaviors is decreased and the argument for alternative education is pushed to the political forefront (National Conference of State Legislatures, 2000).

To summarize, establishment of a safe school climate with prevention efforts and multi-tiered interventions is comparatively cost-effective, can counteract the negative implications of zero tolerance policies, and can lead to long-lasting positive change not only in individuals, but also within the entire system.

Family Educational Rights and Privacy Act

The Family Educational Rights and Privacy Act ([FERPA] 20 U.S.C. § 1232g; 34 CFR Part 99; U. S. Department of Education, 2007b) is a federal law that protects the privacy of student educational records in K–12 educational settings that receive funds from the U.S. Department of Education. Typically, to release any student information, written permission must be received from the parent or eligible student. However, there are a few exceptions to disclosure where consent is not needed such as when a concern regarding the safety of students, staff, or the school environment emerges. Depending on the specificity and severity of the concern, it may fall under one of these exceptions and information may be released to (U. S. Department of Education, 2007b; National Conference of State Legislatures, 2000):

1. School officials with legitimate interest
2. Other schools to which a student is transferring
3. To comply with a judicial order or lawfully issued subpoena
4. Appropriate officials in cases of health and safety emergencies
5. State and local authorities, within a juvenile justice system, pursuant to specific law

In addition, "school officials may disclose any and all education records, including disciplinary records and records that were created as a result of a student receiving special education services under Part B of the Individuals with Disabilities Education Act, to another school or postsecondary institution at which the student seeks or intends to enroll" (U. S. Department of Education, 2007a, p. 2, Individuls with Disabilities Education Improvement Act of 2004). Although consent is not needed, the disclosure statement should indicate these potential exceptions and, if requested, a copy of the disclosed information must be provided. FERPA as now written has supported safe school efforts by not allowing parents to jump from school to school and withhold information when their child is facing disciplinary action or is involved with special education services. Chapter 8 discusses FERPA regulations and their relationship to threats or other dangerous behavior.

Proposed Legislation

In fall of 2007, the Positive Behavior for Effective Schools Act (GovTrack US, 2007b, 2007c) and the Safe Schools Improvement Act of 2007 (GovTrack.us 2007c) were both introduced for federal legislation. The Positive Behavior for Effective Schools Act (Senate Bill 2111) was introduced by then-Senator Barack Obama and a parallel bill was introduced in the House (H.R.

3407). These proposed bills allowed the use of Title 1 funds for Positive Behavior Supports and would promote early intervention services. The Safe Schools Improvement Act of 2007 (H.R. 3132) would have improved school safety by bringing new attention to the need for schools to monitor incidences of bullying and harassment, include bullying and harassment within the federal definition of violence (which is currently not included), and implement prevention programs to remedy these problems. Although neither of these bills became law, it is encouraging that Positive Behavior Supports, early intervention services, and more direct attention to bullying, harassment, and prevention programs were brought forth for federal legislation. There remains the possibility that these could be reintroduced at a later date. In addition, 39 states have already passed anti-bullying legislation (Bailey, 2008), and further inclusion of bullying in the federal definition of violence would strengthen already existing legislation.

THE PRESENT VOLUME

Ninety-two percent of states require schools to have crisis plans (Adamson & Peacock, 2007; National Center for Education Statistics, 2004; SHPPS, 2007), and while over 95% of school districts across the country report having a crisis plan, only 66% of states require that the plans be reviewed and revised (SHPPS, 2007). In our experience, this oversight and accountability gap is concerning, and instead of districts actively reviewing and utilizing their crisis plan, many plans are collecting dust on a shelf. One of the primary goals of this book is to provide the information and resources needed to establish a safe school climate through the use of a dynamic, cooperative, and comprehensive process that involves prevention, crisis preparedness, and planning, and additionally provides a continuum of interventions addressing the educational, physical, and psychological safety needs of students and staff. A second goal of this book is to broaden how school professionals view crisis planning; it is not just planning for a crisis response. The primary focus of crisis planning should be to establish a safe school climate that embeds crisis prevention, preparedness, response, *and* recovery within a school's daily structure and education programming to balance both physical *and* psychological safety while increasing academic achievement. One example of crisis planning that provides this balance comes from the Cherry Creek School District's (2008) comprehensive safe schools model that integrates the recommendations of the USDOE, the National Incident Management System (NIMS), and the Federal Emergency Management Agency (FEMA), which will be discussed further in subsequent chapters, and also balances physical and psychological safety with the four phases of crisis prevention through recovery (Figure 1.3).

Section I and Chapter 1 of this book introduce key concepts that provide the foundation for establishing a safe school climate. As part of this foundation, Chapter 2 identifies the key stakeholders involved, identifies strategies to obtain their support, and discusses physical safety and psychological assessment processes. Section II addresses physical safety and psychological safety through a multi-hazards

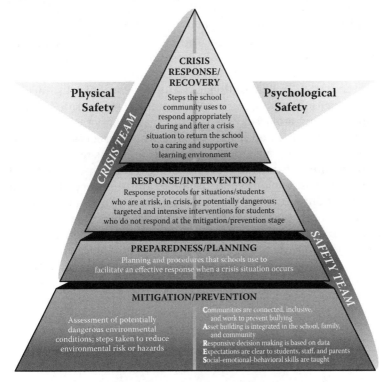

Cherry Creek School District
Comprehensive Safe Schools Plan

Figure 1.3 Cherry Creek School District Comprehensive Safe Schools Plan (2008). *Source*: Reprinted with permission from Cherry Creek School District, Greenwood Village, Colorado (2008).

approach to prevention and preparedness. In this section, Chapter 3 addresses physical safety through the utilization of a multi-hazards approach to establishing a safe learning environment and crisis preparedness plans. Chapter 4 introduces the National Incident Management System (NIMS) and adaptation of the Incident Command System (ICS) to establish an effective district safety team and school crisis team, while Chapter 5 focuses on crisis response plans. The book concludes with Section III, to focus more specifically on psychological safety. Chapter 6 provides guidelines and specific resources for establishing a safe school through universal prevention efforts, with Chapter 7 providing the structure for early and targeted interventions. Chapter 8 discusses students who exhibit risky and potentially dangerous behavior and provides specific structures and procedures to address their intensive needs, with Chapter 9 presenting specific crisis management and recovery efforts needed in the event of a crisis. Table 1.2 provides a summary of key elements provided in this book according to the multi-tiered model, balancing both physical and psychological safety.

It is critical to emphasize that comprehensive safe schools planning encompasses the multiple components introduced in this chapter. In addition, is not a linear process, but a circular process in nature and must be actively reviewed and implemented year after year. Good prevention/mitigation and preparedness leads to good response and recovery, for which good response and recovery leads to the return of a perception of safety and the prevention and mitigation of future events. Figure 1.4 is a visual graphic of the Comprehensive Safe Learning Environments approach advocated for within this book. We encourage the reader to refer back to this model after reading each chapter.

Table 1.2 Physical and Psychological Safe School Measures Spanning a Comprehensive Framework for Creating and Sustaining a Safe Schools Climate

	Universal	Targeted	Intensive
Physical safety	Collaboration with key stakeholders and community agencies (Chs. 2 & 4) Physical safety audits and data analysis (Ch. 2) Multi-hazards approach (Ch. 3) Establishment of safety teams (Ch. 2) and crisis teams (Ch. 4) Development of prevention and preparedness plans (Ch. 3) and crisis response plans (Ch. 5) Universal mitigation activities (Ch. 6)	Implementing further safety measures in response to audits and data analysis (Ch. 2)	Law enforcement collaboration to respond to threats and acts that threaten physical safety (Ch. 8)
Psychological safety	Collaboration with key stakeholders and community agencies (Chs. 2 & 4) Psychological safety assessment and data analysis (Ch. 2) Psychological safety response: planning and training (Ch. 3) Establishment of safety teams (Ch. 2) and crisis teams (Ch. 4) Development of prevention and preparedness plans (Ch. 3) and crisis response plans (Ch. 5) Psychological safety prevention activities: positive behavior supports; school-wide programming regarding positive school climate, culture, and expectations (Ch. 6)	Identification of at-risk students and risk factors (Chs. 7 & 8) Confidential reporting procedures of threatsl (Ch. 7) Evidence-based interventions to teach positive, pro-social skills, in addition to academics (Ch. 7)	Threat and suicide assessment and interventions (Ch. 8) Intensive mental health crisis interventions (Ch. 9)
	Psychological assessment of psychological needs and triage following a traumatic event (Ch. 9) Crisis response and recovery interventions (Ch. 9)		

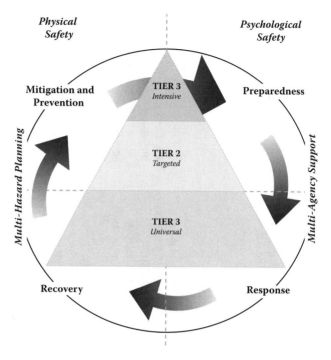

Figure 1.4   Comprehensive safe learning environment: The M-PHAT approach. *Source*: Adapted from Office of Special Education Programs (2009). *Response to intervention and PBS*. Retrieved April 11, 2009, from http://www.pbis.org/rti/default.aspx. In public domain; and U. S. Department of Education, 2007. Practical information on crisis planning: A guide for schools and communities. Washington, DC. In public domain.

Two

System-Wide Considerations: Stakeholder Support and Data-Driven Decision Making

Before considering the specific strategies and procedures that comprise the critical components for establishing safe schools, it is necessary to review general factors that are relevant when undergoing any sort of systemic change within a school. Consideration of these factors will increase the efficiency and maximize the likelihood of success of the safe schools planning efforts that are undertaken. This is particularly important given that schools may be called upon to implement comprehensive safe schools planning under conditions of limited resources, and with overextended staff. This discussion will begin with the importance of stakeholders.

THE IMPORTANCE OF STAKEHOLDERS

Support from stakeholders, or "anyone who has a concern in relation to the problem" (OSEP, 2004), is important for many reasons. Generally, involving stakeholders in a system change effort helps to improve communication, increase accountability, justify funding and resources, and promote sustainability of the efforts over time (OSEP, 2004). More specifically, the support of administrators is repeatedly cited as a critical factor for the success of any intervention within a school (Elliott, 2006; Gottfredson & Gottfredson, 2002; Kam, Greenberg, & Walls, 2003; Lohrmann, Forman, Martin, & Palmieri, 2008). Administrators control the resources, such as money, staff, and time (Elias, Zins, Graczyk, & Weissberg, 2003); their attitude can influence the staff's likelihood to support the intervention;

their commitment over time is needed for sustainability of the intervention (Lohrman et al., 2008); and they serve encouraging and monitoring roles (Han & Weiss, 2005). In addition to support from administrators, support from school staff is also critical as they are often the ones who are called upon to implement changes in the school. Their consensus on the need for the change, beliefs and attitudes toward the new initiatives, and ownership of the proposed changes are clearly critical if changes are to be effective (D'Andrea, 2004; Elias et al., 2003; Fixsen, Naoom, Blase, Friedman, & Wallace, 2005; Lohrmann et al., 2008; Weissberg, 2004).

In addition to garnering support from administration and staff, encouraging all members of the school community (i.e., *all* school staff), parents, and relevant community organizations to be involved in the efforts is of importance (Greenberg, Weissberg, O'Brien, Zins, Fredricks, Resnik, & Elias, 2003; Leadbeater, Hoglund, & Woods, 2003; Weissberg, 2004) as this sets the foundation and relationships necessary for the multi-agency efforts in the preparedness phase, and may be called upon in the response and recovery phases. Given that change in a school can take several years and there is great likelihood of staff turnover, inclusion of all people who have an interest in the change and who can act as change agents is important to ensure sustainability over time (Elliott, Kratochwill, & Roach, 2003). It has also been noted that collaboration by schools with community agency partners is a common trait of the most successful school emergency management programs (U. S. Department of Education, 2007e). This makes sense given that crises are not always contained within a school. Coordination of crisis preparedness and response plans with community agencies can avoid duplication of efforts, ensure open channels of communication, and also help reduce the burden of efforts on planners.

Who Are Key Stakeholders in School Safety?

Stakeholders for safe schools planning are broadly defined by the U.S. Department of Education (2007e) as "the people who are concerned about the safety of the school and the people who call to assist when a crisis occurs" (p. 3-3). Based on this definition and the discussion above, clearly a broad array of people can be included under the title of "stakeholder in school safety." Some of these people are in the school building itself, and some are outside; some are obvious, and others might be thought of as more nontraditional partners (Elliott, Grady, Shaw, Aultman-Bettridge, & Beaulieu, 2000; U. S. Department

Table 2.1   School Safety Stakeholders

Administration: leadership at the top level is critical.
- Building principal and administrative team
- School board/superintendent

School staff: leadership can come from the grass roots level as well as from the top; these are the people who will carry out the plans.
- Teachers
- Mental health staff
- Security staff
- Nursing/medical staff
- Teacher aides/paraprofessionals
- Support staff: office, custodial, cafeteria

Families: as consumers of the plans, their input will be valuable.
- Parents
- Students

Community organizations: coordinate plans, create common vocabulary, utilize their expertise in order to not reinvent the wheel.
- Response agencies: police and fire departments, emergency medical services
- Helping agencies: mental health centers, health care facilities, crisis hotlines
- Social service agencies
- Public health professionals
- Business leaders
- Clergy/churches
- Local media
- Area colleges
- Legal counsel
- Local government officials

Note: This is not an exhaustive list and can very depending on district and school size, resources, and needs.

Sources: Adapted from Elliott, D. S., Grady, J. M., Shaw, T. E., Aultman-Bettridge, T., & Beaulieu, M. T. (2000). U. S. Department of Education. (2007c).

of Education, 2007c). Table 2.1 highlights the key stakeholders in school safety. It is important to note that others may be added depending on unique school or district characteristics and needs.

Barriers to Collaboration With Stakeholders

When stakeholders collaborate, it often requires they alter their normal activities, learn about each other, and decide how they will share responsibilities. According to the U.S. Department of Education (2008), "Schools and first responders each have distinct responsibilities that complement each other in school emergencies, but that foster unique organizational cultures, administrative structures, organizational priorities, and roles" (p. 2). For example, schools typically make many decisions based on a consensus approach among staff; however, first responder agencies require clear lines of authority and the ability to make immediate decisions with minimal time for dialogue and consensus. In addition, first responders are primarily responsible for physical safety and the immediate implications of the event, while schools are responsible for physical safety and psychological safety, in addition to long-term implications of the event. The differences in decision-making approaches and responsibilities are necessary to meet the goals and outcomes of each organization, but if these differences in style are not understood it can lead to challenges for coordination and leadership. Oftentimes "turf" and communication issues emerge due to these differences and professional priorities. These issues may emerge within or among agencies outside of the school, but may also arise within the school. For example, it is not uncommon to find that school counselors and school psychologists, or teachers within different subject area departments, have not had the time to collaborate and communicate about emerging safety issues and/or students of common concern. Therefore, dialogue and collaboration with all key stakeholders in advance of an event occurring is of critical importance.

Integration With Multi-Hazards Approach to Prevention and Preparedness

As part of its multi-hazard emergency planning for schools training, FEMA states that the all-hazards or multi-hazards approach is recommended because "planning issues are the same, regardless of the type of emergency" (FEMA, 2004b, p. 1). FEMA includes emergencies such as natural hazards (e.g., earthquakes or floods), technological hazards (e.g., power outages or nuclear accidents), and human-made hazards (e.g., chemical spills or terrorism). Although the focus of the current volume encompasses more than just the types of "hazards" that FEMA discusses, clearly these incidents are ones that could impact schools. Therefore, schools' use of the multi-hazards approach is also important. In fact, the authors would advocate expanding the multi-hazards approach for schools to include preparedness and response planning for other typical school crises, such as the death of a student or staff member, suicide threats or completions, and other dangerous behavior, such as weapons on campus, mental health emergencies, etc. One assumption of the multi-hazards and multi-agency approach for schools is that many types of emergencies that schools could potentially encounter may necessitate assistance from an outside response agency. Therefore, consultation and communication with outside response and service agencies before a crisis occurs becomes an essential part of safe schools planning and developing a crisis preparedness plan.

According to FEMA (2008a), in order to ensure that first-responder services are delivered to schools in a timely and efficient manner, it is essential that school districts participate in local government National Incident Management System (NIMS) preparedness programs. NIMS is a "comprehensive approach to crisis planning and is a framework for federal, state, local and private agencies to effectively and collaboratively manage incidents using a core set of concepts, principles, procedures, processes, terminology and standards" (U. S. Department of Education, 2006a, p. 1). As part of this framework, it is recommended that common and consistent NIMS terminology be used across agencies to establish communication in plain language (FEMA, 2008b). This is echoed by the U.S. Department of Education's observation that common knowledge of each other's terminology is critical for school staff and emergency responders (U. S. Department of Education, 2007c). In short, FEMA recommends that school emergency planning include training for staff on the importance of shared principles and the use of common terminology when outside agencies are called into the emergency. NIMS provides schools with a starting point for ensuring they will have an approach that is compatible with emergency responders. NIMS and its application for schools are discussed further in Chapters 3 and 4.

In conclusion, support from stakeholders is important for many reasons. From a systemic perspective, many different people need to be "on board" with the safe schools efforts if they are to succeed. Administrators and school staff who will drive the safe schools planning should agree that it is needed and worth attention over time. Students and parents, who will be consumers of the plans, are important for the input that they can give. Members of the surrounding community may not implement all pieces of the plan, but they will be included at critical moments as part of the multi-agency preparedness, response, and recovery efforts. Their expertise can help with planning efforts, and it is clearly necessary that all those who are responding to a crisis share a common language and coordinated procedures. Therefore, all of these players will be needed at the table during some point in the safe schools planning process.

IMPORTANCE OF DATA IN THE PROCESS

Though it is clearly important to involve key stakeholders when planning for safe learning environments, it may not always be the case that all stakeholders are in agreement on the necessity of change. Data can be gathered to demonstrate the degree and nature of concerns with student safety in the school and within the community (Elliott et al., 2000). Quantification of these concerns provides a concrete means of demonstrating which areas of school safety are going well and which areas could be improved. Not only can this information help to facilitate support from stakeholders who might otherwise believe their school is "safe," it also can help to more precisely identify what areas need to be addressed by the school. The goal of creating a safe learning environment can be overwhelming, because it is arguably somewhat subjective and can encompass a large variety of tasks. Assessment data can help narrow down specific targets for change or intervention. Further, effective mitigation and prevention planning require assessment of the school's concerns and common incidents. Needs assessments and other data are also important for effective development of crisis plans (U. S. Department of Education, 2007c). One additional benefit to gathering data is that planning data can serve as a benchmark against which future school safety concerns can be measured (Elliott et al., 2000).

The U.S. Department of Education (2008) summarizes the data-gathering process with the term "vulnerability assessment," described as "the ongoing process for identifying and prioritizing risks to the individual schools and school districts" (p. 1). In order to thoroughly assess schools' susceptibility to threats or hazards, an ongoing team approach to data gathering that includes a variety of types of assessments is recommended. Specifically recommended are

1. Needs assessment to identify areas needing improvement/unmet needs
2. Hazards assessments to determine which hazards are relevant for a given school
3. Threat assessment to assess students who may pose a threat to safety
4. Consequence assessment to delineate potential negative outcomes for schools that would follow a crisis
5. Risk analysis to establish the likelihood of potential hazards or threats

Using a slightly different model, the current discussion will focus on two general areas of data gathering that are warranted, and subsequent chapters will review components of the various assessments listed above. First, a physical safety audit or site assessment should be conducted to determine factors having to do with the physical layout or facilities within the school building that might need to be changed in order to ensure student safety. Factors such as the safety of driveways, parking lots, playgrounds, outside structures, and fencing; control of access to the school building; the presence of/need for cameras; and consideration of how school floor plans impact getting students into and out of the building should be evaluated (U. S. Department of Education, 2007c). Hazards, risk, and consequence assessments as described above are also included in this area of data gathering. The second area to be assessed has to do with the human factors that impact how safe students are and how safe students feel at school. Included in this area are school policies, staff training, and prevention and intervention programs (DeMary, Owens, & Ramnarain, 2000; Elliott et al., 2000; Texas School Safety Center, 2008). Assessment of factors such as the degree of bullying or harassment that occurs; how safe parents, students, and staff believe that students are; how they perceive the climate of the school; and the prevalence of dangerous and or risky behaviors in which students engage can help to complete the picture of student safety (Elliott et al., 2000; U. S. Department of Education, 2007d).

What Does the Data Gathering Look Like?
Physical Safety Audit
Thorough evaluation of all of the physical features of a school building, its grounds, and surrounding area that have a

potential impact on school safety is a potentially lengthy task, particularly for larger school buildings/multiple building complexes. Several states have created safety audit systems (see Table 2.2) recommended by the National Clearinghouse for Educational Facilities (NCEF, 2008) that are available on-line. Also based on the work of NCEF, Table 2.3 provides a more thorough listing of categories, with a brief description of each that should be included as part of a physical safety audit.

Under the U.S. Department of Education (2008a) and the Office of Safe and Drug Free Schools (2008c) vulnerability assessment model, schools also need to determine the degree of likelihood and potential impact of a wide variety of hazards and/or risk factors. Using a process of identifying how likely a hazard is, on what scale it would impact the school, how severe the event would be, and how much advance warning the school would have, schools can prioritize which hazards to address. See Table 2.4 for a sample risk index worksheet where schools can list and rate potential hazards that could impact their schools. Data gathered from both the physical and psychological safety assessments can be used to make these determinations. In addition, collaboration with community partners such as law enforcement, fire agencies, emergency medical services, building inspectors, public health officials, transportation officials, public utility officials, and

Table 2.2   Online Resources for Physical Safety Audits

1. Florida Safe School Design Guidelines: Strategies to Enhance Security and Reduce Vandalism
   Florida Department of Education, 2003
   http://www.fldoe.org/edfacil/pdf/fl_ssg.pdf
2. Safe Schools Facilities Planner
   North Carolina Department of Public Instruction, 1998
   http://www.schoolclearinghouse.org/pubs/safesch.pdf
3. K12 Security and Vulnerability Assessment
   Kentucky Center for School Safety, no date
   http://www.kycss.org/emp/SSVulnerabilityAssessment.doc
4. Campus Safety and Security Audit Toolkit
   Texas School Safety Center, 2006
   http://cscs.txstate.edu/txssc/txssc-safety-audits.htm
5. School Safety Audit Protocol
   Demary, Owens, & Ramnarian—Virginia Department of Education, 2000
   http://www.doe.virginia.gov/VDOE/Instruction/schoolsafety/safetyaudit.pdf

members of the community that provide mitigation for other potential hazards will be helpful in making determinations of the relative importance/degree of risk to the school of the various hazards. According to the U.S. Department of Education (2008a), "Local emergency planning councils regularly assess these elements for community planning and may be able to offer input" (p. 12).

Psychological Safety Assessment

Although much of the information on the physical safety of students can be determined objectively with observation, not all student safety data can be obtained in this manner. For example, determining the impact of school and district policy on student safety, or whether existing prevention and intervention programming is adequate, requires some subjective judgments. Students' experiences with bullying and perceptions of safety are also difficult to evaluate objectively. Students have been noted to be more aware of peer aggression and victimization in school settings than adults, as teachers do not always observe these behaviors and students do not always tell teachers when it has happened (Craig & Pepler, 1997; Pellegrini & Bartini, 2000; Smith & Sharp, 1994). In addition, in the author's district-wide psychological safety surveys of 3rd through 12th grade students given in a large suburban Denver school district (see District Example of Using Data to Establishing a Safe School Climate section below for more information on the district and the survey), when asked, "How safe have you felt at school?" elementary students consistently report that they feel less safe at school than older students. In contrast, parent and staff ratings of student safety reflect perceptions of decreasing levels of student safety with age (Figure 2.1). While approximately two thirds of students reported feeling safe in this survey, it is important to pay attention to those who are reporting otherwise. It is not clear why the younger students are less likely to report that they are safe at school; perhaps it is a reflection of a general sense of less control over the environment for younger students, paired with an elevated sense of invulnerability for adolescents. What is more clear is that at all levels, the degree to which students are perceived as safe at school differs depending on who— parents, students, or staff—is asked. For this reason, for some content areas it is necessary to survey all relevant stakeholders, ideally getting responses from parents, students, and staff. Therefore, assessment of psychological safety variables will

Table 2.3 Domains to Be Included in a Physical Safety Audit
With a Brief Description of Desirable Features for That Domain

School Grounds and Site Access Control

Site Surveillance

- Easy monitoring of all areas

Site Territoriality—Maintenance

- School boundaries and all buildings are clearly marked
- Building and grounds are well maintained
- Entrances to property and main building entrance are clear

Site Access Control

- Minimal entrances (but at least two)
- Access for emergency vehicles
- Entrances can be secured
- Fencing balances access control, territoriality, and surveillance

School Surroundings

- Potential threats (e.g., power plants, transportation lines) near the school evaluated

High-Risk Sites

- Consider vehicle checkpoints, chemical spill risk, fire evacuation, and explosive attack possibility

Earthquake, Wind, and Flood Protection

- For areas prone to these, adequate measures taken to minimize potential risks (safe refuge sites identified, alternate routes into and out of site identified, objects adequately secured against falling, etc.)

Landscaping

- Done to mark boundaries, but not obstruct views/allow for places to hide
- Well kept so as not to become hazardous

Site and Exterior Building Lighting

- Uniform, no pockets of shadows
- Goal = natural surveillance that discourages trespassing and vandalism
- Vandal-resistant and well maintained

Traffic Circulation

- Done to avoid accidents, speeding, and blind spots
- Consider pedestrian safety—separate pedestrian and vehicles at entry/exit
- Emergency vehicle access
- Handicapped parking
- Minimize/eliminate hiding places along pedestrian routes

School Bus Areas, Parent Pick-Up Areas, and Public Transportation

- Designated loading and unloading zone with minimized crowding, prohibited parking, and location separate from parent drop-off and pick-up
- Safe access to public transportation

Table 2.3   (continued) Domains to Be Included in a Physical Safety Audit With a Brief Description of Desirable Features for That Domain

Vehicle Parking
- Clearly marked (who goes where)
- Supervised
- Limited access
- Gates for non-school times
- Separate student/staff parking
- Bicycles secure

Dumpster Enclosures
- Enclosed, cannot be used to climb on building

Site Utilities
- Transformers, generators, and meters have limited access, do not block emergency vehicles, and cannot be climbed on
- Kept locked/secured
- Fire hydrants visible

Storm Water Retention Areas
- Used to mark boundaries
- Nonclimbable fences
- Accessible pipes

Outdoor Athletic Facilities and Playgrounds

Natural Surveillance
- In view of building staff

Boundaries and Setbacks
- Play areas/student gathering places clearly defined, protected by fencing and set back from street

Separation from Vehicular Traffic
- Areas separated from normal vehicular traffic, but accessible to emergency vehicles

Play Areas and Equipment
- Younger and older child play areas separated
- Areas free of potential projectiles
- Protective surfaces surround play equipment
- Equipment well maintained

Joint Use Facilities
- After-hours community areas have own amenities
- Access to school can be limited during non-school hours

Bleachers, Field Houses, and Outbuildings
- Well maintained
- Securable from intruders   *—continued*

Table 2.3   (continued) Domains to Be Included in a Physical Safety Audit With a Brief Description of Desirable Features for That Domain

Water Fountains

- Vandal-resistant
- Well secured
- Wheelchair accessible

Vending Machines and Public Telephones

- Well monitored
- Adequately secured
- Phone available outside building

Building Access Control: Entry Doors, Windows, Walls, Roofs
General

- 100% control of access to building
- Areas not in use secured
- Directions to entry areas clear
- Rules clearly posted

Exterior Doors

- Minimal number
- Designed to prevent unauthorized access
- Sized and arranged to reduce crowding
- Windows not located so, if broken, door could be opened from the inside
- Designed to resist thrown or wind-blown objects

Exterior Walls

- No building niches or blind spots that allow places to hide
- No footholds (nonclimbable)

Windows

- Designed to enhance surveillance
- Locks secure
- In good condition
- Protected from unauthorized entry
- Usable as secondary means of escape

Windows in High-Risk Areas

- Designed to resist explosives, gunfire, or forced entry

Roofs

- Access limited
- Visual surveillance possible from ground
- Heavy roofing materials (tiles) secure

Canopies, Awnings, Breezeways, and Covered Walkways

- Cannot be climbed on
- Adequately lit

Table 2.3 (continued) Domains to Be Included in a Physical Safety Audit With a Brief Description of Desirable Features for That Domain

- Observable
- Well engineered

Courtyards

- Visual surveillance possible
- Access controlled/lockable
- Entry doors prevent congestion

High-Value Targets

- High-security locks for areas holding high-value targets for theft (e.g., offices, computer rooms, music rooms, etc.)

Entry and Reception Areas

Main Entry

- Identifiable
- Supervised
- Well lit
- Designed to prevent overcrowding

Secondary Entries and Exits

- Kept to a minimum
- Don't serve as concealed areas for unwanted activities

Reception Area

- Electronically lockable external doors
- Visitors obliged to confer with receptionist/are seen by reception staff
- Protective features (e.g., panic button, telephone) in place
- Administrators can view area

High-Risk Schools

- Bullet-resistant windows/walls
- Entries, windows, walls designed to be blast resistant

Nonstructural Hazards

- Freestanding heavy objects (e.g., bookcases) adequately secured against falling
- Ceilings, lighting fixtures, and partitions secured in earthquake-prone areas

Corridors, Interior Doors, and Lockers

Corridors

- Well lit
- Allow for natural surveillance/no hiding areas
- No freestanding objects or flammable decorative materials
- Walls decorated to promote ownerships of school
- Wide enough to minimize overcrowding
- Exit routes posted and exit signs visible *—continued*

Table 2.3 (continued) Domains to Be Included in a Physical Safety Audit With a Brief Description of Desirable Features for That Domain

- Water fountains secured and out of traffic flow
- Vending machines well placed and monitored

Interior Doors

- Staff can quickly lock doors without stepping into hall
- Master keys available
- Can open classroom doors from inside if need to exit
- Open doors do not project into corridor
- Doors sized and arranged to minimize crowding

Lockers

- Locked with school-owned locks
- Designed/spaced to minimize crowding

Stairs and Stairwells

- Located and designed to minimize congestion and accidents
- Well lit
- Adequate hand rails
- Natural surveillance or electronic monitoring
- Well designed in high-risk areas

Elevators

- Monitored
- Secured
- Well lit

Exitways

- Clear of obstruction
- Free of locks/chains that would prevent escape
- Number of exits up to fire code
- Exit routes clearly visible

Classrooms

Natural Surveillance

- All parts of classroom visible from door
- No hiding places
- Well lit

Windows in High-Risk Areas

- Designed and located so as to resist explosives, gunfire, or forced entry

Electrical Lighting

- Easy to clean and maintain

Table 2.3 (continued) Domains to Be Included in a Physical Safety Audit With a Brief Description of Desirable Features for That Domain

Communications

- On public address system
- Two-way communications are possible
- Cell phones can be used

Doors and Secondary Escape Routes

- Doors can be locked quickly without stepping into corridor
- Master keys available
- Intruders could not lock doors
- Can be opened from inside in case of emergency exit
- Exterior doors are solid and lockable
- Escape routes clear
- Evacuation possible for mobility-impaired students

Fire Safety

- Heat-producing appliances are guarded
- Materials/artwork on no more than 20% of wall area
- Decorations are flame resistant

Nonstructural Hazards

- Freestanding heavy objects adequately secured against falling
- Ceilings, lighting fixtures, and partitions secured in earthquake-prone areas

Portable Classrooms

- Located to maximize security
- Adequate internal security features
- Clearly identifiable
- Access beneath portable is restricted
- Heavy objects secured
- Proper considerations for earthquake-prone areas

Art, Music, and Dance Rooms

Art Room

- Clear view of entire area
- Kilns properly located, ventilated, and secured
- Proper storage of photography supplies

Music Room

- Clear view of entire area
- Locked storage for instruments
- Alarm system
- Choir risers are safe

—continued

Table 2.3 (continued) Domains to Be Included in a Physical Safety Audit With a Brief Description of Desirable Features for That Domain

Dance Room

- Clear view of entire area
- Locked storage for equipment
- Dressing areas supervised
- Safe flooring and mirrors

Labs, Shops, and Computer Rooms

- Clear view of work and entry areas
- Alarm systems in place
- Equipment and chemical storage locked
- Fire extinguishers in place
- "Kill switches" for hazardous machines
- Eye wash stations in place
- Logs used for chemicals and dangerous substances
- Battery-powered lights for chemical storerooms
- Equipment in good working order
- Proper ventilation
- Freestanding heavy objects adequately secured against falling
- Ceilings, lighting fixtures, and partitions secured in earthquake-prone areas

Offices, Workrooms, and Conference Rooms

School Office

- Confidential records properly stored
- Two-way communication systems in place
- Has a windowless "safe room" with a phone and lockable doors for emergencies

Principal's Office

- Has secondary exit

Guidance Office, Teachers' Workrooms, and Conference Rooms

- One-to-one adult/child conferencing areas are observable

Nonstructural Hazards

- Freestanding heavy objects adequately secured against falling
- Ceilings, lighting fixtures, and partitions secured in earthquake-prone areas

Windows in High-Risk Areas

- Designed to resist explosives, gunfire, and forced entry

Food Service Areas and Student Commons

- Entryways sufficiently large to prevent overcrowding
- Separate entrance and exits
- Well lit
- Designed to keep noise levels low

Table 2.3   (continued) Domains to Be Included in a Physical Safety Audit With a Brief Description of Desirable Features for That Domain

- Clear view of entire area
- Can be secured after school hours
- If in use after hours, access to rest of school restricted
- Evacuation plans, hand-washing instructions, and air to choking victims signs clearly posted
- Equipment does not block exits
- Freestanding heavy objects adequately secured against falling
- Ceilings, lighting fixtures, and partitions secured in earthquake-prone areas
- Windows designed to resist explosives, gunfire, and forced entry

Restrooms

- Visual surveillance/supervision maximized
- Well lit
- Well maintained
- Vandal-proof fixtures
- Main entry doors lockable only from the outside
- Partition doors proper height, bolted to door, and operable
- Sinks located to deter vandalism and encourage hand washing
- Restrooms located to be accessible for after school activities
- Hot water pipes protected
- Hard ceiling and see-through dispensers (to prevent storage of contraband)
- Windows not advised
- Mirrors shatterproof
- Large event restrooms have two means of entry/egress

Library/Media Center

- Separate and secure access from rest of the building
- Well lit
- Reception area located to control traffic and view entire media center
- Storage areas lockable
- Theft deterrents in place
- Storytelling areas or niches designed to prevent accidents
- Freestanding heavy objects and shelving adequately secured against falling
- Ceilings, lighting fixtures, and partitions secured in earthquake-prone areas
- Windows designed to resist explosives, gunfire, and forced entry

—continued

Table 2.3   (continued) Domains to Be Included in a Physical Safety Audit With a Brief Description of Desirable Features for That Domain

Health Services Center

- Medical equipment and supplies locked in an observable area
- Natural surveillance into patient care areas as needed
- Toilet doors swing outward
- Shelving and equipment properly secured against falling

Auditorium/Theater/Performing Arts Center

- Separate and secure access from rest of the building
- Good visual surveillance
- Designed for good traffic flow and reduced likelihood of falls
- Secure and fireproof storage for equipment
- Lighting and scenery equipment in good repair
- Access to catwalks and lighting equipment controlled
- Curtains nonflammable
- Dressing rooms easily supervised
- Freestanding heavy objects adequately secured against falling
- Ceilings, lighting fixtures, and partitions secured in earthquake-prone areas

Indoor Athletic Facilities

Gymnasium, Fitness Center, Weight Room, or Related Facility

- Separate and secure access from rest of building
- Secure area for equipment
- No hiding places
- Retractable partitions can be locked in place
- Basketball courts given proper safety borders
- Weight room/exercise equipment in good working order
- Bleachers safe and in good condition

Locker Rooms

- Coach's room has unobstructed view of locker area
- Solid ceiling (to prevent storage of contraband)
- Mesh-type lockers to avoid concealing prohibited items
- Lockers spaced to avoid overcrowding
- Lockers maintained with school-owned padlocks
- Mirrors shatterproof
- "Visitor" facilities clearly labeled as such

Nonstructural Hazards

- Freestanding heavy objects adequately secured against falling
- Ceilings, lighting fixtures, and partitions secured in earthquake-prone areas

Table 2.3   (continued) Domains to Be Included in a Physical Safety Audit With a Brief Description of Desirable Features for That Domain

Emergency Communication, Power, Fuel, and Water
Building Notification Systems

- Panic button/duress alarm at front desk
- Mass notification system reaches entire building
- Uninterruptible power supply provides emergency backup power
- In earthquake-prone areas, communication systems are adequately braced and supported
- Wiring distributed so as to prevent tampering
- Panic button or intercom buttons available in isolated areas for high-risk sites

Radio/Wireless Communication Systems

- Necessary equipment to ensure radio communication with EMS personnel in place
- Sufficient number of hand-held two-way or cell phones available for staff

Telephone Systems

- Main telephone distribution room secure and protected against extreme temperatures
- Telephone system has uninterruptible power supply

Emergency Power

- Provisions for emergency power in place throughout building
- Exterior connection for emergency power for other sources available
- Emergency and normal electrical equipment installed at different locations

Exterior Utility Lifelines Protection

- Water supply lines and storage adequately protected
- Other utility lifelines (power; voice, data, and Internet communications; fuel; etc.) have restricted access and are adequately protected from natural disasters and vandalism
- Redundant locations for telephone and communication services to the site

Security and Surveillance Systems
Building Security Systems

- Card access systems in place
- Master key control system in place
- Devices used for physical security integrated with computer security systems (used IDs and passwords)
- Effective use of metal detectors/x-rays for high-risk sites
- Access to information on building operations, schematics, and procedures only available to authorized personnel

Building Surveillance Systems

- Cameras cover appropriate areas of the schools, are appropriately set up and maintained, and are protected against vandalism and tampering, and have an uninterruptible power supply
- Surveillance system protected with firewalls so can't be broken into   *—continued*

Table 2.3 (continued) Domains to Be Included in a Physical Safety Audit With a Brief Description of Desirable Features for That Domain

Fire Alarm and Control Systems

- Meet local code and emergency responder requirements
- Fire extinguishers and pull stations in areas where they can be easily monitored
- Alarms can be perceived and recognized against normal light and noise levels
- Sprinkler heads flush with ceiling
- Fire extinguisher cabinets flush with walls
- Pull stations have tamper deterrents
- Fire alarm panels only accessible to authorized staff
- Redundant off-premises fire alarm reporting
- Fire-detection equipment reasonable protected from an incapacitating mechanical or physical impact
- Outdoor fire detection equipment protected against vandalism and the elements
- Backup power will allow system to operate for 24 hours

Mechanical Systems
Fresh Air Intakes and Exhausts

- Properly located and to prevent tampering/vandalism
- Exhaust outlets are downwind of air intakes

Air Handling and Filtration

- Master ventilation shut-off in designated area
- Air systems have been balanced
- Functional, tight-sealing fire dampers installed and operational
- Smoke evacuation system in place for high-risk sites

Ares of Refuge/Community Shelter

- Areas of refuge or community shelter will be heated/cooled during an emergency

Asbestos

- Asbestos management plan in place if applicable

Equipment Stability

- Heavy mechanical equipment secured

Equipment Inspection, Maintenance, Recommissioning, and Testing

- Well-maintained records of inspections
- All systems properly maintained, recommissioned, and tested on a regular schedule by trained staff

Custodial and Equipment Rooms

- All equipment rooms clearly identified
- Secure doors/locks for equipment rooms
- Fire doors tight-fitting and in good working condition
- Chemical storage areas labeled

Table 2.3   (continued) Domains to Be Included in a Physical
Safety Audit With a Brief Description of Desirable Features for
That Domain

- Custodial closets securely locked
- Designed to prevent spread of smoke from custodial or equipment rooms
- Adequate clearance between stored items, equipment, and sprinklers, light fixtures, and heaters

Areas of Refuge/Community Shelter

- Shelter spaces in high-risk or wind hazard areas clearly identified and windowless (or with protective features for windows)
- Objects secure from falling
- Necessary provisions for communications, emergency power, and water in place
- Exterior utility lifelines adequately protected from natural disaster or attack
- Reinforced roofs in earthquake-prone or high-wind areas
- Proper considerations for earthquake-prone areas

Note: This is not meant as a physical safety assessment tool. Please see the original source for a complete survey instrument.

Source: Adapted from National Clearinghouse for Educational Facilities (2008). *Mitigating Hazards in School Facilities.* Retrieved October 29, 2008, from http:// www.ncef.org/pubs/mitigating_hazards.pdf.

include a combination of review of existing policies and pre-vention/intervention practices, examination of more objective behavioral data that schools typically already gather (e.g., office referrals, suspensions/expulsions, and absences), and collection of survey data that together provide a comprehensive view of the safety of the learning environment. See Table 2.5 for a more complete listing of variables that are required for consideration in a psychological safety assessment. An example of a Brief School Climate Survey summary report that addresses psychological safety variables is included on the CD.

Some of the physical safety audit tools that have been developed (e.g., Virginia Department of Education School Safety Audit Protocol and Texas School Safety Center Campus Safety and Security Audit Toolkit; see Table 2.2) also include means of assessing policies and prevention/intervention practices. These address a second component of psychological safety assessment, which involves the review of data on factors that impact school safety, such as behavior referrals, suspension and expulsions, truancy, and violations of district drug and alcohol policy, that a school or district already gathers.

Table 2.4 FEMA/U.S. Department of Education Risk Index Worksheet to Be Used With Categories of Potential Hazards

Hazard	Frequency	Magnitude	Warning	Severity	Risk Priority
	4 Highly likely	4 Catastrophic	4 Minimal	4 Catastrophic	☐ High
	3 Likely	3 Critical	3 6–12 hours	3 Critical	☐ Medium
	2 Possible	2 Limited	2 12–24 hours	2 Limited	☐ Low
	1 Unlikely	1 Negligible	1 24+ hours	1 Negligible	
	4 Highly likely	4 Catastrophic	4 Minimal	4 Catastrophic	☐ High
	3 Likely	3 Critical	3 6–12 hours	3 Critical	☐ Medium
	2 Possible	2 Limited	2 12–24 hours	2 Limited	☐ Low
	1 Unlikely	1 Negligible	1 24+ hours	1 Negligible	
	4 Highly likely	4 Catastrophic	4 Minimal	4 Catastrophic	☐ High
	3 Likely	3 Critical	3 6–12 hours	3 Critical	☐ Medium
	2 Possible	2 Limited	2 12–24 hours	2 Limited	☐ Low
	1 Unlikely	1 Negligible	1 24+ hours	1 Negligible	
	4 Highly likely	4 Catastrophic	4 Minimal	4 Catastrophic	☐ High
	3 Likely	3 Critical	3 6–12 hours	3 Critical	☐ Medium
	2 Possible	2 Limited	2 12–24 hours	2 Limited	☐ Low
	1 Unlikely	1 Negligible	1 24+ hours	1 Negligible	
	4 Highly likely	4 Catastrophic	4 Minimal	4 Catastrophic	☐ High
	3 Likely	3 Critical	3 6–12 hours	3 Critical	☐ Medium
	2 Possible	2 Limited	2 12–24 hours	2 Limited	☐ Low
	1 Unlikely	1 Negligible	1 24+ hours	1 Negligible	

Hazard Categories to Consider

Biological
- Infectious diseases
- Contaminated food

Community
- Hazardous waste sites
- Military installations or other government facilities
- Railroads, highways, airports, or other mass transport sites that are used to transport dangerous cargo or that could be impacted during a community emergency
- Dams or reservoirs; nearby water sources that could flood
- Community venues (arenas) that attract large crowds
- Nearby infrastructure: chemical or nuclear power plants
- Potentially dangerous gathering sites (abandoned buildings, mines)

Climate and Culture of the School
- Drug usage and trafficking
- Crime
- Truancy
- Students, personnel, or intruders who may pose a danger to others
- Sexual misconduct

Natural
- Earthquakes
- Tornadoes
- Lightning
- Wild animals
- Severe wind
- Hurricanes
- Winter precipitation
- Extreme temperatures
- Landslides and mudslides
- Volcanoes
- Wildfires
- Tsunamis
- Floods

Physical Environment
- Structural hazards (roofs, masonry, doors, windows, etc.)
- Maintenance hazards (furniture, appliances, HVAC, fire hazards, chemical labs, etc.)
- Grounds hazards (landscaping, lighting, equipment, etc.)

Technological
- Cyberbullying
- Internet predators
- Electrical fires
- Cyber-attacks to files/computer systems
- Inappropriate use of computers (e.g., on-line gambling)
- Power outages/disruption to communication systems

Terrorism
- Explosions
- Kidnapping/hostages
- Bioterrorism/biological warfare
- Radiological threat
- Chemical threats
- Nuclear blasts

Crime and Violence
- Weapons
- Fights
- Active shooters
- Intruders
- Gang violence

Source: Office of Safe and Drug Free Schools, U. S. Department of Education. (2008). *A Guide to School Vulnerability Assessment: Key Principles for Safe Schools*. Washington, DC (pp. 13–17, 27). Risk Index Worksheet taken from U.S. DOE from FEMA's on-line training program, *IS-362 Multi-Hazard Emergency Planning for Schools*. Public domain.

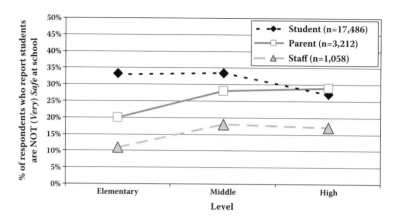

Figure 2.1   Percentage of students, parents, and staff who report that students are *not* safe or very safe at school.

Many of the existing data sources that can be reviewed simply require gathering the particular piece of information and/or relevant number(s) and including them in a summary report that includes all available information. See Figure 2.2 for an example of a potential data summary spreadsheet that compiles information on several safety-related variables on which schools may have available information. In addition to this simple data summary, DeMary et al. (2000) recommend collecting school incident-based safety data and reviewing them for patterns/trends. The PBS-based School-Wide Information System (SWIS; May, Ard, Todd, Horner, Glasgow, Sugai, & Sprague, 2000) data system provides one such system for managing this type of data. The purpose of SWIS is described as "to provide school personnel with accurate, timely, and practical information for making decisions about discipline systems" (May et al., 2000, p. 4). Information on discipline incidents is collected on an ongoing basis. This information is then entered into a Web-based application that allows for summaries of the information that can be used to guide effective decision making for individual students, groups of students, or the school as a whole.

For information that is not already available or available based on review of existing school documents or data collection procedures, it is likely to be necessary to administer a survey. When data are gathered via survey, several issues should be kept in mind. Elliott et al. (2000) recommend that survey tools be developmentally and culturally appropriate,

Table 2.5   Domains to Be Included in a Psychological Safety
Assessment

Review of Psychological Safety Support Structures

Rather than data collection, per se, the purpose of this portion of the safety assessment is to review existing policies and procedures in place that might have an impact on the psychological safety of students. The Virginia Department of Education School Safety Audit Protocol (DeMary et al., 2000) and Texas School Safety Center *Campus Safety and Security Audit Toolkit* (2008) contain assessments of some of these variables.

School and District Policy

- Discipline
- Use of force
- Incident reporting policies
- Policies on reporting of threats
- Alternatives to suspension
- Behavioral expectations/consequences

District and School Vision/Mission Statements

Student Resources

- Before and after school programs
- Mental health support
- Prevention and intervention programming
    - Conflict resolution
    - Anger management
    - Diversity
    - Bullying prevention
    - Character education
    - Suicide prevention

Staff Training (for All Staff)

- Conflict resolution/problem solving
- Crisis planning
- Personal safety
- Early warning signs of dangerous/suicidal students
- Appropriate responses to fighting
- Bullying prevention

Review of Existing Data

These are data that schools are likely to gather already. The goal of this review is to look for patterns (e.g., locations, type of incident, times of year/day, particular staff involved) and identify areas of concern.

—continued

Table 2.5   (continued) Domains to Be Included in a Psychological Safety Assessment

Attendance Data
- Absences
- Tardies
- Drop out

Academic Achievement Data
- End of grade-level assessments
- State assessments
- Progress monitoring data
- Benchmarking data
- Classroom data

Office Referrals
- Type of incident
- Number of referrals for individual students
- Specific referral teacher

Suspension/Expulsions
- In-school suspensions
- Out-of-school suspensions

Accident Reports
- Bus
- Science labs
- Staff injuries
- Athletic fields
- Student injuries

Bus Referrals

Special Education Referrals
- Behavior
- Learning
- Attentional concerns
- Developmental concerns

Parent Questions/Concerns

Ongoing Incident-Based Data (SWIS data taken from www.swis.org)
- Number of office discipline referrals per month
- Type of problem behaviors leading to office referrals
- Locations of problem behavior events
- Problem behavior events by time of day
- Students contributing to office discipline referrals

Danger/Suicide Risk Assessments
- Threat
- Weapons
- Suicide

Substance Use Violations
- Alcohol
- Drugs

Table 2.5   (continued) Domains to Be Included in a Psychological
Safety Assessment

Subjective Data

These are variables that are difficult to assess without surveying at least the student
population. Obtaining reports from multiple informants (i.e., parents and staff) will help
improve the accuracy of the data.

School Climate

- Perceptions of safety
- Attitudes toward school
- Parent involvement in school
- Fairness of rules
- School engagement

Violence and Victimization

- Bullying/harassment
- Aggression and conflict
- Witnessing of bullying/violence
- Gang activity

Problem Behaviors

- Drug and alcohol use
- Truancy
- Sexual activity
- Vandalism/graffiti

Mental Health

- Depression
- Attention deficit/hyperactivity disorder
- Suicidality

Protective Factors

- Positive self-concept and self-efficacy
- Problem solving, conflict resolution, and social skills
- Involvement in school and other pro-social activities
- Social support
- Supportive relationships with parents and non-family adults
- Academic motivation
- Sense of purpose and future

Community Perceptions of the School/Students

- Parent involvement in schools
- Parent view of the school
- Community view of the school

Community Climate

- Community conditions
- Community values
- Availability of firearms
- Rates of community violence (and degree of student exposure)

Sources: Center for Mental Health in Schools. (2006). Cherry Creek School District. (2008).
DeMary, J. L., Owens, M., & Ramnarain, A. K. V. (2000). Elliott, D. S., Grady, J. M.,
Shaw, T. E., Aultman-Bettridge, T., & Beaulieu, M. T. (2000). Peterson, R. L., &
Skiba, R. J. (2002). Texas School Safety Center. (2008).

2007-2008 Risk Factor Summary: MS2
CONFIDENTIAL

Alcohol & Drug Use Violations 8/07-6/08

Offense (multiple offenses possible)	Substance
Use	MJ
Possession	Alcohol
Other	Other
Total # of Students with First Offenses:	
Second Offenses:	
Third Offenses:	

SWIS Data

	05-06	06-07	07-08
Administrative Days (gain/loss):	n/a		
Instructional Days (gain/loss):	n/a		
SET Behavior			
SET Mean			
Avg Referrals/Day			
ISS Incidents			
ISS Days			
OSS Incidents			
OSS Days			

Danger Assessments

	Total			Level of Risk 07-08				
	05-06	06-07	07-08	Low	L-M	Med	M-H	High
6								
7								
8								
Total								

Attendance

	06-07	07-08
>10 Unexcused:		
>100 Unexcused:		
>200 Unexcused:		
Sanction Letters:		
Review Board Hearings:		
1st Court Appearance:		

Expulsions

	05-06	06-07	07-08
Manifestations			
Expelled Sp.Ed			
Weapons			
Assault			
Drug/Alcohol			
Threats			
Disruptive/Willful			
Total			

Suicide Risk Assessments

	05-06	06-07	07-08
6			
7			
8			
Total			

Suspensions

Total Number of:	06-07	07-08
# of Suspended Students		
# of Suspended Classes		

School Demographics

	06-07	07-08
Free & Reduced Lunch	%	%
Stability	%	%
Mobility	%	%

SpEd/Out-of-School Placements

	07-08
# SED	
In-district/Out-of-school	
Home Hospital	
Out-of-District	

Child Abuse Reports

07-08

Brief School Climate Survey

	% Who feel safe or very safe			% Who are sometimes afraid to go to school		% Who report they were bullied/harassed (at least once per week over the past month)			% Who observed bullying/harassment (at least once per week over the past week)		% Who reported the climate item was true or very true		% of Staff
	04-05	06-07	07-08	04-05	06-07	04-05	06-07	07-08	04-05	06-07	04-05	06-07	
Student Report 6													
7													
8													
Staff													

Climate Questions (Student Report)
Rules are clear
Adults respect students
Adults help bullied/harassed students
Student respect each other
Student help bullied/harassed students
Students include other students
I care about school

Figure 2.2 Example of a Potential Data Summary Worksheet.

be relatively easy to use, and have adequate reliability (or the ability to yield the same measurement over repeated administrations) and validity (or the ability to accurately measure what it is supposed to measure). Determination of adequate reliability and validity is not always possible; sometimes schools will develop their own measures, and reliability and/or validity have not been determined for all available measures. Even so, it is clearly preferable to use a survey instrument that will result in an accurate and repeatable measurement of the variable in question. Other practical considerations include who to survey (parents, students, staff), how frequently to survey, how extensively to survey, how to distribute reports, and how to help schools make use of the data that they receive. Several surveys of school climate and psychological safety have been developed and are available on the Internet. A description of these surveys is presented in Table 2.6.

Comprehensive School Safety Assessment: Real-World Example

Comprehensive safe schools data collection is more of a process than an event; what is thought to be important to assess can change over time. As school safety incidents occur locally, nationally, and internationally, the focus of what are thought of as threats to school safety can broaden and/or change. For example, following the shootings at Columbine High School, bullying received a major focus; following the terrorist attacks on September 11th, schools began to consider threats from outside terrorists; following the SARS coronavirus, "Bird Flu," and "H1N1 Flu" scares, schools began considering implications of potentially deadly contagious and infectious diseases, not only in persons, which could result in school closings, but also if school buildings were chosen to house quarantined victims. In addition to a potential change in focus over time, data collection can be time consuming to conduct. Although one critical function of data collection is to provide information at the outset to bring key stakeholders on board, it also provides guidance and direction to the most immediate safety needs that will take priority. Ensuring that all relevant pieces of data are collected can take time and should occur prior to and during the implementation of a school's safety efforts. It is important to remember that once safety prevention efforts are implemented, these efforts must be given sufficient time to have an impact before data are collected on the effectiveness.

Table 2.6   Resources for Psychological Safety Assessment

Barometers of School Safety Assessments (BSSA)

http://www.colorado.edu/cspv/safeschools/assessments/index.html

Variables assessed: school climate, bullying, violence-perpetration/victimization, dating violence, weapon carrying/use, smoking and drugs, truancy, gang involvement, mental health, bonding time with family, parental control and monitoring, parents value pro-social behavior, trust, involvement in school and community activities, health and wellness, physical safety, and self-efficacy

Surveys are available for elementary, middle, and high school students. Staff and parent/community surveys are in development.

California Healthy Kids Survey (CHKS)

http://www.wested.org/pub/docs/chks_surveys_summary.html

Variables assessed: school safety; environmental and individual strengths; alcohol, tobacco, and other drug use; physical activity and nutrition

Surveys for students (grades 5–12) and staff can be downloaded using the link above; additional data collection and analysis services are available from WestEd for a fee.

The CHKS was developed for the California Department of Education by WestEd with input from an expert panel of researchers, prevention practitioners, health experts, policy makers, and school community members. WestEd (2004) reports that it was developed so as to "ensure that the survey met the highest research standards" (p. 2) with procedures that ensure the reliability and validity of the survey results.

California School Climate Survey—Short Form (CSCS-SF)

Variables assessed: school climate, global safety and security, violence/victimization, hostile attitude, social support, and social desirability

The CSCS-SF is for 6th through 12th grade students only.

The CSCS was designed specifically for use by school safety planning teams; several subscales (Campus Disruption, Substance Use and Weapon Carrying, School Climate, Schools Safety, Physical-Verbal Harassment, Weapons and Physical Attacks, and Sexual Harassment) have been supported with factor analysis (Furlong, Greif, Bates, Whipple, Jimenez, & Morrison, 2005).

Communities that Care Survey (CCS)

http://download.ncadi.samhsa.gov/Prevline/pdfs/ctc/CTC_Youth_Survey_2006.pdf

Variables assessed: incidence and prevalence of substance use, delinquency, and related problem behaviors and the risk and protective factors that predict those problems

The CCS is for 6th through 12th grade students only and can be downloaded from the above link. The CCS was designed to measure 21 risk and 11 protective factors in the development of antisocial behavior identified by the Communities That Care prevention planning framework. Arthur, Hawkins, Pollard, Catalano, and Baglioni (2002) reported that the factor structures of the scales were coherent and that reliability values for most of the scales were good (about 0.78 on average).

Table 2.6 (continued) Resources for Psychological Safety Assessment

Youth Risk Behavior Surveillance System (YRBSS)

http://www.cdc.gov/HealthyYouth/yrbs/questionnaire_rationale.htm

Variables assessed: alcohol, tobacco, and other drug use; weapons, violent incidents, sexual behavior, health and activity levels, obesity and asthma

Surveys for 6th through 12th grade students only can be downloaded at the above link. The YRBSS was designed to "determine the prevalence of health-risk behaviors among high school students" (CDC, 2004, p. 2). No validity data are available on the YRBSS, though test-retest reliabilities have been found to be "substantial or higher" (61%–100%; CDC, 2004, p. 5). It should be noted that others have described the test-retest reliability of the YRBSS as "marginal at best" and have questioned the use of the YRBSS without screening for response sets such as selection of the most extreme responses, inconsistency of responses, or multiple omissions (Furlong, Sharkey, Bates, & Smith, 2004).

The example below, from a large suburban Colorado school district, demonstrates that each component of data collection provides a necessary piece of the puzzle that contributes to effective safe schools planning over time.

District Example of Using Data to Establish a Safe School Climate

The following example is taken from the Cherry Creek School District (CCSD) in suburban Denver, Colorado. CCSD reported an enrollment of approximately 48,679 students in the 2007–2008 school year at 38 elementary schools, 10 traditional (plus one alternative) middle school, and 6 traditional (plus one alternative) high schools (Cherry Creek School District, 2007). Sixty-four percent of students were Caucasian, 14% African American, 13% Hispanic, and 8% Asian/Pacific Islander; 19% of students spoke a primary language other than English, and 20% were eligible for free and reduced lunch.

Physical Safety Data

The outset of comprehensive safe schools planning in this district began in the summer of 1999, following the Columbine High School shooting incident. Schools were given crisis plan templates that encouraged a review of physical safety-related factors in each school; the Colorado Safe Schools Act of 2000 (C.R.S. 22-32-109.1) provided some of the content for this evaluation as it required some review of physical safety plans and equipment. A district-wide physical safety audit was then conducted by an external auditing agency in 2000, which recommended physical security operations improvements. Schools began implementation of these recommendations. As part of this audit, it was also recommended that a staff position be created to ensure ongoing monitoring of physical safety planning and practices and also ensure sustainability in the future. A Director of Safety and Security was added to district administration in 2002. Individual schools have continued to review their building's physical safety components including factors such as working radios, intercoms, and other communications equipment; updated crisis response and communication plans; updated floor plans; use of identification badges; and updated crisis team information and calling trees. This information is now submitted to the district on a yearly basis as part of their preparedness plan and then reviewed for completion before final acceptance by the district. This template will be discussed in greater detail in Chapter 3 and a copy of the template can be found on the CD.

Psychological Safety Data

As the collection of physical safety data changed somewhat over time, so too did the collection of psychological safety data. Initial efforts included intermittent district-administered surveys that asked schools to quantify safety-related policies, practices, and prevention and intervention efforts. Questions were asked about structure and function of school safety teams, types of prevention and intervention efforts and how these were implemented, thoroughness of training of staff and students in early warning signs of troubled students, the use of danger (threat) assessments, and presence of a crisis plan and a process for reviewing the plan's effectiveness if the school had implemented their plan in the preceding school year. In order to make review of these factors more systematic both at the school and district level and to help schools view their prevention and intervention efforts as an integral part of their safety planning and not as two separate tasks for which the school was responsible, this process was adapted. To accomplish this, a planning template focused on prevention and intervention was included as part of their yearly preparedness template (Figure 2.3). This document then serves both as a data collection tool and monitoring tool at the district level and as a prevention planning tool at the school level.

The "CARES" model behind this template will be discussed in greater detail in Chapter 6.

The second component of psychological safety assessment, the gathering of existing safety-related data, was initially recommended to schools, but not systematized. To help make this task more consistent across schools, two tools have been put into place. The first is a simple data summary spreadsheet (see Figure 2.2) that allows schools to quickly see all safety-related data together in one location and to look for patterns in the data over time. The second tool that several schools throughout the district have utilized is the SWIS data system described above. A third sample tool titled Psychological Safety Progress Review—Revised is on the CD.

District-wide safety planning efforts also included the use of survey data to complete the picture of psychological safety within the district. When planning began in 1999, risk behaviors and supportive factors were already being assessed every other year using the Profiles of Student Life: Attitudes and Behavior Survey (PSLB; Search Institute, 1996). However, several safety-related variables, specifically bullying, perceptions of safety, and school climate, were not included in this survey. Because the district was using the Bully-Proofing Your School (BPYS) prevention program, the Colorado School Climate Survey (CSCS; Porter, Jens, Epstein, & Plog, 2000; developed as part of the BPYS program) was also given in order to provide information on these variables based on student, parent, and staff report. Over time, the survey has changed both in process and content and has allowed for more efficient and comprehensive assessment of school safety variables.

On a basic level, technological advances have allowed for administration of the survey over the Internet. This greatly streamlines the data collection process and allows for increased capacity of the number of people surveyed. Customized surveys can be entered into Web sites such as Stellar Survey, Survey Monkey, or Zoomerang; the surveys can be taken online, and simple summaries of the responses are immediately available. This method does require that students, parents, and staff have access to computers; for this reason, parents in this district are still given the option of taking the survey via paper and pencil and students complete the survey at school.

Content of the parent and staff surveys also has been changed over time. Initial parent and staff surveys directly paralleled the student surveys; however, adults reported they could not always answer the detailed questions about bullying

CARES Prevention Action Plan for Safety Team Planning

School: _____   Date: _____

Projected Outcomes	Safe Schools Prevention/ Intervention Activity	Person(s) Responsible for Implementation	Timelines (by what date will each item be completed)	Evaluation Methods (how will you measure changes in adult and/or student behavior as a result of this outcome/activity)	Mid-year Progress Monitoring (to be completed when reviewing the Action Plan)	End-of-year Progress Summary
Communities are connected, inclusive, and work to prevent bullying						
Asset-building is integrated in the school, family, and community						
Responsive decision-making is based on data						
Expectations are clear and communicated to students, staff, and parents						
Social-emotional-behavioral Skills are taught						

Figure 2.3 Cherry Creek School District Prevention and Intervention Planning Template.

or school climate the students could answer. Because of this, these detailed questions were removed and more general questions regarding adult awareness and the perceptions of the effectiveness of district safety efforts were added. This allows for comparison of student and adult, as well as parent and staff perceptions of bullying and safety along with more direct feedback from adults on how well the district efforts are going.

In another effort to make the assessment process more efficient, the content areas of the two student surveys (the PSLB and CSCS) were combined to create one survey that assessed risk behaviors, bullying, perceptions of safety, and protective/resiliency factors. The protective/resiliency portion of the survey was modeled after the Healthy Kids Colorado Survey (OMNI, 2005) and the California Healthy Kids Survey (WestEd, 1997, 2004). Risk factors questions were pulled directly from the Youth Risk Behavior Survey (CDC, 1990). The resulting student survey provides a comprehensive look at the school safety variables listed in Table 2.5. Because this survey is new and its reliability and validity are not yet known, it is not included in the current book. The surveys from which it was created are referenced and should be considered as valuable resources, along with the surveys described in Table 2.6 for schools or school districts conducting a survey of psychological safety-related variables.

Further adaptations of the survey process are likely as school safety concerns change and data are further analyzed. As stated above, comprehensive school safety data collection is an ongoing process. Schools need to decide whether to use existing surveys, which can have the important benefit of fewer resources needed to conduct the assessment along with proven reliability and validity, or to develop their own, which allows the school or district greater adaptability and control. Some of the assessment resources listed in Table 2.6 provide data collection, management, and reporting support, though typically for a fee. For those schools with limited resources to develop their own assessment tool, these sources could be particularly helpful. The current example has focused primarily on what information was gathered and how it was gathered. An additional critical consideration of a psychological safety assessment is how the results will be disseminated. Ideally, each school should receive a report that gives them feedback on their school's results and how those results compare to the district as a whole and/or other comparable schools.

When statewide or national data are available, these comparisons can also be helpful. In addition, schools are likely to need some guidance in what to do with their data to help develop targets for improvement. Table 2.7 contains some examples of questions that schools were encouraged to consider when looking at their survey results. These questions were designed in reference to the Brief School Climate Survey data summary sheet (see CD) and are included here as examples of the types of questions that can help schools make use of their data. In order to address any areas of concern, available school and district resources should be presented along with survey data. These resources can be ones already in place or ones that have been discussed as part of the stakeholders' planning efforts.

DEVELOPMENT OF DISTRICT-LEVEL SAFETY TEAM

In addition to support from all relevant stakeholders and collection of physical and psychological safety data, to help develop and guide the data-gathering process discussed above, the establishment of a leadership team at the district level responsible for overseeing the safety efforts is critical. School-level safety teams are also critical and are discussed below. Membership of the district-level team, called here either a safe schools design team or safety team, should include representation from relevant district stakeholders (Fixsen et al., 2005). Inclusion of relevant stakeholders on this committee helps to ensure common language and common vision as described above, improves ongoing buy-in from school community members, and distributes the responsibility for sustaining the safety efforts over time among many people (Elliott et al., 2000; Elliott et al., 2003; OSEP, 2004). Given that implementation of new programs can take 2 to 4 years and that staff turnover during this time period is a definite possibility (Fixsen et al., 2005), this shared responsibility helps to maintain the efforts when key players step down from their positions.

Taken largely from the list of school safety stakeholders above, potential members of the district-level safe schools design team include administrative representatives from each of the following positions when applicable for a given school district:

- Central office administration
- Mental health staff

Table 2.7 Questions to Consider When Looking at the Student Survey Report

- Look at the number of students in each grade and for each gender. Did an adequate number of students complete the survey so that the results are likely to be representative of the school population (overall, by grade, and by gender)?
- Does the overall picture of the student data (general perceptions of safety, levels of bullying/harassment, and portrayal of school climate) fit with how adults in the school community see the school? Are there responses that stick out or don't make any sense?
- Are the reported percentages at acceptable levels: are sufficient numbers of students reporting they feel safe or very safe, is the number of students who report they experience/observe bullying/harassment consistent with school goals, do the student responses to climate questions present a picture of climate as the school would like it to be?
- Are ratings of safety and bullying/harassment consistent across the grades or are there grades that stand out either positively or negatively?
- Are there locations that stand out as needing attention (i.e., are more frequently mentioned) based on reports of student safety and experienced and observed bullying/harassment (in particular pay attention to locations that appear to be of concern on all three questions)?
- What reasons for not feeling safe are students most frequently reporting?
- Are there some types of bullying/harassment behaviors that occur at higher levels than others for the school?
- How do perceptions of safety, bullying/harassment, and school climate compare with 2004 data? Because of the number of comparisons, almost all schools will see some changes in their data. Remember that it is a different group of students who were surveyed in 2006 versus 2004. Also, consider the magnitude of and the patterns to the data:
- Are changes consistently positive/negative or does it depend on the type of question or the grade of the students?
- Are there changes in the grade levels that have concerns about safety or bullying/harassment?
- Are there changes in reasons students give for not feeling safe (as the questions changed from 2004 to 2006, direct comparisons are possible only for some reasons)?
- Are there changes in locations students report bullying/harassment or not feeling safe?
- What factors might have contributed to changes in the student data from 2004 to 2006? Consider both changes within the school (e.g., programs that have been added or removed or changes in staff or curriculum) and changes/events outside the school.

Note: Whether or not the differences from 2004 to 2006 are statistically significant depends on the number of students surveyed. For smaller schools differences need to be larger in order to achieve statistical significance. Please interpret small changes (1%–5%) with caution; changes this small in size could be due to chance variation and most likely do not reflect actual changes in the variable in question.

- Safety and security staff
- Nursing/medical staff
- General education and special education administrators
- Prevention or intervention services
- Transportation services
- Families
- Research and data support personnel

Other representatives that might be included are

- Before- and after-school program directors
- Multi-cultural office
- Legal services
- Risk management

Input from community organizations, such as response and helping agencies, is also critical. Ways to improve collaboration with community agencies will be discussed below as it may not always be practical for representatives from these agencies to have ongoing membership on this school district team.

This team can serve several different functions. Generally, the team should meet regularly to provide leadership around data collection, develop plans and problem-solve, and implement and manage particular strategies such as training, coaching, and evaluation that are related to the district and school safety efforts (Elias et al., 2003; OSEP, 2004). Decisions around what data will be collected, how the assessment will take place, and how the information will be disseminated will come from this team. Based on that data, this team researches possible policies, procedures, and interventions, and determines the most appropriate recommendations for their schools. A second role that follows from this is to provide schools with needed support (information, training, and resources) related to preparedness/planning, prevention/mitigation, intervention/response, and crisis response/recovery. It should be noted that although support can occur across all four stages, the district safety team is primarily responsible for the prevention and preparedness/planning stages. It may or may not respond to specific events (as would a crisis response team), but does providing training and resources to schools that help prevent crises from occurring. Figure 2.4 delineates the overlap and differences between the roles of a safety and a crisis team. It should be noted that in smaller districts or individual schools, these two teams could completely overlap. For larger schools

Integration of Safety and Crisis Team Roles

Figure 2.4   Integration of safety and crisis team roles. *Source:* Adapted from Cherry Creek School District. (2008). *Emergency response and crisis management guide.* Greenwood Village, Colorado: Author.

and/or districts, separating these two teams may help reduce the workload on the individual team members. Crisis teams will be discussed in greater detail in Chapter 4.

Comprehensive safe schools planning is not a one-time event, but rather an ongoing process that requires continual attention. From this it follows that the district-level safety team will also be responsible for promoting the sustained implementation of the efforts over time. This task includes ensuring ongoing support, both financial and political/administrative, and keeping community partners involved in the multi-agency coordination. The safe schools design team also works to ensure that team membership roles are filled, and ensuring that efforts stay visible and relevant to current safety concerns in the schools (Fixsen et al., 2005; OSEP, 2004).

A final role for the district safety team is evaluative. This team provides schools with descriptions of necessary components (e.g., school level safety teams, crisis plans) for effective safe schools planning and monitors the schools to ensure that they implement the needed steps. Related to this, they can oversee the implementation fidelity of prevention and intervention strategies that are used by schools (Elliott et al., 2000). It should be clear from the description of the functions of the safety team that representation of many different areas is not only important to ensure that all key stakeholders are at the table, it is also necessary to ensure a wide variety of expertise on the team in order carry out all the roles. These teams will require more intensive efforts during initial stages when models are created and plans are developed. Although these efforts may become less intense over time, the importance of the team will not diminish. The other roles—data collection, support/training, monitoring, and evaluation—are ongoing and will require continual attention.

District-Level Safe Schools Design Team: Real-World Example

As described above, the Cherry Creek School District began its safe schools efforts in 1999. One of the very first steps was to convene a district-level safety team, called the Safe Schools Design Team. As was true for the data collection process, this team has changed, both in its roles and membership, in the years since its inception. At the outset, the team had representation from administration, mental health, nursing, and prevention, and included people with expertise in data collection, supportive factors/resiliency, bullying, threat assessment, crisis response, and recovery. These roles were derived largely from the initial charge of this team that was primarily focused on psychological safety. Though physical safety was an important element in the district's safe schools model that was created, responsibility for physical safety was held by a separate group in these early stages. Because of the overlap and interplay between the physical and psychological components of schools safety, it became clear that it was necessary to have these groups merge. The Director of Safety and Security (the position developed in response to the physical safety audit described in the District Example of Using Data to Establish a Safe School Climate section above) as well as the administrator in charge of the district's physical plant were added to the team. Administrative representation also increased over time. A district-level administrator who oversees principals, as well as a principal from each level (elementary, middle, and high school) was also added to the team. These additions were based both on the necessity of input and on the need to improve communication with and buy-in from individual school administrators. Although some initial members of the team also happened to be parents in the district, a non-employee parent was added to the team to represent this perspective of parents. The multi-agency partnerships with responding agencies and helping agencies were established through the Director of Safety and Security (law enforcement connections) and the mental health representatives (mental health centers, social service agencies) in order to ensure the necessary two-way communication, preparedness, and response with these agencies. This team has gone on to write grant proposals to support its efforts, and maintained co-management (physical and psychological safety team leaders) of the Emergency Response and Crisis Management (ERCM) grant from the Office of Safe and Drug Free Schools, which solidified its coordinated efforts in preparedness, response, and recovery planning.

The original responsibilities of the team were to bring together knowledge and resources, to develop the district safe schools model and ensure that resources were in place to support this model, and to guide schools in both short-term and long-term safe schools planning. As part of performing this role, this team has been responsible for the creation and ongoing maintenance of several resources that are available to the school community. These include

Comprehensive Safe Schools Planning Manual—provided initial information to all schools on the original district safe schools model based on the four areas: assessment, prevention, intervention, and crisis response; printed resources were included for each area

ERCM Response and Crisis Management Guide—provided information on later district safe schools model based on four areas: prevention/mitigation, preparedness/ planning, intervention/response, and crisis response/ recovery; printed resources were included in each area including the ERCM Preparedness Template and CARES Action Plan (see Figure 2.3)

Intranet-based Safety Folder—accessible to staff via district Web site; contains resources and safety-related information; recommended templates made available electronically

Safe Schools Update—an electronic quarterly publication of the Safe Schools Design Team that allows for communication about current safety issues and upcoming trainings for district staff

Training Videos—available to teach staff about district's overall model and provided curriculum materials, and to conduct staff development training regarding caring community, early warning signs, anonymous reporting line information, child abuse signs and reporting, and crisis plans

Safe Schools Parent Web site—includes description of district's safe schools model, directory of relevant district-level safe schools contacts, and links and resources for parents

Crisis Recovery Manual—copy-ready handouts and other resources to provide in times of crisis

In addition to creating these material resources to support schools, the Safe Schools Design Team coordinated several district-wide meetings each year to disseminate this information and to provide schools the opportunity to learn from each other. Safe Schools Design Team members have also provided ongoing yearly training, consultation, and support, and/or have coordinated these efforts with relevant experts. The data collection role has been fulfilled through district-wide psychological safety assessments that have included feedback for each school preparedness. A template is also submitted to the safety team for review in order to ensure that all necessary safety planning steps are implemented by each school and that feedback is given when necessary. This information is also helpful in designing ongoing programming at the district level.

Because the district's efforts are ongoing, even though much of the model design work has been completed (and revised when needed), the team continues to support, train, monitor efforts, and revise and update the available materials as the national knowledge base on safe-schools planning increases. It is the job of this district-level team to integrate this knowledge and school safety tasks into individual school staff's roles so it is a part of what they do every day and not just one more thing for which they are responsible, particularly given a climate characterized by high-stakes testing. Also, school staff continues to turn over and there are always new hires in the district who are not familiar with the district's model or who do not have the necessary knowledge of a particular prevention strategy or danger assessment process that they need to fulfill their role. Thus, despite some change in the roles and responsibilities of this team, the importance of this team has not diminished over time.

Parallel Process at the School Level

Just as a district is encouraged to form a team of key stakeholders with a variety of forms of expertise, so too should an individual school. This is true whether or not such a safe schools design or safety team exists at the district level. The membership description and the roles of the school-based team are similar to those reviewed above. The school team is expected to meet regularly, complete the prevention and crisis planning templates, coordinate with other school teams (e.g., the school crisis team, PBS team), take input from and communicate with all facets of the school community, and take steps to ensure that the school is addressing safety concerns in the areas of prevention/mitigation, preparedness/planning, intervention/response, and crisis response recovery (Cherry Creek School District, 2008). Also, just as these efforts must be continually monitored at the district level, the efforts at the schools are ongoing and in need of oversight in order to ensure that resources are available and tasks are completed. Logically, the makeup of the team would look different at elementary, middle, and high school levels and in a smaller school versus a larger school. In smaller school settings, one person may fill many roles and/or the school safety team may also be the school crisis team. In a larger school, these two teams may be separate, yet work collaboratively together with certain individuals serving on both teams (crisis teams will be discussed further in Chapter 4). Clearly, though, given the variety of responsibilities that it is given, this school-based safety team will function better with members with expertise in administration, discipline, mental health and prevention, nursing or health, data analysis, crisis response, and crisis recovery paired with consultation with relevant outside community agencies.

EFFECTIVE COLLABORATION WITH COMMUNITY AGENCIES

A final general factor that warrants attention is effective collaboration with community agencies for the multi-agency efforts. The importance of including community collaborators has been described in the discussion of the importance of gaining support from key stakeholders (Brock, 2006; Reeves, Nickerson, Jimerson). According to the U.S. Department of Education (2007c), it is not just in the planning stage that this multi-agency collaboration is important, but rather collaboration during the "entire emergency management process" is the common trait of successful school emergency management programs. More specifically, in the mitigation/prevention stage involvement of community collaborators can be beneficial in designing data collection in their area of expertise and with interpretation of the data once collected. Further, their knowledge of information on potential hazards that could impact the school can prove invaluable. These professionals are likely to look at school safety through a different lens than school personnel. As they may play a role in an actual crisis situation, it makes sense to include outside agencies when planning and conducting drills and exercises. The selection of off-campus evacuation sites may require communication with a nearby business or church. Finally, in the response and recovery stage, schools may need to depend upon the resources that these outside agencies can offer students and families in order to return their school to regular functioning. The remaining chapters of this book address these activities further in-depth.

Despite the importance of including community agencies and the potential benefit of adding a different perspective to safe schools planning with a multi-agency collaboration, this is not without its challenges. Though different perspectives can be helpful, it can also be difficult to agree upon common goals given that outside agencies may bring their own terminology and mission to the conversation (U. S. Department of Education, 2007e). The administrative style of school district personnel and law enforcement, for example, may be different. Conversations that focus on shared goals/what is agreed upon can help to moderate these differences. On a practical level, it can be difficult to find the time to make sure that these conversations occur and it can be seen as one more responsibility for personnel, both in the school and the community agency, who are already feeling spread thin. Periodic review to ensure that all relevant people are at the table and trying to make sure that responsibilities are clearly specified can help with this concern. One additional recommendation from the U.S. Department of Education (2007e) is to utilize existing connections when possible. For example, if mental health personnel in the district already have connections with individuals in a community mental health agency, then conversations about safe schools planning can take place within the context of already ongoing discussions. Despite the potential challenges, the importance of being able to work together with community agencies around a shared goal utilizing a common language is critical to ensuring that safe schools planning efforts are successful.

CONCLUSION

The remaining chapters in this book focus on more specific steps and strategies of safe schools planning. The current chapter focused on more general, systemic factors that are important regardless of the specific safe schools model that a school or district uses or the particular strategy employed. In order for safe schools efforts to be successful, key stakeholders need to be brought in to lend their support. Data collection can help to provide information that can help stakeholders see the necessity of safe schools planning and can help to focus these efforts on the areas that are of greatest need for the school or district. With the support of stakeholders and guidance from the data, a district-level team should be formed that is responsible for planning, guiding, and supporting the efforts of the organization as a whole and to provide coordinated guidelines and efforts for all schools. A school-based safety team is also essential to plan for all components of safe schools on a site level. Finally, given the importance of multi-agency cooperation in all stages of safe schools planning, it is imperative that attention be paid to ensuring that collaboration with these agencies occurs.

II

PHYSICAL SAFETY: MULTI-HAZARD PREVENTION AND PREPAREDNESS

Three

Integrating and Expanding a Multi-Hazards Approach to Establish a Safe Learning Environment

While schools continue to be safe places for children and staff, all schools and communities must take steps to enhance their level of readiness for a variety of potential crises, threats, or hazards. Federal, state, and local governments across the country have taken steps to establish homeland security departments to augment their emergency management capabilities. In light of recent world and national events, such as the attacks on September 11, 2001, there is the recognition, expectation, and obligation for schools to care for students, staff, and sometimes the community, in the event of any type of emergency or natural disaster. Yet, some school districts do not yet have an effective emergency management plan, have not received any preparedness training, lack coordination with local emergency agencies, and/or have not established an effective communication system within the school or linked to the community. The involvement and coordination of schools with community emergency preparedness efforts is critical to ensure that needs of students and staff are met throughout the planning process.

WHAT DOES IT MEAN TO USE A MULTI-HAZARDS APPROACH FOR SAFETY PLANNING?

The multi-hazard approach, as discussed in Chapters 1 and 2, is one shared by many agencies (FEMA, 2008a) that are engaged in the task of preparedness and planning for crisis and potential threats to safety situations. The framework is based on the notion that many types of emergencies or crisis situations have shared elements that each community and school may anticipate and should be prepared to manage. Officials involved in emergency management tend to describe multi-hazards planning as including preparedness for a variety of incidents or situations that affect public safety, health, and property; and much of the focus with a multi-hazards approach is on physical safety concerns, both from natural and human-caused (either intentional or unintentional) disasters. This multi-hazards framework has been used for many years as best practice for development of preparedness and response plans in communities across the country. Schools are also now encouraged to approach their vulnerability to physical risks and preparedness for emergencies and disasters in the same manner.

This multi-hazard framework for safety planning as used by a variety of agencies can be agency or location specific and tends to include such physical and property hazards as

- Natural disasters
  - Flooding
  - Tornado
  - Hurricane
  - Lightning strikes
  - Avalanche
  - Winter storms
  - Earthquake
- Infectious disease outbreaks
- Chemical spills and disasters
- Fire (including wildfire)
- Terrorism attacks
- Utility disasters
- Transportation accidents

To ensure that protocols are consistent with the expectations of emergency management and public safety officials, schools are now also using the Federal Emergency Management Agency (U. S. Department of Education, 2007c; FEMA, 2004b) recognized phases of emergency management (prevention and mitigation, preparedness, response, and recovery). Moreover, the U.S. Department of Education has strongly encouraged schools to engage in crisis management work within that framework (FEMA, 2008a; U. S. Department of Education, 2007e). Creating and strengthening relationships with community partners such as law enforcement, fire safety, and public health and mental health agencies is best facilitated when all speak the same preparedness language.

In 2004, the National Incident Management System was established as the standardized uniform system for managing domestic incidents for federal, state, local, and private agencies. The core set of management concepts are suitable for schools to use in crisis and safety planning. Since 2005, schools have been included in the adoption of NIMS (see Chapter 4) so that incidents involving school crisis and safety may be jointly managed in a multi-agency response (U. S. Department of Education, 2006c). The National Response Framework developed by the Department of Homeland Security now includes schools (United States Department of Homeland Security, 2008). It is recommended that school preparedness plans and safe school planning align with the language from the federal government for coordinated action and communication.

HOW IS THE MULTI-HAZARD APPROACH EXPANDED OR MODIFIED FOR SCHOOLS?

School safety plans that incorporate multi-hazard protocols will increase the likelihood that school staff and students are equipped to prepare for, respond to, and recover from a disaster or emergency (U. S. Department of Education, Emergency Response and Crisis Management [ERCM], 2006b). The U.S. Department of Education does not recommend a "cookbook approach" to crisis preparedness for schools, but rather advocates that each school and community consider its own definition of crisis, threats to potential safety and well-being, and its own laws and resources (U. S. Department of Education, 2007d, 2007e). Therefore, adapting the multi-hazards thinking to school safety planning, especially within the framework of an integrated physical and psychological safety approach, requires expansion from the traditional natural and human caused disaster approach used by local, state, and national disaster response agencies. The U.S. Department of Education Technical Assistance Center Readiness and Emergency Management Web site (www.rems.org) includes examples of lessons learned from a variety of school and community crisis events (U. S. Department of Education, ERCM, 2006). A review of this site helps delineate the broad categories of events that may also influence the safety and security, school climate, and well-being of students and staff. The multi-hazards framework can then be adapted and expanded to be applicable to various types of school crises that can affect the safety and well-being of students and the functioning of a school as a learning environment, not just more traditional physical hazard concerns.

Comprehensive multi-hazard planning for schools should include plans for these additional and more common school-based crises or emergencies. While some of these events may overlap with traditional multi-hazards planning, many call for unique preparedness, planning, and response on the part of a school community. Common school emergencies and crises that require prior planning and best-practice response may include

- Bomb threat
- Fire
- Severe weather: hurricane, tornado, flooding, earthquakes (depending on community location)
- Utilities emergency
- Medical emergency, including when to call 911
- Hostage situation
- Hazardous materials, chemical spills, gas leaks
- Infectious disease or pandemic outbreak
- Weapons on campus or in school building
- Suicide threats or completion
- Active shooter incident
- Outside intruders
- Death of a student or staff member
- Multiple deaths or injuries
- Abduction of a student
- Vehicle crashes
- Violent student behavior
- Threats against others or the school
- Bullying/harassment
- Violent crime or other safety threat in the community

THE IMPORTANCE OF MULTI-AGENCY COLLABORATION FOR MULTI-HAZARD PREPAREDNESS AND RESPONSE READINESS

School administrators and staff are likely to be first responders to many school-based crisis situations. Examination of violent incidents on school campuses reveals that in a majority of cases, most events were of a brief duration and required administrative or staff response before law enforcement arrival (Vossekuil et al., 2002). For some schools in more rural regions, community emergency response may take considerable time. In addition, school-based mental health professionals are most often first responders to address emotional issues and conduct psychological triage (Chapter 9). However, comprehensive and coordinated multi-hazard preparedness and response readiness must also include planning with community agency partners, as schools most certainly will need assistance with events that require law enforcement intervention, fire protection, or emergency medical assistance.

One of the greatest challenges in effective collaboration with protection and response agencies (i.e., police, fire, emergency medical services) is the different perspectives used to approach school safety (U. S. Department of Education, 2007e). The use of the multi-hazard approach and knowledge of other preparedness language used by community agencies will help schools to bridge the gaps. With the integrated physical and psychological safety model, agencies also need to understand the impact of their preparedness plans on children, as many of those involved in safety planning outside of schools have little or no training regarding developmental stages of childhood or specialized needs of children with disabilities. For instance, preparedness and response plans involving a school that includes a special program for autistic children must take the unique needs of those children into account. Collaboration with the protection agencies may include visits to the site and suggestions for moving children quickly, or addressing specific needs during time of evacuation or shelter-in-place situations.

Collaboration and communication is also needed with community mental health agencies for recovery planning if the emotional needs overwhelm the internal system of the school or the district after a crisis situation. Those plans are also best prepared in advance, as a variety of community mental health providers may rush to a crisis site to provide assistance in an uncoordinated manner, with potential to cause more chaos and distress than to provide help. Predetermined plans for requesting community mental health agency assistance, accepting requested help, assuring the credentials of providers, and clarifying expectations on the school site and with students and staff are best developed before a need occurs. In some cases, a pre–agreed-upon memorandum of understanding may best help to clarify expectations and duties of outside agencies (Poland & McCormick, 1999; Reeves et al., 2006; Schonfeld & Newgrass, 2003).

SCHOOL MULTI-HAZARD PREPAREDNESS AND PLANNING: TYPES OF GENERAL AND SPECIFIC PLANS

One of the challenges for schools has been applying and making the multi-hazard language applicable for the school setting. To help overcome this challenge, general crisis preparedness and response protocols should be established and reviewed regularly so schools are better equipped to effectively and efficiently respond to a variety of safety needs. To assist with this task, schools can pre-plan many common elements to be used in a variety of multi-hazard responses; for instance, many types of crises may necessitate the need for evacuation from the school to an outside safe area, for transport of injured students or staff to a medical facility, or require go-kits. Table 3.1 demonstrates how the Cherry Creek School District has organized common key elements of general preparedness into ten steps. Specific documentation is provided to district officials at the beginning of each school year to assure these ten general preparedness steps were completed by each school (see Emergency Preparedness Template). In addition to the common preparedness elements suggested, it is also advised that plans be developed for

- Building control and general system procedures
- Accidents and medical emergencies
- Weather and other natural disasters
- Hazard-specific building safety responses
- Specific psychological safety responses

Table 3.2 summarizes specific aspects to consider for each type of the general and specific plans mentioned.

Building Control and General System Procedures

Building control and system procedures are those that enable a school to respond in a rapid, coordinated, and effective method in the event of an emergency (Cherry Creek School District, 2008). The procedures and practices developed in this part of the multi-hazards preparedness plan include communication within the school system and with other "outside"

Table 3.1   10-Step Preparedness Plan for Schools

1. Identify a command post and update communication resources

- Identify a primary command post and a back-up command post that have access to various modes of communication
- Establish successful communication:
  - Ensure various communication modes are in working order (i.e., two-way radios, intercom, tones/buzzers, megaphones, weather radio, district emergency phone)
  - Update contact numbers and calling trees and ensure these are accessible at all times
- Establish physical safety measures
  - A master set of keys and building floor plans area accessible
  - Staff IDs are being worn
  - Parents have been notified in advance of emergency procedures
- Establish psychological safety measures
  - Crisis and/or safety team meets monthly to discuss climate of the school and specific areas and programming that need attention

2. Assign crisis roles according to Incident Command System

- Depending on the size of the school, the staff resources available, and geographic location, some staff may need to fill more than one role
- Each role needs a back-up person who is trained to fulfill that particular role
- Crisis team coordinators and leaders need to be clear who they report to and whom they oversee according to the Incident Command Structure
- Identify staff who have obtained first aid, CPR, and EMT training

3. Identify and review inside safe assembly areas

- These safe areas are typically for shelter-in-place situation, such as a tornado
- Most often it entails moving students away from rooms on the perimeter of the school building to an internal area

4. Designate on-site outside assembly areas

- In the event a school needs to be evacuated, assembly areas on school grounds but outside the building need to be identified
- With a larger student body, multiple sites may need to be identified
- All staff must be trained in where these sites are located

5. Identify and contact two off-site emergency evacuation locations

- Sites need to be near school and able to house students and staff until they can be released to parents or return to school
- Sites should be contacted yearly to coordinate arrangements and ensure ongoing agreement

6. Print student roster, emergency cards, and student/staff photos

- Office manager or designee assembles complete student and staff lists and schedules
- Rosters and schedules need to be updated regularly as these are used to account for all students and staff in an emergency situation

—continued

Table 3.1   (continued) Ten-Step Preparedness Plan for Schools

- Emergency contact cards need to be completed; main office and health clinic should each have a set of emergency cards
- On the staff emergency cards, attending school(s) for each staff member's child(ren) attend need to be listed
  - In an emergency, the office may need to contact a school for which a staff member's child attends and notify them of the concern; that child's emergency card may also then need to be activated

7. Check and replenish contents of emergency go-kits

- In an evacuation, the administration, classroom, and medical emergency response go-kits need to be taken
- Nurse maintains the medical go-kit
- It is critical that supplies are checked and maintained regularly

8. Identify emergency evacuation staging areas for individuals needing evacuation assistance

- Principals work with fire department, district safety and security, health services, and risk management to designate emergency evacuation staging areas in the building
- Signs must be posted to mark these locations
- Special education classrooms should be clearly marked on the school map

9. Identify individuals needing evacuation assistance and develop individualized evacuation plans

- Additional assistance may be needed by the following staff due to needs of the students (e.g., children in wheelchairs) with whom they work: nurses, mental health staff, special education staff, and counselors
- Individual students and staff with specialized needs should have an individualized evacuation plan developed and a copy of that plan placed in all emergency response go-kits
  - Staff who need assistance must ask for assistance and be included in the planning
  - If appropriate, the student also needs to be involved in designing and practicing their own evacuation plan

10. Establish a crisis drill/exercise schedule for the year

- Various types of crisis drills and exercises need to be practiced throughout the year
- Type of drill/exercise, date, and time of the drill needs to be recorded
  - Ensure a variety of drills and time frames are considered

Note: This Preparedness Plan must be updated yearly.

Source: Adapted from Cherry Creek School District. (2008). *Emergency response and crisis management guide.* Greenwood Village, CO: Author.

Table 3.2   Multi-Hazard Planning Needs for Schools—Types of General and Specific Plans

Building Control and General System Procedures

1. Notification and warning procedures; communication with
   a. Emergency agencies needed for response
   b. Building administration
   c. District administration
   d. Staff
   e. Students
   f. Parents/community
2. Securing the building in case of danger or threat
   a. Secure perimeter
   b. Lockdown
   c. Return to normal conditions
3. Evacuation protocol
4. Family reunification plan
5. Emergency response kits
6. Media protocols

Accidents and Medical Emergencies

1. Fire
2. Hazardous materials, gas leak, bioterrorism
3. Medical emergencies
   a. Injury/illness/death
   b. Reasons to call 911
   c. Guidelines for medical transport
   d. Medical transport plan
4. Transportation accidents
5. Utility failures

Weather and Other Natural Disasters

1. Flooding
2. Tornado
3. Hurricane
4. Lightning strikes
5. Avalanche
6. Winter storms
7. Earthquake

Specific Building Safety Responses

1. Bomb threats
2. Civil disturbance
3. Hostage or barricade   *—continued*

Table 3.2   (continued) Multi-Hazard Planning Needs for Schools—Types of General and Specific Plans

4. Intruder/suspicious person
5. Missing student/kidnapping
6. Report of a weapon on campus
7. Suspicious packages
8. Threats
9. Weapons/violent incidents

Specific Psychological Safety Responses

1. Child abuse
    a. Child abuse reporting procedures
    b. Tips for school personnel: questioning when child abuse is suspected
2. Death of staff member
3. Death of student
4. Memorials at school
    a. Contagion effect
    b. Questions for the school crisis team about memorials
5. Restraint/physical intervention procedures
6. Self-injury or other risk behaviors
7. Sexual assault
8. Suicide
    a. Suicide threat/ideations
    b. Suicide attempt
    c. Suicide completion
    d. Memorials after suicide

Source: Adapted from Cherry Creek School District. (2008). *Emergency response and crisis management guide.* Greenwood Village, CO: Author.

agencies (i.e., emergency response agencies), access control to the building, movement of students and staff within the building or in an evacuation to provide for safety, and reunification of students with their caregivers after an emergency event. It also includes having ready the essential materials necessary in the event of an emergency evacuation or shelter-in-place and for family reunification needs.

The first essential component is the need for emergency notification and warning procedures for all levels of communication. Multi-hazard planning should prepare for efficient and clear communication to

- Emergency agencies needed for response
- The school district main administrative office

- Staff in the building
- Students in the building
- Parents/community
- The media

When creating communication plans for schools, it is essential to consider the levels and types of notification that may be needed for both physical safety and psychological safety events. For example, emergency notification for a fire necessitates a different notification system than does a notification of a death of a student or staff member (U. S. Department of Education, ERCM, 2007a, 2007b). Care must be taken for developmentally appropriate information and schools should always consider the "circle of impact" of the event. For instance, a death of a former teacher may have great impact on the teachers in the building, but may have less impact on the students, who were not at the school when the former teacher was there. So, in that case, information should be shared with the teaching staff in an appropriate way, rather than the student body as a whole.

Schools need multi-hazard standard language for securing the building when danger or threat exists to the students and staff. Several levels of building control best meet the needs of schools. The first type of building control is needed when the threat is outside the building and securing staff and students inside is all that is necessary. This is sometimes referred to as a secured perimeter (see Chapter 5 for further discussion; Cherry Creek School District, 2008; United States Department of Homeland Security, 2007). Student and staff safety needs are assured by securing them inside with locked outside doors, and in some cases moving them to safer areas (i.e., moving students in mobile classrooms inside the building). This can be used in the event of any safety threat that is outside the building. In most cases, educational programming will continue, except for outside activity. In some elementary schools, these situations have been known to occur with minimal educational or programming disruption, as students are told it is an "inside day" and no outside recess will occur. In some cases, a shelter-in-place situation may be needed where students and staff remain in the building for a longer period of time, due to a situation of a prolonged nature, like a terrorist attack or chemical spill in the community (U. S. Department of Education, 2007d).

A second type of building control is referred to as a lockdown. This includes situations where danger may be present inside a school building from an intruder or someone on the campus with a weapon, for instance. These full lockdown situations should be used only in the case of immediate threat of violence in or on school grounds. They typically include some type of movement away from windows and doors and locking of interior doors to secure safety within the classrooms or offices (refer to Chapter 5 for further discussion).

It is critical that secured perimeter and lockdown terminology are clearly defined and understood so confusion is eliminated among the school and emergency agencies. Typically, these terms are used by school staff to indicate the level of security needed. It has been the authors' experience that police agencies may not be familiar with the secure perimeter level of school security and may request a school "lockdown," when they really mean lock the outside doors as in a secured perimeter situation. This again highlights the need for good communication and drill and practice (see Chapter 5 for further discussion on drills/exercises) that includes community partners.

In preparation for events that require students and staff to leave the school building in order to maintain their safety, evacuation plans (see Chapter 5 for further discussion) must be made with forethought and community cooperation and planning. Large schools or those located in more isolated areas have a particular challenge when thinking about possible evacuation sites where students and staff might be housed for a period of time until safety is assured and reunification with families can be made. Most often, sites in two different directions away from the school are recommended, in case of a community-wide disaster or blocked roads. These evacuation sites may be used in the event of a school building hazard that requires that the students and staff remain off the school grounds and away from the area, or when they need to evacuate the building but can remain on school grounds, weather permitting.

After an evacuation or after a particularly traumatic or disruptive event, plans are needed to reunify large numbers of students with their parents or caregivers. These plans should include preestablished reunification sites, assigned personnel, and necessary materials to manage the dismissal of students to appropriate adults. As part of a physically and psychologically integrated and comprehensive plan, the students' needs for emotional and physical well-being should be communicated to caregivers upon reunification. Chapter 5 discusses specific aspects to be included in a reunification plan.

Crisis Go-Kits

Emergency response kits should also be prepared for the administrative or office staff and for teaching staff to take in the event of an emergency that requires evacuation from the school. These are sometimes referred to as "go-kits" (U. S. Department of Education, Readiness and Emergency Management for Schools [REMS], 2008a; U. S. Department of Education, 2006b, 2007d). The administrative go-kit includes basics that may be needed by administrators or office staff to work in a coordinated effort and communicate efficiently with others in the event of an emergency. It also includes materials needed for the reunification of students and their caregivers. The administrative go-kit should be stored in an easily accessible location in the main office. This location should be visible to ensure that the kit is taken along as part of each evacuation and drill from the building. If feasible, it is also recommended a second administrative go-kit be placed in an alternative location in case the main office is inaccessible during an incident. Table 3.3 suggests the content of this Administrative or Office Go-Kit, which is often stored in a bag, backpack, or cart for easy transport by office staff. In addition, a second administrative go-kit should be kept off campus in case the first go-kit cannot be accessed. Classroom teachers need their own go-kits. Table 3.4 contains essential elements to be included in the classroom go-kit. Finally, first aid and other supplies needed in a medical emergency should also be prepared into a medical "go-kit." The contents of medical kits are best determined at the district level by the nursing or health coordinator, in consultation with community partners. Some schools have several levels of first-aid or medical go-kits, as trained nurses may have a need for and are qualified for materials that may not be appropriate when a school has only first-aid trained staff.

Accidents and Medical Emergencies

The multi-hazard planning for accidents and medical emergencies should be done at the school level and also with community response agencies. As mentioned above, certain school sites may have populations of students or programs with unique needs. At a minimum, the multi-hazard planning for medical and accident emergencies should include procedures for the school staff's first response and also for after medical assistance arrives (i.e., medical transport of students). This

Table 3.3   Administrative Go-Kit Contents

Check the contents of the administrative go-kit. Replenish any items that have been used. Always provide *new batteries* for flashlights and megaphones.

- Copy of the school's Emergency and Crisis Preparedness Plan/Template
  - Includes contact information for district and crisis team personnel, etc.
- Copy of District Emergency Response and Crisis Management Manual
- Floor plans of the school and each building on campus
- Updated student and staff rosters, schedules, and photos
- Emergency cards for students and staff with contact names and phone numbers
- Megaphone(s) with additional batteries
- Flashlights with additional batteries
- IDs for key school crisis team staff members (name tags, vests, etc.)
- List of individuals with special needs for evacuation assistance and individualized plans
- Main office cell phone and/or district two-way radios
- Student release and sign-out sheets
- First aid supplies (depending on availability of nurse and trauma kits)
- Clipboards, paper, and writing utensils

Source: Adapted from U. S. Department of Education, Readiness and Emergency Management for Schools. (2008). *School emergency supplies and "Go-Kits."* Retrieved November 12, 2008, from http://rems.ed/gov/views/documents/ EmergencySupplies_n_GoKit101705.doc; and Cherry Creek School District. (2008). *Emergency response and crisis management guide.* Greenwood Village, CO: Author.

planning will need to be site specific depending on the availability of a school nurse to help with medical triage in cases of injury (see Chapter 5). The medical plans should also outline documentation of emergency calls and accidents. See Table 3.2 for a more specific list of the types of accidents and medical emergencies for which schools need to make plans.

Weather and Other Natural Disasters

Preparedness planning for weather or other natural disasters is also critical, as some areas of the country have unique needs requiring extensive coordination of efforts with community responders. Each public and private pre-school, K–12, and post-secondary school across the country has been provided with public alert radios, commonly referred to as NOAA Weather All Hazards Alert radios (National Weather Service, 2008; U. S. Department of Education, 2006a). These radios sound an alarm to alert school personnel about hazardous weather and other community emergencies, even when other means of

Table 3.4   Classroom Go-Kits Contents

- Updated class lists
- Student emergency cards and emergency phone numbers
- List of students with special needs and description of specialized needs (medical, dietary, mobility/evacuation)
- Copy of the School Staff Crisis Response Plan: list of school emergency procedures to include evacuation procedures
- Identification for teachers (e.g., staff ID cards)
- Battery-operated flashlight
- Colored status cards (green, yellow, red)
- Clipboards, paper, and writing utensils
- Student release and sign-out sheets
- Student activities (games, books, etc.)
- First-aid kit

Source: Adapted from U. S. Department of Education, Readiness and Emergency Management for Schools. (2008). *School emergency supplies and "Go-Kits."* Retrieved November 12, 2008, from http://rems.ed/gov/views/documents/ EmergencySupplies_n_GoKit101705.doc.

communication are disabled. These radios have been provided at no cost through the Department of Homeland Security's FEMA agencies since 2005.

The installation and use of such radios provides schools with early alerts, so that response can be timely. However, school personnel need direction about the placement and use of radios and alerts. Radios need to be periodically checked to make sure they are in working order, and they should be placed where they can be monitored by staff in the event of an emergency communication. If natural disasters or weather-related events occur while children and staff are in school, the school and district personnel are the first responders charged with decision making regarding safety. With the help of the NOAA radios, early and accurate information can be used to make good decisions about correct response. In the event students need to be evacuated due to weather-related concerns, preparedness also requires coordination with school transportation staff.

Safety areas and inside shelters for tornadoes, hurricanes, and other weather emergencies should be preplanned, designated, and marked. Within the multi-hazard plan, safety areas away from windows and glass may be also used in other types of physical safety emergencies, such as the event of outside threats to safety. Orderly movement to these inside shelter areas is best accomplished by the drill and practice necessary for multi-hazard preparedness. Crisis drills are discussed further in Chapter 5.

Hazard-Specific Building Responses

While schools can and should engage in multi-hazard planning and response and develop plans to provide consistency in leadership, roles, and responses, the federal government also advocates that hazard-specific planning needs occur for other types of likely school crises (United States Department of Homeland Security, 2008; refer to Table 3.2).

Recent events across the country remind schools that threats to safety can come from both within and outside of the school. School staff need preparedness training related to the types of events that might occur in a school building, including some that may not typically be emphasized in other multi-hazard agency response plans. For example, bomb threats can be extremely concerning and unsettling to a school given that the goal of such a threat is most likely disruption to the learning environment. School secretarial personnel need training about the use of threat recording cards and specific response protocols that provide guidance about how to respond in the event of a bomb threat. Unfortunately, the necessity of some building-specific response categories has been confirmed by known incidents of school intruders and hostage situations that have resulted in emergency situations and loss of life in schools such as those in the Platte Canyon High School, Colorado, and the West Nickel Mines School, Pennsylvania. Although response to these incidents definitely involved law enforcement, staff training was also seen as essential in response. Each day, schools across the country may be faced with situations involving missing students and possible kidnappings, in addition to reports of weapons, which need clear reporting and response procedures for all staff and students.

Specific Psychological Safety Response Planning

Hazard-specific preparedness and response planning is also required for those situations that involve a threat to a student or staff's emotional or psychological well-being. While some psychological safety situations in Table 3.2 clearly overlap with physical safety of students, training of school staff for best practice response to these emotional or behavioral situations is a key component to comprehensive school multi-hazard preparedness. Staff must be knowledgeable about signs of child abuse and their reporting requirements under the law. Other psychological safety areas for which schools need to prepare include training in school staff response to suicide threats, sexual assaults, self-injury, or other dangerous behavior. In addition, district and school guidelines for physical restraint of students must be clear and training must occur. Finally, preparedness training should be included about best practices in response to deaths of students or staff and the use of memorials at schools (see Chapter 9).

Psychological Safety Preparedness and Response Training: Real-World Example

The Cherry Creek School District (described in Chapter 2) conducts yearly trainings for administrators and crisis teams in Emergency Response and Crisis Management (ERCM). This training includes the need for a multi-hazards approach and provides guidance on preparedness for both physical and psychological safety issues. Existing and new administrators have been trained in best practice response. In addition, each school is given copies of the Emergency Response and Crisis Management Guide (Cherry Creek School District, 2008), which includes documentation in support of the trainings, for both physical and psychological safety topics. The ERCM Preparedness Template required by the district also requires that schools provide documentation of training and plans for prevention and other psychological issues, such as school staff training in child abuse awareness and reporting. Finally, all school building staff receives yearly updates on topics such as child abuse awareness and reporting, early warning signs of troubled students, and universal precautions against dangerous disease. Most recently, the yearly updates were systematized through the production of a DVD with standardized training, scripts, and handouts in order to facilitate the update process in the schools.

CONCLUSION

Schools' use of the all-hazards approach and use of other safety language now adopted by other government and response agencies will align efforts and allow for good communication and coordination to prepare for emergencies and disasters likely to occur on school sites across the nation. It is recommended that schools pre-plan the common essential elements that may be used in a variety of multi-hazard responses. While schools have now been provided with many materials to support multi-hazard emergency preparedness, a comprehensive school safety plan requires additional preparedness and response planning for other types of school crises situations that are commonly faced in schools. The authors advocate such preparedness and response planning and training in the areas of psychological safety as well.

A comprehensive multi-hazards plan for a school or district is recommended to have five broad categories of planning:

1. Building control and general system procedures
2. Accidents and medical emergencies
3. Weather and other natural disasters
4. Hazard-specific building safety responses
5. Specific psychological safety responses

School districts and all schools need accountability for their preparedness efforts in the required areas, and a yearly update requirement for all plans. Turnover in leadership staff in schools requires ongoing training for preparedness. In addition, many of the preparedness plans need ongoing collaboration with outside response agencies (police, fire safety, emergency medical, mental health agencies, etc.) for coordinated planning, as personnel changes occur. Schools are important in their communities because of the care they provide for their students and staff in the event of emergencies or crisis, but also because they may be a safety center for the community in the event of a community-wide disaster. All-hazards thinking, ahead of events, combined with crisis team development and drills and practice will help schools best prepare for events that may impact student and staff safety and welfare. Information in Chapters 4 and 5 will more specifically describe how to develop and implement a comprehensive plan for safe learning environments to encompass specific crisis response plans.

Four

Establishing an Effective School Crisis Team Using Incident Command System Principles

C rises have the potential to affect every student and staff member in a school building. Despite everyone's best efforts at crisis prevention, it is certain that some type of crisis or emergency will occur in schools. Good planning and preparedness will facilitate a rapid, coordinated, and effective response when a crisis situation happens. Although being well prepared involves an investment of time and resources, the potential to reduce injury, save lives, minimize trauma and its after effects, and ensure the appropriate and efficient return to learning is well worth the effort.

Emergency planning includes the creation of a comprehensive safe school plan that includes a crisis team response plan and a school staff crisis response plan. These plans should be tailored to each school's unique characteristics and community needs. Also, they need to be designed with input from various stakeholders, including local, county, and state emergency responder agencies and with consistent components that have been identified as essential. All schools in a district should use a common language in order to ensure understanding of terminology, effectiveness in response, and accountability for preparedness. It is essential that these plans find the right balance between school, district, and community responsibility and that they clearly define those roles for each.

Development of a crisis plan is only part of what is needed for effective crisis response. The most effective way of responding to a critical incident or crisis situation at a school site is through the development of a multi-disciplinary crisis team.

This chapter focuses specifically on the roles and responsibilities pertaining to both a District Crisis Team (DCT) and a School Crisis Team (SCT), while Chapter 5 will discuss the specific comprehensive safe schools plan, to include the crisis response team plan and the school staff crisis response plan. It is difficult for any district superintendent to manage an incident occurring at a school site or multiple schools without a team effort from key district level personnel, nor can a single principal or assistant principal manage the many aspects associated with a critical event at an individual school. Therefore, the most important component of effective safe schools comprehensive plans and crisis response plans is to have each member of the crisis team identified, comfortable, and competent in executing his/her role long before a crisis or critical incident occurs.

Depending on the type of incident, there are many tasks that will need to be carried out and coordinated using input from both the school and district administrative personnel, and in many cases, community responders. Principals and site administrators must also rely on key school personnel to perform tasks during a crisis situation that will ensure the physical safety and psychological well-being of students and staff at the school. In addition, there are crisis incidents when effective communication and multi-agency coordination between responding agencies may be required. The structure of National Incident Management System (NIMS) can help facilitate coordination and communication between agencies. It is also now a requirement for organizations that receive federal preparedness assistance and all local response agencies, including K–12 schools and higher education institutions (OSDFS, 2008a). Therefore, schools need to utilize the concepts, principles, and terminology consistent with the National Incident Management System and the Incident Command System. However, many school districts are still unfamiliar with the NIMS Incident Command System and/or struggle to apply this structure to the school setting. Therefore, this chapter provides specific guidance in regards to the common language and structure of the NIMS Incident Command System and specific adaptations to be considered when applying the language to a school setting and developing crisis teams and response plans.

THE NATIONAL INCIDENT MANAGEMENT SYSTEM

The U.S. Department of Homeland Security released the National Incident Management System in March 2004 as a comprehensive national approach to incident management in an all-hazards context (FEMA, 2006). According to the Federal Emergency Management Agency (FEMA), NIMS provides a consistent framework for all aspects of emergency management that enables public and private entities to work together effectively and efficiently in preparation for, prevention of, response to, and recovery from crisis incidents, regardless of cause, size, or complexity. Within the comprehensive framework of NIMS, a structure and management concept called Incident Command System (ICS) supplies the common language for crisis team functions and organizational processes. A 5-year training plan has been developed by FEMA and compliance objectives for implementation at all levels of federal, state, and local government have been phased in (FEMA, 2008c, 2008d). Departments and agencies in the private sector and nongovernmental agencies have also been encouraged to use the concepts, as they can be used to guide the response to daily occurrences to incidents requiring coordinated federal response to a national emergency (FEMA, 2008c).

In July 2008, the U.S. Department of Education and the U.S. Department of Homeland Security specifically *recommended* that *all* schools and higher education institutions implement NIMS (OSDFS, 2008e). The U.S. Departments of Education, Homeland Security, and Health & Human Services are required to support the implementation of NIMS, which means that award recipients of grants from these agencies are *required* to implement identified NIMS compliance activities (OSDFS, 2008a, 2008e). This recommendation is based on recognition that providing for a safe school environment includes integration with agencies outside of the school that contribute to the safety and welfare of the entire community. Recognition of the importance of this integration is not a new concept for many schools. Implementation of NIMS simply formalizes partnerships, procedures, and activities already taking place in numerous schools across the country.

NIMS Training for School Personnel

The U.S. Departments of Education and Homeland Security encourage schools to determine which key personnel on emergency or crisis teams need NIMS training based on their role in the overall school or crisis management structure (OSDFS, 2008a, 2008d). It is recommended that all "key personnel" take at least some of the NIMS training courses. The Federal Emergency Management Agency and its training branch, the Emergency Management Institute (EMI) now offer numerous on-line, independent study courses that are free and include a certificate of completion for documentation after a course exam is completed. Schools are also encouraged to work with community partners as part of their preparedness efforts and to conduct joint training led by an instructor qualified by the National Integration Center (NIC). Whether on-line or as part of a workshop training, the U.S. Department of Education suggests that the NIMS IS-100.SCa, *Introduction to the Incident Command System for Schools*, and the IS-700, *NIMS: An Introduction*, be required for personnel with any role in emergency preparedness or response at the school level. Additional instruction is suggested for those with critical or leadership roles (OSDFS, 2008d); these supplementary courses are accessible through the EMI Web site at http:/training.fema.gov.

Real-World Example

The Office of Safe and Drug Free Schools (July 2008e) and the U.S. Department of Education (July, 2006d) suggests that NIMS compliance be coordinated with local governments and that educational leadership should help provide guidance to individual schools and campuses. In 2008, the Colorado General Assembly passed legislation requiring NIMS compliance in all Colorado schools and higher education institutions (also known as Colorado Senate Bill 08-181) to improve coordination among agencies when responding to school incidents (Colorado Senate Bill 08-181, 2008—C.R.S. 22-32-109 revised). The legislation required that links to resources for training be posted and that NIMS principles be institutionalized into the operations of school emergency planning. All schools' emergency management plans were to be coordinated with community emergency agencies, and memoranda of understandings between agencies were recommended, to the extent possible. There was some confusion on the part of schools following the legislation, in part because it did not specify what training was required. To assist with guidance to schools, a joint position statement was authored by the Colorado School District Self-Insurance Pool, the Colorado Association of School Boards, the Colorado Department of Public Safety, the Colorado Department of Education, and the Division of Emergency

Management, Colorado Department of Local Affairs (2008).
The position statement recommends training on IC-100.SCa, *An Introduction to ICS for Schools*, for all personnel on "safety" teams in schools. The personnel referenced as needing training has been described in this book as members of the safety team and the crisis teams. It also specifically recommends IS 362, Multi-Hazard Emergency Planning for Schools, for school leadership personnel responsible for developing the district's all-hazards plan. Other courses were seen as beneficial but not required under the legislation. The position statement provided direction to schools to establish a timeline for compliance before July 1, 2009. This example demonstrates how coordination in training requirements and adoption of NIMS compliance need to be clearly stated and realistic for schools, given time demands for other duties.

INCIDENT COMMAND SYSTEM

The NIMS structure includes six integrated components that are the foundation of the systematic approach to incident response (Federal Emergency Management Agency, March 2006, June 2007; U. S. Department of Education):

1. Command and management
2. Preparedness
3. Resource management
4. Communications and information management
5. Supporting technologies
6. Ongoing management and maintenance

The command and management component, known as the Incident Command System (ICS) will be the focus of this chapter as it has the most applicability to establishing effective school crisis teams. The ICS helps to outline roles and responsibilities of the district and school crisis teams, and facilitates communication with community responders. For information on the other five components, the reader is referred to the *IC-100.SC* introductory course for schools.

When a school-based crisis incident occurs, school personnel are the immediate responders. They are first to give command and management directives, provide for safety and first aid, and begin notification and communication with students, staff, and emergency response personnel. ICS was developed to efficiently and effectively manage all types of crisis incidents, from small events to large disasters, and has been shown to be effective in more than 30 years of emergency and non-emergency applications by federal agencies and in the private sector (FEMA, 2007). The major concept behind ICS is that every emergency requires that certain tasks or functions be performed, and that in a crisis situation staff will transition from their day-to-day jobs to a similar function in addressing the crisis (FEMA, 2007). For example, in an emergency the principal will become the "Incident Commander." The model can expand or contract according to the size of the emergency and the staff available, and in addition the key principles can be used to provide organization for planned events in schools, such as homecoming activities, graduations, etc. (FEMA, 2007).

ICS can help to outline the role and functions of the district and school crisis teams. Crisis and emergency management in the schools is no exception to the notion that every complex job needs to be organized. There are five major management functions that are the foundation of the Incident Command System, and these functions apply to routine emergencies, nonemergency organizing, and/or major disaster response. The main functions are incident command, operations, planning, logistics, and finance. Each role on the team should also have a back-up person designated in the event of an absence or inability to perform the function.

School application of these terms is described below (FEMA, 2007):

- *Incident Commander*: Sets the priorities and has overall responsibility for the incident. The Incident Commander establishes command, works to protect life and property, and directs overall management of emergency response activities. In a school this is typically the principal or site administrator (or designee), and at the district level this would be the superintendent. In some instances with school emergencies or crisis situations, the command may transfer from one Incident Commander to another. A transfer of command should always include discussion and update of the incident.
- *Operations Leader*: Makes it happen by "doing" (California Governor's Office of Emergency Services, 1998). They conduct the actions to reach the objectives outlined in the crisis plan. On a school campus, most

staff will be assigned roles under the operations section. The operations section is responsible for care of students, carrying out response activities according to established crisis and emergency procedures, and the specific emergency management and response protocols. The Operations Leader coordinates these various efforts and the staff involved.

- *Logistics Leader*: Makes it possible by "getting" (California Governor's Office of Emergency Services, 1998). Provides resources and needed services to support the crisis plan operations and other activities necessary to manage the crisis. At the school team level, this leader is responsible for communications and transportation, as well as securing and providing needed materials, resources, services, and personnel. This section may take on a major role in extended emergency situations.
- *Planning Leader*: Makes it rational by "thinking" (California Governor's Office of Emergency Services, 1998). Supports the incident action planning by tracking resources, collecting and evaluating information, and maintaining documentation related to the development of the incident and status of resources. In smaller school emergencies or crises, the Incident Commander (IC) is typically responsible for planning, but in a larger emergency, the District Crisis Team (DCT) may support the school through planning functions. The School Crisis Team (SCT) may also establish a planning section, or assign the tasks to Logistics Leader, as needed.
- *Finance Leader*: Makes it fiscally accountable by "recording" and "paying" (California Governor's Office of Emergency Services, 1998). Finance is critical for monitoring and tracking incident costs and for reimbursement accounting. This is especially important in tracking costs where a state or federal "disaster area" may be declared and reimbursement for disaster-related expenses is available. Again, depending upon the crisis situation, financial assistance may be provided by district-level personnel. At the school level, the finance leader tracks all planning, preparation, response, and recovery costs and helps to project the next year's budget in regards to supplies and resources needed to support the school's comprehensive safety and crisis plans.

- *Additional roles*: Within the Incident Command Structure, there are other needed staff functions, such as a Public Information Officer, a Safety Officer, and possibly someone to provide other liaison functions (Reeves et al., 2006). These command positions report directly to the Incident Commander.
  - *Public Information Officer (PIO)*: This person serves as the information conduit to media, parents, and the community. In many school districts, the PIO function is performed by district-level personnel. If there is no district PIO, preparedness planning should include designation of a district spokesperson for crises or emergencies. In some cases, a school spokesperson will be designated, with district approval. This school-level spokesperson is typically the principal, who serves as Incident Commander. Other school staff should refer all media inquiries to the designated PIO for the incident, as media communication may require specialized training from the school district.
  - *Safety Officer/Coordinator*: Monitors safety conditions and develops measures for assuring the safety of all response personnel. In the school ICS, this Safety Officer serves as a liaison to law enforcement and other emergency response agencies, and is usually a School Resource Officer, School Security staff, or other administrative-level designee. The safety officer meets community responders upon arrival and continues to serve as liaison, as needed.
- *Other Liaison Officer*: Serves as the primary contact for other supporting agencies assisting at the site. This function on many school teams may be performed by the Safety Officer or by the principal or an assistant principal. In larger schools or at the district level, a community liaison person may fulfill this role, depending on the nature of the crisis situation.

One of the most important reasons for schools to use ICS is the common terminology. Response agencies will communicate more effectively with schools if similar roles are described with similar wording. In many ways, Incident Command has been in place since the formation of the first modern schools when, in an emergency, the principal has assumed control or management responsibility, and has activated others as needed. For relatively small incidents or with a smaller school setting, the school principal may perform many of the functions of the ICS structure. When an incident grows in complexity or is in a larger school, it is best practice for the principal to activate other personnel who have assigned responsibilities on the School Crisis Team (SCT). In turn, once activated, each individual below may activate others needed to complete the necessary functions. This multi-disciplinary nature of the team allows for people to focus on their particular area of responsibility in a crisis, for which they have received training and have practiced through drills and exercises.

This leads to the introduction of the ICS concept of "Span of Control." The ICS structure suggests that no one person should be in charge of more than seven other people. The optimum number is five, unless a large number of people are all performing the same function. For example, one person might be in charge of 10 teachers, if all are caring for students. This principle is important when designing the District Crisis Team (DCT) or SCT and considering the implementation of the crisis response plan. Figure 4.1 outlines the basic school incident command flow chart.

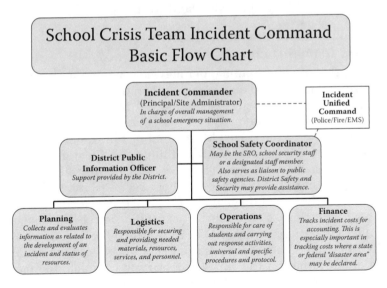

Figure 4.1   Basic Incident Command Flowchart. *Source*: Adapted from Cherry Creek School District. (2008). *Emergency response and crisis management guide*. Greenwood Village, CO: Author.

COMMAND STRUCTURE

Integrated or Unified Command

In some school emergencies additional support or response agencies need to be involved; therefore, the School Crisis Incident Command Structure must also link into the larger Unified Command System. The Integrated or Unified Command System is specifically designed to complement the methods that responding emergency agencies will use, and to allow for seamless transmission of authority for an incident from the school to the responding agency and back to the school. In a Unified Command scenario involving a school, the Incident Commander at the school (principal or designee) may work together with the superintendent in the incident command. When city, county, or state response agencies are involved, or in an emergency with a community-wide response, the Unified Command will also include the Incident Commander established by those agencies. Public information may also be coordinated in the Unified Command structure. Finally, crisis teams from the school, the district level, and the public mental health or victim's assistance agencies may also need to coordinate to provide needed recovery assistance (Cherry Creek School District, 2008). Figure 4.2 provides a flow chart of the integrated/unified command structure.

School Incident Command System Crisis Team Structure

While the Incident Commander may be occupied with duties in Unified Command and in communicating with the superintendent or emergency personnel, the School Crisis Team (SCT) must perform activities associated with managing and containing the crisis. Most functions of the SCT in the event of a crisis or emergency fall under the Operations and Logistics sections of ICS. Therefore, leadership roles in the management of the functions of those sections are critical to good functioning of the team in a time of crisis or emergency. They will then coordinate the specific activities needed under Operations and Logistics as outlined below. The careful selection of the leader positions should be based not on job title, but rather on the skills necessary to complete the task and also on personality characteristics to effectively respond in a crisis situation (e.g., the ability to remain calm, provide stable leadership, and make rational and effective decisions). For instance, an assistant principal, who is an expert

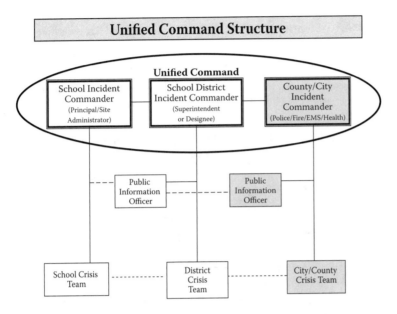

Figure 4.2   Integrated/Unified Command Structure. *Source*: Adapted from Cherry Creek School District. (2008). *Emergency response and crisis management guide*. Greenwood Village, CO: Author.

in curriculum and instruction, may or may not not have the personality or all the skills necessary to manage operations during a crisis; therefore, he/she may not necessarily be best in the Incident Commander back-up role or the Operations or Logistics Leader roles without additional training. The roles of Finance and Planning Leaders may be filled at the school for some crises situations, or may be filled by district personnel who have expertise and can provide guidance to the school in these areas.

Next, it is important to identify other staff on the team and determine roles based on their skills, training, and appropriateness during a time of crisis. Additional certified and non-certified school personnel can also be assigned roles based on their skills and training. For instance, if there is not a school nurse on site each day, medical response may need to be supplemented by personnel who have had some level of first aid or other medical training. If no other school personnel have had first-aid training, this training will need to be provided. Table 4.1 provides a sample of a medical triage planning sheet. The roles and functions that *may* be needed on a school crisis team are listed below. While this list seems long, many duties

Table 4.1 Identification and Planning for Medical Triage and Support

The Emergency Medical Care Coordinator (Nurse) Will:

• Conduct a staff survey yearly to determine those with first aid/CPR/EMT/AED training and complete a list of trained staff. They may be used for back-up medical care and triage.

Staff with First-Aid/CPR/EMT/AED Training (Note "Trained" or "CERT" if currently certified.)

Name	School #	Cell/ pager	First Aid	CPR	EMT	AED

may be completed by the same person, and many crisis situations will not need all roles or functions, due to the nature of the crisis. This list should be tailored to each school site, but all should be considered as the possible tasks that may be needed in the event of a larger scale crisis situation.

• Emergency Medical Coordinator
• Student and Staff Communication Coordinator
• Student Care and Recovery Coordinator
• Student Supervision Coordinator
• Student and Parent Reunion Coordinator
• Translation/Cultural Mediator Coordinator
• Facilities and Building Coordinator
• Supplies and Equipment Coordinator

- Transportation Coordinator
- Food and Water Coordinator
- Staff and Community Volunteer Assignment Coordinator

Real-World Example

One of the authors worked in a school during a crisis that involved the death of a student due to a long-term illness. Her colleague, a mental health professional, had recently lost her husband to a long-term illness. It was too emotionally difficult for her colleague to provide direct mental health interventions to students; however, she was able to skillfully perform many of the duties found in the logistics section. In a second example, one of the authors worked in a school where the principal was great at providing leadership around long-term goals and vision, but was not as strong with operational or logistical details. Therefore, the assistant principal and the principal had agreed to a unified command in all events with the two of them working closely together to ensure all details were addressed.

Figure 4.3 outlines the structure and roles of a typical school crisis team, as designed by one school district (Cherry Creek School District, 2008). This outline is an adaptation of a suggested team composition from the National Association of School Psychologists' PREPaRE Workshop #1: Crisis Prevention and Preparedness (Reeves et al., 2006). However, in a small school some operations and logistics activities may need to be combined under one person as a coordinator of the combined activities. In addition, finance and planning functions may also occur under another's roles and responsibilities. See Figure 4.4 for a modification of a typical ISC to accommodate a smaller sized school. Schools are encouraged to tailor the flowchart to best meet their school and crisis team size and needs. An additional consideration is that some crisis team coordinator activities may need to be carried out by non-teaching staff. Further explanation of the roles and responsibilities of the School Crisis Team as they pertain to ICS are provided in Table 4.2.

Each SCT staff member must adequately be trained to carry out the duties of their role(s) on the team. In the event of a staff absence, or inability to perform the duties assigned, a back-up system is needed, so that all tasks are accomplished. This back-up plan takes careful thought, because the absence of the principal (Incident Commander) or operations or logistics leadership

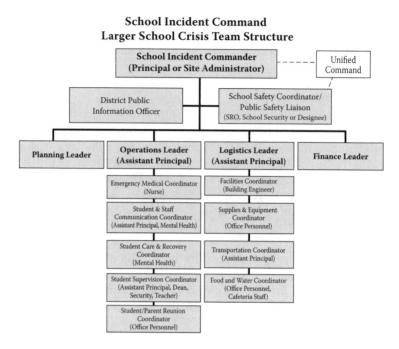

Figure 4.3 Example of how to modify the ICS to fit a larger school setting. *Source:* Adapted from Cherry Creek School District. (2008). *Emergency response and crisis management guide.* Greenwood Village, CO: Author.

may cause a shift in roles. Given that principals are called out of school buildings to attend many various meetings, and that many schools do not have full-time mental health (psychologist, social worker, or counselor) or nursing staff, this back-up plan is clearly important. Table 4.3 provides a planning sheet to help designate specific roles and also identify back-up personnel. It is the responsibility of the SCT chair or Incident Commander to clarify any role substitution. A chart with a quick reminder of the responsibilities of each position should be readily available. Any preparation that can occur to assist in the carrying out of the tasks of the team is encouraged. For instance, the release log for student/parent reunification may be created in advance, in anticipation of a need. Creation of communication plans may also be done in advance: How will the crisis team be informed? Who will deliver messages to the classrooms, if needed? In the case that student movement is necessary, to what specific location(s) will the teachers move their students? Where will counseling services be offered?

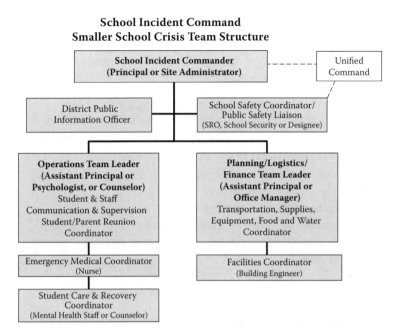

Figure 4.4   Example of how to modify the ICS to fit a smaller school setting. *Source*: Adapted from Cherry Creek School District. (2008). *Emergency response and crisis management guide*. Greenwood Village, CO: Author.

These and other duties must be preplanned to ensure the best response. Templates for activities are encouraged, as needed activities must all be considered.

CONCLUSION

The SCT and DCT are critical foundations to an effective crisis plan, and comprehensive preparedness efforts require that the school crisis team be organized, trained, and ready to respond in times of need. However, the crisis team is only one component of a comprehensive safe schools plan. Further preparedness activities linking the multi-phase, multi-hazard, and multi-agency components (M-PHAT) of a comprehensive plan, in addition to response plan components, will be discussed in the next chapter.

Table 4.2   School Crisis Teams Roles/Responsibilities Within the ICS

Some of the roles and responsibilities that each school crisis team member may assume in the event of a crisis situation are listed below. Some personnel may assume more than one role and perform several tasks. Required tasks may depend on the type of crisis situation a school is experiencing. Please note the suggested staff members who might be assigned the roles below, but training and personality characteristics should be taken into consideration when selecting specific staff members to fulfill role.

School Incident Commander (*Principal or Site Administrator*)
- Assesses the situation and engages appropriate crisis response protocol
- Communicates with higher level administrators
- Monitors implementation of the response plan
- Implements crisis team phone tree to assemble the team
- Serves as liaison with public safety and response agencies to coordinate responses in a unified command
- Assigns duties to team according to ICS structure
- Reviews and approves public information releases with District Public Information Officer
- Coordinates with School Security and Safety Officer for the safety of students and staff
- Reviews and approves communication with staff and students
- Approves appropriate requests for additional resources
- May also serve as Finance Leader ("the payer") and approve funds

District Public Information Officer
- Works as the media contact for the district and/or school
- Coordinates with the principal or site administrator for statements to the press, as needed
- Briefs the media, if necessary
- Reviews public information releases with the principal or site administrator
- Serves as link with the City/County/State Public Information Officers

School Safety Officer/Coordinator (*SRO, School Security, or Designee*)
- Assigns, supervises, and coordinates school security (with local law enforcement if necessary)
- Secures incident site, perimeter
- Maintains liaison with public safety agencies on operational issues
- Briefs incident commander and key officials on security issues and investigation
- Collaborates with local law enforcement
- Supervises crowd and traffic control and access management
- Supervises safe and organized movement of students and staff, as needed
- Assembles students and staff for information sharing and/or safety
- Knows evacuation plans/routes/procedures, security measures, alternative site plans

Table 4.2   (continued) School Crisis Teams Roles/Responsibilities
Within the ICS

- Reports weather, emergency conditions, obstacles or others concerns
- Other duties associated with protection of life, property, and information

Operations Team Leader (*Assistant Principal, Mental Health Staff—Psychologist,
Social Worker, or Counselor***)**

- Assists Incident Commander (principal or site administrator)
- Chairs or co-chairs the school crisis team meetings
- Facilitates or co-facilitates discussions and decision making with team
- Provides expertise in linking team to the appropriate crisis response protocols and guidelines
- Leads the development of the response and intervention plan to include physical and psychological interventions
- Leads or provides the functions in the operations section
- Reviews effectiveness of response and interventions
- Coordinates with planning and logistics coordinator to ensure resources are available
- Communicates with district- and/or community-level team(s)
- Leads team in debriefing after a crisis occurs
- Documents activities

Operations Team

Emergency Medical Coordinator (Nurse)

- Identifies and coordinates staff who have first-aid/CPR/EMT training
- Coordinates the emergency card/emergency information procedure with the principal/ site administrator
- Maintains trauma bags and supplies with beginning of year and midyear check
- Works with special education staff, school mental health staff, and counselors to identify and plan for individuals who may need evacuation assistance
- Coordinates medical triage in the event of an emergency
- Provides direct medical care
- Arranges for additional medical support from trained staff
- Liaisons with emergency medical responders
- Requests additional supplies, as needed
- Knows and provides for student and staff medical needs
- Documents medical and transport activities
- Evaluates for additional training needs

Student and Staff Communication Coordinator (Assistant Principal, Mental Health)

- Implements crisis team and/or staff phone tree, as needed
- Coordinates the communication content and dissemination to student and staff during a crisis event   *—continued*

Table 4.2   (continued) School Crisis Teams Roles/Responsibilities Within the ICS

- Works with principal/site administrator and Student Care and Recovery Coordinator to determine appropriate content and means of communication
- Provides written statements to use for student, staff, and parent notification (works with district PIO as needed) (i.e., fact sheet, parent letter)
- Monitors communication dissemination plan
- Considers information and responses needed by office personnel
- Engages and monitors communication with victims and families
- Keeps records of communication requested and released

Student Care and Recovery Coordinator (Mental Health Staff)
- Determines the psychological impact on students and staff and the nature of care and recovery services needed
- Contacts District Crisis Recovery Coordinator when incident occurs to discuss care and recovery needs
- Develops a plan for care and recovery using appropriate resources
- Maintains a crisis resource notebook with readily available resources and handouts
- Works with district and/or community resources
- Mobilizes mental health/counseling resource personnel
- Establishes and coordinates best practices in classroom information meetings, caregiver trainings, and classroom-based and individual psychological first aid throughout the event to reduce panic and minimize trauma impact
- Identifies resources to manage grief and the healing process, as needed
- Coordinates best practice psychological recovery services, as needed
- Prepares for memorial services and long-term support, as needed
- Communicates resources available to administration, staff, students, and parents/guardians
- Maintains records of referrals and services provided
- Assesses additional training needs regarding recovery

Student Supervision Coordinator (Assistant Principal, Dean, Security, Teacher)
- Accounts for all students and staff
- Works with safety officer
- Coordinates supervision and duties of teachers not with students

Student and Parent Reunion Coordinator (Office Personnel)
- Develops system for releasing students to parents
- Designates a reunion site/center
- Checks emergency cards for name of person(s) authorized to pick up student
- Releases student to authorized person (checks and verifies ID with name listed on student emergency card)
- Maintains a student release log

Table 4.2   (continued) School Crisis Teams Roles/Responsibilities Within the ICS

Possible Alternate Role Needed: Translation/Cultural Mediator Coordinator (as needed)
- Translates and serves as a cultural interpreter for the crisis team and/or community
- Helps with culturally competent responses and trains staff on cultural awareness
- Helps facilitate meetings with students, parents, and community, as needed

Logistics Team Leader (*Assistant Principal*)
- Leads or provides the functions of the Logistics section
- Works with Building Engineer for facilities needs
- Works with office personnel for supplies and equipment needs
- Monitors supplies and equipment needs
- Coordinates access with district personnel
- Coordinates access to and distribution of supplies during an emergency
- Documents activities of Logistics section

Logistics Team

Facilities Coordinator (Building Engineer)
- Locks entrances/exits, helps secure building (supplemented by security and staff in secondary schools)
- Knows floor plan of building and locations of shut-off valves (e.g., gas, electrical, furnace, alarm system)
- Communicates with district maintenance
- Helps move objects to help with response

Supplies and Equipment Coordinator (Office Personnel)
- Coordinates requests for copying, documentation instruments, parent letters, etc.
- Locates identified support supplies to help implement crisis plan and response
- Purchases necessary supplies
- Maintains the emergency response kits (go-kits)

Transportation Coordinator (Assistant Principal)
- Coordinates the assembly and transport of students with Executive Director and District Transportation Services

Food and Water Coordinator (Office Personnel, Cafeteria Staff)
- Coordinates the acquisition, preparation, and distribution of food and water during shelter-in-place

Possible Alternate Role Needed: Staff and Community Volunteer Assignment/Coordinator
- Establishes and implements the contact plan for both during and after school hours contact
- Establishes plan to rapidly disseminate information to staff or volunteers during school hours   *—continued*

Table 4.2   (continued) School Crisis Teams Roles/Responsibilities
Within the ICS

- Maintains an accurate directory of community resources and staff
- Helps coordinate volunteer assignments

Planning Leader *(Assistant Principal, Teacher, or Role May Be Filled by District Personnel)*

In a small emergency or small school another team leader or district personnel may fulfill these duties; in a larger emergency or larger school this position may be assigned, as needed.

- Collects and evaluates information related to development of the crisis
- Evaluates status of resources
- Helps to think ahead of current status and prepare for future change to situation

Finance Leader *(Assistant Principal, Office Manager, Teacher, or Role May Be Filled by District Personnel)*

In a small emergency or small school another team leader or district personnel may fulfill these duties; in a larger emergency or larger school this position may be assigned, as needed.

- Gathers and documents anticipated crisis-related planning expenses
- Documents and tracks expenses related to crisis planning and development
- Tracks and records expenses incurred when a crisis event occurs
- Completes paperwork to seek reimbursement, if available

Source: Adapted from Cherry Creek School District. (2008). *Emergency response and crisis management guide.* Greenwood Village, CO: Author; and Reeves, M., Nickerson, A., & Jimerson, S. (2006). *PREPaRE Workshop #1—Prevention and preparedness: The comprehensive school crisis team.* Bethesda, MD: National Association of School Psychologists.

Table 4.3   Assigning School Crisis Team Roles for School Incident
Command System (ICS)

As directed by the Principal/Site Administrator (School Incident Commander), the School
Crisis Team will respond to any emergency that affects the school building, students,
staff, and/or visitors. The essential roles are listed below. In case of absence, each role
should have back up personnel listed. Consider which roles may need more than one
back up if personnel shift roles due to the absence of others. Some staff may fill more
than one role and complete various functions. Ful-time personnel are suggested for
primary roles.

The **School Incident Commander** will designate staff members to fill essential roles.

Crisis Team Role	Name	School Phone	Cell/Pager	Home Phone
Site Incident Commander (Principal/Site Administrator)				
Alternate #1 Site Incident Commander				
Alternate #2 Site Incident Commander (optional for smaller schools)				
District Public Information Officer				
School Safety Coordinator				
Alternate #1 School Safety Coordinator				
Alternate #2 School Safety Coordinator				
Operations Team Leader (Principal or Asst. Principal)				
Alternate #1 Operations Team Leader				
Alternate #2 Operations Team Leader				

—continued

Table 4.3 (continued) Assigning School Crisis Team Roles for School Incident Command System (ICS)

Crisis Team Role	Name	School Phone	Cell/Pager	Home Phone
Operations Team Roles				
Emergency Medical Coordinator				
Alternate #1 Emergency Medical Coordinator				
Student & Staff Communications Coordinator				
Alternate #1 Student and Staff Communications Coordinator				
Student Care & Recovery Coordinator				
Alternate #1 Student Care & Recovery Coordinator				
Student Supervision Coordinator				
Alternate #1 Student Supervision Coordinator				
Student/Parent Reunion Coordinator				
Alternate #1 Student/Parent Reunion Coordinator				
Translation/Cultural Liaison Coordinator				
Logistics Team Leader				
Alternate #1 Logistics Team Leader				
Alternate #2 Logistics Team Leader (optional for smaller schools)				

Table 4.3   (continued) Assigning School Crisis Team Roles for
School Incident Command System (ICS)

Operations Team Role	Name	School Phone	Cell/Pager	Home Phone
Logistics Team Role				
Facilities Coordinator				
Alternate #1 Facilities Coordinator				
Supplies and Equipment Coordinator				
Alternate #1 Supplies & Equipment Coordinator				
Transportation Coordinator				
Alternate #1 Transportation Coordinator				
Food & Water Coordinator				
Alternate #1 Food & Water Coordinator				

Source: Adapted from Cherry Creek School District. (2008). *Emergency response and crisis management guide.* Greenwood Village, CO: Author.

Five

Comprehensive Safe School and Crisis Response Planning

Developing quality crisis preparedness and response plans takes good leadership, time, and resources. While over 95% of schools and/or school professionals report having a crisis plan (Adamson & Peacock, 2007), a Government Accountability Office (U.S. GAO, 2007) survey of school districts found that many school crisis plans did not integrate recommended practices and that district officials struggle to balance priorities and resources pertaining to educating students and ensuring student safety. In addition, schools lacked equipment, training, and expertise in emergency planning (U.S. GAO, 2007). The team approach using the organizational principles of the Incident Command System (as discussed in Chapter 4) is one of the most efficient ways to utilize the talent and expertise of school personnel to assist in development of quality plans, under conditions of oftentimes limited resources.

One of the most important outcomes of good prevention and preparedness utilizing a multi-phase, multi-hazard, multi-agency, and multi-tiered (M-PHAT) model is a well-developed comprehensive safe school plan. Both the district- and school-level comprehensive plans for safe schools should integrate physical and psychological safety throughout all phases to include prevention efforts, the preparedness steps, response protocols, and the recovery plan. This chapter provides a sample of a comprehensive safe school plan in addition to a discussion of the various elements of specific crisis response plans. The need for crisis response plans to be practiced within a variety of drills and/or exercises to ensure effective and efficient activities associated with the plan and the familiarity of the crisis team and other staff with their roles during crisis is emphasized. Finally, release and reunification planning and strategies for working with the media are discussed.

COMPREHENSIVE PLANS FOR SAFE SCHOOLS

Effective safe schools planning encompasses both district- and school-level comprehensive safe school plans, in addition to specific crisis response protocols (Figure 5.1). As discussed above, the comprehensive safe schools plan encompasses all phases of prevention/mitigation, preparedness, response, and recovery. This comprehensive plan is often developed by the district-level safety team, as a model to assist schools in developing the school level comprehensive plan, and may take the form of a district notebook and accompanying trainings. It provides an outline and specifics of the multiple elements needed to establish and maintain a safe schools climate. It can also serve as a long-range planning and sustainability tool to ensure that the comprehensive nature of safe schools planning is attended to on a consistent basis. The Incident Command Structure model (Chapter 4) may also be used to

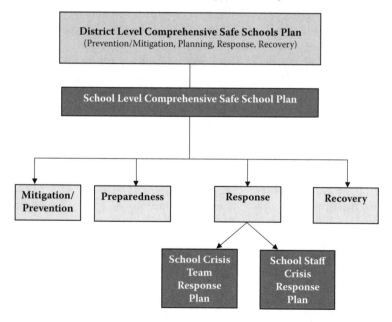

Figure 5.1 Overview of district and schools plans for comprehensive safe schools.

assign roles and responsibilities in the Comprehensive Safe School Plan, as planning of all types of major events or activities can be thought of as having the basic components of operations, logistics, planning, and finance. The purpose of the structure is to preassign duties and roles and to ensure task completion at all phases. Table 5.1 provides an overview of the essential components to be included in a multi-phase comprehensive safe school plan and outlines possible staff roles to complete the tasks.

In addition, the CD provides a more specific example in a checklist format of a comprehensive safe school plan that districts and schools can utilize in developing and reviewing their own comprehensive safe schools plan.

CRISIS RESPONSE PLANS

Crisis response plans are a subcomponent of the Comprehensive Safe School Plan and are developed both at the district and individual school level in the preparedness phase. While every school and school-based crisis team needs a response plan tailored to its own unique characteristics and setting, a district-level safety team provides the leadership and guidance to ensure certain components and common elements are included among individual school response plans (Cherry Creek School District, 2008). This can be accomplished by developing district-level protocols for the multi-hazards that might typically be faced by a school (i.e., bomb threats, chemical spill, etc.; Chapter 3). Schools will then integrate these protocols into their school-level response plans. District-level crisis response plans also need to be created to ensure coordination among schools, to provide for assistance to schools in a crisis that requires a unified command situation, and to address needs for individual administrative office buildings. As mentioned in the previous chapters, it is critical that all schools and administrative buildings interface with each other and local agencies in a consistent and cohesive manner.

School/Building-Level Crisis Response Plans

The school/building-level crisis response plans are linked to the preparedness, response, and recovery section of the district's overall comprehensive safe school plan. These school and building plans need to be readily available and frequently reviewed, so that they do not become another notebook sitting on a shelf, but rather plans that are easily and correctly

Table 5.1   Essential Components to Be Included in the Multi-Phase Comprehensive Safe Schools Plan

Prevention and Mitigation

• Incident Commander	• Take leadership role in emphasizing both physical and psychological safety
	• Facilitate safety assessments
• Planning Section	• Develop a physical safety assessment/audit to determine how problems may impact physical vulnerability to certain crises
	• Review the last safety audit to examine school buildings and grounds
	• Develop a psychological safety assessment/audit to determine how problems may impact psychological vulnerability to certain crises
	• Determine common themes regarding major problems in your school
	• Determine who is responsible for overseeing violence prevention strategies in your school
• Logistics Section	• Conduct an annual physical safety assessment
	• Evaluate buildings and sites to identify potential hazards—request assistance for hazard mitigation actions to increase disaster resistance
	• Survey school premises to identify and address safety issues and areas vulnerable to security breaches
	• Conduct an inventory to check quality of stored emergency response go-kits: administration, classroom, and medical (nurse)
	• Assess and analyze criminal activity pertaining to school safety and/or on school grounds
	• Conduct a psychological safety assessment
	• Evaluate discipline data, office referrals, teacher, parent, student concerns
	• Review and collate data
• Operations Section	• Encourage staff to provide input and feedback during the crisis planning process (surveys, questionnaires, focus group meetings)
	• Help assess how the school is currently addressing problems
	• Dialogue with community emergency responders to identify local hazards and identify services needed
• Finance	• Identify current monetary resources available and those needed as a result of the physical and psychological safety assessment

Preparedness

• Incident Commander	• Take leadership role in preparing school/district safety and crisis plan
	• Submit school crisis plan to district office

Table 5.1   (continued) Essential Components to Be Included in
the Multi-Phase Comprehensive Safe Schools Plan

• Planning Section	• Determine what crisis plans exist in the district, school, and community and identify key elements to be included in school/district crisis plan
	• Identify all stakeholders involved in crisis planning
	• Identify key staff members to fulfill ICS roles (including back-up staff)
	• Identify specific sites to include
	• School Command Post
	– Command post serves as a base for emergency operations—access to telephones, FAX, intercom, and other building controls
	• Safe Assembly Areas: shelter-in-place, protective areas within building, on-site outside assembly areas, off-site emergency evacuation locations
	• Emergency evacuation staging areas
	• Gather information about the school facility
	• Floor and site plans to include location of utility shutoffs
	• Topographic, floodplain, and street maps
	• Identify the necessary equipment that needs to be assembled to assist staff in a crisis
	• Develop classroom emergency go-kits (class lists, emergency cards, flashlight, etc.)
	• Identify emergency transportation resources
	• Number and capacity of assigned buses
	• Number and capacity of private cars that can park on campus
	• List of all drivers
	• Primary, alternative, and emergency evacuation bus routes
	• Develop mutual aid/emergency transportation arrangements with other jurisdictions
	• Plan and implement training and drills
	• Identify types of drills to be practiced and schedule drill practice
	• Schedule dates for staff training
	• Coordinate with local response agencies and involve in drill practice, if appropriate
	• Develop a plan for recovery phase and identify potential short-term and long-term interventions and assistance needed

—*continued*

Table 5.1 (continued) Essential Components to Be Included in the Multi-Phase Comprehensive Safe Schools Plan

• Logistics Section	• Develop a description of preparedness, notification, and response protocols for each type of crisis to include clear, concise language, communications and warnings, and various response protocol options for activation
	• Develop procedures for how to activate the response protocol when school or district receives a message of an impending actual or perceived emergency/disaster/threat
	• Develop procedures for communicating with staff, students, families, and the media
	• School district should make arrangements in advance with local television and radio stations to broadcast emergency bulletins
	• Provide every family with information about the school's emergency and family reunification plan (to include list of TV and radio stations, and district and school Web site addresses they can monitor)
	• Update communication resources
	• Develop and update resource lists to include:
	• Organizational chart with names, job titles, addresses, and phone numbers of key ICS and back-up personnel
	• Building and district Crisis Team members, addresses, and phone numbers
	• Emergency telephone numbers, to include emergency response agencies
	• Establish procedures to account for students during a crisis (color-coded emergency status cards)
	• Assemble classroom emergency go-kits
	• Develop protocols and procedures to include transitioning to assembly, shelter-in-place, and/or evacuation locations
	• Obtain the necessary equipment that needs to be assembled to assist staff in a crisis.
	• Monitor notification and warning systems
	• Test at least annually the effectiveness of communications equipment (intercoms, telephones, radios, e-mail distribution lists, cell phones, pagers, etc.)
	• Obtain emergency communications equipment
	– Battery operated weather alert radios
	– School office cell phone and "red phone" (emergency line that is used only by school officials and not made public)
	– Hand-held two-way radios
	– Megaphones to serve as secondary communication warning devices

Table 5.1   (continued) Essential Components to Be Included in the Multi-Phase Comprehensive Safe Schools Plan

	• Coordinate with transportation
	• Work with transportation department to develop emergency transportation plans and routes
	• Develop specialized transportation plans for children or staff with special evacuation needs
	• Plan and implement training and drills
	• Develop protocol and practice scenarios for drills
	• Conduct staff training on crisis plan, emergency procedures, awareness, roles, reporting procedures, and coordination efforts with response agencies
	• Document all on-campus incidents that violate law
	• Plan how anniversaries of events will be commemorated
• Operations Section	• Practice and train in order to execute assigned roles and responsibilities
	• Provide feedback to Logistics and Planning Team leaders on what needs to be addressed to further ensure a safe schools climate
	• Obtain training in various crisis response strategies and interventions that may need to be employed, to include assessing the emotional impact (psychological triage) and needs of staff and students
• Finance Section	• Record all current expenditures and identify costs of future expenditures

Response

• Incident Commander	• Assess and identify the type of crisis, along with its magnitude and location
	• Ascertain type of response needed (i.e., evacuation, reverse evacuation, lockdown, or shelter-in-place)
	• Activate the incident management system by notifying crisis team, district personnel, and additional responders, if needed
	• Make immediate decision regarding first actions needed
	• Take active leadership—portray a calm, confident, serious attitude
	• If necessary, yield leadership to others (e.g., if Incident Commander is personally impacted) or engage in a joint command
	• Monitor staff response and personal impact on responders—be ready to offer a break to responders if necessary
• Planning Section	• Communicate with staff who are managing students and providing direct response to students to assess current and future needs, both with physical and psychological safety issues

—continued

Table 5.1   (continued) Essential Components to Be Included in the Multi-Phase Comprehensive Safe Schools Plan

	• Communicate to logistics section the student, staff, and family needs so they can obtain resources to meet needs (i.e., need to conduct a caregiver training so will need to reserve space and develop parent handout of resources)
	• Document actions being taken by crisis team as this:
	• Provides record of appropriate implementation of crisis plan
	• Records damage for insurance purposes
	• Tracks financial expenditures
	• Can become legal documents
• Logistics	• Maintain communication among all relevant staff at officially designated locations
	• Establish what information needs to be communicated to staff, students, families, and the community
	• Communicate accurate and appropriate information – Verify! Verify! Verify!
	• Monitor how emergency first aid is being administered to the injured
	• Keep supplies nearby and organized
	• Decide if more equipment and supplies are needed
	• Communicate to Planning Leader the resources needed to carry out interventions
• Operations Section	• Teachers take immediate attendance and display emergency status cards
	• Red = immediate help and/or medical emergency needed
	• Yellow = need to receive or communicate information, concerns, or have an unaccounted for student
	• Green = all persons assigned are present and no needs or concerns
	• Conduct triage to determine crisis interventions needed and deliver continuum of interventions—first priority is physical safety followed by psychological safety
	• Administer medial triage to victims, if needed
	• Activate student release and family reunification plan, if needed
• Finance Section	• Record and track all expenditures
Recovery	
• Incident Commander	• Assemble school crisis team
	• Listen to Operations section feedback regarding student and staff recovery needs
	• Provide leadership in how to meet these needs and/or form partnerships with other agencies to help meet needs

Table 5.1   (continued) Essential Components to Be Included in the Multi-Phase Comprehensive Safe Schools Plan

	• Allocate appropriate time for recovery
	• Strive to return to learning as quickly as possible and provide necessary support (i.e., modify bell schedule for a few days, provide substitute teachers)
• Planning Section	• Evaluate care and recovery efforts
	• Evaluate for additional training and resources needed to better prepare for next response
• Logistics Section	• Continuously communicate with Planning and Operations sections to gather needed supplies and resources to carry out recovery efforts
• Operations Section	• Monitor how staff is assessing students for the emotional impact of the crisis
	• Continue psychological triage
	• Identify what follow-up interventions need to be available to students, staff, and first responders and deliver these interventions
	• Identify the types of individual, small group, and large group interventions needed (psycho-education, individual and/or classroom-based psychological first aid)
	• Provide caregiver training, if appropriate, and provide resources to caregivers regarding helping self and students
	• Assess curricular activities that can help address the crisis
	• Repair building or enhance physical atmosphere of building (repainting, landscaping)
	• Capture "lessons learned" and incorporate them into revisions and trainings
• Finance Section	• Continue recording and tracking expenditures
	• Complete and submit paperwork for potential reimbursable expenses

Note: Assign tasks as needed to specific individuals. These tasks can also be used to plan for various types of school events (e.g., graduation ceremonies, prom, large assemblies, sporting events, etc.).

Sources: Cherry Creek School District. (2008). *Emergency response and crisis management guide.* Greenwood Village, CO: Author; and U. S. Department of Education. (2007c). *Practical information on crisis planning.* [Brochure]. Retrieved on August 13, 2008, from http://www.ed.gov/admins/lead/safety/crisisplanning. html.

implemented in the event of an emergency or crisis. Response plans should include detailed information on the following: (a) specific roles, responsibilities, and procedures for building-level crisis teams and school staff; (b) integration of all areas of the ICS into steps necessary for crisis response; (c) full details of specific response protocols to include type of emergency, safety, and communication needs (i.e., essential phone numbers, administrative go-kit); and (d) clearly defined roles and expectations of community partners (Armstrong, Massey, & Boroughs, 2006).

School Crisis Team Response Plan

A school crisis team response plan focuses the crisis team on best practice responses and the school protocol to be used in the event of a crisis or emergency situation. It can be developed in a checklist format that includes the outlines of essential steps to be taken in the event of any crisis, roles and responsibilities utilizing the ICS, specific protocols for the type of crisis, and communication and reunification procedures to be followed. This checklist is used by the team in the event of a crisis or emergency, and helps ensure each response choice is considered, relative to the nature of the specific crisis. For instance, does the nature of the crisis require communication to the local response agencies, directly to parents or community, or is the nature of the crisis one that is handled internally and does not require immediate outside notification, etc.? The crisis team response plan checklist also builds in the ongoing assessment of the impact of the crisis on students and staff, and follow-up planning for a multi-day response. The overall elements included in a school crisis team response plan are consistent between schools in a district, as directed by the district-level team, but specific elements need to be tailored to each individual school. Figure 5.2 highlights an example of a school crisis team response plan checklist.

Once initial response interventions have been implemented, the recovery process begins. First and foremost, restoring psychological safety is just as important as restoring the physical structure of the school. Throughout the recovery phase, good communication is needed between the school, parents, and community as ongoing needs, support, and resources are identified. It is critical to provide suggestions for staff members, students, and parents regarding how to support one another and how to improve understanding of the various reactions. Appropriate memorial activities can also be helpful and

RESPONSE PLAN (i.e., School Crisis Team Response Plan)

☐ Identify type of crisis
☐ Call 911, secure safety, if necessary
☐ Assemble crisis team
☐ Verify facts
☐ Identify type of emergency response needed
    ☐ Secured perimeter
    ☐ Lockdown
    ☐ Evacuation
    ☐ Respond with medical triage, if needed
    ☐ Other _____
☐ Activate appropriate crisis response protocol
☐ Communication/notification considerations
    ☐ Notify district administration
    ☐ Notify staff
    ☐ Notify students
    ☐ Notify feeder or other affected schools
    ☐ Notify parents/community
    ☐ Activate Public Information Office to communicate with community, media
    ☐ Communication with family of affected students/staff
    ☐ Identify and develop communication to parents (i.e. letter, Web site, etc...)
☐ Provide immediate crisis interventions to ensure physical safety measures
    ☐ Secure building
    ☐ Move students away from physical harm, scenes, and images
    ☐ Transportation needs
    ☐ Building/physical plant considerations
    ☐ Other: _____
☐ Account for safety of all students and staff
☐ Identify needed supplies/materials
☐ Once physical safety established, begin implementation of immediate psychological
☐ support (e.g. emotional support for victims, those impacted)
☐ Begin initial psychological triage and assessment to identify crisis exposure
☐ Make contact to activate district/community crisis teams, if appropriate
☐ Activate release and reunification plan, if needed
☐ Conduct staff meeting at the end of the day to share update and preview of tomorrow (if possible)
☐ Hold crisis team meeting to debrief immediate crisis intervention and plan for next day and near future

Figure 5.2   School Crisis Team Response Plan.

anniversary dates need to be considered. Recovery can take days, months, or years so schools need to be flexible and able to sustain these efforts or seek other agency help if needed. Lastly, evaluating and reflecting upon care and recovery efforts by identifying what worked and what didn't helps to better prepare for the next crisis (Cherry Creek School District, 2007). Table 5.1 and the Comprehensive Safe School Plan lists specific elements to be considered in the recovery phase. The CD also contains a checklist titled "Evaluating the Crisis Response" that can be used to evaluate the level and effectiveness of crisis plan response and recovery implementation.

School Staff Crisis Response Plan

Much of this chapter has focused on response plans needed by the school and crisis team, but just as important is a well-developed crisis response plan for teaching and office staff. The Staff Crisis Response Plan is developed for school staff and focuses on the immediate execution of specific roles and responsibilities of staff to ensure safety of all (Armstrong et al., 2006). It should be placed in all common areas and classrooms of the school in a visible location (e.g., near every classroom door). It should be taken in the event of an evacuation, as part of the classroom go-kit, and contain necessary crisis information for teachers and other staff to use in typical crisis situations that might be encountered. It should be clearly understood and substitute teachers should be informed of its existence. In many schools, these plans are seen in the format of a color-coded and easily referenced flip chart. Figure 5.3 is a checklist highlighting the essential components to be included in a staff crisis response plan, and the CD contains a sample staff crisis response plan in flip chart format.

TYPES OF PRACTICE EXERCISES AND DRILLS

Crisis preparedness and response plans have often been something schools develop, but rarely use or practice. For schools that do practice, 83% practice natural disaster drills; 58% and 52% practice drills for shootings or bomb threats, respectively; and only 38% and 28% practice for hostage and chemical/biological/radiological threats, respectively (Neiman & DeVoe, 2009). To ensure well-executed response plans, the U. S. Department of Education has encouraged schools to develop and practice crisis exercises and drills on a regular basis (National School Safety and Security Services, 2008;

School Staff Response Plan

☐ Response signal for each type of crisis
☐ Means of communication
  ☐ Phone, e-mail, walkie-talkie procedures
☐ Specific response protocol for each type of crisis (e.g., secured perimeter, lockdown, fire, tornado, reverse evacuation, etc.)
☐ Student and staff accountability procedures
☐ Evacuation routes identified
☐ Procedures for using color-coded cards, if applicable
☐ Modified procedures for lunch time incidents
☐ Dismissal and reunification procedures
☐ Before and after school program emergency procedures

Figure 5.3   Essential components to be included in a school staff response plan.

U. S. Dept. of Education ERCM, 2006). The purpose of the exercises and drills is to test the preparedness and response plans in action, and revise as needed before a crisis or emergency occurs. The Homeland Security Exercise and Evaluation Program (HSEEP) has established a national standard, common policies, and guidelines for emergency exercises (United States Department of Homeland Security, 2007). The goals of exercises are to (a) assess and validate policies, plans, procedures, training, equipment, assumptions, and interagency agreements; (b) clarify roles and responsibilities; (c) identify gaps in resources and procedures; (d) measure performance; (e) improve interagency coordination and communication; and (e) identify areas of needed improvement (United States Department of Homeland Security, 2007). To properly execute exercises and drills, HSEEP has identified the following elements to be in place: an organized structure; development of plans and timelines; clear definition of roles and responsibilities; selection of correct exercises and insurance that resources are available to manage the exercise/drill; leadership focused on time management, mentoring, motivation, discipline, and training personnel; and emphasis on teamwork to strive for the accomplishment of common goals. Table 5.2 summarizes the essential objectives and training forums involved in various types of exercises and drills, while Table 5.3 overviews general procedures. The distinction between the various types of exercises and drills is as follows:

Table 5.2   Essential Learning Objectives and Potential Training
Forum Involved in Each Type of Crisis Drill/Exercise

Type of Drill/ Exercise	Learning Objectives	Potential Training Forum
Discussion Based		
• Orientation seminar	• Introduces new programs, policies, or plans • Provides overview of crisis plan, and roles and responsibilities within the plan	• Staff meeting • Grade-level meeting • District-level meeting • Support staff meeting
• Workshop	• Achieves specific training goal or skills (exercise objectives, policies, plans) • Serves as a foundation for more detailed drills and exercises	• Crisis team attends workshop together
• Tabletop exercises	• Validate plan and procedures by using a hypothetical scenario to discuss plans and procedures in a non-threatening environment • Troubleshoot any anticipated areas of concern • Discuss various viewpoints or possible issues of contention before an event occurs • Clarify roles, responsibilities, and procedures • Facilitate engagement of public safety personnel or community agencies in discussion of plan • Clear goals and objectives for practice	• Written scenario read, followed by discussion within a crisis team meeting • Diagrams of floor plans and handouts with roles and responsibilities outlined are used to discuss procedures
Operations Based		
• Emergency drills	• Practice and achieve mastery of emergency procedures • Practice *one* specific type of drill or operation/function at a time • Provide experience with new procedures and/or equipment • Identify strengths and concerns with plan	• Practice drills with school, district, and/or community teams

Table 5.2   (continued) Essential Learning Objectives and
Potential Training Forum Involved in Each Type of Crisis Drill/
Exercise

Type of Drill/ Exercise	Learning Objectives	Potential Training Forum
• Emergency drills	• Involve response agencies to assess collaboration and clarity of roles and responsibilities	• Types of drills: • Drop, cover, hold • Fire drill • Tornado drills • Earthquake drills • Shelter-in-place drills • Evacuation drills • Reverse evacuation drills • Secured perimeter drills • Lockdown drills
• Functional exercise	• Simulates real emergency • Periodic event updates drive activity at management level • Complex and realistic problems are simulated in a time-constrained environment • Assesses coordination among school personnel and various response agencies • Evaluates capabilities, functions, plans, and staff of the Incident Command System and other multi-agency coordination • Assesses strengths and weaknesses in plan • Assesses needed materials and supports to carry out roles and responsibilities	• School and public safety exercises • Medical emergency exercises
• Full-scale exercise	• Most complex • Multi-agency, multi-jurisdictional, multi-organizational exercises • Tests an entire community's capacity to respond • Focuses on implementing and analyzing plans, policies, and procedures • Cooperative agreements developed in a previous discussion-based exercise	• Large community emergency drills—often held during summer or on weekend at a school site • May use students as actors; however, be aware of prior trauma history to not unknowingly retraumatize actors

—continued

Table 5.2 (continued) Essential Learning Objectives and Potential Training Forum Involved in Each Type of Crisis Drill/Exercise

Type of Drill/ Exercise	Learning Objectives	Potential Training Forum
• Full-scale exercise	• Exercises are simulated in real-time, highly stressful, time-constrained environment that is as close to real life as possible • Actual mobilization of resources and personnel—use real equipment, props, and multi-agency personnel	• Public notice of exercise is necessary so they don't mistake it for an actual event

Sources: Adapted from Reeves, M., Nickerson, A., & Jimerson, S. (2006). *PREPaRE Workshop #1—Prevention and preparedness: The comprehensive school crisis team.* Bethesda, MD: National Association of School Psychologists; and United States Department of Homeland Security. (2007). *Homeland security exercise and evaluation program (HSEEP).* Washington, DC. Retrieved August 14, 2008, from https://hseep.dhs.gov/pages/1001_HSEEP7.aspx.

1. *Orientation seminars*: provide an overview of the crisis plan procedures, crisis roles and responsibilities, and policies; can be conducted within a staff meeting.
2. *Workshop*: a training that focuses on specific training goals and building skills; can be done through staff development offering.
3. *Tabletop exercises*: typically done by a school crisis team or district crisis team where a hypothetical or real-life situation is presented and the team discusses how they would implement their crisis plan and what considerations would need to be taken into account.
4. *Emergency drills*: practice of one specific type of drill (i.e., lockdown) to practice and achieve mastery of emergency procedures.
5. *Functional exercise*: simulates a real emergency in a time-constrained environment; involves public safety and emergency agencies.
6. *Full-scale exercise*: multi-agency, multi-jurisdictional, and multi-organization exercises; tests entire community's capacity to respond.

The CD describes additional specific steps for each type of drill.

One of the most asked questions by administrators is, "If we practice lockdown drills won't we just increase the anxiety of students and make them fearful?" Best practice guidelines have been identified for conducting drills so as to help decrease potential anxiety. First and foremost, the staff must stay calm as their attitudes and actions will be mirrored by students (Brock, 2006a; Prevention Tools, 2008; Reeves et al., 2006). The regular practice of crisis drills enables staff to become proficient in executing the crisis procedures, which in turn enables them to remain calm in a true crisis event. How the drill is presented to the students has a lot to do with level of anxiety regarding the drill. In the authors' experience, equating the new drill to already established crisis drills such as fire, tornado, and evacuation drills also can help decrease anxiety as the students are already familiar with many of the steps. For example,

> We are going to be practicing a new drill called a lockdown drill. We will need to use these procedures if there is a safety issue and we need to keep you all safe. I am going to go over the procedures and many of the steps you already know as some of the procedures are similar to a fire or tornado drill.

If students have questions, answer them truthfully, but in a developmentally appropriate manner.

In addition, a study conducted by Nickerson and Zhe (2007) found there were no differences in state of anxiety or perceptions of school safety between the intervention group who participated in an intruder drill and the control group who did not participate in such a drill. The intervention group actually acquired the skill of moving quickly to a safe location and increased their short-term knowledge and skill acquisition without altering anxiety or perceived safety. From this study, it follows that if crisis drills are done in a well-planned, thorough, and calmly executed manner that takes developmental appropriateness into consideration, they do not increase the students' anxiety, but actually increase student knowledge of what to do in a particular situation (Nickerson & Zhe, 2007; Pitcher & Poland, 1992). Poland (1994) also emphasizes that students and staff will not be able to do what is needed in a moment of crisis unless it has been practiced and staff have emphasized to students the importance of following the directives of adults. In support of this, the Office of Safe and Drug

Table 5.3   General Crisis Drill and Exercise Procedures

Type of Drill/ Exercise	General Procedure
Drop-cover-hold	Students and staff take cover under a nearby desk, table, or sturdy doorframe in order to cover their body. Then cover eyes by leaning face against arms while holding onto the legs of the desk or table until the event ceases. *Potential events*: earthquake, nuclear weapon Students and staff move to windowless interior rooms or hallways of the first floor or basement. Student and staff kneel on the ground, bend over with their face dropped into their lap and arms covering their head and neck. *Potential event*: tornado
Evacuation	Students and staff leave the school building or facility using the predetermined evacuation routes. Relocation is at a predetermined, alternative setting, typically off school grounds. *Potential events*: fire, bomb threat, contaminated air inside school, gas leak
Reverse evacuation	Staff and students move from school grounds back into the school building. This may then lead into a lockdown or shelter-in-place. *Potential events*: safety concern outside, unsafe weather, environmental hazard close to school (e.g., chemical plant spill)
Lockdown	Students and staff remain in the school building when there is a threat outside or within the school, or when moving throughout the school is unsafe. Blinds are closed over windows. All sit quietly in room (preferably a locked room) positioned away from windows and doors and sit against a wall. *Potential events:* dangerous intruder in school or in immediate school vicinity or act of violence or potential violence
Secured perimeter	All staff and students outside the building are returned to the building or other safe area. All exterior doors are locked and secured. Blinds are closed; however, movement within the school is allowed. No outside activity is allowed but inside activity and schedules are allowed, as authorized. Access inside and outside the building is controlled and limited to authorized individuals only. *Potential events*: Major crime or police chase near school; custody battle and a parent is threatening to come to school to pick up child unauthorized; lockdown has been implemented at another nearby public or private school in response to violent incident; fight outside that involves numerous individuals; intruder or suspicious person on campus, but not inside school; extremely disruptive student who appears to be potentially violent or emotionally unstable on campus; dangerous animal (e.g., bear); to begin securing in preparation for potential lockdown

—continued

Table 5.3 (continued) General Crisis Drill and Exercise Procedures

Type of Drill/ Exercise	General Procedure
Shelter-in-place	Participants move into lockdown procedure and relocate to predetermined rooms that have minimal to no windows and vents. Disaster go-kit is utilized in the event of chemical/radiological/biological emergency; all windows and doors are sealed with duct tape and plastic sheeting and mechanical building systems are turned off.
	Potential events: severe weather, chemical/radiological/biological emergency

Sources: Adapted from Cherry Creek School District. (2007). *Emergency response/crisis management training.* Workshop presented to staff as part of a Title IV Safe and Drug Free Schools grant. Greenwood Village, CO; Reeves, M., Nickerson, A., & Jimerson, S. (2006). *PREPaRE Workshop #1—Prevention and preparedness: The comprehensive school crisis team.* Bethesda, MD: National Association of School Psychologists; and Prevention Tools. (n.d.). *All hazards approach: School crisis management guide for timely response to school emergencies.* www.prevention-tools.net.

Free Schools (2007) recommends that drills be practiced until each person can successfully execute their assigned duties.

RELEASE AND REUNIFICATION PLANNING

After an emergency or serious crisis incident, students and families will need to be reunited in an orderly and thoughtful manner. Well-designed and executed reunification plans at the school level help decrease the traumatic impact of an event on students, staff, and parents while also demonstrating to the community the school is well organized and prepared to deal with a crisis event. Release plans are used when students are allowed to leave the school building and reunification plans when parents come to collect their child from a predetermined non-school location. There are many factors to consider when establishing a good release and reunification plan, from activating buses to transport students to a specific reunification site and setting in motion the specific tasks necessary to release students to caregivers. Again, basic components and structure are often set by the district response plan, with specifics designed for the individual school. Table 5.4 outlines the specific factors to consider in a release and reunification plan.

Table 5.4 Essential Elements to a Release and Reunification Plan

Off-Site Reunification Location

1. Incident Commander advises Student/Parent Reunion Coordinator and Transportation Coordinator of decision to implement off-site evacuation and reunification procedures.
2. Begin setting up bus staging area and begin routing buses to staging area.
3. Local law enforcement and other needed personnel should proceed to site to help with traffic and crowd control.
4. The Public Information Officer will provided needed details and instructions to media and webmaster to be conveyed to parents and community.
5. While en route to site, a school staff member needs to prepare a list of all evacuees on bus to be delivered to Student/Parent Reunion Coordinator upon arrival.
6. Crisis team members shall facilitate the unloading of students and school staff and direct them to assigned waiting location.
7. School district will designate an individual to be the Commander-in-Charge for this site.
8. Activate dismissal procedures.

On-Site Reunification Location

1. Incident Commander makes decision to use alternative dismissal procedures and activate reunification crisis plan.
2. Teachers and students are notified of plan.
3. The Public Information Officer or Incident Commander will provide needed details and instructions to media and webmaster to be conveyed to parents.
4. Parents are notified of need to come and pick up their child (reverse 911, local media outlets, Web site, e-mail).
5. Local law enforcement and other needed personnel should proceed to site to help with traffic and crowd control.
6. Staff are activated to help with parent verification and procedures.
7. Authorized adult/parent must print and sign their name, in addition to the time, on a sign-out sheet (must require a printed name as you often cannot read signatures). Two different ways to facilitate check-out:
   a. Parents must check in at a central location, show ID, sign child out, and wait for child to be called down to area to be released
      i. Pro = Parents are not provided access to building
      ii. Con = Hard to keep up with demand if large numbers of parents arrive at once and parents get frustrated with waiting for child to be called down to parent waiting area
   b. Parents must check in at central location, show ID that is matched to student emergency release card, and are then permitted access to classroom and allowed to sign child out with teacher
      i. Pro = Able to keep up with demand better and accelerates dismissal process
      ii. Con = Parents have access to building

—continued

Table 5.4   (continued) Essential Elements to a Release and Reunification Plan

Specific On-Site Duties to Facilitate Reunification Process

1. Establish an Incident Command Post.

2. Organize response if multiple agencies are involved.

3. Check identification of all personnel and staff who arrive to provide assistance.

4. Secure area for student and staff away from where parents will be arriving.

5. Set up student release sign-out area.

6. If needed, set up media staging area.

7. Have mental health and medical staff available for medically and emotionally fragile students.

8. Only release students to authorized persons who show ID and are listed on the student's emergency release card (ensure there are not custody disputes).

9. Have multiple tables ready to accommodate large demand of parents signing in and out.

10. Provide handouts to parents on traumatic stress reactions and resources.

11. Provide supervision for those students whose parents do not come and pick up until an authorized person can arrive.

12. Make every effort to maintain order and ease fears and anxiety. Be prepared for emotional parents that may feel a need to circumvent process to get to child faster.

13. Have additional staff and security to help with crowd control and maintaining order.

    a. Do not have parents entering and exiting out same doors as this creates a traffic jam. Consider traffic flow pattern.

Sources: Adapted from: Cherry Creek School District. (2007). *Emergency response/crisis management training.* Workshop presented to staff as part of a Title IV Safe and Drug Free Schools grant. Greenwood Village, CO; Prevention Tools. (n.d.). *All hazards approach: School crisis management guide for timely response to school emergencies.* www.preventiontools.net.

WORKING WITH THE MEDIA

Planning ahead of time for how to collaborate effectively wih the media is a critical component to any district and school comprehensive safe schools plan and crisis response plan. The district and/or school spokesperson for the incident (i. e., public information officer) must be clearly designated and should align with the planning that occurs in the preparedness phase as many events have similar media issues. The media can be a great ally in disseminating helpful information in the response and recovery process, but they can also be very critical. In the authors' experience, the prior collaboration and sharing of helpful information (i.e., media coverage of suicide can lead to potential contagion effects) between the school district and media venue in the preparedness phase can have a great influence on how information is reported by media when crisis occurs. The CD contains multiple handouts that provide information on how to work cooperatively and collaboratively with the media. Some general guidelines are as follows: provide a media area off school grounds where regularly scheduled press conferences are held (even if no new information is available, still report that no new information is available); assign only one to person to talk with media (e.g., designated public information officer) or in a large-scale event, coordinate and plan the release of information with various agencies in the Unified Command; school principals (school incident commander) are trained or coached in best practices of media discussion in the preparedness phase. Other suggestions include: confirm all information before releasing; always tell the truth; focus on facts; use a prepared fact sheet; develop 3 to 5 key messages for parents and community; use media to relay information about support services and school's plan for addressing physical and psychological safety; do not feel obligated to answer all questions, instead it is acceptable to say that you do not have that information at this time or you cannot cannot release that information; minimize exposure to the media for students, staff, and families; and control access to caregiver/parent or community meetings (Brock, et al. 2009; National Association of School Psychologist, 2006; Poland & McCormick, 1999; U. S. Dept. of Education, ERCM, 2007c).

CONCLUSION

As evidenced by Chapters 1 through 5, comprehensive safe schools planning and preparation involves a team of school and community-based professionals who are willing (a) to work together for the common goal of establishing a safe schools climate; (b) conduct both physical and psychological safety assessments and use the results to make data-driven decisions; (c) develop and train a crisis team according to the ICS; and (d) develop comprehensive plans for safe schools to encompass well-practiced preparedness and response plans. The subsequent chapters of this book will focus primarily on the psychological safety components to developing a safe school by implementing multi-tiered prevention and intervention programming for all students, and the book will conclude with an overview of specific crisis interventions to help in recovery efforts and the mitigation and prevention of future events.

III

PSYCHOLOGICAL SAFETY: MULTI-LEVEL PREVENTION, INTERVENTION, AND RECOVERY

Six

Universal Prevention Efforts in Schools

The first two sections of this book focused primarily on balancing physical and psychological safety to address the multi-phase, multi-hazard, and multi-agency approach to crisis planning, preparation, and response. This final section of the book will focus on the remaining component of the comprehensive safe school (M-PHAT) approach we have proposed—multi-tiered interventions. These interventions help to establish a safe schools learning environment while also preparing schools for response interventions in the event of a crisis. Programming ideas will be presented that not only help reduce the likelihood of school violence and other negative consequences, but also serve as the basis for quality response efforts and interventions that help to mitigate the negative impact of a crisis event. In turn, interventions and response efforts enhance positive school climate by supporting and building individual resiliency factors, which then in turn serve as protective factors for future negative events, thus the circular nature of the model proposed in Chapter 1 of this book (see Figure 1.4). In addition, the Center for Mental Health in Schools (2008a) advocates for adopting a broader, transactional perspective, which suggests that emotional and behavioral problems do not only reside within the individual student, but are also impacted by environmental factors (school, family, community). Therefore, in addition to programs that support individual students, efforts should also be directed at providing universal, targeted, and intensive interventions to address the environmental factors. Various programs and interventions to facilitate the establishment of a safe school climate, in addition to meeting the needs of the individual student, will be discussed further.

While schools are not able to control all internal and external factors that lead to crisis situations, they can take mitigation and prevention actions to reduce the likelihood and/or lessen the impact of events that cannot be avoided (U. S. Department of Education, ERCM, 2007a; OSDFS, 2008b). Universal mitigation and prevention encompasses the full range of actions focused on the whole school (universal) climate that schools can take to achieve these goals. As discussed in previous chapters, prevention refers to the actions taken to keep events from taking place while the role of mitigation is to reduce or eliminate the negative effects of hazardous events in terms of saving lives, property, and money (Lassiter & McEvoy, 2008; FEMA, 2004a).

From Table 6.1 it can be seen that mitigation and prevention efforts include a wide variety of tasks, from ensuring the safety and integrity of the facilities, implementing proper security (both in terms of technology and people), and establishing a positive culture and climate in the school (Lassiter & McEvoy, 2008; OSDFS, 2007b). In other words, the various aspects of mitigation and prevention are complementary to each other and include taking steps to ensure both the physical and psychological safety of the students. Although schools can be vulnerable to crisis events due to improper physical security, it is important to stress that complex factors affect the climate and safety of schools. Therefore, schools must address not only the physical aspects of the safety of students, but also the administrative and management practices of the school, the nature of the student population (including problems such as bullying/harassment, and drug and alcohol use), and the characteristics of the neighborhood served by the school as well (Sprague, 2007; Sprague & Walker, 2002). Mitigation and prevention build on what schools are already doing and are part of an ongoing, long-term process, the success of which is dependent on variables such as support from stakeholders, thorough assessment of the physical environment and the climate, effective planning teams, and collaboration with community agencies as discussed in previous chapters (Lassiter & McEvoy, 2008).

MITIGATION AND PHYSICAL SAFETY

Prevention includes both physical and psychological safety (Sprague, 2007; Sprague & Walker, 2002). In contrast, mitigation efforts, particularly as presented within the U.S. Department of Education's guide, *Practical Information on Crisis Planning* (OSDFS, 2007), are focused primarily on physical safety and

Table 6.1　Prevention and Mitigation Efforts

Mitigation	Prevention
Evaluate the internal and external school environment for the presence of dangerous areas, hazardous materials or substances, policies/procedures, etc.	
Evaluate the types of outside threats, community events, and natural disasters that may occur	Assess the school climate/psychological safety variables
Set up a school environment that is less susceptible to and/or impacted by crisis situations through	
• Crime Prevention Through Environmental Design (CPTED)[a]	
• Security personnel and technology	
Develop a written crisis response plan	Develop a written comprehensive safe schools plan
	Implement multi-tiered comprehensive prevention and intervention programs for students
	Create an inclusive and caring school environment

[a] CPTED is based on the principle that school environmental factors can be used to prevent crime on school campuses. These factors are (a) the ability to see what is occurring in and outside of the school, (b) the ability to control entry and exit from the school environment, (c) the ability to demonstrate ownership of and respect of the property, and (d) prohibited access to the school through window locks, deadbolts, and interior door hinges (Lassiter & McEvoy, 2008; Schneider et al., 2000; U. S. Department of Education, 2007a). More information on CPTED can be accessed at the National Clearinghouse for Educational Facilities Web site: www.edfacilities.org/rl/cpted.cfm#10905.

Sources: Based on Lassiter, B., & McEvoy, P. (2008). Sprague, J., & Walker, H. (2002). Sprague, J. (2007). Hamilton Fish Institute on School and Community Violence. Washington, DC; U. S. Department of Education. (2007).

include a thorough physical safety audit (refer to Table 2.3 for a complete description of a physical safety audit).

At the universal level, concerns that emerge from a physical safety assessment may be addressed through the set of principles known as Crime Prevention Through Environmental Design (CPTED). According to CPTED principles, school buildings should be set up to maximize natural surveillance or visibility, guide people effectively (with signs, landscaping, barriers, etc.) to the areas they can and cannot go, and clearly demonstrate ownership of and respect for the property through effective repair and upkeep of the space (CDC, 2008c; Lassiter & McEvoy, 2008; Schneider, Walker, & Sprague, 2000; U. S. Department of Education, ERCM, 2007a). The U.S. Department of Education (ERCM, 2007a) also suggests that schools should prohibit access to the school by installing window locks, dead bolts, and interior door hinges.

In addition to the use of CPTED, security technology and personnel can also play a role in mitigation (Sprague & Walker, 2002; Sprague, 2007). Security technology can include video cameras, metal detectors/hand-held scanners, baggage-type x-ray machines, entry control devices such as electronic identification card readers, and duress alarm devices. A complete discussion of each of these types of devices is beyond the scope of this book; see Green (1999) for such a discussion. In general, each form of security technology has strengths and weaknesses. For example, video cameras have the benefit of recording incidents as they happen and preserving evidence of what transpired. On the downside, they can be expensive and require maintenance and operational support; they can be circumvented and/or may not be able to view an entire area or all school areas; and they can be stolen or vandalized. A general caution for any type of security technology is that in use, care must be taken to ensure that the technology is properly applied, that it is not expected to do more than it is capable of, and that it is well maintained (Green, 1999). Further, some evidence has suggested that intrusive security measures such as metal detectors can have a negative emotional impact on students, including increased fear and anxiety (Juvonen, 2001; Peterson, Larson, & Skiba, 2001). As with security technology, there are positives and negatives to the use of security personnel. Green (1999) notes that good security personnel can be difficult to find and can be expensive. In addition, the critical event can happen so fast that the physical presence of security technology and personnel may not serve as a deterrent and/or can lead to a false sense of security. For example, in the March 2005 Red Lakes, Minnesota, school shooting incident, the perpetrator got past the metal detector and killed the unarmed security officer before targeting other victims. In addition, oftentimes surveillance tasks can be mundane and repetitive and can be difficult for any quality of personnel to do well for an extended period of time.

Therefore, no one device or person will "solve" all of a school's physical safety concerns and the consequences, both positive and negative, of each method need to be considered and devices/personnel selected based on the results of the safety assessment (Green, 1999; Schneider et al., 2000). Not surprisingly, many discussions of security technology include some statement that the intent of these technologies should be only *one part* of a school's safety planning. Security technology and personnel need to be complemented with measures such as the implementation of empirically supported curricula that help to create a positive and inclusive school climate, school policies and procedures that support a safe school environment, and comprehensive written crisis plans (Peterson et al., 2001; Schneider et al., 2000; Sprague, 2007). As stated previously, physical safety is only one component to establishing a comprehensive safe learning environment; psychological safety is also critical.

PREVENTION AND PSYCHOLOGICAL SAFETY

Whereas mitigation efforts are primarily concerned with keeping students physically safe and free from bodily harm, prevention efforts are those that focus on the psychological health and safety of students. As described in Chapter 1, psychological safety efforts refer to efforts that focus on the emotional well-being and positive social development of students. More specifically, it includes the idea that students *feel* safe (which can be independent of adults' evaluations of whether the students *are* safe), perceive their environment as a safe place in which they can learn, and are free from emotional or psychological harm. Overall safety, therefore, is impacted both by physical security and freedom from fear or anxiety about being harmed by others (Rigby, 2007). When children are afraid in their environment, their academic performance can be impacted and they are not likely to develop to their cognitive or emotional potential (Ratner et al., 2006; Rigby, 2007).

Based on this definition, efforts to ensure psychological safety overlap with what generally have been thought of in schools as prevention efforts focused on a myriad of social-emotional concerns, not just the prevention of emergencies or crises. Using terms outlined in the Positive Behavioral Interventions and Supports (PBS/PBIS) model, interventions for students should be available on a multi-tiered continuum to include the universal level (applied to all students, all staff, all settings), targeted level (applied to students, generally in small groups, who demonstrate concerning patterns of behavior that could lead to more restrictive responses), and intensive level (reserved for students who require the most intensive behavior support) (Lohrmann et al., 2008; Sugai & Horner, 2006). This chapter focuses on universal school-wide interventions, whereas Chapters 7 and 8 will discuss targeted and intensive interventions in addition the identification of risk factors and warning signs and the importance of reporting concerns.

Universal interventions have been found to be effective for approximately 80%–85% of the general school population (Burns & Gibbons, 2008; Lewis, Sugai, & Colvin, 1998; OSEP, 2004; Sprague, Walker, Golly, White, Meyers, & Shannon, 2001; Taylor-Greene, Brown, Nelson, Longton, Gassman, Cohen, Swartz, Horner, Sugai, & Hall, 1997). A review of the literature revealed five critical universal elements that are thought to be important in school-based universal prevention efforts designed to engender a safe learning environment.

School Policies and Management Strategies

The first factor includes school policies and management strategies that can play a role in exacerbating or diminishing violent and disruptive student behavior. Schools need to establish a clear code of behavior that outlines the rights and responsibilities of adults and students, describes expected positive student behaviors as well as problem behaviors, delineates positive consequences for appropriate behaviors, and introduces motivational systems for these behaviors (Gottfredson, Wilson, & Najaka, 2002; Juvonen, 2001; Peterson et al., 2001; Sprague & Walker, 2002). The Positive Behavioral Interventions and Supports (PBS/PBIS) model, in use in many schools across the country, provides an example of concrete ways in which schools can achieve these goals. One of the first tasks to implement the PBS/PBIS model is for schools to determine the behavioral expectations for all students and staff. These expectations are often stated in the form of an acronym that is easy to remember and may be related to a school theme or mascot. The behavioral expectations are then posted in every classroom and in common areas of the school. Next, the behavioral expectations should be taught to students with examples to ensure understanding. See Figure 6.1 for examples. Another component is to implement a system-wide positive reinforcement system where students earn verbal praise, coupons, tickets, or other types of reinforcement (see Figure 6.2 for one example) from any staff member in the school at any time. This allows for intermittent recognition and reinforcement of good behaviors in any setting. Some schools have also used their collaborative relationships with local businesses to have items donated that students can then win by placing their positive reinforcement coupons in a weekly or monthly

drawing. In the authors' experience, this has been successful in many schools but is not without the argument of those
who are against rewarding "expected" behavior. In response
to this argument, it can be noted that the use of rewards to
elicit expected behaviors with the eventual goal of decreasing the frequency of reinforcements is a common behavioral
management strategy (Martin & Pear, 2007). More concretely it
can also be argued that most adults receive regular reward for
"expected" behavior in the form of a paycheck. Some secondary schools that have resisted the coupon or ticket idea have
used "good news" messages or post cards sent home to parents; in the authors' experience, schools that have used these

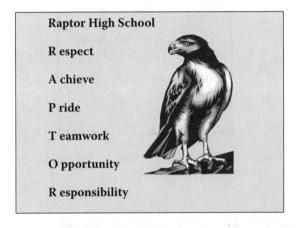

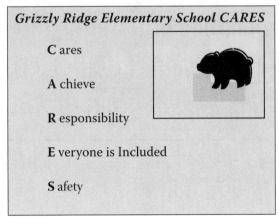

Figure 6.1   Examples of acronyms utilizing the PBS/PBIS structure to help facilitate
universal school policies and management strategies.   *—continued*

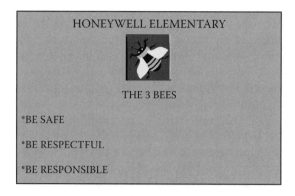

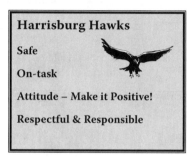

Figure 6.1   (continued) Examples of acronyms utilizing the PBS/PBIS structure to help facilitate universal school policies and management strategies.

Figure 6.2   Example of a positive reinforcement that can then be exchanged for other prizes/reinforcements.

types of reinforcers have received positive feedback from both parents and students. Schools have also used "get in the front of the line" passes for lunch or recess, or rewards for an entire class based on no tardies, fewest absences, etc. Schools have shown great creativity in reinforcing student behavior while hopefully countering some of the arguments against reinforcing expected behavior.

An additional recommendation related to school behavior codes and motivational systems is that the rewarding of positive behaviors should be paired with the teaching and modeling of the expectations and relevant skills by teachers and students (Sprague & Walker, 2002). This helps to maximize the students' chances for earning rewards for expected behaviors and helps facilitate the generalization of acquired skills.

A final area of school policies and management strategies that is worth noting is the use of "zero tolerance" policies. Research has shown that reliance on consequence-based "zero tolerance" policies and on suspension and expulsion alone should be discouraged as these types of approaches lack evidence of effectiveness at best and may in fact exacerbate the student behavior problems (Greene, 2005; Juvonen, 2001; Peterson et al., 2001; Skiba et al., 1997; Sugai & Horner, 2006). Further, although situations may exist where removal of a child from the school is necessary for safety reasons, students who are not in school are not available to learn alternative approaches (Peterson et al., 2001). A system of graduated sanctions that are commensurate with the infraction is the recommended alternative to zero tolerance policies (Greene, 2005). Once in place, policies need to be supported with monitoring of and follow-through with the consequences as outlined in the policy (Gottfredson et al., 2002).

Social-Emotional Skill Building Instruction

A second important component of schools' prevention efforts is a focus on addressing aspects of the students' attitudes, beliefs, and norms that can impact student safety. Interventions that clarify behavioral norms, increase exposure to pro-social beliefs, and correct misperceptions about the prevalence of harmful or illegal behavior have been found to be effective in reducing antisocial behavior, aggression, and delinquency (Coyle, 2005; Gottfredson, et al., 2002). Specific instructional programs focused on the areas of bullying prevention, social skills, conflict resolution, anger management, impulse control, and empathy are also recommended components of a school's prevention programming (CASEL, 2008; Coyle, 2005; Elliott et al., 2000; Hawkins, Farrington, & Catalano, 1998; Juvonen, 2001; Peterson et al., 2001; Sprague, 2007; Sprague & Walker, 2002; Walker, 2001). General recommended strategies for these programs to be successful are to (a) teach skills in a sequential, step-by-step fashion; (b) include active forms of learning, modeling, and practice; (c) provide specific feedback about the new behavior(s); (d) provide cues to prompt the behavior; and (e) include specific techniques to ensure the skills generalize to the school setting (Gottfredson et al., 2002; National Center for Mental Health Promotion, 2008). Table 6.2 provides a more detailed description of the type of interventions in each area along with a brief summary of research that supports the importance of each.

Overall Climate and Culture

The third factor that should be addressed in the school's prevention efforts is the school's overall climate or culture. Intervention with the student population and the implementation of school-wide rules and expectations (as mentioned above) both support the creation of a positive school climate. Additional efforts that impact the school climate are those that encourage students to treat each other with "civility, caring, and respect for the rights of others" (Sprague, 2007; Sprague & Walker, 2002; Walker, 2001). Also, caring relationships between adults and students, an overall sense of community and connectedness to others, and feelings of student ownership of and belonging to the school contribute to a positive school climate (CASEL, 2008; Elliott et al., 2000; Hawkins et al., 1998; Peterson et al., 2001). These variables overlap with those that are often cited as part of asset building or positive youth development.

Positive Youth Development

Through the lens of positive youth development, schools are encouraged to focus on students' strengths and pro-social skills rather than deficits and risk factors (Benson, Scales, Hamilton, Sesma, Hong, & Roehlkepartain, 2006; Smith & Sandhu, 2004). Skills and strengths are bolstered in several ways. First, young people's environments are changed so as to foster supportive relationships and increase the developmental "nutrients" available to students (Benson et al., 2006; Catalano, Berglund, Ryan, Lonczak, & Hawkins, 2002; Greenberg et al., 2003). Second, youth are encouraged to take

Table 6.2 Brief Summary of Research Pertaining to Universal Prevention and Intervention Programs

Prevention Focus	Type of Program/Intervention	Why It's Important
Bullying prevention	Generally recommended to use a whole-school systemic approach that includes assessment of levels of bullying in the school paired with education for all members of the school community about the dynamics of bullying; establishment of rules and a policy regarding bullying; interventions for bullies and victims; and mobilization of peer bystanders to bullying[a]	Bullying is a pervasive form of violence and preventing bullying is thought to be critical to violence prevention efforts; research has clearly shown that bullying negatively impacts the social, emotional, behavioral, and academic functioning of victims and bullies, lowers attendance and connection to school, and increases substance use[b]
Social skills	Interventions typically involve didactic teaching, modeling and role play; opportunities to practice and apply skills are important; skills typically involve communication, assertiveness, refusal and resistance, conflict resolution, and interpersonal negotiation strategies[c]	Deficits in social skills have been linked to aggressive/violent behavior; social skills interventions have been found to have a positive impact; improved social skills may be one way of diminishing the likelihood of becoming a victim of bullying; "relationship skills" have been identified by CASEL as one of the core areas of social emotional learning[d]
Conflict resolution	Different types of programs: skills/problem-solving process taught through curricula; process taught with assistance of a mediator (peer or adult); skills and process taught as part of ongoing curriculum and with classroom management strategies; school-wide approach where all members of school community teach and enforce skills[e]	Teaches students attitudes and skills needed to avoid violence; shifts responsibility for conflict from adults to students; interventions have been found to lead to "impressive results" such as positive impact on academic achievement, social cognitive processes, and aggressive behavior at school; part of CASEL's social emotional core area of relationship skills[f]

—continued

Table 6.2   (continued) Brief Summary of Research Pertaining to Universal Prevention and Intervention Programs

Prevention Focus	Type of Program/Intervention	Why It's Important
Self-management skills: • Anger management • Impulse control	Wide variety of strategies. Generally focused on identification of anger and its triggers; development of skills to moderate the duration, intensity, and frequency of anger expression; and facilitation of socially appropriate, nonaggressive responses in interpersonal situations. Also important to address impulsive responding and to work to generalize skills to the school environment in order to be effective[g]	Self-regulation/self-management identified by CASEL and others as one of the core social-emotional competencies necessary for healthy and successful development; poor anger management skills and impulsivity linked to increased violence and aggression; anger management interventions found to reduce aggressive behavior[h]
Empathy	Improve skills in the ability to recognize emotional cues, take another's perspective, and to be responsive to another person's emotional state; done through instruction and role play[i]	Empathy has been shown to be related to negative attitudes toward violence and to be inversely related to violent and aggressive behavior; part of CASEL's broader core social emotional skill are of self social awareness; empathy training thought to be useful component for programs aimed at reducing aggression[j]

[a] Porter, Plog, Jens, Garrity, & Sager, in press.

[b] Batsche & Knoff, 1994; Buckley, Storino, & Sebastiani, 2003; Furlong, Felix, Sharkey, & Larson, 2005; Glew, Rivara, & Feudtner, 2000; Juvonen, Nishina, & Graham, 2000; Limber & Small, 2003; Miller, Swearer, and Siebecker, 2003; Nansel, Overpeck, Pilla, Ruan, Simons-Morton, & Scheidt, 2001; Orpinas, Horne, & Stanizweski, 2003; Schwartz & Gorman, 2003.

[c] Catalano et al., 2002; Thornton, T. N., Craft, C. A., Dahlberg, L. L., Lynch, B. S., Baer, K., Potter, L., Mercy, J. A., & Flowers, E. A., 2002.

[d] Browning, Cohen, & Warman, 2003; CASEL, 2008; Juvonen, Graham, & Schuster, 2003; Taub, 2002; Thornton et al., 2002.

[e] Crawford & Bodine, 1996; Graves, Frabutt, & Vigliano, 2007; Jones, 2004.

[f] Aber et al., 2003; Brown, Roderick, Lantieri, & Aber, 2004; Crawford & Bodine, 1996; Graves et al., 2007; Skiba, 1999.

[g] Coyle, 2005; Feindler & Wesiner, 2006; Smith, Larson, & Nuckles, 2006.

[h] CASEL, 2008; Feindler & Weisner, 2006; Fong, Vogel, & Vogel, 2008; Guerra & Williams, 2002; Payton et al., 2000; Wittmann, Estibaliz, & Santisteban, 2008.

[i] Björkqvist, Österman, & Kaukiainen, 2000; Sams & Truscott, 2004.

[j] Björkqvist et al., 2000; CASEL, 2008; Jagers, R. J., Morgan-Lopez, A. A., Howard T.-L., Browns, D. C., Flay, B. R., & Aya, A., 2007; Sams & Truscott, 2004; Stone & Dover, 2007.

action to improve their own contexts and are given frequent opportunities for self-direction and participation in positive pro-social activities (Benson et al., 2006; Catalano et al., 2002; Greenberg et al., 2003). The final aspects of asset building and positive youth development include specific instruction of social-emotional skills and reinforcement of the application of these skills and positive behaviors in real-world settings (Catalano et al., 2002; Greenberg et al., 2003). Strategies for asset building/positive youth development and school safety-related prevention efforts overlap considerably. However, the unique feature of a positive youth development approach is the idea that promoting healthy development is an important end in and of itself and not just important due to the countering of risks or engendering of protective factors. Students who are provided with the resources for healthy development are likely to have strengths and skills that are incompatible with negative behaviors (Center for Mental Health in Schools, 2008a; Smith & Sandhu, 2004).

Parent Involvement

The final component to schools' prevention efforts is the involvement of parents. The importance of including parents as part of safe schools planning was previously discussed in Chapter 2. In addition to this role, parents also play an important role in partnering with the school to help students learn effective, nonviolent ways of responding to bullying and helping to ensure that weapons are secured at home. Finally, effective parenting strategies in general are thought to contribute to safe school environments (Sprague & Walker, 2002; Walker, 2001). Table 6.3 summarizes these key components to prevention that need to be addressed in order to create a climate of psychological safety in schools. Figure 6.3 provides a visual model of how all these components are interrelated.

IMPORTANCE OF COORDINATED EFFORTS

Based on the discussion above, it is clear that a wide variety of programs will potentially be needed to help schools build a sense of psychological safety. This can present a particular challenge as it is often the case that schools implement poorly coordinated, short-term, fragmented interventions (Greenberg et al., 2003). When multiple programs are implemented in a way that is poorly coordinated, they can compete among themselves and are less likely to lead to positive change (Center for

Table 6.3   Key Universal Components to Psychological Safety Prevention Efforts

1. School policies and management strategies
   - Clear code of behavior that is taught, monitored, consistently enforced, and emphasizes reinforcement of positive behaviors
2. Social-emotional skill building instruction for students
   - Include modeling, practice, and focus on generalizing skills to school setting
   - Bullying prevention
   - Social skills
   - Conflict resolution
   - Self management
   - Empathy
3. Address overall climate/culture
   - Increase sense of community and connectedness; foster civility among students
4. Positive youth development/asset building
   - Ensure environment provides all students with resources needed for healthy development
5. Involve parents in prevention efforts
   - Gather parent input in planning stages, provide them with the information and skills needed to support school safety efforts

Mental Health in Schools, 2006; Greenberg et al., 2003; Payton, Wardlaw, Graczyk, Bloodworth, Tompsett, & Weissberg, 2000). Comprehensive, coordinated, and multi-faceted approaches are thought to be more effective (Dusenbury, Falco, Lake, Brannigan, & Bosworth, 1997). Many of the problem behaviors occur together and can be addressed by similar strategies (Payton et al., 2000) as demonstrated in Table 6.2. For example, social skills interventions can include conflict resolution, and conflict resolution can include social problem-solving skills, which can also be part of social skills intervention. Recognition of emotions is part of both anger management intervention and empathy intervention. Several models, presented in Table 6.4, can be used to organize many or all of the areas that are important for psychological safety. The first two models (CASEL, 2008; Guerra & Williams, 2002) are based in research and provide comprehensive listings of skills that are critical for effective violence prevention and healthy social emotional development. Although both of these authors discuss the importance of opportunities for engagement, connectedness, and support, their organizational models do not specifically include these environmental variables that need to be addressed for effective prevention. The third model (Catalano et al., 2002) addresses

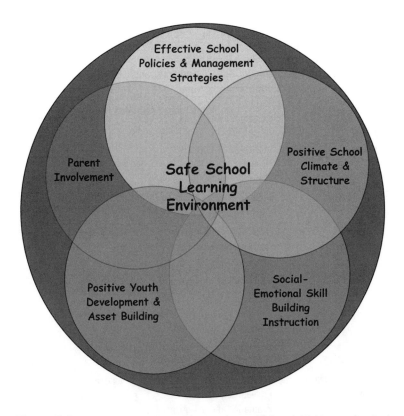

Figure 6.3 Universal prevention and intervention model for establishing a safe school learning environment.

environmental variables, though its ten separate goals may prove overwhelming for schools. Below is an example of a model developed both from research on critical components of effective prevention programming and from practical experience working within a large school district to organize the variety of prevention efforts in place across schools.

Real-World Example of Organizing a District-Wide Universal Prevention Program in Schools: The CARES Model

The CARES model was created within the Cherry Creek School District (CCSD; see Chapter 2 for a description of this district) to summarize the variables that are necessary for a comprehensive model of prevention efforts that facilitate the psychological safety of students (Cherry Creek School District, 2008). CARES stands for

Table 6.4 Models for Organizing Psychological Safety Prevention Efforts

(1) Collaborative for Academic, Social, and Emotional Learning Description of the Core Social-Emotional Learning Areas (CASEL, 2008)

Core Area	Knowledge, Attitudes, Skills
Self-awareness	Identifying and recognizing emotions
	Accurate self-perception
	Recognizing strengths, needs, and values
	Self-efficacy
Self-management	Impulse control and stress management
	Self-motivation and discipline
	Goal setting and organizational skills
Social awareness	Perspective taking
	Empathy
	Difference recognition
	Respect for others
Relationship skills	Communication, social engagement, and relationship building
	Working cooperatively
	Negotiation, refusal, and conflict management
	Help seeking
Responsible decision making	Problem identification and situation analysis
	Problem solving
	Evaluation and reflection
	Personal, social, and ethical responsibility

(2) Core Competencies for Healthy Social and Emotional Development (Guerra & Williams, 2002)

Core Competency	Related Terms
Positive identity	Positive self-concept
	Hopefulness
	Future goals
Personal agency	Self-efficacy
	Effective coping
	Attributional style
Self regulation	Affective, behavioral, and cognitive self-regulation
Social relationship skills	Social problem solving
	Empathy
	Conflict resolution
	Capacity for intimacy

Table 6.4 (continued) Models for Organizing Psychological
Safety Prevention Efforts

System of belief	Attitudes
	Norms
	Values
	Moral engagement

(3) Goals of Positive Youth Development (Catalano et al., 2002)

Goal	Strategies
Promote bonding	Develop relationships with healthy adults, positive peers, school community, and culture
Foster resilience	Emphasize strategies for adaptive coping responses to change and stress
	Psychological flexibility
Promote competence	Social competence: train appropriate interpersonal skills and rehearse strategies for these skills
	Emotional competence: develop skills for identifying feelings, managing emotions, self-management, empathy, self-soothing, and frustration tolerance
	Cognitive competence: influence cognitive abilities, processes, or outcomes
	Behavioral competence: teach skills and reinforce effective behavior choices and action patterns
	Moral competence: promote empathy, respect for rules and standards, a sense of right and wrong, and moral justice
Foster self-determination	Develop the ability to think for oneself and take action consistent with that thought
Foster spirituality	Support youth in exploring spiritual beliefs/practice
Foster self-efficacy skills	Teach strategies such as personal goal setting, coping, and mastery
Foster clear and positive identity	Develop healthy identity formation and achievement
Foster belief in the future	Influence child's belief in his or her future potential, goals, options, choices, or long-range hopes and plans
Provide recognition for positive behavior	Create reward systems for rewarding, recognizing, or reinforcing children's pro-social behaviors
Foster pro-social norms	Encourage youth to develop clear and explicit standards for behavior that minimizes health risks and supports pro-social involvement

Communities are connected, inclusive, and work to prevent bullying.

Asset building is integrated in the school, family, and
community.

Responsive decision making is based on data.

Expectations are clear to students, staff, and parents.

Social-emotional-behavioral skills are taught.

For each item in the model, a description of the area of prevention that is encompassed is presented along with some examples of specific strategies that were used to address this area
within CCSD.

Communities Are Connected, Inclusive, and Work to Prevent Bullying

The first area includes efforts to create a positive school climate and sense of connectedness for students. Bullying prevention is included here to emphasize the importance of this
type of intervention in creating a positive school climate.
Within CCSD, many schools have taught the "Bully-Proofing
Your School" curriculum (Epstein, Plog, & Porter, 2002; Garrity,
Jens, Porter, Sager, & Short-Camilli, 2004) at the elementary
and middle school levels. This involves both direct instruction, typically by the school psychologist and/or school social
worker, and emphasis of the concepts by teachers on a daily
basis throughout the year. In addition, regular staff in-service
time and district-wide trainings have been devoted to more
specific bullying issues, such as cyberbullying, social aggression, and integrating PBS with bullying prevention.

Asset-Building Is Integrated in the School, Family, and Community

This aspect of the CARES model encompasses two areas identified above as important for prevention efforts. The first is
the emphasis on positive youth development and the recommended focus on ensuring that students' environments contain the necessary resources for optimal development. The
second area is parent involvement, which here more specifically refers to the critical role parents play in providing students with necessary resources. To support this aspect of the
CARES model, the district's prevention office has provided
schools with materials (including information for parent
newsletters) and trainings to teach the assets framework and

has offered parenting workshops consistent with the model. It should be noted that parent involvement is also included under the discussion of expectations.

Responsive Decision Making Is Based on Data

This component, described as responsive decision making, has not typically been included as part of prevention models. Data-driven decision making was specifically included in the CARES model to underscore the importance of utilizing data in safe schools planning. As discussed in Chapter 2, site-based data can help ensure that prevention efforts are tailored to the needs of a particular school, district, or community and can serve as a benchmark for evaluating the effectiveness of safety efforts. In addition to outcome data, it is also recommended that schools assess how fully and faithfully the strategies they choose are being implemented (Blasé & Fixen, 2006; Elias et al., 2003; Greene, 2005). Fidelity of intervention has received considerable attention in research on effective intervention in schools; in order for interventions to repeat their proven positive effects, they need to be implemented as designed (in terms of content and dosage) in a quality manner (Elliott, 2006). Data on how well the intervention was implemented, paired with data on what changes have followed since the inception of the intervention, can help schools determine whether the intervention is effective and if not, whether the failure to produce the desired results was due to problems with the intervention itself or with the quality of the implementation (refer to Chapter 2 for further discussion on CCSD's utilization of data).

Expectations Are Clear to Students, Staff, and Parents

The next component outlined in the CARES acronym is that "expectations are clear to students, staff, and parents." This corresponds to the two areas reviewed above that are important in prevention efforts, school policies, specifically management strategies, and a clear code of behavior that outlines expectations and provides for recognition of positive behaviors. The Cherry Creek School District has worked toward communication of clear expectations through its conduct code and discipline policies that are distributed in written form to each student at the beginning of the school year. Both the *parent and the student* sign and return the form stating they are aware of and will abide by the conduct code and discipline policies. Ensuring clear communication of expectations to parents is a second way that parent involvement is critical in the CARES model. Parents, students, and staff are also expected to partner in the maintenance of a safe school environment by reporting behaviors of concern to school administration or to an anonymous reporting line. Additional ways in which expectations are communicated and taught and positive behaviors are recognized is through use of the PBS model in many of the CCSD schools.

Social-Emotional-Behavioral Skills Are Taught

The CARES acronym concludes with "social-emotional-behavioral skills are taught." This area includes instruction in recommended areas of student pro-social attitudes, beliefs, and norms, as well as conflict resolution, anger management, impulse control, and empathy. In order to address this component of the CARES model, CCSD schools implement universal, targeted, and intensive academic and social-emotional interventions. These include bullying and violence prevention programs at the universal level (which reinforces the "C" in CARES); targeted interventions that include counseling groups and small group instruction focused on anger management, social skills, student support and social-emotional skill building groups, and other identified areas of need; and intensive interventions that include intensive individualized support and counseling, direct instruction, alternative educational placements to better meet academic and social-emotional needs, and use of systems of care in partnership with community agencies, if appropriate.

IMPORTANCE OF EVIDENCE-BASED INTERVENTIONS

Prevention and intervention efforts are more likely to be effective when they are comprehensive and coordinated. The careful selection of evidence-based programs to fit into the school's prevention model is critical to ensure the effectiveness of these efforts. Not all prevention programs that schools select have been shown to be effective and, in fact, several violence prevention strategies have been determined to be ineffective or even to produce negative outcomes. These include placing aggressive/antisocial kids together in a group, adding a new program to a system that is already overwhelmed, and using programs that only provide information (instead of skill building) or are brief and not supported by climate changes (Dusenbury et al., 1997). Peer counseling and peer mediation (United States Department of Health & Human Services [DHHS], 2001) are also cited as ineffective means of reducing youth violence. It should be noted that these findings have been criticized for focusing only on violent/aggressive behavior outcomes and, although these programs may not prevent violence per se, they may be able to help students improve their skills and find better ways to handle their problems (Aber, Brown, & Jones, 2003). Finally, generic counseling, social work, and other therapeutic interventions not focused on specific skills deficits, as well as recreational, community service, enrichment, and leisure activity interventions have not been found to effectively impact violent behavior (Gottfredson et al., 2002; DHHS, 2001). In summary, a general intervention or program without a specific focus on teaching replacement behaviors to counteract skills deficits, coupled with implementation by a nontrained professional, will not help to address violent behaviors. Given the scarcity of resources within schools, it is important that time is not spent on an intervention that is less likely to lead to a positive impact. For this reason, it is typically recommended that schools implement *evidence-based* prevention practices (Greenberg et al., 2003; DHHS, 2001).

It should be noted that there are several terms such as "empirically supported" or "science based" that have been used to indicate the concept of "evidence based" (Center for Mental Health in Schools, 2006). Although some disagreement exists on how to define evidence based (Walker, 2004), it is generally thought that the term evidence-based interventions refers to interventions that have been shown to be effective via data gathered using methods that meet rigorous scientific standards (Center for Mental Health in Schools, 2006; DHHS, 2001). In addition, it is argued that the effects of the intervention need to have been replicated in a real-world school setting (DHHS, 2001; Center for Mental Health in Schools, 2006; Kratochwill & Shernoff, 2004; Schaughency & Ervin, 2006). In fact, the belief by school practitioners that an intervention that has been shown to work under controlled conditions will not be effective in the real world is cited as one of the barriers to implementation of evidence-based interventions (Center for Mental Health in Schools, 2006; Schaughency & Ervin, 2006; Walker, 2004). Other barriers that have been discussed include an objection to a prescriptive rather than an individualized functional behavior approach, questions about the adaptability of the intervention to a diverse student population, and

practical concerns such as the expense of (in terms of financial and staffing resources) implementing interventions that
have been found to be evidence based (Schaeffer, Bruns, Weist,
Stephan, Goldstein, & Simpson, 2005; Schaughency & Ervin,
2006; Walker, 2004). In order to address these types of concerns, research has begun to look beyond just the evidence
base for programs and practices to the science behind implementing programs with fidelity and with good outcomes for
consumers (Fixsen et al., 2005). Implementation factors such
as training, coaching, and supervision of staff; leadership and
organizational infrastructure; full involvement of community;
and sufficient dosing (or an appropriate number of sessions
and/or time devoted to the intervention) have been identified
as important variables that may impact the outcome of an
intervention and therefore need to be considered by program
developers and practitioners in the schools (CASEL, 2008;
Fixsen et al., 2005).

Resources for Finding Evidence-Based Interventions

In order to help schools select universal, targeted, or intensive
programs that are evidence based, several "model lists" (see
Tables 6.5 and 6.6) have been created to help schools distinguish between programs with and without thorough evaluation of their evidence base (Greenberg et al., 2003). Two types
of listings are available to schools. The first are on-line sites
that evaluate programs on an ongoing basis. These sites vary
somewhat in the criteria that are used to list programs (for
example, whether or not a program has been shown to have
an impact in multiple studies or has studies that have been
reported in peer-reviewed journals), but most are searchable
by particular concerns/problem behaviors and provide at least
a general overview of the program and the outcomes that have
been demonstrated following implementation of the intervention. In addition, there are other one-time publications that
have reviewed outcome research and rated the potential benefit of violence prevention and/or positive youth development
programs.

It should be noted, though, that these lists do not always
agree as to what are effective programs. Elliott (2008) com-
pared programs across eight federal program lists and found
that only one program was rated at the highest level on all of
the lists; only one additional program appeared on seven of the
lists. Despite this, schools are encouraged to consult these lists
as they generally have been compiled by organizations with

expertise in prevention, intervention, and research design, and contain a wealth of information on which programs are likely to have a positive impact in schools and on the research that supports each intervention they include.

Even with the clear listing of programs with an evidence base, it is possible that schools will either select a program that is not on one of the lists or not find programs on the lists that meet their needs as "only a handful of violence prevention approaches have been evaluated and fewer have been determined to be effective or promising" (Juvonen, 2001, p. 5). In addition, schools receiving elementary and secondary education state grant funds, which require schools to use programs with proven effectiveness, can apply to their state for a waiver, which would allow them to use innovative activities or programs that have the potential to demonstrate a substantial likelihood of success (U. S. Dept. of Education, n.d.). When a program that a school is considering is not on one of the lists, schools are encouraged to consider whether the prevention program is based in theoretical research, as interventions based firmly in theories that have empirically linked the concern and the intervention are more likely to be effective (Nation, Crusto, Wandersman, Kumpfer, Seybolt, Morrissey-Kane, & Davino, 2003; Sugai & Horner, 2006). In addition, when schools select intervention programs without demonstrated effectiveness, they should "be prepared to conduct their own evaluations" (Elliott et al., 2000, p. 19). As described above as part of the CARES model, data need to be gathered on implementation variables related to the fidelity of the intervention (what content was given, by whom, for what duration, and at what level of intensity) as well as on outcome variables that are likely to be impacted by the intervention. This way schools can determine whether the intervention has a positive impact for their students and in the absence of a positive impact, schools will be able to consider whether the intervention did not succeed due to its content or to the way it was delivered (fidelity of implementation).

It is beyond the scope of the current volume to evaluate and recommend specific prevention programs; however, it is realized that for schools that are in the early stages of safe schools planning a list of programs to consider can be helpful. The listing of programs in Table 6.6 was adapted from the University of Maryland School of Medicine, Center for School Mental Health's summary (Steigler & Lever, 2008) of recognized evidence-based programs based on analysis and synthesis of

Table 6.5 Online Web Sites Providing Reviews of Evidence-Based Programs

Internet-Based Resources That Evaluate Programs on an Ongoing Basis

Center for the Study and Prevention of Violence (CSPV)

http://www.colorado.edu/cspv/blueprints/

This Web site overviews the Blueprints for Violence Prevention project, which has identified prevention and intervention programs that meet a strict scientific standard of program effectiveness and have been shown to reduce or eliminate problem behaviors such as delinquency, aggression, violence, substance abuse, and school behavioral problems. Program effectiveness is based upon an initial review by CSPV and a final review and recommendation from an advisory board. Programs selected are based on "evidence of deterrent effect with a strong research design, sustained effect, and multiple site replication" and programs are determined to be "promising" or "model." The 11 model programs, called Blueprints, have been effective in reducing adolescent violent crime, aggression, delinquency, and substance abuse; another 18 programs have been identified as promising programs. There is also a matrix posted on the Web site (http://www.colorado.edu/cspv/blueprints/matrixfiles/matrix.pdf) that provides the category rating for the specific programs across the different listing sites.

Helping America's Youth—Program Tool

http://www.findyouthinfo.gov/cf_pages/programtool-ap.cfm

The Helping America's Youth Program tool, the result of a collaboration among several federal agencies (e.g., the U.S. Departments of Education, Health & Human Services, and Justice) features evidence-based programs that prevent and reduce delinquency or other problem behaviors (i.e., drug and alcohol use). Level 1 rating is given to programs with more rigorous research designs (i.e., experimental with random assignment) and evidence of behavioral decreases or changes in risk or protective factors; Level 2 programs have demonstrated change to youth behavior or risk and protective factors using quasi-experimental design and a comparison group; and Level 3 programs have a strong theoretical base but limited research methods.

The Office of Juvenile Justice and Delinquency Prevention's (OJJDP) Model Programs Guide

http://www.dsgonline.com/mpg_non_flash/mpg_index2.htm and http://www.dsgonline.com/mpg2.5/mpg_index.htm

The OJJDP Model Programs Guide site provides a searchable database of scientifically tested and proven programs that address a range of issues across the juvenile justice spectrum. The guide profiles more than 175 prevention and intervention programs and helps communities identify those that best suit their needs. Users can search the guide's database by program category, target population, risk and protective factors, effectiveness rating, and other parameters. Using four summary dimensions of program effectiveness (conceptual framework, program fidelity, evaluation design, and empirical evidence demonstrating positive impact on behavior), programs are rated as "promising," "effective," or "exemplary."

Table 6.5 (continued) Online Web Sites Providing Reviews of Evidence-Based Programs

Internet-Based Resources that Evaluate Programs on an Ongoing Basis

Promising Practices Network (PPN) on Children, Families, and Communities

http://www.promisingpractices.net/

This network, comprised of a partnership between the Rand Corporation and several state-level intermediary organizations, is dedicated to providing quality evidence-based information regarding programs to help the lives and outcomes of children. Programs are rated "proven" or "promising" based on the rigor of the research and the magnitude of the impact of the intervention on outcomes, or "screened" for programs that have not been reviewed by PPN staff, but have been shown to be effective by one or more credible organizations.

Substance Abuse and Mental Health Services Administration's (SAMHSA) Model Programs—The National Registry of Evidence-Based Programs and Practices (NREPP)

http://nrepp.samhsa.gov/index.htm or http://www.nrepp.samhsa.gov/

This site attempts to provide information both on the scientific and the practical; therefore, numerical ratings are given on a four-point scale based on the quality of research (reliability, validity, intervention fidelity, missing data and attrition, potential confounding variables, and appropriateness of analysis) and the readiness for dissemination (availability of implementation materials, training and support resources, and quality assurance resources). The programs have been tested in communities, schools, social service organizations, and workplaces, and have provided solid proof that they have prevented or reduced substance abuse and other related high-risk behaviors. It should be noted that NREPP's ratings do not reflect an intervention's effectiveness, but rather the quality of the research for each outcome. However, the impact of the intervention on each outcome variable is described. Another part of the Web site (http://modelprograms.samhsa.gov/) has information on a variety of programs that were previously evaluated using a different rating system. These programs were rated "model," "effective," or "promising," and although this list is no longer being updated, it can still be helpful.

Suicide Prevention Resource Center (SPRC): Best Practices Registry (BPR) for Suicide Prevention

http://www.sprc.org/featured_resources/bpr/index.asp

The BPR is divided into three sections. The first lists evidence-based programs that have "demonstrated successful outcomes (generally, reductions in suicidal behavior) and have well-designed research studies" based on the NREPP and the SPRC/American Suicide Foundation Evidence-Based Practices Project. The second section lists expert and consensus statements that "summarize the best knowledge in suicide prevention in the form of guidelines and protocols." The third section lists programs that have been reviewed and determined to adhere to standards and recommendations in the field. Please note this is not a comprehensive inventory of all suicide prevention initiatives.

—continued

Table 6.5   (continued) Online Web Sites Providing Reviews of Evidence-Based Programs

Internet-Based Resources that Evaluate Programs on an Ongoing Basis

U. S. Department of Education Institute of Educational Sciences (IES)—ED Registry (www.whatworks.ed.gov)—What Works Clearinghouse

Programs reviewed are those which have been nominated or suggested by experts based on the following criteria: potential to improve important student outcomes; applicability to a broad range of students or to particularly important subpopulations; policy relevance and perceived demand within the education community; and availability of scientific studies. A wide range of materials may be found under each topic area to include topic reports, intervention reports, practice guides, quick reviews of single studies, and research review protocols. When you log onto the home page, click on Topics Areas and various topics can be chosen: beginning reading, elementary math, character education, English language learners, middle school math, early childhood education, and dropout prevention. Within each area is a searchable database of interventions; when the quality of the research is determined to be of sufficient quality to draw conclusions, interventions are rated as having "positive," "potentially positive," "no discernible," "mixed," "potentially negative," or "negative" effects.

One-Time Publications that Rate Violence Prevention and/or Positive Youth Development Programs

Catalano, Bergulund, Ryan, Lonczak, & Hawkins. (2002). Positive Youth Development in the United States: Research Findings on Evaluations of Positive Youth Development Programs

http://psycnet.apa.org/journals/pre/5/1/15a.pdf.

This summarizes programs that addressed one or more positive youth development constructs, included youth between 6 and 20, involved youth not based on need for treatment, and addressed at least one youth development construct in multiple socialization domains or multiple constructs in a single socialization domain. Programs have adequate study design and outcome measures, adequate description of research methodologies, descriptions of the population served, the intervention, and the implementation, had to have effects demonstrated on behavioral outcomes. It provides program description, research design, and results of the intervention.

Collaborative for Academic, Social, and Emotional Learning (CASEL). **(2003). Safe and Sound: An Educational Leader's Guide to Evidence-Based Social and Emotional Learning (SEL) Programs** http://www.casel.org/downloads/Safe%20and%20Sound/1A_Safe_&_Sound.pdf or http://www.casel.org/pub/safeandsound.php.

CASEL published the *Safe and Sound Report*, which reviews 80 school-based programs that are nationally available, intended for a general population, and have at least eight lessons for at least two consecutive grades. The report provides information on the following: (a) capacity of classroom-based programs to develop social and emotional competencies; (b) program ratings based on sound SEL practice; (c) program effectiveness and implementation supports (evidence of effectiveness, professional

Table 6.5   (continued) Online Web Sites Providing Reviews of
Evidence-Based Programs

**One-Time Publications that Rate Violence Prevention and/or Positive Youth
Development Programs (continued)**

development, student assessment measures, and classroom implementation tools); (d)
ratings of safe and sound learning environments (school-wide coordination, school-
family partnerships, and community partnerships); and (e) program design information.
It also includes a listing of review Web sites, the area of interest that is covered, and a
brief description of the ratings that are used (p. 32 of *Safe and Sound*). The CASEL Web
site offers many additional resources that highlight the effectiveness of social
emotional learning (SEL) programs (http://www.casel.org).

U.S. Department of Health & Human Services. (2001). **Youth Violence: A
Report of the Surgeon General**

http://www.surgeongeneral.gov/library/youthviolence/chapter5/sec1.html

This report includes programs based on determination of rigorous experimental design,
evidence of significant deterrent effect, and replication of effects at multiple sites or in
clinical trials, and classifies strategies as ineffective, promising, and model.

Source: Adapted from Steigler, K., & Lever, N. (2008). *Summary of evidenced-based program registries.* Center for School Mental Health. University of Maryland School of
Medicine: Author.

outcome findings. Only programs that received recognition
from more than one of the evidence-based program registries (Table 6.5) were included in Table 6.6, unless otherwise
noted. Please note this is *not* an all-inclusive list, and given the
existence of organizations that have rigorously evaluated the
evidence base of prevention programs, it makes sense for the
reader to refer to these specific on-line Web sites for additional
in-depth information. As mentioned above, these lists do not
always agree and it is not always the case that the prevention
program a school has selected will be on the list. When determining existing research to support a selected program, these
lists can save schools time in their preliminary research and
can prove an invaluable resource.

Real-World Example: Examination of CARES
Model Fit and Research Base for Programs in
Use in a Large Suburban School District

As mentioned above, it is not always the case that programs
selected for use within a school or district will appear on one
of the lists (see Table 6.5). Under those circumstances, it is

Table 6.6 Overview of Universal Evidence-Based Social-Emotional Programs and Interventions

	Universal Prevention Programs	
Program Name	**Age Level Targeted/Topics Addressed**	**Program Recognition Program Web Site**
Psychological Safety Component		
Al's Pals	• Preschool through first grade	• Helping America's Youth Registry Level 2
Social-Emotional Skills Building:	• Develop social-emotional skills and create caring, cooperative classroom environment	• Reviewed by NREPP
• *Social Skills*	• Designed to increase social-emotional competence and decrease aggressive/antisocial behavior	• OJJDP Effective
• *Conflict Resolution*		http://www.wingspanworks.com/ educational_programs
All Stars	• Middle school	• Reviewed by NREPP
• *Positive Youth Development*	• Prevention of high-risk behaviors (drug use, violence, sexual activity)	• OJJDP Promising
	• Reinforce positive qualities in youth and connections with adults at home and school that are inconsistent with high-risk behaviors	http://www.allstarsprevention.com
Bully-Proofing Your School	• Preschool through high school	• U.S. Department of Health Resources Services Administration—Stop Bullying Now Resource
Social Emotional Skills Building:	• Systemic bullying prevention program that enlists staff and students in the creation of a caring school environment that is not conducive to aggression and bullying	• *Under review by OJJDP*
• *Bullying Prevention*		
• *School Climate and Culture*		

* BPYS is not yet included on more than one evidence-based registry. It is included here due to (1) initial evidence of program effectiveness and (2) the authors' favorable experience working with this program in schools.
www.bullyproofing.org

• Has been found to reduce bullying behavior, improve perceptions of safety at school, and favorably alter attitudes toward bullying and physical aggression (Menard, Grotpeter, Gianola, & O'Neal, 2007)

Caring School Community
• *Social-Emotional Skills Building:*
  • *Empathy*
• *School Climate and Culture*
• *Positive Youth Development*
• *Parent Involvement*

• Kindergarten through elementary
• Builds classroom and school community; strengthens students' connectedness to schools
• Fosters empathy and understanding of others
• Focus on helpfulness, respect, and responsibility

• CASEL Select Program
• Catalano et al. (2002)—Effective - Schools and Families domain
• Helping America's Youth Registry Level 2
• Reviewed by NREPP
• OJJDP Effective Program
• What Works Clearinghouse: Potentially Positive Effects
http://www.devstu.org/csc/videos/index.shtml

Good Behavior Game
• *School Policies and Management*

• Elementary schools
• Classroom management strategy designed to improve aggressive/disruptive classroom behavior

• CSPV Blueprints Promising Program
• Helping America's Youth Registry Level 2
• OJJDP Exemplary
• Surgeon General's Report Promising

Guiding Good Choices
• *Social-Emotional Skills Building:*
  • *Refusal Skills*
• *Parent Involvement*
• *+ Drug Prevention*

• Grades 4–8
• Drug use prevention program aimed at parents; strengthens and clarifies family expectations and improves family bonding
• Teaches students resistance skills

• CSPV Blueprints Promising Program
• Helping America's Youth Registry Level 2
• Reviewed by NREPP
• OJJDP Exemplary
• PPN Proven
• Strengthening America's Families Exemplary
• Surgeon General's Report Promising
http://www.channing-bete.com/ggc   *—continued*

Table 6.6 (continued) Overview of Universal Evidence-Based Social-Emotional Programs and Interventions

I Can Problem Solve: Raising a Thinking Child • *Social-Emotional* Skills Building: • *Social Skills*	• Preschool through elementary school • Violence prevention program focusing on nonviolent ways to solve everyday problems to resolve interpersonal problems and prevent antisocial behaviors	• CSPV Blueprints Promising Program • CASEL Select Program • Helping America's Youth Registry Level 2 • NREPP Legacy Program • OJJDP Effective Program • SAMHSA Promising Program http://guide.helpingamericasyouth.gov/programdetail.cfm?id=458 http://www.researchpress.com/product/item/4628/

Lion's Quest Skills for Adolescence
 	
• *Social-Emotional Skills* Building:
  • *Social Skills*
  • *Parent Involvement*
  • *Positive Youth Development*
	• Grades 6–8
	• Comprehensive life skills and drug prevention program emphasizing character development, communication, decision making, and also includes a service-learning component; good prevention program for guiding towards healthy choices and drug and violence free lifestyle
		• Reviewed by NREPP
		• OJJDP Effective Program
		• PNN Screened Program
		• SAMHSA Model Program
		• USDE's Safe, Disciplined, and Drug Free Schools Promising Program
		http://www.nrepp.samhsa.gov/programfulldetails.asp?PROGRAM_ID=99
		http://casat.unr.edu/bestpractices/view.php?program=56

Olweus Bully Prevention Program
 	
• *Social-Emotional Skills* Building:
  • *Bullying Prevention*
  • *School Climate and Community*
	• Grades K–9
	• Goals are to reduce and prevent bullying problems and improve peer relations
	• Found to reduce bullying, improve school climate, and reduce related antisocial behaviors
		• OJJDP Effective Program
		• Blueprints Model Program
		• SAMHSA Model Program
		http://www.clemson.edu/olweus/

Peace Works
- *Social-Emotional Skills Building:*
  - *Conflict Resolution*
  - *Self-Management*
- *School Climate and Culture*
- *Parent Involvement*

- Kindergarten through high school
- Teaches students and parents conflict resolution skills and enhances the school climate through caring and support

- CASEL Select Program
- OJJDP Promising Program
http://www.peace-ed.org/

Promoting Alternative Thinking Strategies (PATHS)
- *Social-Emotional Skills Building:*
  - *Social Skills*
  - *Self-Management*

- Pre K–5th grade
- Can use activities with parents
- Promotes emotional and social competencies and reduces aggression and behavior while enhancing classroom processes

- CSPV Blueprints Model Program
- CASEL Select Program
- Helping America's Youth Registry Level 1
- Reviewed by NREPP
- OJJDP Exemplary Program
- USDE's Safe, Disciplined, and Drug Free Schools Promising Program

http://www.channing-bete.com/prevention-programs/paths/
http://www.modelprograms.samhsa.gov/pdfs/model/PATHS.pdf
- http://www.prevention.psu.edu/projects/PATHS.html
- http://www.nrepp.samhsa.gov/programfulldetails.asp?PROGRAM_ID=127
- http://www.colorado.edu/cspv/blueprints/modelprograms/PATHS.html

—continued

Table 6.6 (continued) Overview of Universal Evidence-Based Social-Emotional Programs and Interventions

Positive Action

• *Positive Youth Development*

- Ages 5–18
- Based on Thoughts-Actions-Feelings Circle
- Program teaches that positive actions related to physical, intellectual, social, and emotional areas of self lead to and are influenced by feeling good about oneself
- Some lessons are aligned to state standards

- Helping America's Youth Registry Level 2
- Reviewed by NREPP
- OJJDP Effective Program
- PNN Screened Program
- SAMHSA Model Program
- USDE's Safe, Disciplined, and Drug Free Schools Promising Program

http://www.positiveaction.net/

Positive Behavior Supports

• *School Policies and Management*

• *Climate and Culture*

- Kindergarten through high school
- Change student behavior through changes in the school environment; provide direct instruction and a continuum of behavioral support to all students

- Improvements in classroom and hallway behavior and decreased discipline referrals have been noted following implementation of PBS
- * Because it is not an intervention program per se, PBS is not included on any of the registry listings, but is included here due to its positive impact on School Policies and Management and School Climate and Culture and based on the authors' experience of positive results using PBS in schools. Also this framework provides support for any universal program being implemented

Project ACHIEVE

• *Social-Emotional Skills Building:*

- Ages 3–14
- A school improvement program focusing on academic and social/emotional/behavioral success of all students

- CSPV Blueprints Promising Program
- Helping America's Youth Registry Level 1

• *Social Skills* • *Conflict Resolution* • *Self Management* • *Positive Youth Development* • *Caring Climate and Culture*	• Integrates strategic planning, professional development, on-site consultation, and technical assistance for student achievement and positive school and classroom climates • Meaningful parent involvement and community outreach • Helps schools implement PBS/PBIS and response-to-intervention processes	• Reviewed by NREPP • OJJDP Exemplary Program • PNN Proven Program • SAMHSA Model Program • USDE's Safe, Disciplined, and Drug Free Schools Exemplary Program http://www.projectachieve.info/
Project ALERT • *Substance Abuse Prevention*	• Ages 12–14 • Classroom-based adolescent substance abuse prevention program • Provides skills and strategies for resisting drug use and establishing non-use attitudes and beliefs • Can compliment other health, sex education, physical education, science, and social studies curricula	• CSPV Blueprints Promising Program • Helping America's Youth Registry Level 1 • Reviewed by NREPP • OJJDP Exemplary Program • PNN Proven Program • SAMHSA Model Program • USDE's Safe, Disciplined, and Drug Free Schools Exemplary Program http://www.projectalert.best.org/Default.asp?bhcp=1
Responding in Peaceful and Positive Ways • *Social-Emotional Skills Building:* • *Social Skills* • *Conflict Resolution*	• Middle school • Teaches students to use a social cognitive problem-solving model to choose nonviolent strategies for resolving conflict	• Catalano et al.—Effective School, Family, and Community domains • Helping America's Youth Registry Level 1 • Reviewed by NREPP • OJJEP Exemplary Program http://www.preventionopportunities.org

—continued

Table 6.6 (continued) Overview of Universal Evidence-Based Social-Emotional Programs and Interventions

SOAR (Skills, Opportunities, and Recognition) • *School Policies and Management* • *Parent Involvement*	• Kindergarten through middle school • Training for teachers in classroom management and cooperative learning • Family management training for parents, along with strategies to improve communication with school	• CASEL Select • CSPV Promising Program • Catalano et al.—Effective School and Family domains • Helping America's Youth Registry Level 2 • OJJDP Effective Program • PPN Promising • Surgeon General's Report Model Program
SOS Signs of Suicide • *Suicide Prevention*	• Ages 14–18 • Students taught to increase help-seeking behavior and recognize warning signs within self and others	• NREPP Reviewed • OJJDP Promising Program • SAMHSA Promising Program • SPRC Reviewed Evidence-Based Practice http://guide.helpingamericasyouth.gov/programdetail.cfm?id=656 http://www.nrepp.samhsa.gov/programfulldetails.asp?PROGRAM_ID=66
Steps to Respect • *Social-Emotional Skills Building:* • *Bullying Prevention* • *Conflict Resolution*	• Grades 3–6 • Whole school approach to bullying and includes staff and parents. Teaches it's safe to come forward when there is a problem • Skills taught to recognize and refuse bullying, maintain friendships, resolve conflicts • Family trainings and materials to reinforce at home	• OJJDP Effective Program http://www.cfchildren.org/programs/str/overview/ http://guide.helpingamericasyouth.gov/programdetail.cfm?id=698 *This program is currently only listed on one program recognition list, but is included due to the author's favorable experience with this program.

Teaching Students to Be Peacemakers	Ages 9–14	Helping America's Youth Registry Level 2
Social-Emotional Skills Building: • *Conflict Resolution* • *Climate and Culture*	• Students, faculty, and staff are taught conflict resolution procedures by teaching social-emotional competence. Also reduces antisocial and aggressive behaviors	• OJJDP Promising Program • PNN Proven Program • SAMHSA Model Program • USDE's Safe, Disciplined, and Drug Free Schools Promising Program http://www.co-operation.org/pages/peacemaker.html http://guide.helpingamericasyouth.gov/programdetail.cfm?id=49

Note: Please note this is not an all-exhaustive list. Programs were included based on their impact on factors critical to psychological safety in schools and their inclusion on more than one evidence-based program registry listing. The authors are not specifically endorsing a particular program(s), nor is it meant to substitute for one of the rigorous reviews of programs conducted by the organizations listed in the third column of this table. See Table 6.5 for further information regarding program qualifications and how to find program recognition qualifications. CASEL = Collaborative for Academic, Social, and Emotional Learning; CSPV = Center for the Study and Prevention of Violence; NREPP = SAMHSA's National Registry of Evidenced Based Programs and Practices; OJJDP = Office of Juvenile Justice and Delinquency Prevention; PNN = Promising Practices Network on Children, Families, and Communities; SAMHSA= Substance Abuse and Mental Health Services Administration; SPRC = Suicide Prevention Resource Center; USDE = U. S. Department of Education.

Source: Adapted from Stiegler, K., & Lever, N. (2008). *Summary of recognized evidence-based programs implemented by expanded school mental health programs center for school mental health.* University of Maryland School of Medicine. Retrieved November 29, 2008, from http://csmh.umaryland.edu/resources.html/index.html.

Additional sources: Benson et al., 2006; Beran & Tutty, 2002; Christensen, Young, & Marchant, 2004; Committee for Children, n.d.; Epstein et al., 2002; Frey, Hirschsttein, & Guzzo, 2000; Garrity et al., 2004; Gottfredson, Gottfredson, & Hybl, 1993; Grossman, Neckerman, Koepsell, Liu, Asher, Beland, Frey, & Rivara, 1997; Limber, 2006; Luiselli, Putnam, Handler, & Feinberg, 2005; McMahon & Washburn, 2003; Oswald, Safran, & Johanson, 2005; Safran & Oswald, 2003; Scales & Roehlkeparain, 2003; Scott & Barrett, 2004; Steigler & Lever, 2008; Warren, Edmonson, Griggs, Lassen, McCart, Turnbull, & Sailor, 2003.

important for the school to consider the research base of the program (or how well it fits within theoretical research linking the concern with the intervention) as well as any evidence for the program that exists outside of the recognized lists. Table 6.7 demonstrates how the Cherry Creek School District evaluated the research base of several prevention programs to align within their CARES prevention model presented above. This grid serves several purposes. It allows for visual examination to ensure that all aspects of the CARES model are being addressed. Through discussion of the underlying philosophy of each of the programs, it allows for examination of overlap among the programs to ensure that efforts are coordinated and implemented toward one cohesive goal. Finally, it lays out the research and evidence in support of each of the programs. Therefore, this type of grid can be used to ensure that programs selected fully support the conceptual model of prevention and, to the greatest extent possible, are based in research with a process for collecting and evaluating program effectiveness.

CONCLUSION

Mitigation and prevention work hand in hand to ensure that the likelihood of crisis situations in schools is reduced and that, given that no school can ever prevent all crisis situations, the impact of the crisis situation on the school is lessened. This is done through universal efforts that help address the physical and psychological safety of the school. Physical safety is addressed largely through efforts organized under the concept of Crime Prevention Through Environmental Design (CPTED), security technology, and security personnel. It is also accomplished by mitigating any identified physical hazards from the site vulnerability assessments discussed in earlier chapters. Psychological safety is addressed through the components of good policy and management strategies and implementing quality programs and models to address positive school climate and positive youth development, build social-emotional skills for all students, and encourage parental involvement. Together, all of these maximize the likelihood of a safe learning environment. The discussion of prevention efforts was largely focused on universal intervention strategies focused on the entire school population. Chapter 7 will focus on more targeted interventions designed for youth not responding to universal interventions and supports.

Table 6.7 Research Base CARES Prevention Model

Model Component	Prevention Program			
	Bully Proofing Your School[a]	Search Institute 40 Developmental Assets[b]	Positive Behavior Supports[c]	Second Step[d]
Communities are connected,	Caring Community a main focus; also stresses engagement of bystanders and responsibility of all students to help reduce bullying	Focus on relationships, especially adults (not just professionals) connecting with youth and engaging and empowering youth	Common expectations for all members of the school community	Social skills and empathy training can help build relationships
inclusive,	Encourages students to include ALL students, including outsiders	All youth benefit from assets; positive values asset includes emphasis on equality and social justice; social competence asset includes emphasis on cultural competence	Includes an emphasis on respect—some schools may choose to deal with diversity more directly	Indirectly addressed only (through social skills and empathy training)
and work to prevent bullying	Main emphasis. Works to prevent bullying through systemic approach plus teaching about bullying and involvement of bystanders	Some assets relate: positive values (helping others); commitment to learning (cares about school); caring school climate, but no direct mention of bullying	Can be included as an expectation (though expectations *alone* are not sufficient to prevent bullying)	Empathy training, asking for help, impulse control, problem-solving, anger management (also Steps to Respect program more specifically focuses on bullying)

—continued

Table 6.7 (continued) Research Base CARES Prevention Model

		Prevention Program		
Model Component	**Bully Proofing Your School**[a]	**Search Institute 40 Developmental Assets**[b]	**Positive Behavior Supports**[c]	**Second Step**[d]
Asset-building is integrated in the school, family, and community	Caring school climate, safety, school boundaries, caring, integrity, interpersonal competence, cultural competence, peaceful conflict resolution	Focus on all youth—not just "at risk"—strategies include "mobilization of citizens and realignment of social systems" (Leahy & Judge Nearing, 2003); also engage youth as partners in asset building	Addresses several assets (e.g., clear expectations)	Caring school climate, service to others, responsibility, planning and decision making, interpersonal competence, resistance skills, and peaceful conflict resolution are all addressed
Responsive decision making is based on data	Includes student, parent, and staff survey of bullying, perceptions of safety, and overall school climate	Profiles of Student Life: Attitudes and Behavior Survey data available	SWIS data system is part of PBS's emphasis on data-based decision making; has immediate responsiveness	Data not part of program
Expectations are clear and communicated to students, staff, and parents	School and classroom rules about bullying/inclusion are one of the main components (expected to be communicated to parents, staff, and students)	Related assets: boundaries and expectations, school boundaries (school provides clear rules and consequences)	Requires 3–5 positive and clearly stated expectations; teaching matrix (expected to be communicated)	Expectations of behavior within the curriculum

Social-emotional-<u>behavioral skills are taught</u>	Some skills taught: taking a stand/strategies for bystanders, strategies for victims	Five Social Competencies assets: planning and decision making interpersonal competence cultural competence resistance skills peaceful conflict resolution; no direct skills taught	Importance of skill teaching is emphasized, no direct tools for teaching	Empathy training, impulse control, problem-solving, anger management, (developmental specific skills related to these areas)
Underlying philosophy	Bullying prevention needs to be systemic; all members of the "caring community" work together to prevent bullying. Structure, clear rules, and information on bullying + skills for students are also key	Focus on all kids—not just "at risk"; look at strengths, not risks; focus on relationships not on problems that kids have. Creating an asset-rich environment helps kids thrive	Reduction of behavioral challenges and increased constructive behaviors is best accomplished through compassionate, constructive, and direct teaching; changing environments to change behavior; application of behavior analysis—a continuum of behavior support for all students	Changing attitudes and behaviors through skills training will decrease violent behavior

—continued

Table 6.7 (continued) Research Base CARES Prevention Model

	Prevention Program			
Model Component	Bully Proofing Your School[a]	Search Institute 40 Developmental Assets[b]	Positive Behavior Supports[c]	Second Step[d]
Evidence of impact/research base	Four-year, longitudinal study (no control group) found decreases in bullying behaviors and improved perceptions of safety (Epstein et al., 2002). Another study found decreased witnessed bullying in intervention (not control) school; and no decline in positive attitudes in intervention (not control) school (Beran & Tutty, 2002); multi-year, multi-site evaluation demonstrated reductions in bullying behavior, improved perceptions of safety at school, and favorable impact on attitudes toward bullying and relational aggression at the elementary level (Menard et al., 2007). Also, the principles of BPYS follow what research has suggested is necessary for effective bullying intervention (Porter et al., in press)	Strong correlational research that demonstrates the link between assets and decreased risk behavior and more positive behaviors. No outcome evaluation of assets model, but this is not surprising as there is no assets "program"	Review of research on PBS notes positive changes at the school-wide level (more classroom organization, rule clarity, and decrease in suspensions) and in specific settings (hallways, playground, etc.). Evaluations of universal school-wide PBS interventions said to offer very promising results; however, concerns exist about the ability of universal school-wide supports to improve individual chronic behavior	SAMHSA-NREPP Listing (2.4 of 4); OJJDP Model Programs guide—effective; U.S. Dept. of Ed. Safe Schools—exemplary. Sprague et al. (2001) found decline in office referrals for 4 of 6 treatment schools + no change in control; Grossman et al. (1997)—decreases in physical aggression found in 2nd–3rd grade treatment kiddos, but not in control; 2nd–5th graders in intervention schools had improved social competence, but not in controls

	(Gottfredson et al., 1993; Safran & Oswald, 2003; Warren et al., 2003), improved hallway behaviors (Oswald et al., 2005), decreased discipline referrals (Luiselli et al., 2005), and classroom behavior (Christensen et al., 2004)	Frey, Hirschstein & Guzzo (2000); Van Schoiack-Edstrom, Frey, & Beland (2002) found less social exclusion and verbal aggressions in tx versus control middle schools		
		No studies found		
	Scott and Barrett (2004) found increased instruction times; improved standardized test scores and math "skills" (Luiselli et al., 2005) (no control group for either)			
	All			
Connection with academic success	Indirect; victimization is related to poorer school performance	Kids with more assets have higher GPAs (GPA assessed 3 years after assets) (Scales & Roehlkepartain, 2003)		
Age group	Curricula exist for Pre-K through high schools	All	Designed for Pre K–5, but also found effective in middle school (Van Schoiach-Edstrom et al., 2002; McMahon & Washburn, 2003)	

—continued

Table 6.7 (continued) Research Base CARES Prevention Model

Model Component	Prevention Program			
	Bully Proofing Your School[a]	Search Institute 40 Developmental Assets[b]	Positive Behavior Supports[c]	Second Step[d]
Is there a parent component	Parent materials available; parent information on Web site	Parents play a critical role	Family-school collaboration thought to complement PBS (Minke & Anderson, 2005). Parent trainings/materials available	

[a] Garrity et al., 2004.
[b] Benson, Scales, Leffert, & Roehlkepartain, 1999.
[c] Sugai, G., Horner, R. H., Dunlap, G., Hieneman, M., Lewis, T. J., Turnbull, A. P., Turnbull, H. R., III, Wickham, D., Wilcox, B., & Ruef, M., 2000.
[d] Committee for Children, n.d.

Seven

Early and Targeted Interventions

Universal interventions as described in Chapter 6 will be effective for approximately 80%–85% of the general school population (Burns & Gibbons, 2008; Lewis et al., 1998; Sprague et al., 2001; Taylor-Greene et al., 1997; United States Office of Special Education Programs [OSEP], n.d.). However, for those students who come to school with more complex academic, social, and emotional difficulties, additional and targeted interventions are needed (Hawken & Horner, 2003). Targeted* intervention efforts are for those students who have been identified as having multiple risk factors that place them at a higher likelihood for future aggressive or antisocial behaviors (Larson, 2008) or academic failure and for whom universal interventions have not proven effective. Targeted intervention efforts most often include academic and/or behavioral skills training delivered in a small group format as a supplement to universal prevention efforts. To be most effective, targeted interventions should be paired with the universal school-wide psychological and physical safety prevention efforts discussed in previous chapters.

Given the many academic demands that are placed on schools today, educators may be concerned that taking the time to teach social-emotional skills deters from academic instruction. Targeted interventions do not come at the expense of academic performance—quite the contrary; teaching social-emotional skills to children has been found to increase academic achievement and performance on standardized achievement tests relative to peers who do not receive this type of intervention (CASEL, 2007a, 2007c).

---

* Targeted interventions can also be referred to as Tier 2, secondary, or selected intervention. For this book, targeted interventions will be used throughout.

DEFINITION OF EARLY AND
TARGETED INTERVENTIONS

It is first important to define "early and targeted" interventions. These interventions are offered soon after it is determined that a student or groups of students are not responding to the universal interventions as should be expected. "Early" does not necessarily mean that the intervention takes place for younger, elementary-aged students, but rather that interventions are implemented as soon as indicated without having to wait for a full diagnostic (i.e., special education) assessment before the student can receive intervention services. Until recently (and still found in many parts of the country) this has often been the case. Students have been denied access to intervention services or do not qualify to receive additional supports for academic or social-emotional concerns because their scores on the assessments did not contain enough of a discrepancy and/or fall under a particular diagnosis. This has been deemed the "wait-to-fail" model (Lichtenstein, 2008; Pfohl, 2006) as often schools were essentially telling parents, "Sorry, your child is struggling, but not struggling enough to receive additional services." In essence, the special education comprehensive assessment has served as the "gatekeeper" to ensure the number of students receiving additional services remained manageable, and therefore this model has kept many students from receiving the services they desperately needed. Clearly it is preferable to lessen the impact of behavioral and academic struggles for students through early identification and intervention of those students needing assistance. In an environment where the needs of children are paramount and students are successful, school safety is enhanced. Further, when students' emotional and behavioral needs receive early intervention, the need for future crisis response efforts is diminished.

Targeted interventions are those that help to mediate behavioral/or academic problems and are generally only needed for a minority of students (approximately 15%; Burns & Gibbons, 2008; Lewis et al., 1998; Taylor-Greene et al., 1997; OSEP, n.d.; Sprague et al., 2001). Even so, depending on the size of the school and scope of student needs, it is possible that a school may experience an "inverted triangle" where over 80% of students need targeted and intensive services (e.g., high-needs school, alternative schools). If this is the case, then staff would need to be trained to deliver targeted interventions at the universal level to all students. Certainly under many circumstances, it is not always feasible to deliver individualized targeted interventions due to the resources that would be required. Generally, however, targeted interventions are delivered in a small group setting (e.g., up to 10–15 students) where more students can receive services. The targeted interventions are also considered part of the general education curriculum (Burns & Gibbons, 2008), where they are accessible to all students, not just special education students.

Concerns such as poor peer relations, low academic achievement, and/or chaotic home environments often lead to a student being selected for targeted interventions (Lewis & Sugai, 1999). More specifically, students who are likely to benefit from targeted intervention demonstrate a need for more direct instruction and support in learning social skills, emotional regulation, problem-solving skills, and specific academic skills. In a recent study conducted with middle school students, Suldo and Shaffer (2008) demonstrated the importance of looking at a dual-factor model of mental health in youth. The authors assessed both positive indicators of wellness (or subjective well-being [SWB]) and more traditional negative indicators of well-being; hence the name "dual-factor model." Indictors of SWB and wellness were life satisfaction (including family and school), own cognitive appraisals of one's happiness, and positive affect (including stable emotions and mood state). Negative indicators included negative affect (such as sadness, guilt, anger) potentially coupled with indicators of mental illness or psychopathology. They found that students with low psychopathology and high SWB had better reading skills, school attendance, academic self-perceptions, academic-related goals, social support from classmates and parents, self-perceived physical health, and fewer social problems than students who had low SWB. Students who exhibited higher levels of psychopathology, yet also had higher SWB, reported a higher positive quality of life than those with a lower sense of subjective well-being in absence of mental health issues. Therefore, the authors concluded the reliance on negative indicators of mental health alone may over- or underidentify youth who could potentially benefit from targeted intervention as subjective well-being variables can mitigate the negative impact of psychopathology. On the contrary, those individuals without psychopathology, but who demonstrate negative affect, can also be at higher risk. Looking at both subjective well-being *and* negative indicators of well-being can potentially lead to more accurate identification of students who could benefit from support.

Chapter 6 discussed the importance of directly teaching skills and also promoting positive youth development at the universal level. In regards to targeted interventions, strategies focused on promoting well-being, while also addressing psychopathology (if present), can promote the greatest outcomes and may be essential to attaining positive academic achievement and a safe schools climate.

WHY ARE TARGETED INTERVENTIONS NEEDED?

One of the most frequent questions the authors of this book hear from educators is, "Why do schools need to address mental health? That is not our job; our job is to teach academics." High-stakes testing has placed students' ability to meet academic standards in the spotlight. As much as schools might feel the need to draw the line and only focus on teaching academics, it is naïve to think that teaching of academic skills occurs in isolation from teaching of social-emotional skills. There is not a single aspect of life that is not impacted by social-emotional factors, and the mental health needs of students must be addressed in order to maximize academic success. As stated in Chapter 1, interventions that address social-emotional needs of students also improve academic achievement (CASEL, 2008a; Johns et al., 2008; McKevitt & Braaksma, 2008; OSDFS, 2006). In addition, as described in Chapter 6, ensuring that students have strong social-emotional skills is one of the cornerstones of creating a psychologically safe school environment (CASEL, 2008a; Sprague, 2007; Sprague & Walker, 2002; Walker, 2001).

After a 12-year fight, mental health advocates finally won passage of the federal Mental Health Parity Act of 2007, which requires insurance companies to treat mental health on an equal basis with physical illnesses, when policies cover both. Yet recent educational legislation (i.e., No Child Left Behind, Individuals with Disabilities Education Improvement Act 2004) continues to emphasize academic progress (AYP) and academic interventions, not students' behavioral or social-emotional needs. Pressures on schools to improve academic performance have also increased focus on standardized testing, accountability, the strength of a school's curriculum, and the promotion of sound instructional practice. Yet considerable evidence indicates that nonacademic factors influence academic achievement (OSDFS, 2006).

According to the Substance Abuse and Mental Health Services Administration (SAMHSA, n.d.[a]) at least one in five children and adolescents have a mental health disorder. This includes depression, attention deficit/hyperactivity disorder, and anxiety, conduct, and eating disorders. One in ten youth (or about six million) has a serious emotional disturbance, which refers to the above-mentioned disorders when they severely disrupt home, school, and/or community functioning. Therefore, the frequency with which children and youth are diagnosed with a mental health disorder provides the first reason that it is important for schools to provide targeted intervention.

Even in the absence of a diagnosable disorder, children are often exposed to stressors that place them at risk for emotional disturbance and/or lead to behaviors that come to the attention of the school. A longitudinal study that assessed 1,420 randomly selected children when they were ages 9, 11, and 13 years, found that by age 16, over 68% reported having experienced at least one traumatic stressor (Copeland, Keeler, Angold, & Costello, 2007) to include an isolated traumatic event (one-time occurrence, e.g., an act of violence) or chronic trauma situations (long-term, e.g., domestic violence, child abuse, crime-ridden neighborhood). As a result of these experiences, negative behaviors can emerge that are related to underlying trauma, yet the student may be seen as oppositional and consequences may be applied without thorough assessment and attempts to address the underlying traumatic impact. Because trauma exposure has been found to correlate with lower academic achievement and mental health disorders (Nickerson, Reeves, Brock, & Jimerson, 2009), schools need to address these mental health concerns. Because not all students will experience exposure to trauma, nor will all those exposed to trauma necessarily develop intensive reactions or behaviors, many of these concerns can be best addressed through targeted interventions.

In addition, symptoms of adult disorders are often traceable back to the existence of childhood disorders and stressors. Approximately half of adults with anxiety disorders had symptoms of some type of psychiatric illness by age 15; those with obsessive-compulsive disorders tended to have delusions and hallucinations as children, and adult phobias were linked to specific phobias that occurred in childhood

(National Institute of Mental Health [NIMH], 2007). The failure to treat the above named symptoms and situations can lead to school failure, family conflicts, drug abuse, violence, and even suicide; ultimately these factors will contribute to safety concerns at school (SAMHSA, n.d.[c]).

Given the number of youth affected by mental health concerns, stressors, or symptoms that could lead to later concerns in the absence of intervention, only 12% of youth aged 12 to 17 (three million) are receiving school-based mental health services for emotional or behavioral problems (SAMHSA, 2008). Among these youths, 9.9% received mental health services from a school counselor, school psychologist, or through regular meetings with a teacher for emotional or behavior problems and 3.9% received special educational services for emotional or behavior problems. These statistics speak to the great need for targeted interventions (and as will be discussed in Chapter 8, intensive interventions). However, these services are often not enough as schools do not have the monetary or staffing resources to meet all the needs.

The above statistics and the potential impact of mental health concerns on academic and social-emotional growth clearly point to a strong need for more efficient use of services and to better identify those in need of targeted interventions. It is in the best interest of schools to address the mental health and academic needs of students in conjunction with their overall safe schools climate and safety planning, as developing meaningful social and emotional connections with students and creating a climate of mutual respect are essential to keeping schools safe and making them successful (United States Secret Service and U. S. Department of Education, 2008).

THE BENEFITS OF PROVIDING TARGETED INTERVENTIONS

In addition to quality universal interventions, targeted interventions are needed to help further the academic and social/emotional success of students. The positive impact of targeted interventions has been found in students' academic performance, educational outcomes, and social skills; these interventions have proven successful in helping students learn well with others, increasing student engagement, and decreasing behaviors that interfere with learning (CASEL, 2007b). This is critical given that when students are defiant, aggressive, or threatening to others, these negative behaviors may also contribute to a perception of an unsafe environment.

Academic Performance and Educational Outcomes

Programs that focus on social-emotional learning have been found to decrease the number of suspensions and expulsions, increase school attendance, improve attitudes towards school, improve grades, and also improve performance on academic achievement tests (CASEL, 2007a, 2007c); Hawkins, Smith, & Catalano, 2004). Smith, Adelman, Nelson, Taylor, and Phares (1987) found that academic failure and or the lack of academic competence can underlie anger and hostility expressed by students in a school setting, therefore supporting the need to provide targeted interventions to help support academic performance and decrease the likelihood of potentially unsafe behavior.

Helping Students Learn Well With Others

Cooperative learning is integrated into many classrooms. A review of 164 cooperative learning articles conducted by Johnson, Johnson, and Stanne (2000) found that cooperative learning can significantly improve academic performance and prevent and treat a wide variety of social problems such as racism, sexism, delinquency, drug abuse, bullying, violence, lack of pro-social values, alienation and loneliness, psychological pathology, and low self-esteem. However, if students do not have good social and emotional skills, the benefits of a cooperative learning group can be minimized and potentially even negated (Munro, O'Brien, Payton & Weissberg, 2006). Students who do not possess the social and emotional skills needed for cooperative learning can be taught these skills through targeted interventions, which then in turn better prepares them to benefit from learning in the general education (universal) classroom setting.

Increasing Student Engagement

Teachers have great influence over students' perception of school. If teachers promote and model positive and respectful interactions and students perceive teacher support, this can significantly impact student's academic motivation, engagement, and performance (Bryk & Schneider, 2002; Osterman, 2000; Ryan and Patrick, 2001). School engagement has also been linked to violence (Karcher, 2002; Sandhu, Arora, & Sandhu, 2001) and delinquency (Morrison, Cosden, O'Farrell,

& Campos, 2003). Schools where students feel most alienated have been noted to have the highest levels of violent behavior (Warner, Weist, & Krulak, 1999). Not surprisingly, building connections and relationships between adults and students is one component to a comprehensive approach to decreasing school violence (Kneese, Fullwood, Schroth, & Pankake, 2003).

Decreasing Behaviors That Interfere With Learning

Interventions that focus on social-emotional learning can also decrease high-risk behaviors such as substance abuse, student misconduct, rebellious behaviors in school, and propensity towards violence (Osterman, 2000; Ryan & Patrick, 2001; Zins, Weissberg, Wang, & Walberg, 2004). In a recent meta-analysis of over 700 programs focusing on social-emotional learning in preschool through high schools, schools that used a social-emotional learning program reported a 44% decrease in suspensions and a 27% decrease in other disciplinary actions (CASEL, 2007b). It follows that such a reduction in negative behavior will likely increase the perceptions of a safe and orderly environment and allow for greater focus on academics.

In summary, interventions targeting the teaching of social-emotional skills do not divert schools from the primary focus of academic achievement, but rather these interventions enhance academic achievement by improving and sustaining a safe schools climate and educating students to be good problem solvers and caring, responsible, and engaged students. In addition, not only do these interventions enhance basic skills but they also teach students skills they need to be successful in life (CASEL, 2007a).

EVIDENCE-BASED INTERVENTIONS

As discussed in Chapter 6, it is important that the potentially limited resources of schools be spent on interventions that have been proven to be effective (Greenberg et al., 2003). Evidence-based interventions are those that are empirically supported with research findings that demonstrate their ability to produce predictable, beneficial, and effective results (Forman & Burke, 2008) and have been replicated in a real-world school setting (Kratochwill & Shernoff, 2004; Schaughency & Ervin, 2006). The 2004 reauthorization of the Individuals with Disabilities Education Act (IDEA) and No Child Left Behind

(NCLB) both require the use of evidence-based interventions. Therefore, in addition to academics, schools should also focus their efforts to increase the social-emotional skills of students with the use of programs and strategies that have demonstrated effectiveness.

SELECTING TARGETED INTERVENTIONS

It can be overwhelming to know where to begin when trying to select targeted inventions. The on-line resources listed in Table 6.5 for finding prevention programs that have been demonstrated to positively impact students can also be used to select targeted interventions. In addition, Forman and Burke (2008) offer guidelines, highlighted below, that can be used to select targeted interventions. A more comprehensive review can be found in their book chapter.

First, the targeted population needs to be identified along with intervention goals. A functional assessment can be done in order to understand why the behavior problem or social-emotional need is occurring. These results lead to identified goals and determining if an individual or group intervention strategy is most appropriate. Whether or not these strategies are evidence-based can be determined by analyzing the type of research design and evaluating the quality of evidence. Because of requirements such as those in IDEA and NCLB, many program developers will apply the label "evidence based" or "research based" to their intervention. It is important to do one's homework on the validity research behind the program and not be lured or enticed by fancy packaging or a good salesperson that makes a program "look good" despite little or no empirical research to support program effectiveness. The many on-line resources that are now available catalogue evidence-based interventions through objective review rather than based on the developer's own determination. However, due to the rapid growth in interventions being labeled evidence or research based, Web sites are finding it hard to keep current with these lists. The pace of good quality research can be slow and the fact that a program is not on a list does not mean there is no research or evidence to support it. Therefore, it is acceptable to consider interventions not listed on a published list, but again it is critical to pay particular attention to study design, validity and reliability, number and type of participants used, and the potential generalizability of findings to a particular school population and setting. Additional data should be gathered on such programs as they are used.

Various Web sites listing evidence-based interventions relevant to mental health, safety, social and emotional learning, behavioral health, as well as academic interventions are listed in Table 6.5. As stated in Chapter 6, there is minimal consistency and uniformity in regards to the applied scientific standards used between the professional and government affiliations (DHHS, 2001) and the quality of the research and study designs can vary tremendously. It is important to be a knowledgeable consumer when researching programs and to conduct a good evaluation of the school's and students' needs to select a quality program that will best address those particular behavioral and/or social-emotional needs.

CONSIDERATIONS FOR IMPLEMENTATION OF TARGETED INTERVENTIONS

Participant Selection

Once the program or curriculum has been selected, intervention participants need to be selected carefully in order to ensure compatibility with the programs' recommended targets. For example, grouping aggressive peers together for counseling and social skills intervention has been discouraged, as it may create more problems, especially if it inadvertently reinforces deviant behaviors and criminal activity (Arnold & Huges, 1999). It will take a skilled and trained educator or mental health professional to successfully manage these group dynamics.

Staff Training

Schools often make the mistake of putting their least qualified staff (i.e., teaching assistants) with their most challenging students. Students who need targeted interventions need the most qualified professionals teaching these interventions; therefore, sufficient staff development should be provided to ensure that adults have obtained the necessary skills. For example, some schools tend to put teacher assistants in charge of detention hall with no direct instruction occurring to teach replacement skills, and detention essentially becomes a babysitting service.

Staff Resources

Staff resistance and lack of time are challenges that must be addressed by a strong educational leader (Hunter, Elias, & Noms, 2001). Staff resources often need to be creatively reallocated to include more direct service while scheduling modifications can be made to ensure time to deliver targeted interventions. For example, in one elementary school, the principal shifted teacher assistants (TAs) from primarily doing clerical duties (i.e., making photocopies) to providing direct service to students. In one middle school, the gym teacher wanted to co-facilitate an anger management group with the school-based mental health professional. He received curriculum training and gave up a planning period to co-facilitate this group. It was very successful, as he was excellent at building rapport and encouraging students to make positive changes. The principal found money in the building budget to offer the gym teacher curriculum pay for giving up his planning period. The gym teacher said he would have done this without the extra money, as it was one of the most rewarding activities of his career due to the positive changes he had seen in students.

SCHOOL DEMAND AND EXPECTATIONS VERSUS STUDENT FUNCTIONING

When a student struggles in a school setting it is often due to a discrepancy between what the school is asking the student to do (school demand and expectations) and what he/she is able to do (student functioning) (Neel, n.d.). Academic frustration underlies numerous behavior issues and instead of analyzing the academic issues, it is often the case that the problems are assumed to be purely behavioral. In addition, schools tend to approach academic instruction differently than social skills instruction. Academic instruction has a content, context (Neel, n.d.), and specific scope and sequence. However, the same approach is not always taken when it comes to teaching social-emotional skills; instead, social skills instruction is conducted in isolation from academic instruction or from real-world, classroom contexts. This hinders the learning of social skills as effective instruction of any kind needs clear instructional content, context, and sequence. As demonstrated by Figure 7.1, when student problems arise there typically is a large gap between the school's demands and expectations and the level of where the student is currently functioning. In

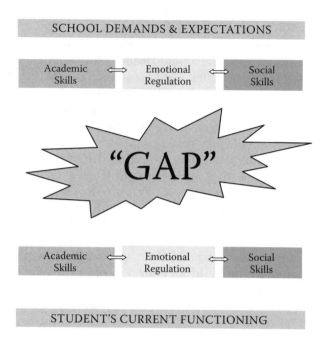

Figure 7.1   Instructional gap between target performance and current level of functioning. *Source:* Adapted from Neel, R. (n.d.). A presentation given to the Colorado Society of School Psychologists.

addition, there are three interconnected areas that are needed for students to be successful in school and for the creation of a safe school environment: academic skills, emotional regulation, and social skills (Neel, n.d.). Schools must provide direct instruction (just as is done with academic problems) in all three areas in order to build specific skills for lasting change. Providing the setting is not enough without direct instruction. As Rick Lavoie (1989) so eloquently stated in a video he produced on learning disabilities, telling a student to "look at it harder" will not teach the student how to read. Just as placing a student in a social situation without necessary skills or implementing punishment will not *teach* those needed social skills or how to regulate and manage their emotions.

The small number of students who continue to struggle after these skills are taught may need individual and intensive intervention (see Chapter 8). In the early intervention phase, schools need to work to close the instructional gap (what the student can do vs. what the school expects him/her do) to decrease frustration and increase academic and social-emotional skills. Targeted instruction can help teach at-risk students about appropriate school behavior so they are actually able to execute the newly learned behaviors under specific circumstances (Larson, 2008).

TYPES OF TARGETED INTERVENTIONS

Children who need targeted interventions are generally thought of as having difficulty performing a specific skill(s). It is important to understand the reasons why they are having difficulty in order to choose the best intervention to match their need. The National Association of School Psychologists (NASP, 2002b) outlines four hypotheses as to why children may have difficulty performing a skill:

1. *Lack of knowledge* (acquisition deficits)—The child does not know the skill(s) or cannot discriminate when to appropriately use the skill. For example, a child grabs a book from a peer in class when she wants one because she does not know how to appropriately ask to borrow it. The child does not understand how to add two-digit numbers with regrouping as it is a newly taught skill.
2. *Have knowledge but difficulty performing consistently* (performance deficits)—The child knows how to perform the skills but fails to do so consistently or at an acceptable level of competence. For example, the child understands the class rule that he should raise his hand to speak, and does so most of the time, but yet sometimes blurts out a comment. The child knows how to write a five-sentence paragraph but struggles to organize thoughts and construct sentences when the topic is not familiar.
3. *Knows how to perform skill and motivated but lacks practice or feedback* (fluency deficits)—The child can perform the skill and is motivated to perform, but has not had enough practice or direct feedback on how to improve delivery of skill. For example, a student has learned what to say and do when confronted with bullying behavior, but needs more practice to have a confident and strong response.
4. *Internal or external factors are interfering* (competing skills)—Competing skills and factors are interfering with the child demonstrating a learned skill

appropriately. For example, depression, anxiety, or negative motivation can interfere with use of appropriate conflict resolution skills, even though the skills have been taught and learned. A child's hyperactivity can interfere with work completion even though the child possesses the academic skills.

ACADEMIC INTERVENTIONS

Although academic interventions are not the primary focus of this book, they are critical to ensuring safe schools. When students are frustrated academically, they are more prone to acting out. Therefore, academic intervention at all three tiers of a service delivery model is equally important as social-emotional programming. Students who demonstrate academic success have fewer behavioral issues that negatively impact school climate and safety (CASEL, 2007a, 2007b, 2007c; Suldo & Shaffer, 2008). Offering flexibility within the general education to meet a variety of educational levels, teachers being trained in differentiating the curriculum to meet diverse learning styles, and targeted academic supports that utilize direct instruction to teach remedial skills are all necessary in ensuring student success and, ultimately, school safety.

ALTERNATIVES TO SUSPENSION

As stated earlier, punishment and consequences alone do not teach positive replacement behaviors. Furthermore, there is increasing evidence to suggest that most behavior problems that result in suspension and expulsion can be prevented through proactive procedures (Metzler, Biglan, Rusby, & Sprague, 2001; Sprague et al., 2001). Therefore, if a school setting imposes consequences without direct instruction of more appropriate alternatives, most likely the maladaptive behaviors will only continue. For example, some schools suspend students for truancy. The rationale behind this is questionable, as the school has not only given permission for the student to remain out of school, but they have reinforced the truancy behavior by providing a positive reinforcement for choosing to not be in school. Although it is beyond the scope of this book to review all alternatives to suspension, Peterson (n.d.) provides a good overview of various alternatives to suspension to consider (see Table 7.1).

Table 7.1 Alternatives to Suspension

1. *Problem Solving/Contracting*—Problem-solving approaches can help students to identify their difficulties and alternative behavior choices. The development of a contract asking them to make good faith effort to utilize the problem solving process instead of choosing maladaptive means can be effective in securing their commitment to try. Reinforcers for success and consequences for continuation of problem behaviors need to be integrated.

2. *Restitution*—In-kind restitution allows the student to help restore or improve school environment. For example, if a student vandalized the building, the student can help to repair damage or improve the environment more broadly (e.g., picking up trash). If the student was bullying another student, the student could write a letter of apology and/or help educate others about the negative impacts of bullying.

3. *Mini-courses or Skill Modules*—Short courses or self-study modules related to the student's inappropriate behavior could be designed. Outcome goals are to increase student awareness about their own behavior to facilitate positive behavior change. Examples include readings, watching a video, or developing an oral report. Some schools have integrated mini-courses while students are serving in-school suspensions (ISS).

4. *Parent Involvement/Supervision*—Parents are invited to be a part of the problem-solving process and work collaboratively with the school to be more involved in their child's schooling. Increased communication with school and increased supervision, in addition to coordinated behavior change approaches, are effective.

5. *Counseling*—Counseling supports can be offered either at school by trained professionals such as school psychologist, counselor, or social worker or by mental health professionals outside of the school. Counseling should be focused on problem solving or personal issues interfering with academic and/or social success.

6. *Community Service*—Student works for a specific amount of time in a supervised community service activity. For example, volunteering to clean up an elderly person's yard or tutoring younger students.

7. *Behavioral Monitoring*—Have the student self-chart behaviors and/or provide feedback sessions. For example, check in and check out with an adult at the beginning and end of each day.

8. *Coordinated Behavior Plans*—Create structured and coordinated behavior plans based on a functional assessment of the specified behavior. Supports and reinforcement for appropriate behaviors need to be integrated. For example, a functional behavioral assessment is conducted by the school psychologist and then a meeting is held between teachers, student, and parents to outline behavior plan with specified outcome goals, intervention, and supports to be provided in addition to a positive reinforcement schedule.

9. *Alternative Programming*—Provide short-term or long-term changes in schedule, seating, content of classes, or alternative learning environment. For example, an independent study, smaller class, or a change of programming.

—continued

Table 7.1   (continued) Alternatives to Suspension

10. *Appropriate In-School Suspension (ISS)*—In-school suspension should include academic tutoring instruction and skill building related to problem behavior. There should also be a clearly defined procedure for returning to class or earning back privileges contingent on student progress or behavior. However, ISS is not a good alternative to out-of-school suspension if student wants to avoid attending class as this only reinforces the class avoidance.

Source: Adapted from Peterson, R. L. (n.d.). *Ten alternatives to suspension.* Impact. Retrieved on November 29, 2008, from http://www.ici.umn.edu/products/impact/182/over5.html.

Skiba and Rausch (2006) also emphasize universal interventions such as school-wide positive behavior supports, conflict resolution, bullying prevention, social-emotional learning, and improved classroom management as important precursors to alternatives to suspension. At the targeted level, early screening and identification in addition to direct alternative skills instruction through programs such as anger management and mentoring are important.

SOCIAL-EMOTIONAL INTERVENTIONS

There are a many interventions that teach social-emotional skills. The programs/interventions reviewed in this section have been highlighted due to being listed on one or more Web sites found in Table 6.5 and having research conducted regarding the effectiveness of the intervention. Table 7.2 highlights evidence-based programs specifically pertaining to emotional regulation, anger management/aggression reduction, social skills/problem solving, substance abuse, and suicide prevention. Please note this is not an all-inclusive list, nor are the programs specifically endorsed by the authors. As was discussed in Chapter 6, given that such a list can be helpful to schools that are in the early stages of safe schools planning, it is included here. Schools are encouraged to consider multiple means of selecting interventions, including consulting the Web sites in Table 6.5; evaluating the quality of research available for other programs of which they are aware, but that are not on these lists; and gathering their own data to determine the impact of the intervention in their particular school setting.

Table 7.2 Overview of Specific Targeted Evidence-Based Social-Emotional Programs and Interventions

Program Name	Age Level Targeted and Topics Addressed	Program Recognition
Emotional Regulation		
• Coping Power	• Late elementary to middle school years • Based on empirical model of risk factors for substance abuse and delinquency. Addresses social competence, self-regulation, and positive parental involvement. • Targeted and/or Intensive Program	• NREPP Legacy Program • OJJDP Exemplary Program • SAMHSA Model Program http://www.copingpower.com
• Incredible Years	• 2–12 year olds • Parent component strengthens parenting competencies and fosters parent involvement in children's school experience • Child component teaches how to understand and communicate feelings, use effective problem solving, manage anger, friendship skills • Teacher training component focuses on strengthening classroom management strategies, promoting school readiness, reducing aggressive and noncompliant behaviors in the classroom • Targeted or Intensive Program	• OJJDP Model Program • PNN Proven Program • SAMHSA Model Program • Strengthening America's Families Exemplary 1 Program www.incredibleyears.com www.samhsa.gov

—continued

Table 7.2 (continued) Overview of Specific Targeted Evidence-Based Social-Emotional Programs and Interventions

Emotional Regulation

Anger Management/Aggression Reduction

• Too Good for Violence	• Grades K–5, 6–8 • Promotes character values, social-emotional skills, and healthy beliefs (conflict resolution, anger management, respect for self and others, effective communication) through role playing, cooperative learning games, small group activities, and classroom discussions • Universal or targeted intervention level • Optional parent and community involvement elements	• Met the What Works Clearing House evidence standards (USDOE—Institute of Educational Sciences) http://ies.ed.gov/ncee/wwc/reports/character_education/tgfv • http://www.modelprograms.samhsa.gov/pdfs/model/TGFV.pdf

• Aggression Replacement Training (ART)	• Ages 12–17
	• Teaches adolescents to understand and replace aggression and antisocial behavior with positive alternatives; three components: pro-social skills, anger management, moral reasoning
	• Targeted and/or Intensive Program
		• OJJDP Effective Program
		• Extensive research reviews and modification for school setting can be found at:
		  • www.researchpress.com
		  • www.mcgill.ca/crcf/projects/art
		  • www.wiley.com (Wiley Series in Forensic Clinical Psychology)

• Second Step Violence Prevention Program	• Preschool–8th grade (ages 4–14) • Learn a variety of social skills to include empathy, emotional control, problem solving, and cooperation; also teaches how to identify and understand own and other's emotions, reduce impulsiveness, choosing positive goals, managing emotional reactions to make positive decisions	• Helping America's Youth Registry Level 2 • OJDDP Effective Program

Table 7.2   (continued) Overview of Specific Targeted Evidence-Based Social-Emotional Programs and Interventions

Emotional Regulation

Anger Management/Aggression Reduction

• Second Step Violence Prevention Program	• Universal or Targeted Program	• PPN Promising Program • SAMHSA Model Program • USDOE's Safe, Disciplined, and Drug Free Schools Exemplary Program http://www.cfchildren.org/programs/ssp/overview/ http://guide.helpingamericasyouth.gov/programdetail.cfm?id=422

Social Skills/Problem Solving

The Stop and Think Social Skills Programs for Schools	• Pre K–8th grade • Teaches interpersonal, problem solving, and conflict resolution skills to include listening, following directions, asking for help, ignoring distractions, accepting consequences • Targeted Program	• OJJDP Promising Program • SAMHSA Model Program http://www.projectachieve.info/productsandresources/thestopthinksocialskillsprogramschool.html
• Incredible Years	• 2–12 year olds • Parent component strengthens parenting competencies and fosters parent involvement in children's school experience • Child component teaches how to understand and communicate feelings, use effective problem solving, managing anger, friendship skills	• OJJDP Model Program • PNN Proven Program • SAMHSA Model Program

—continued

Table 7.2   (continued) Overview of Specific Targeted Evidence-Based Social-Emotional Programs and Interventions

Emotional Regulation

Social Skills/Problem Solving

• Incredible Years	• Teacher training component focuses on strengthening classroom management strategies, promoting school readiness, reducing aggressive and noncompliant behaviors in the classroom • Targeted and Intensive Program	• Strengthening America's Families Exemplary 1 Program www.incredibleyears.com www.samhsa.gov

Substance Abuse

• Life Skills Trainining	• Ages 8–14 • Substance use prevention, which focuses on decreasing use of alcohol, tobacco, drugs, and violence; teaches drug resistance skills, personal self-management, general social skills to include building self-esteem confidence, and coping skills • Universal or Targeted	• Helping America's Youth Registry Level 1 • OJJDP Exemplary Program • PPN Proven Program • USDOE's Safe, Disciplined, and Drug Free Schools Exemplary Program http://www.lifeskillstraining.com/

Suicide Prevention

• CARE (Care, Assess, Respond, Empower)	• High school • Provides empathy and support, safe context for sharing personal information, reinforce positive coping and help-seeking behaviors, and contact with a positive adult.	• Reviewed by NREPP • Targeted and Intensive • PNN Promising Program http://www.nrepp.samhsa.gov/programfulldetails.asp?PROGRAM_ID=225

Table 7.2 (continued) Overview of Specific Targeted Evidence-Based Social-Emotional Programs and Interventions

Suicide Prevention (continued)

• CARE (Care, Assess, Respond, Empower)	• Goals are to decrease suicidal behaviors, decrease related risk factors, increase personal and social assets

Note: Please note this is not an all-inclusive list. Programs were included based on their impact on factors critical to psychological safety in schools and their inclusion on more than one evidence-based program registry listing. The authors are not specifically endorsing a particular program(s), nor is it meant to substitute for one of the rigorous reviews of programs conducted by the organizations listed in the third column of this table. See Table 6.5 for further information regarding program qualifications and how to find program recognition qualifications. NREPP = SAMHSA's National Registry of Evidence-Based Programs and Practices; OJJDP = Office of Juvenile Justice and Delinquency Prevention; PNN = Promising Practices Network on Children, Families, and Communities; SPRC = Suicide Prevention Resource Center; USDE = U. S. Department of Education.

Source: Adapted from Steigler, K., & Lever, N. (2008). *Summary of recognized evidence-based programs implemented by expanded school mental health programs center for school mental health.* University of Maryland School of Medicine. Retrieved November 29, 2008, from www.schoolmentalhealth.org and http://csmh.umaryland.edu.

Emotional Regulation

The ability to self-regulate emotions underlies everything people do. Managing frustration, anger, and anxiety, and also knowing what level of emotion is appropriate to express in a specific social situation all involve emotional regulation. Not only does emotion regulation play a role in all that we do, it also is directly associated with how other view us and how successful we are with specific tasks. For example, high levels of anxiety can have a negative impact on academic performance and also negatively impact organization, memory, concentration, and test performance (Airaksinen, Larsson, & Forsel, 2005; Miesner & Maki, 2007; Veenman, Kerseboom, & Imthorn, 2000). Anxiety also leads to significant social difficulties such as initiating and maintaining social relationships and oftentimes leads to withdrawal from social situations due to fear of rejection; plus, comorbidity with depression has been found to be as high as 50% (Huberty, 2008).

Hawken and Horner (2003) conducted a multiple baseline study of a targeted intervention called the Behavior Education Program (BEP) that used a "check-in, check-out" system. BEP requires that students check in with an adult at the beginning and end of each day and with teachers throughout the day. A Daily Progress Report is signed by teachers at the end of each class period providing immediate feedback regarding students' behavior. Points for positive behaviors are earned each day, traded for tangible rewards, and the Daily Progress Report is taken home, signed by parents, and returned the next day. The authors found that the BEP intervention was associated with a reduction in problem behavior and an increase in academic engagement; in addition, the students were more consistent with class participation without behavior problems. Hawken and Horner concluded that a simple, cost-efficient system that utilizes prompts for appropriate behavior (check-in, check-out), provides adult attention contingent upon appropriate social behavior, and teaches self-monitoring/regulation can improve problem behavior, especially if the problem behavior is being maintained by peer or adult attention and the adult is a reinforcer for behavior.

Anger Management/Aggression Reduction

Aggression and anger have been found to be associated with conduct disorders, depression, anxiety, difficulties in social relationships, higher levels of academic problems, and higher rates of school dropout (Lochman, Powell, Clanton, McElroy, 2006; Risi, Gerhardstein, & Kistner, 2003). A review and meta-analysis of anger management programs (some school based and some not) found that anger management programs in general were effective in decreasing anger. Those that included self-awareness and regulation, problem solving, development of alternative means for expressing feelings, and specific strategies to ensure maintenance and generalization were most promising. In addition, those that were able to intervene early with younger children showed more lasting effects (Smith, Larson, DeBaryshe, & Salzman, 2000). A more extensive review of various anger management intervention programs can be found in Risi et al. (2003).

Social Skills/Problem Solving

Social skills instruction is just as important as academic skills instruction as there are many students coming to school without the repertoire of social skills they need to be successful in school and strengthen interpersonal relationships (Knoff, 2002). Social skills encompass the ability to know what to say, how to make good choices, and how to behave in diverse situations (Elliott, Roach, & Beddow, 2008; NASP, 2002b). Students' possession of good social skills is linked not only to the quality of the school environment, but also to school safety, as students who have good social skills have higher academic performance; positive behavior, social, and family relationships; and more involvement in extracurricular activities (NASP, 2002b). Students who can convey information; relate to other people; appropriately express their thoughts, knowledge, and feelings; and are able to work collaboratively with others will succeed well beyond their K–12 schooling years and be productive members of society.

Regardless of the political and philosophical debates regarding whether social skills are the responsibility of schools to teach, educators and school mental health professionals need to be reinforcing positive social skills though direct and indirect instruction (NASP, 2002b) utilizing both universal and targeted interventions and parent involvement. A student with adequate social skills is able to perform a variety of behaviors to include specific, discrete, verbal, and nonverbal behaviors and behaviors that initiate and maintain relationships, and can demonstrate behavioral performance that includes responding to situation-specific environmental demands (Elliott et al., 2008). Several targeted interventions can help students acquire these skills. The National Association of School Psychologists (2002b) highlights specific components to an effective social skills program (see Table 7.3). However, it should be noted that these components can apply to all types of skills-based targeted interventions that may be provided.

Coping Skills Regarding Grief and Loss

Loss is universal and everyone grieves (reacts to) the loss in some way (Mauk & Sharpnack, 2006). Whether it be the death of someone who was cared about or grieving the loss of the way life used to be prior to an event (e.g., natural disaster, significant physical injury, divorce of parents, relocation, breakup of a relationship), grief responses can vary greatly. Grief can have a substantial impact on a student's educational performance and behavior as it can lead to increased anxiety and stress, impaired memory, diminished ability to concentrate, increased absenteeism, increased fear of the future and other potential losses, and an increase in acting out behaviors or

Table 7.3 Components of Effective Skills Training

- Utilizes a behavior and social learning teaching approach
- Utilizes universal language or set of steps that facilitates learning a new behavior (scaffolding)
- Uses a systematic approach
- Clearly defines goals and objectives
- Provides a structure that builds upon existing supportive and responsive relationships to help reinforce students as they learn new skills
- Includes training and support for parents
- Integrates targeted skills training within general education curriculum and universal supports/program already in place
- Provides instruction in positive skills, not just punishment of inappropriate behaviors, by focusing on facilitating the desirable behavior as well as eliminating the undesirable behavior
- Utilizes modeling, coaching, and role-playing to promote learning, performance, generalization, and maintenance of appropriate behaviors; this facilitates active student engagement in the lesson
- Provides students with immediate, constructive performance feedback that is stated in positive terms
- Utilizes positive strategies and adds punitive strategies only if the positive approach is unsuccessful and the behavior is of a serious and/or dangerous nature
- Provides training and practice opportunities in a variety of settings with different groups and individuals in order to encourage generalization of new skills to real life situations
- Utilizes functional assessments of behavior to identify specific outcome goals and to also identify children who may need additional intensive interventions beyond the targeted interventions
- Increases the frequency of an appropriate behavior in a particular situation by addressing naturally occurring causes, consequences, and reinforcements
- Integrates self-monitoring, self-reflection strategies for students to enhance generalizability and sustainability of newly learned skills
- Includes parents/caregivers as active participants

Source: Adapted from National Association of School Psychologists. (2002). Social skills: Promoting positive behavior, academic success, and school safety. [Electronic version.] www.nasponline.org/resources/factsheets/socialskills_fs.aspx.

excessive withdrawal (Mauk & Sharpnack, 2006). For many students, grief reactions will be a natural process of the grieving process and they will be able to successfully work through their grief by utilizing their naturally occurring support systems (Brock, 2006a). However, for others, they may need assistance through targeted interventions that may include counseling or group support. In addition, the integration of creative arts (i.e., drawing or painting), literature and music, and/or written expression have been found to be powerful avenues of expression for children and adolescents (Mauk & Sharpnack, 2006).

Coping Skills Regarding Divorce

Divorce impacts up to 40% of children by the time they are 18 years old (Greene, Anderson, Doyle, & Riedelbach, 2006). Hetherington and Kelly (2002) report that children of divorce are at double the risk for experiencing clinically significant behavior problems. They may experience initial negative outcomes (e.g., adjustment issues due to moving or sharing time between parents), yet if supports are available to children and families after the divorce these negative outcomes often improve 1 to 2 years after the divorce as families adjust (Hetherington & Kelly, 2002). A review of specific divorce intervention programs by Greene et al. (2006) demonstrated that school-based programs have the potential to reach greater numbers of children than community-based programs, and can offer support within the naturalistic setting and provide students with a network of teachers, counselors, and peers to offer support. In addition, their research indicated that when supports are offered following a divorce, the negative implications of divorce—academic, social, and in regards to adjustment—can be mitigated. Divorce support groups in schools are most often conducted in a small group setting which allows students to meet others who are experiencing similar circumstances and reactions, and they often integrate anger management, relaxation training, communication skills, and problem-solving abilities while also utilizing role playing, art projects, skits, bibliotherapy, discussions, and puppets.

Substance Abuse and Suicide

Due to presenting or anticipated concerns, substance abuse and suicide prevention programs may also be offered at the targeted level. Chapter 8 will further discuss the implications of substance abuse and suicide; however, Table 7.2 includes samples of targeted intervention programs with positive outcomes to address these issues.

AWARENESS OF RISK FACTORS AND EARLY WARNING SIGNS FOR EARLY INTERVENTION

When selecting students to participate in targeted interventions, school staff need to pay attention to the specific risk factors and warning signs students can display as these help identify which students need additional support beyond universal interventions.

Risk Factors and Warning Signs

Risk factors increase the likelihood that a young person will become violent, and the larger the number of risk factors the individual is exposed to, the greater the probability the individual will engage in violent behavior; however, it is important to note that risk factors are not direct causes of violence (CDC, 2009; U. S. Dept. of Health & Human Services, 2001). Risk factors for violence are also not static, as their predictive value changes depending on in what developmental stage they occur, in what social context, and under what circumstances (DHHS, 2001). To ensure a safe schools climate, school staff need to understand and identify potential risk factors in students. Table 7.4 lists potential risk factors that may indicate the need for early, targeted interventions and support. Again, it is important to emphasize that risk factors are *not* causes of potentially concerning behaviors nor does the presence of one risk factor alone necessarily indicate a severe concern. However, multiple risk factors and the accumulation of factors increase the likelihood of behavioral concern and propensity towards actual violence (Lewis, Brock, & Lazarus, 2002).

Early warning signs are concrete manifestations of behavior that indicate immediate need for intervention (Brock, 2006a, 2002c) to mitigate something more serious occurring. Oftentimes early warning signs (e.g., threats) can lead to disciplinary actions (Bailey, 2002), but more often they are an indicator that a student needs help. (Chapter 8 further discusses specific warning signs and interventions.)

Staff Awareness Training

A critical component to prevention and early intervention is staff awareness training. This should be conducted at the beginning of each year with all staff and with new staff as hired throughout the year. Staff awareness training should include information about the signs of child abuse, risk factors and early warning signs of concerning behavior, reporting

Table 7.4   Potential Risk Factors

Personal Characteristics/Individual Risk Factors
- History of aggression/physical violence
- Risk taking behaviors
- Low intelligence and/or deficits in social cognitive or information processing abilities
- Psychological conditions (i.e., impulsivity, hyperactivity)
- Antisocial behaviors, attitudes, beliefs (i.e., lack of empathy, remorse, delinquent acts)
- Academic decline or persistent academic failure (i.e., poor attitude, performance)
- Lack of connectedness to school and/or positive peer groups
- Medical or physical challenges
- Poor coping skills
- Poor self-regulation of emotion/behavioral control
- Low self-esteem
- External locus of control
- Excessive worry, anxiety, anger, sadness (i.e., high emotional distress)
- Withdrawal or extremely introverted
- Exposure to violence and conflict in the family
- History of violent victimization
- Physical or emotional proximity to a crisis event (i.e., victim of crime, natural disaster)
- Prolonged exposure to chronic crisis situations (i.e., domestic violence)
- Involvement with drugs, alcohol, or tobacco

Family Risk Factors
- Antisocial parents/parental criminality
- Poor parent-child relationships (i.e., ineffective, uncaring, or overly rigid/ authoritarian parenting)
- Harsh, lax, or inconsistent disciplinary practices
- Low parent involvement/monitoring/supervision
- Low emotional attachment to parents or caregivers
- Poverty
- Low parental education
- Parental substance use
- Parent history of prior mental health problems
- Dysfunctional/"broken" home environment
- Family conflict

Peer/School Risk Factors
- Weak social ties to peers and/or school
- Social rejection
- Delinquent peer group/siblings
- Social isolation

—continued

Table 7.4   (continued) Potential Risk Factors

- Exposure to violence and/or crime (i.e., TV, in neighborhood)
- Lack access to positive role models
- Poor academic performance
- Low commitment to school
- Truancy/drop out of school
- Frequent school transitions
- Exposure to violence and racial prejudice

Community Risk Factors

- Poverty
- High concentrations of poor residents
- Low levels of community participation
- Socially disorganized neighborhoods
- Gang involvement
- Availability of drugs and firearms

Sources: Brock (2002c); Centers for Disease Control and Prevention (CDC). (2009). *Youth violence prevention scientific information: Risk and protective factors.* Retrieved on February 9, 2009, from http://www.cdc.gov/ncipc/dvp/YVP/YVP-risk-p-factors.htm; Nickerson, A. B., Reeves, M. A., Brock, S. E., & Jimerson, S. R. (2009). *Identifying, assessing, and treating posttraumatic stress disorder at school.* Developmental Psychopathology at School Series. New York: Springer; Surgeon General's Report of Youth Violence (U.S. Department of Heath & Human Services, 2001.

procedures, and how to get help for a troubled student. There have been numerous instances across the country that when the warning signs were noticed and reported, tragic events were prevented and in many cases the students received interventions that were desperately needed. The authors' school district developed an early warning signs staff training video that was required to be shown to all staff early in each school year and also to all new staff hired throughout the year. This video was 12 minutes long and designed to be shown in a staff meeting. Time for discussion and question and answer session followed the video and was facilitated by administrator/dean, school mental health staff, and/or school nurse. The video was specific about the need to report the warning sign behavior in order to get early intervention for students.

BREAKING THE CODE OF SILENCE: METHODS OF REPORTING CONCERNING BEHAVIORS

Research shows that in over 81% of violent school incidents, someone other than the attacker knew it was going to happen but failed to report it (Vossekuil et al., 2002). Students often hesitate to report concerning behaviors of their friends for the fear of "narking." Staff may hesitate to report as they are fearful of the negative perception that concerning behaviors or incidences can bring upon an individual staff member or the negative reflection on the climate and culture of the school. In both cases "retribution" underlies the fear that leads to not reporting or seeking help. Therefore, it is critical that schools break the "code of silence" and have in place a confidential method for students, staff, parents, and community members to report concerning behaviors, and when they do so anonymity and/or confidentiality is guaranteed and they are supported in their effort to report. Similar to "Crime Stoppers," which is known nationally for community members to report concerns to local police departments, schools need a similar process. In addition, when schools receive tips about illegal or concerning behavior, school officials must take steps to verify the reliability of information (e.g., interviewing the student[s] regarding the concern). At times this can lead to a need for a more formalized threat and/or suicide assessment (see Chapter 8), an investigation, and/or a search (for example, of lockers or backpacks) and seizure (as in the case of contraband). (For additional detailed guidelines on search and seizure, see Bailey, 2002.)

SPECIFIC REPORTING GUIDELINES FOR TIP LINES

Individual schools and school districts can establish tip lines or tip boxes that ensure confidential reporting. Approximately 25% of schools report having a hotline or tip line to report problems, with more high schools having this in place (41.8%) than elementary schools (19.2%) (Neiman & DeVoe, 2009). It is critical to establish a system where confidential reporting can take place and incoming calls or tips are consistently monitored. In addition, staff and students need to be trained to be as specific as possible when making a report, and that when a threat is involved verbatim language is especially important (see Chapter 8 for more information regarding threats and threat assessment process).

Real-World Example: One State's Tip Line

The state of Colorado is one of a small number of states that have developed a statewide confidential reporting hotline (www.safe2tell.org). Parents and students can report threats to the hotline, operated by the state patrol, via a toll-free number or e-mail and be guaranteed anonymity. Reports can also be made on the Web site. Calls are answered at a Colorado State Patrol communication center and when action is needed and appropriate, information is immediately forwarded to local school officials and law enforcement agencies. Safe2Tell then follows up with the school that received the tip to ensure that it was investigated and that action was taken. It is believed that due to the fact that calls cannot be tracked and that those who use the hotline trust that appropriate action will be taken, young people are moving away from a code of silence and are reporting their concerns (www.safe2tell.org). These referrals to schools have resulted in early intervention services at the school, interruption of potentially violent behavior, and the reporting of illegal behavior to law enforcement.

SUMMARY

In summary, targeted interventions focused on both academics and social-emotional skills can help to increase student achievement and improve social relationships to facilitate a safe schools climate. Identifying students who need specific targeted interventions early and training staff to delivery quality interventions is critical to meeting the needs of all students and closing the gap between what is expected of students and what they can actually do that often leads to behavioral concerns due to frustration. Research has demonstrated the importance of targeted interventions as part of a multi-tiered service delivery system. Delivery of such targeted intervention services in small group formats have proven to be effective in social, emotional, and behavior improvement and efficient for schools to implement. There will inevitably be students who need more intensive services than can be provided by universal and targeted interventions. Therefore, Chapter 8 will now discuss the intensive level interventions to ensure all student needs are being met and that additional threats to the safety of school campuses can be addressed.

Eight

Managing Risk Behaviors and Other Intensive Interventions

By implementing quality universal and targeted interventions, schools can minimize the need for more intensive interventions. However, it is unrealistic to think that schools can prevent all types of behavior that necessitate more intensive interventions. Therefore, as part of the multi-tiered intervention service delivery model and to further ensure a safe learning environment, schools need to be prepared to intervene with students who exhibit intensive level concerns and behaviors. Managing risk behaviors that signal possible risk to self or others necessitates an intensive and individualized approach.

As mentioned previously in this volume, the perception of school safety is dependent on many things including the observable negative behaviors of students. While data do not necessarily support an increasing rate of more serious school violence or out-of-control behavior, when such behavior does occur, it can be alarming to school officials, students, and parents alike (DeVoe, Peter, Kaufman, Miller, Noonon, Snyder, & Baum, 2004; National Center for Educational Statistics, 2006). In addition, violence and negative behaviors that may be tolerated in schools can alienate many students and contribute to a hostile learning environment (Dupper & Meyer-Adams, 2002). A negative school climate has also been linked with student dropout, drug use, delinquency, victimization, school failure, psychosomatic problems, and depression (Gallay & Pong, 2004; Perkins & Borden, 2003; Reid, Peterson, Hughey, & Garcia-Reid, 2006).

RISK BEHAVIORS AND THREATS
TO SCHOOL SAFETY

High-risk behaviors are often an outward manifestation of more serious emotional or behavioral difficulties that are not likely to respond to universal prevention or targeted intervention in schools; thus, individual or intensive support utilizing a multi-agency effort may be needed. Because the mental health needs of children and adolescents are greatly under-identified and untreated (SAMHSA, n.d.[a]), schools are in a perfect position to address this concern and function both as a support system for youth and as a critical avenue for providing first identification and access to needed interventions for individuals.

Unfortunately, many schools have used the philosophy of zero tolerance as a solution to issues of disruption and potentially unsafe behavior. As previously described, this philosophy typically includes predetermined consequences for and removal of students engaging in negative behavior and is used as a deterrent to negative behavior in others and as one means of improving the school climate. These policies have caused controversy, however, especially when mitigating circumstances or situational context is ignored. In addition, there is evidence that these policies may unfairly target students of color and those with emotional or behavioral disorders (Skiba, 2000; Skiba & Peterson, 2000; Skiba et al., 1997; Tobin & Sugai, 1996). As an alternative, recent findings from the American Psychological Association's Zero Tolerance Task Force support preventative measures, threat assessment procedures, a planned continuum of alternatives to suspension and expulsion, and improved collaboration between schools and other agencies to provide needed services to students who demonstrate risk behavior (American Psychological Association Zero Tolerance Task Force, 2008). Therefore, schools' prevention efforts should include systems and processes for early identification of students who pose a danger to themselves or others (OSDFS, 2007). Response efforts in the multi-stage phase should also include procedures for the appropriate response to and intervention with the risk behaviors and other intensive needs of children such as threats to harm self or others, substance use or abuse, and child abuse, that may be observed in schools.

LEGAL AND POLICY ISSUES

School-based procedures for identification and intervention with students who demonstrate risk behaviors or other intensive needs are best guided by principles derived from federal and state guidelines. The 2002 publication by the U.S. Secret Service and the U.S. Department of Education provides guidance to schools in responding to and managing threats of targeted school violence (Fein, Vossekuil, Pollack, Borum, Modzeleski, & Reddy, 2002). This document clearly delineates that effective management of such behavior can only occur in a larger context of school safety, with a positive climate that includes respect and emotional support. Within this context, three essential elements are recommended to guide the development of an effective threat assessment procedure in a school: (1) authority to conduct an assessment; (2) capacity to conduct inquiries and investigations; and, (3) systems relationships. Authority, capacity, and relationships are often outlined in policy and memorandums of understanding between agencies. These interagency agreements can also help to outline the process for the sharing of information and provision of needed services.

Sharing of information has caused confusion for schools when student privacy issues conflict with safety concerns. As mentioned in Chapter 1, the Family Educational Rights and Privacy Act (FERPA) was designed to protect the privacy of student educational records in K–12 educational settings (U. S. Department of Education, 2007b). However, in a health or safety emergency, *FERPA* permits schools to disclose education records, including personally identifiable information, without consent in order to protect the health or safety of students or other individuals. At such times, records and information may be released to appropriate parties such as law enforcement officials, public health officials, and trained medical personnel. This exception is limited to the period of the emergency and generally does not allow for a blanket release of personally identifiable information from a student's education records (U. S. Department of Education, 2007a).

FERPA has additional exceptions, which are also designed to support safety in schools (U. S. Department of Education, 2007a). Schools may disclose information from "law enforcement unit" records, such as records of off-duty police officers employed as school security officers (SROs), and to outside law enforcement agencies without parental consent as such records are not considered educational records. Video camera images may be shared with parents of students whose images are on the video and also with law enforcement authorities, as appropriate. School officials may also disclose information about a student that is obtained through personal knowledge or observation. A recent publication for schools regarding school safety and FERPA exceptions specifically states that "if a teacher overhears a student making threatening remarks to other students, *FERPA* does not protect that information, and the teacher may disclose what he or she overheard to appropriate authorities" (U. S. Department of Education, 2007a). Therefore, specific guidance now exists as to a school official's authority to disclose such safety-related information heard in schools.

BREAKING THE CODE OF SILENCE
FOR HIGH-RISK BEHAVIORS

Schools and other agencies have encouraged reporting of potentially dangerous behavior through the use of anonymous reporting lines. Those report lines, mentioned previously, are seen as a means of prevention of more serious behavior and also as an avenue for early intervention. School climate may also influence a student's decision to report information about threats. In 2008, the U.S. Secret Service and the U.S. Department of Education released information from a study of 15 individuals who had prior knowledge of a potential school threat and either reported or did not report their information (Pollack, Modzeleski, & Rooney, 2008). Those students who participated in the "bystander study" and had reported threats to safety indicated that their reporting of concerns was influenced by positive relationships with adults at school and a feeling that the information would be taken seriously (Pollack et al., 2008). Such reporting lines have been shown to be used for reporting both lower level violence, such as bullying and harassment, and also potentially life-threatening behaviors, such as suicide threats and threats of lethal violence against a school or individual (www.Safe2Tell.org).

Teachers and other school staff also play an important role in identification and intervention with students at risk for violence or other dangerous behavior. They are on the front lines with children and adolescents every day, and have the potential to observe and/or overhear warning signs or threats that may indicate a serious threat of harm or other dangerous behavior. Increased awareness by all members of the school community is essential to the safety and well-being of all. Repeatedly, schools are called on to train *all* members of their school community to help prevent violence (Goldstein, 1999; Rozalski & Yell, 2004). This also includes school staff such as paraprofessionals, bus drivers, cafeteria workers, and custodial staff who observe, listen, and work with students *outside* the classroom. All adults employed by the school need to be taught to identify risk factors and warning signs of depression, suicide, violence, substance abuse, and child abuse as part of comprehensive planning for a safe learning environment. Severe threats, such as those that include weapons, tend to get reported, but identification of other types of threats, such as written threats, may be less likely to be reported by some individuals in schools (Robinson & Clay, 2005).

Early warning signs of troubled students have been identified by the U.S. Departments of Education and Justice and other professional organizations, and refer to a broad range of troubling behaviors that may lead to violence against self or others, including serious aggression, physical attacks, suicide, dangerous use of drugs, and other dangerous interpersonal behaviors (Dwyer et al., 1998); thus, they are more concrete behavioral and emotional indicators than risk factors. Schools have been cautioned *not* to use this list as a checklist or to use the signs to unnecessarily label or stigmatize students, as all behavior must be considered in a developmental and situational context. In regards to violence, no single sign or set of early warning signs can *predict* whether a child will be violent; however, when warning signs are connected to a progressive pattern of concerning or escalating behaviors, immediate and multiple interventions may be necessary (Dwyer & Jimerson, 2002). The list of warning signs can be used as awareness training for all staff so that they may better refer students for individualized or other services. These signs include

- Social withdrawal
- Isolation, alienation
- Feelings of rejection
- Being a victim of violence
- Feelings of being picked on and persecuted
- Low school interest and performance
- Violent expressions in writings and drawings
- Uncontrolled anger

- Patterns of chronic and impulsive hitting, intimidating, bullying
- History of discipline problems
- History of violence and aggression
- Intolerance and prejudicial attitudes
- Drug and alcohol use
- Affiliation with gangs
- Access, possession, and use of firearms
- Threats of violence or suicide

In addition to the early warning signs, there are six imminent warning signs that include behaviors that teachers and other staff should seek assistance for immediately. These include

- Serious physical fighting
- Severe destruction of property
- Severe rage for minor reasons
- Detailed and serious threats of lethal violence
- Possession and/or use of weapons
- Serious threats of suicide or self-injurious behaviors

Training all school personnel for awareness of the varying degrees of serious and potentially dangerous behavior will protect children and enable intervention services to occur.

Reporting of Dangerous Student Behavior: Real-World Example

In a large suburban school district that trained all staff in early warning signs of dangerous and suicidal behavior and utilized an anonymous tip line, referrals from staff members have included student writings signaling unusual preoccupation with violence or violent events, poems with themes of despair or suicide, and students with characteristics of depression. In one situation, a coach called the school district tip line after receiving an e-mail from a student in the early evening, talking about hopelessness and not continuing on with his life. The teacher feared the student was considering suicide. The principal, district intervention coordinator, and the school psychologist were informed of the threat that evening. Intervention for the student included both a phone call at home that night and an early morning suicide risk assessment by the psychologist that led to individualized and family intervention for the student outside the school related to some ongoing family issues. Fortunately, the student was not considered suicidal, but was identified as having symptoms of depression, and a potentially dangerous situation had a successful outcome of increased connection with helping adults at school and provision of important intervention services for the student.

SUICIDE AS A SCHOOL SAFETY ISSUE

In 2004, suicide was the third leading cause of death among youth ages 10–19 (NIMH, 2008b) and for every youth who dies by suicide, 100–200 suicides are attempted (Lieberman, Poland, & Cassel, 2008). The 2007 Youth Risk Behavior Survey (YRBS) of students grades 9–12 found that 14.5% seriously considered attempting suicide in the 12 months before the survey was completed, 11.3% had made a plan about how they would attempt suicide, and 6.9% had attempted suicide within the past 12 months (CDC, 2008d). These statistics show that preventing teen suicide is a real issue facing schools on a regular basis. There is a need for best practice prevention and intervention strategies to prevent harm to teens. Suicidal tendencies overlap with many other psychological disorders such as depression, bipolar disorder, and alcohol and other substance abuse, in addition to problematic parenting and home-life environments/stressors, and situational factors (e.g., access to firearms in the home, break-up with significant other) (Brock, Sandoval, & Hart, 2006; Lieberman et al., 2008). The YRBS results also showed that 28.5% of high school students reported that they were so sad or hopeless almost every day for two or more weeks in a row that they stopped doing some usual activities during the 12 months before the survey (CDC, 2008d). Teens who report such mental health–related risk factors may be in need of early or intensive interventions to include an evidence-based suicide prevention and awareness curricula, a suicide risk assessment process that involves parents, a system for providing referrals, possible school-based interventions and supports, and postvention activities to help students and staff cope in the unfortunate even of a completed suicide (Brock, Sandoval, et al., 2006; Lieberman et al., 2008). Suicide prevention programs in schools have shown promising results in decreased self-reported suicide attempt rates and increased awareness of depression (Aseltine & DeMartino, 2004). Suicide "gatekeeper" training is recommended for all those who work with youth. This type of training raises awareness of the warning signs for suicide and helps adults know when there might be reason to bring students to the attention of school psychologists, social workers, and counselors. Table 8.1 reviews the warning signs for suicide that should be part of gatekeeper training and considered in evaluation of risk.

In addition to the importance of suicide in its own right, suicide also overlaps with targeted violence seen in schools. In the joint study by the U.S. Secret Service and the U.S. Department of Education examining 25 years of targeted school violence events, 78% of students who perpetrated school violence were found to have a history of suicidal thoughts or attempts prior to their act of violence, and more than half (61%) had documented histories of feeling extremely depressed or desperate (Vossekuil et al., 2002). Only 34% had ever received a mental health evaluation prior to the event, which may indicate that the warning signs of depression or suicide were not identified. Less than one fifth (17%) had ever been diagnosed with a mental health or behavioral disorder, which highlights the importance of referring students who are having difficulty to needed services and resources. Another key finding was that in 82% of the events, the attackers' behavior indicated to others that they were having difficulty coping with a loss. The importance of identifying and obtaining resources

Table 8.1   Warning Signs of Youth Suicide

- Statements that threaten to or talk of wanting to hurt or kill him/herself
- Behaviors that suggest the youth is looking for ways to kill him/herself such as seeking access to firearms, pills, or other dangerous objects
- Talk of or written statements about death, dying, or suicide
- Increased substance (alcohol or drug) use
- Expressions of no reason for living or no sense of purpose in life
- Anxiety, agitation
- Disrupted sleep—either difficulty sleeping or sleeping all the time
- Statements that indicate the youth is feeling trapped or as if there is no way out
- Hopelessness, helplessness
- Withdrawal from friends, family, and society
- Rage, uncontrolled anger, vengeful behavior
- Reckless behavior or engaging in risky activities, seemingly without thinking
- Dramatic mood changes

Source: Adapted from American Association of Suicidology. (n.d.). *Warning signs.* Retrieved February 8, 2008, from http://www.suicidology.org/web/guest/stats-and-tools/warning-signs

for potentially suicidal students was also clearly seen in both the Columbine and Virginia Tech school shooting episodes where the perpetrators had expressed and acted on thoughts of suicide. The Columbine Review Commission Report (State of Colorado, 2001) and the Report of the Virginia Tech Review Panel (Commonwealth of Virginia, 2007; U.S. Departments of Health & Human Services, Justice and Education, 2007) made clear that suicide is a matter that needs continued attention in relationship to school attacks, both in terms of the mental health of the attacker and the potential issues that follow in the aftermath of such an incident. Clearly, schools need systems and procedures in place to assess and properly intervene with potentially suicidal or homicidal students.

Best Practices for Suicide Intervention

Best practices for suicide intervention with students exhibiting warning signs or making suicidal threats are more likely to be implemented when a school's procedures are clearly outlined and staff are thoroughly trained (Reeves, Nickerson, & Brock, in press). Table 8.2 gives an example of a school suicide threat response process, including the supervision of the student and documentation required. Assessment of risk should be completed by trained school psychologists, social workers, or counselors only, as schools have been found liable in situations regarding actions by untrained staff (Leiberman & Davis, 2002).

General recommendations for the assessment and intervention process include staying with the student, not promising confidentiality, and comprehensively assessing risk based on the functioning of the student, the plan, the level of dangerousness, presence of and ability to use resources, previous behavior and significant history, and ability to problem solve. It is also considered prudent to check level of risk determination and intended actions with another professional, when others with appropriate training are available in a school. Phone consultation can also be used when needed, in particular when no other staff with appropriate training are available in the school building. Finally, action plans should be developed based on level of risk and parent(s) should be notified (Brock, Sandoval, et al., 2006; Davis & Brock, 2002; Leiberman & Davis, 2002; Lieberman et al., 2008; Poland & Leiberman, 2002). A sample suicide threat action plan is shown in Figure 8.1.

The use of personal suicide contracts, after a relationship is established with the student, is recommended for low-risk

Table 8.2   Sample Process for Response to Suicide Threat

☐ Assemble Suicide Assessment Team (SAT). Risk level must be confirmed by more than one person.

☐ SAT determines level of concern.

☐ Use the Suicide Threat Flowchart to determine specific action steps based on risk concern (Figure 8.1).

☐ On all/any level of concern, parent/guardian will be involved and notified.

☐ On all/any level of concern, student will be supervised until disposition is settled.

☐ A plan to keep the student safe will be determined by the Suicide Assessment Team.

☐ SAT will coordinate immediate and long-term safety plan with parent/guardian, appropriate mental health professionals, emergency rooms, etc.

☐ On all/any level of concern, parent/guardian will be given "Parent Tips: Keeping Your Child Safe" handout and outpatient resources (handout can be found on accompanying CD).

☐ On all/any level of concern, SAT will document incident on Suicide Documentation Form and in student's confidential health or behavioral record. Document with Notification of Emergency Form depending on high level of concern (Suicide Documentation Form sample can be found on accompanying CD).

☐ SAT will coordinate reentry to school and development of school safety plan and follow-up.

Chronic Suicide Threat/Ideation/Attempt

☐ Each incident of threat/ideation/attempt must be taken seriously.

☐ The Suicide Assessment Team must be involved in the assessment of each incident.

☐ Each assessment must be documented.

☐ If a parent is uncooperative or does not take suicidal assessments seriously, consider having the parent sign the Notification of Emergency Form with each evaluation.

☐ After repeated suicide assessments (depends upon the situation), the school may move toward more targeted and intensive interventions including, but not limited to,

  • Problem-Solving Team meeting
  • Social Service referral
  • Other actions as determined by Administration and Mental Health personnel

Source: Adapted from Cherry Creek School District. (2008). *Emergency response and crisis management guide.* Greenwood Village, CO: Author.

situations where immediate action is not necessary. More specifically, caution should be exercised so that the suicide contract is not a substitute for a careful assessment of the student (Sandoval & Zadeh, 2008).

Table 8.3 outlines Sandoval and Zadeh's (2008) five-step protocol for suicide intervention in schools recently published by the National Association of School Psychologists in the School Psychology Forum. In addition to the steps outlined in

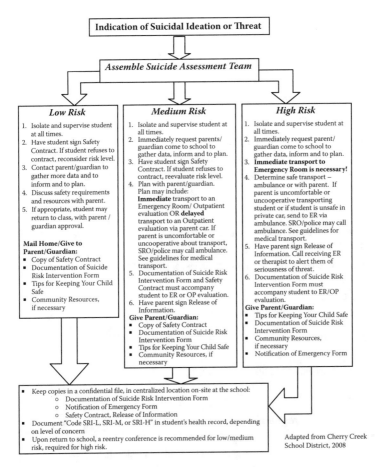

Indication of Suicidal Ideation or Threat

Assemble Suicide Assessment Team

Low Risk	*Medium Risk*	*High Risk*
1. Isolate and supervise student at all times. 2. Have student sign Safety Contract. If student refuses to contract, reconsider risk level. 3. Contact parent/guardian to gather more data and to inform and to plan. 4. Discuss safety requirements and resources with parent. 5. If appropriate, student may return to class, with parent / guardian approval. **Mail Home/Give to Parent/Guardian:** ▪ Copy of Safety Contract ▪ Documentation of Suicide Risk Intervention Form ▪ Tips for Keeping Your Child Safe ▪ Community Resources, if necessary	1. Isolate and supervise student at all times. 2. Immediately request parents/guardian come to school to gather data, inform and to plan. 3. Have student sign Safety Contract. If student refuses to contract, reevaluate risk level. 4. Plan with parent/guardian. Plan may include: **Immediate** transport to an Emergency Room/ Outpatient evaluation OR **delayed** transport to an Outpatient evaluation via parent car. If parent is uncomfortable or uncooperative about transport, SRO/police may call ambulance. See guidelines for medical transport. 5. Documentation of Suicide Risk Intervention Form and Safety Contract must accompany student to ER or OP evaluation. 6. Have parent sign Release of Information. **Give Parent/Guardian:** ▪ Copy of Safety Contract ▪ Documentation of Suicide Risk Intervention Form ▪ Tips for Keeping Your Child Safe ▪ Community Resources, if necessary	1. Isolate and supervise student at all times. 2. Immediately request parent/guardian come to school to gather data, inform and to plan. 3. **Immediate transport to Emergency Room is necessary!** 4. Determine safe transport – ambulance or with parent. If parent is uncooperative or uncooperative transporting student or if student is unsafe in private car, send to ER via ambulance. SRO/police may call ambulance. See guidelines for medical transport. 5. Have parent sign Release of Information. Call receiving ER or therapist to alert them of seriousness of threat. 6. Documentation of Suicide Risk Intervention Form must accompany student to ER/OP evaluation. **Give Parent/Guardian:** ▪ Tips for Keeping Your Child Safe ▪ Documentation of Suicide Risk Intervention Form ▪ Community Resources, if necessary ▪ Notification of Emergency Form

▪ Keep copies in a confidential file, in centralized location on-site at the school:
  ○ Documentation of Suicide Risk Intervention Form
  ○ Notification of Emergency Form
  ○ Safety Contract, Release of Information
▪ Document "Code SRI-L, SRI-M, or SRI-H" in student's health record, depending on level of concern
▪ Upon return to school, a reentry conference is recommended for low/medium risk, required for high risk.

Adapted from Cherry Creek School District, 2008

Figure 8.1   Suicide Risk Intervention (SRI) steps. *Source*: Adapted from Cherry Creek School District. (2008). *Emergency response and crisis management guide*. Greenwood Village, CO: Author.

this protocol, it is also advised that actions, recommendations, and referrals given should be documented and kept in a confidential file, for needed reference in case of another incident. A reentry meeting is recommended for any student sent for further evaluation or hospitalization. The CD accompanying this text includes a sample of one district's suicide risk assessment documentation form. This can be modified to help schools develop their own process and documentation form. In addition, Table 7.2 highlights one evidence-based suicide prevention program that can be utilized in schools. Finally, the need for use of best practice for suicide prevention and intervention in schools is also supported by legal cases in which schools

Table 8.3 Sandoval and Zadeh's Five-Step Protocol for Responding to Suicidal Behavior in Schools

STEP 1. PREPARATION

Review information and resources on suicide
- Compile a list of local agency and professional resources
- Consider relevant cultural issues

Know and assess warning signs
- Determine if the warning signs are sufficient to trigger further action
- Determine reliability and validity of the sources of these warning signs
- Determine if warning signs should be cross-validated

Be free to take action
- Determine if action needs a more qualified person
- Seek supervision, when needed
- Assess whether there are conflicts of interest or other obligations that may interfere with time needed for suicide intervention
- Use a suitable environment, free from distractions
- Summon others if help is needed

Avoid impulsive action
- Control own emotions
- Do not exacerbate the situation

STEP 2. ENGAGEMENT

Be appropriately responsive
- Nonverbal behavior should be appropriate to the situation
- Established a clear contract and explain the limits of confidentiality
- Assess your cultural competence to engage with this student

Active listening
- Reflect feelings effectively
- Use accurate and helpful restatements and reflections
- Use silence effectively and do not talk too much

Honesty
- Be honest, and keep the focus on the student
- Use caution with self-disclosure

STEP 3. EVALUATION

Ego functioning
- Determine if the student is thinking clearly
- Detect any errors in thinking
- Consider the student's characteristic coping mechanisms

Table 8.3   (continued) Sandoval and Zadeh's Five-Step Protocol for Responding to Suicidal Behavior in Schools

- Consider the student's use of problem-solving skills
- Consider the signs of resilience and strengths the student possesses

Lethality: Use questioning to assess the following

- Has the student attempted suicide before?
- Does the student have a plan?
- Does the student have the means, such as a weapon or poison?
- What is the student's understanding of death?
- Is the student willing to seek help?
- Is the student using drugs of any kind?
- Can the student identify suicide-provoking situations?
- Does this student need to be hospitalized?
- What is the status of the warning signs?

Spiritual beliefs

- What are the student's religious beliefs?
- Is the student connected to a religious/spiritual congregation?

Support network

- Does the student have friends who may be helpful?
- Are there immediate or distant family members who can be supportive?
- Has the student bonded with any school or community personnel?
- Has the student been abused?

STEP 4. ACTION

Contracting

- Consider if a contract is appropriate for this student
- Use available and recommended format for a contract
- Provide a lifeline or hotline number that can be used for emergencies
- Assess whether student will comply with the contract

Problem solving

- Determine if the student can think of alternative solutions to problems faced
- Determine if the student can think of ways to avoid suicide-provoking situations

Referral

- Determine if the student can be left alone, or if should someone remain with him or her at all times
- Consider the possible suicide resources available in your community
- Determine if the student will participate in the referral
- Determine if parents will and are able to participate in the referral

—continued

Table 8.3 (continued) Sandoval and Zadeh's Five-Step Protocol for Responding to Suicidal Behavior in Schools

- Help parents access resources through their medical insurance company, if warranted
- Assess whether anxiety, abuse, or other forms of victimization need to be dealt with

Safe environment

- Recommend that dangerous items be removed from the home or secured (e.g., firearms, other weapons, prescription medications)
- Find a place in the school where the student can be monitored
- Consider if the student is in need of an out-of-home placement
- Consider what changes in the school environment are needed for the student

Informing and documentation

- Inform school and other personnel about what has transpired, as needed
- Keep a record of the interview
- Inform the parents as needed
- Double-check with external supports such as private therapists or others who are involved with the case

STEP 5. FOLLOW-UP AND MONITORING

Supporting psychopharmacology, if included in treatment

- Establish a working relationship with the physician and obtain permission to share information
- Consider whether the medications had a positive impact on the student's thoughts and behavior
- Determine if the student has been taking the prescribed medication correctly
- Observe any side effects that may be interfering with the student's functioning
- Determine if a therapeutic adjunct to medication is needed

Supporting therapy

- Determine how the school can best comply with therapist requests
- Determine if therapy has had a positive impact on the student's thoughts and behavior
- Learning that occurs in therapy should be reinforced in the school environment
- Continue monitoring the student, as needed

Direct services

- Consider if you are qualified to counsel this student, and if supervision is available, if needed
- Consider alternative resources available to help the student
- Consider whether you have the necessary time to work with this student
- Facilitate the support from parents and others

Source: Adapted from Sandoval, J., & Zadeh, S. (2008, Winter). Principles for intervening with suicide. *School Psychology Forum: Research in Practice, 2(2),* 67–79.

have been found liable for negligence when school staff are not properly trained to protect students and intervene with best practices (Lieberman & Davis, 2002).

Suicide Risk Documentation: Real-World Example

Documentation of suicide risk can play a critical role in ensuring proper intervention with students who express or exhibit suicidal thoughts or behaviors. Another use of a documentation form might be to compile school or district data related to suicide interventions. These data can then be used to drive prevention efforts, guide staff training, and even influence staffing decisions. In one district, suicide intervention data gathered over 4 years showed that the highest numbers of suicide risk assessments repeatedly occurred in 8th–10th grade, and more specifically, concerns were highest with 9th grade girls (Cherry Creek School District, 2008). These data provided documentation of the need for awareness training for students in 9th grade and prevention efforts in middle school. Funding was obtained through grants and through support from a nonprofit agency connected to the school district to provide both of these services to students.

OTHER HIGH-RISK BEHAVIORS

Students in schools may also exhibit other risk behaviors that indicate a need for intensive and individualized interventions.

Self-Injury

Researchers and school personnel agree that the rates of self-injurious behavior among teens appears to be increasing (Muehlenkamp, 2006; Purington & Whitlock, 2004; Wester & Trepal, 2005; Whitlock, Powers, & Eckenrode, 2006; Yates, 2004). Surveys of high school students have shown that from 3.9%–39% of students have engaged in some form of self-injury (Lloyd, 1997; Nock & Prinstein, 2004; Patton, Hamphill, Bond, Toumbourou, McMorris, & Catalano, 2007). Schools need additional and specific training to have best practice response to this behavior, including an emphasis on suicide screening for students who self-injure. In addition, self-injurious behavior in youth has been shown to be highly "contagious" or copied from peers, and therefore, individualized interventions are preferable to group interventions. Many myths and much misinformation surround this behavior. It is important for school personnel to have an accurate understanding of self-injury; for example, self-injury can serve a variety of functions to help manage or control emotions and may also be complicated by the presence of co-morbid disorders. Understanding the nature of any co-morbid symptoms is important to describing the problem and needs to parents or caregivers, and to providing appropriate referrals and treatment recommendations. Evaluation by trained school personnel is the first step in the link with effective treatment. School personnel can also be helpful in designing short-term safety plans and assisting youth in gaining appropriate coping skills and effective alternatives for the management of emotions. Table 8.4 outlines recommended steps to effective management of self-injurious behavior in schools.

Victims of Child Abuse, Sexual Abuse, and Sexual Assaults

Youth who are victims of child abuse, sexual abuse, or sexual assault are also at great risk of harm to self and in need of individualized intervention in schools (Glassman, Weierich, Hooley, Deliberto, & Nock, 2007). Schools must train personnel to recognize signs of such abuse and about their legal obligation to report. Schools should also support students through the process of referral to human service agencies and monitor their progress after such a report. While schools' role is not to provide the individualized treatment some of these victims of abuse or assault may need, they serve an important role in providing the connection to needed and appropriate help agencies or individuals.

Substance Abuse

The National Survey on Drug Use and Health (NSDUH) questioned youth ages 12–17 across all 50 states about substance use, and risk and protective factors that can affect substance use (SAMHSA, 2005). One risk factor that was assessed was perception of risk related to use. Perception of risk of use has been found to be linked to substance use, in that the higher the perceived risk associated with use, the lower the rates of use. NSDUH results demonstrated that perceived risk of heavy alcohol use has remained stable from 2002–2004, but declines were seen in the perceived risk of more serious drugs, such as cocaine and heroin (SAMHSA, 2005). This decreasing perception of risk may put more young people at risk for dangerous

Table 8.4   Nine Recommendations for Responding to Self-Injury in Schools

1. Provide awareness and knowledge to school personnel	• Physical signs • Emotional signs • Obligation to report behavior to parents • Understanding self-injury as a coping attempt
2. Educate students about the need to report	• Large awareness campaigns are not recommended • Educate students to report *all dangerous behavior* and early warning signs
3. Use a team approach to responding to students	• Collaborate with school nurse when needed • Consultation is encouraged
4. Provide appropriate school support for students	• Listen and acknowledge feelings • Individualized support is recommended
5. Screen for co-morbid disorders and suicidal ideation	• Determine indicators of co-morbid disorders • Behavior should be differentiated from suicidal behavior unless screening indicates otherwise
6. Notify and provide resources to parents	• Gather additional relevant history • Document contact • Refer to knowledgeable community therapists
7. Develop short-term plans for safety	• Identify possible triggers and physical cues • Identify alternative behaviors to try to interrupt cycle of self-injury • Identify at least one supportive adult at school if impulse to self-injure returns • Plans should not require a promise to do "no-harm" until replacement behaviors are in place • Introduce healthy coping techniques, stress management, anger management skills
8. Collaborate with community support	• Communicate with treatment providers • Reinforce treatment goals and techniques in the school environment

—continued

Table 8.4 (continued) Nine Recommendations for Responding to Self-Injury in Schools

9. Control the contagion effect, as needed	• Identify the leader of peer group engaging in self-injury
	• Identify interventions for that student
	• Set limits on behavior at school when needed

Source: Adapted from Kanan, L., Finger, J., & Plog, A. (2008, Winter). Self-injury and youth: Best practices for school intervention. *School Psychology Forum: Research in Practice, 2(2),* 67–79. Retrieved January 9, 2009, from http://www.nasponline. org/publications/spf/Issue2_2/kanan.pdf.

Additional sources: Alderman, 1997; Conterio, Lader, & Kingston Bloom, 1998; Heath & Beettam, 2005; Heath, Beettam, & DeStefano, 2005; Kanan & Finger, 2006; Lieberman, 2004; Nock & Prinstein, 2004; Onacki, 2005; Purington & Whitlock, 2004; Simeon & Favazza, 2001; Walsh, 2006; White Kreiss, Gibson, & Reynolds, 2004; Whitlock & Knox, 2007; Whitlock et al., 2006.

use of drugs. The Substance Abuse and Mental Health Services Administration (SAMHSA) reports that of first-time users of marijuana, 63.8% were younger than age 18 when they first used (SAMHSA, 2005), and increased rates in the abuse of prescription and nonprescription drugs also account for keeping the "drug problem" as part of the discussion of intensive interventions needed for youth (Johnston, O'Malley, Bachman, & Schulenberg, 2006). Current research indicates the concerning prevalence of substance use:

- Overall rate of substance abuse or dependence was estimated at 8.8% for youth ages 12–17, with the rate of dependence or abuse similar for males and females (SAMHSA, 2005).
- 41% of adolescents who were admitted to treatment for alcohol or other drug use also had a co-occurring mental health disorder (Johnston et al., 2006).
- 29.1% of high school age youth have ridden with a driver who had been drinking alcohol in the past 30 days (CDC, 2008d).
- 44.7% of high school age youth had at least one drink of alcohol and 26% had five or more drinks in a row within a couple of hours in the preceding 30-day period (CDC, 2008d).
- Over 4% reported alcohol use on school property in a 30-day period (CDC, 2008d).

Whether or not they are using on school property, clearly these teens bring drug use problems to school. Awareness of the substance abuse issues and trends for youth, access to prevention and intervention at all levels, clear and consistently enforced school policies, assessment of substance use severity and provision of resources to families are all important for the future health and well-being of our youth and in establishing a safe learning environment. The reader is also referred to the evidence-based prevention program list in Chapter 7 (Table 7.2) for additional resources. Treatment for drug use and dependence is outside the scope of the regular educational environment, but again, identification of problems and referrals to appropriate treatment are essential.

THREATS OF HARM TO OTHERS OR THE SCHOOL

Much has been written on this topic in response to the highly publicized events of targeted school violence around the country. The 2002 Final Report and Findings of the Safe School Initiative: Implications for the Prevention of School Attacks in the United States, a joint research project by the U.S. Secret Service and the U.S. Department of Education (Fein et al., 2002) and other publications (Commonwealth of Virginia, 2007; Vossekuil, et al., 2000, 2002) have helped shed light on some of the key points that direct schools to take appropriate action when a threat or other potentially dangerous behavior occurs. The Safe School Initiative reviewed 37 school violence incidents and 41 attackers from around the country during the period of 1974–2000. The 10 key findings and their implications for schools in preventing and managing such incidents are outlined in Table 8.5.

Those findings also led to the development of the threat assessment process outlined in the accompanying publication *Threat Assessment in Schools: A Guide to Managing Threatening Situations and to Creating Safe School Communities* (Fein, et al., 2002). Six principles from that document support the foundation of a school threat assessment process:

1. Targeted violence is the end result of an understandable, and oftentimes discernible, process of thinking and behavior.
2. Targeted violence stems from an interaction among the individual, the situation, the setting, and the target.

Table 8.5   Ten Key Findings of the Safe School Initiative and Their Implications for Comprehensive Planning and Intensive Interventions

1. Incidents of violence at school are rarely impulsive acts.	Thought processes and behavior may be discernable from observation and communication. The time frame may be short, so quick inquiry and intervention is needed.
2. Prior to most incidents, other people knew about the attacker's ideas and/or plan to attack.	Students are an important part of prevention efforts. Schools need to encourage reporting of potentially dangerous threats or behavior. Schools need to ensure they have a fair, thoughtful, and effective system to respond to information when it is brought forward.
3. Most attackers did not threaten their targets directly prior to advancing the attack.	Schools should not wait for a threat to begin an inquiry. Schools should also inquire about behaviors and communications of concern.
4. There is no accurate or useful "profile" of students who engage in targeted school violence.	Schools should focus not on profiles of students, but rather on behavior and communication. Ask, "Is the student on a path towards violent action?"
5. Most attackers engaged in some behavior, prior to the incident, that caused concern or indicated a need for help.	When behavior of concern is noticed, additional probing by caring adults may find cause for notification or referral. Inquiry may determine a more comprehensive picture of a student's past and current behavior and any indications that the student is planning an act of violence.
6. Most attackers were known to have difficulty coping with significant losses or personal failures. Many had attempted or considered suicide.	Inquiry should include questions about recent losses or perceived failures, and feelings of hopelessness and desperation. Aspects of a student's life that may either increase or decrease the potential for violence must be considered. Screen for suicide risk.
7. Many attackers felt bullied, persecuted, or injured by others prior to the attack.	Schools should support ongoing efforts to reduce bullying and harassment. Assessing a student's history of bullying and harassment should be part of the inquiry.

Table 8.5   (Continued) Ten Key Findings of the Safe School Initiative and Their Implications for Comprehensive Planning and Intensive Interventions

8. Most attackers had access to and had used weapons prior to the attack.	Schools should inquire about any efforts to acquire, prepare, or use a weapons or ammunition, including bomb-making components. Pay attention to access to and communications about weapons.
9. In many cases, other students were involved in some capacity.	Inquiry should include attention to the role that a student's friends or peers may be playing in the student's thinking about and preparation for an act of violence. The climate of a school can help students see that adults can be called upon in times of need and that violence doesn't solve problems.
10. Despite prompt law enforcement responses, most shooting incidents were stopped by means other than law enforcement interventions.	Preventative measures and good emergency planning are both needed. Schools must have protocols and procedures for responding to and managing threats and other behaviors of concern.

Sources: Adapted from Fein, R., Vossekuil, F., Pollack, W., Borum, R., Modzeleski, W., & Reddy, M. (2002; revised, 2004). *Threat assessment in schools: A guide to managing threatening situations and to creating safe school climates.* Washington, DC: U.S. Secret Service and Department of Education; and Vossekuil, B., Reddy, M., Fein, R., Borum, R., & Modzeleski, W. (2002). *The final report and findings of the safe schools initiative: Implications for the prevention of school attacks in the United States.* Washington, DC: U.S. Department of Education, Office of Elementary and Secondary Education, Safe and Drug Free Schools Program and U.S. Secret Service, National Threat Assessment Center.

3. An investigative, skeptical, inquisitive mind-set is critical to successful threat assessment.
4. Effective threat assessment is based upon facts rather than characteristics or "traits."
5. An "integrated systems approach" should guide threat assessment inquiries and investigations.
6. The central question in a threat assessment inquiry or investigation is whether a student poses a threat, not whether the student has made a threat.

The FBI has recommended a four-pronged approach to threat assessment in schools that also emphasizes the multifaceted nature of a good threat assessment process suggested in the principles listed above (O'Toole, 2000). This includes assessing the personality and behavior of the student making the threat, the student's family dynamics, the current school climate and dynamics of the situation, and the larger social dynamics. Use of a multi-disciplinary team has also been recommended by the FBI to review the severity of the threat and determine the course of action. The Report of the Columbine Review Commission (State of Colorado, 2001) also supported establishment of a threat assessment team at each middle and high school for evaluating threats of violence as a group utilizing various sources of information. These teams should include trained staff, law enforcement, and other involved community personnel united in the purpose and process of threat assessment inquiry. More specifically, the goal of the team is to determine if the student who *makes* a threat actually *poses* a threat (Fein et al., 2002). A clear response protocol is needed so that school personnel have a consistent and fair response to such concerns. Table 8.6 provides an example of a school-based threat assessment protocol. At higher levels of risk, law enforcement can and should be used for investigation of threats.

School-based teams have been recommended by many additional authors and school practitioners and are considered the best practice to response to threats or other danger concerns in schools (Cornell & Sheras, 2006; Cornell & Williams, 2006; Cornell, Sheras, Kaplan, McConville, Posey, Levy-Elkon, McKnight, Branson, & Cole, 2004; Jimerson & Brock, 2004; Kanan, 2008a, 2008b; Nicoletti, 2007; Reddy Ranzano, Borum, Vossekuil, Fein, Modzeleski, & Pollack, 2006). These teams should operate under several guidelines. First, school teams should operate with approval of and within the process determined by the school district administration. They should also operate within their levels of expertise and ethical guidelines to assure no harm and fairness to students (Griffiths, Sharkey, & Furlong, 2008). The school-based threat assessment team and process should be initiated by any communication or behavior that indicates a concern about potential to commit violence toward another, and it is recommended that the process not be delayed until a threat is actually expressed (Reddy Ranzano et al., 2006). The school-based team accomplishes several tasks: it acquires all needed information from a *variety* of sources, determines the level of concern after evaluating the information, develops appropriate action plans for students who make threats or have other potentially dangerous behavior, and monitors the effectiveness of such plans to reduce behavior of

Table 8.6   Steps in a Threat/Danger Assessment Process

☐ Secure safety, as needed. If presence of imminent warning signs, contact school resource officer (SRO) or police.

☐ Assemble the School Threat (Danger) Assessment Team.

☐ Determine the facts of the incident.

☐ Gather, triangulate, and document information.

☐ Use the district threat/danger assessment form to guide information gathering and level of concern determination (Sample Threat/Danger Assessment Form can be found .on accompanying CD)

☐ Gather and verify information from records, law enforcement, victim(s), and witnesses.

☐ Interview the student of concern to give them an opportunity to tell their side of the story and to evaluate their thinking. What is their response when confronted?

☐ Interview the parents, if possible, to further gather concerns, risk factors, warning signs, and protective factors.

☐ Assess risk factors, warning signs, and possible mitigating protective factors.

☐ Consider situational and developmental context of the statement or incident.

☐ Review and evaluate the information gathered as a team.

☐ Determine the level of concern, and take appropriate action.

☐ Develop an Action and Supervision Plan.

☐ Document the school, student, and parent expectations on a behavior contract, if appropriate.

☐ Review the plan with the parents and if a behavioral contract is developed, have parents and student sign the contract.

☐ File the original in the discipline file at the building level, along with your intervention plan.

☐ A copy of the Threat/Danger Assessment should be stored in a central location in the designated administrator's office at the school.

☐ Fax a copy to the confidential fax at the District Administrative Offices.

☐ Monitor the effectiveness of the plan over time and continue to gather information.

☐ For students with repeated Threat/Danger Assessments, use the RTI/Problem-Solving Process to further assess and prescribe effective interventions.

☐ Obtain consultation at any time from the Intervention Coordinator or the Office of Safety and Security.

Source: Adapted from Cherry Creek School District. (2008). *Emergency response and crisis management guide*. Greenwood Village, CO: Author.

concern over time. After information is gathered, that evaluation of information should be guided by key questions about the incident and person(s) involved (Fein et al., 2002).

1. What are the student's motives and goals?
2. Have there been any communications suggesting ideas or intent to attack?
3. Has the student shown inappropriate interest in school attacks or attackers, weapons, incidents of mass violence?
4. Has the student engaged in attack-related behaviors?
5. Does the student have the capacity to carry out the act?
6. Is the student experiencing hopelessness, desperation, or despair?
7. Does the student have a trusting relationship with at least one responsible adult?
8. Does the student see violence as an acceptable or desirable way to solve problems?
9. Is the student's conversation and "story" consistent with their actions?
10. Are other people concerned about the student's potential for violence?
11. What circumstances might affect the likelihood of violence?

Information can also be classified in the categories of threatening risk factors, behavioral risk factors, and protective factors (or factors that might reduce risk) (Cherry Creek School District, 2008; Kanan, 2008a, 2008b; Kanan & Lee, 2004). Examples of these factors include how direct or planned was the threat; what evidence is there that the student has the ability to carry out the threat; what previous violence history is present; are hopelessness, helplessness, and/or suicidal ideation present; what behaviors seem to indicate that the student uses appropriate support when available; and what ability does the student have for self-restraint? The CD accompanying this book contains a sample of a threat assessment documentation form that helps to outline various considerations to be attended to during a threat or danger assessment process. (The reader is also referred to Cornell and Sheras [2006] for additional information regarding guidelines for a threat assessment team and steps to be included in a student threat assessment).

Interventions Equal to the Level of Concern

After gathering information, a school team is next charged with determining an appropriate course of action. These actions are best documented in a behavior contract agreed upon and signed by the student and parent. Relatively little has been written about suggested options for intervention after a lower level threat or behavior concern. The CD accompanying this text includes suggested actions or "trees" that can be used in a school setting to help reduce or eliminate concerns for safety and may be considered as part of a behavioral contract to be established upon a student's return to the school setting after a threat assessment. This notion of "planting trees" has been presented to schools by John Nicoletti (2007) as a way to stop a student from heading down a path toward violence. He describes various types of "trees" that can be effective: questioning the student about their actions or communications, confronting them about behavior that is inappropriate or potentially dangerous, and giving consequences that are appropriate. In addition, increased monitoring of students, treatment when indicated, and increased protective measures at school are also suggested as interventions depending on the seriousness of the threat or danger.

School intervention plans should consider the appropriate level of "tree" and also use other interventions in four basic categories, depending upon the needs of the student and the motives for the behavior (Cherry Creek School District, 2008; Kanan, 2008a, 2008b; Kanan & Lee, 2004).

1. Discipline and legal consequences (including written letters of apology, suspension, expulsion, police issued ticket, etc.)
2. Monitoring and supervision (including reduction of free time and before and after school unsupervised time, increased supervision at school, checking in and out with school staff, etc.)
3. Skill building (including development of anger management or coping skills, or participation in counseling, etc.)
4. Relationship building (including seeking support from school or other adults, participation in school activities, participation in community activities, etc.)

These four components of intervention planning may be sufficient for most regular education students; however, functional analysis of behavior and development of formalized behavior support plans are necessary for students in special education after incidents of threat assessment (Cornell & Sheras, 2006) and should be part of response to threats or behaviors of concern by those students. The data from the Virginia Threat Assessment Study (Cornell et al., 2004) indicated that 45% of students who made threats were students in special education. Similarly, 5 years of data from a large suburban school district (approximately 50,000 students) in Colorado indicated that 36% of the danger assessment incidents were with students identified as special education (Kanan, 2008b). Such data substantiate the need for staff at schools who are involved in the threat assessment process to have good awareness and training about their responsibilities for assessment and intervention planning under the law for both regular and special education students.

Documenting Interventions After Threat Assessment

As mentioned above regarding suicide assessment documentation, it is equally important that a school document any type of threat and assessment process. These incidents are best tracked and monitored over time, and effectiveness of the intervention plan must be re-evaluated to determine the impact on the student's behavior. The documentation from previous assessments has been shown of value in numerous cases where a student transitioned to another school and then had continued or similar concerns. Using data to drive prevention, training for staff and intervention options can also be an outcome of such data collection.

Real-Life Example: Danger Assessment and Intervention Plan

Five years of data kept on threat/danger assessments have helped one school district learn much about the issues with students and also to assure staff about the safety in schools. In the Cherry Creek School District, serving approximately 50,000 students, 709 threat/danger assessment incidents were documented over 5 years (Kanan, 2008b). Of incidents reported, approximately 58% were incidents of low-level concern. Another 36% of incidents were of medium concern, requiring specific intervention planning. Finally, only 5%

were incidents of high concern requiring law enforcement action, incarceration, or hospitalization. The threat assessment process helped to determine appropriate action in response to a threat or potentially dangerous behavior. The documentation form served to promote an organized review of data when conducting the assessment, determination of level of concern based on these data, and to provide records of actions by the school-based team. During the 2006–2007 school years, additional data were tracked on specific information provided on the documentation form. Among other patterns observed, it could be seen that teams were almost always involving the school psychologist or social worker, but staff in secondary schools were not involving the School Resource Officer to the extent as was hoped. In addition, classroom teacher input was not uniformly obtained in secondary schools. Specific and additional training was then designed to address the composition of threat assessment teams and the use of data from multiple sources to guide the assessment process.

STUDENTS WITH SIGNIFICANT EMOTIONAL AND BEHAVIORAL ISSUES

As previously mentioned, the Substance Abuse and Mental Health Administration estimates that as many as one in five children may have a mental health disorder that can be identified and requires treatment (SAMHSA, n.d.[a]; SAMHSA, 1996). One in ten may have a serious emotional disturbance that severely disrupts their interactions at school, at home, and in the community. However, the most recent report from the U.S. Department of Education Institute for Education Sciences (IES, n.d.) showed that in 2003–2004, only 489,000 students were receiving services under the special education category emotional disability; therefore, it is evident that not all of those students with emotional disturbances are receiving formal services in the school setting. While IDEA provides for education of students with significant emotional or behavioral disorders, providing appropriate service to effectively address needs in the educational setting have challenged school administration, teachers, and support services staff. Schools are able to meet the emotional needs of many students, but at the same time, there are also students whose needs require more intensive support than can be given in the school setting.

Collaborating With Community Agencies for Intervention

Some children diagnosed with severe mental health disorders may best obtain comprehensive and community-based services through "systems of care" for mental health. Systems of care are designed to help children with serious emotional disturbances and their families cope with the challenges of very difficult mental health, emotional, or behavioral problems. In a system of care model, schools, mental health services, child welfare agencies, juvenile justice, and other agencies work together to ensure that children and adolescents with mental, emotional, and behavioral problems and their families have access to the services and supports they need to succeed. These services and supports may include diagnostic and evaluation services, outpatient treatment, emergency services case management, intensive home-based services, day treatment, respite care, therapeutic foster care, and vocational services that will help young people make the transition to adult systems. Children might be attending special education classes at school, but they may also need access to after-school or recreation programs. Effective systems of care can improve how children behave and function emotionally, improve school performance, reduce the number of costly hospital and out-of-home residential treatment placements, reduce violations of the law, and provide more services to those who need them (SAMHSA, n.d.[b]).

Wraparound Services   Many agencies are now providing intensive (Tier 3) treatment in a wraparound model of comprehensive, community-based services. This multi-component treatment adheres to a well-defined planning process that blends school and community services with less formal supports and is based in strengths and systems theories. The basic principles of wraparound care include providing for family voice and choice, using formal and informal team-based services including the use of natural supports, providing for collaboration among community providers and the school in a community-based effort, the use of culturally competent providers, individualized treatment planning that includes strengths-based thinking, and focusing on outcome-based efforts for the student and family. While research is preliminary, the wraparound model has been found to improve attendance and school engagement and to increase placements in less-restrictive school environments (Quinn & Lee, 2007; Wyles, 2007). This blend of perspectives and services also seems to be related to improved adaptive behavior, reduced emotional and behavioral deficits, improved functioning in the classroom and community, and avoidance of more restrictive placements for students with serious emotional and behavioral disorders (Quinn & Lee, 2007; Scott & Eber, 2003). Schools must be knowledgeable about opportunities that exist in their community to refer students in need of intensive and individualized care to such services. Further, schools are essential in the planning and provision of needed services in the wraparound model of care.

Functional Family Therapy

Functional Family Therapy (FFT) is a family-based intervention program that has been found successful in treating youth, ages 11–18, for a wide variety of risk behaviors, including delinquency, violence, substance use, conduct disorder, and oppositional defiant disorder. It is designed to help reduce problematic behaviors by helping families to understand the functionality of both positive and negative behaviors over 8 to 26 weeks. This flexible intervention can be delivered in a variety of settings and by a variety of professionals and is another excellent example of an intervention that uses a multi-agency collaboration approach to providing services to youth who require individualized and intensive treatment. More specifically, intensive intervention occurs in phases:

1. Engagement—emphasizes factors that prevent dropout from program
2. Motivation—designed to change maladaptive reactions and increase motivation for change
3. Assessment—designed to clarify relationships and interpersonal function of behavior
4. Behavior change—communication training, parenting skills, problem solving, and conflict management techniques
5. Generalization—therapist and case management help to provide community resources necessary to support change

Over 30 years of data reflect positive outcomes for FFT in reducing problem behavior, delinquency, criminal behavior, and the need for more intensive and costly placements (Center for the Study and Prevention of Violence, n.d.). Functional Family Therapy is a Center for the Study and Prevention of Violence Blueprints Model Program, a SAMHSA effective program, and an OJJDP exemplary program (Sexton & Alexander, 2000).

The Safe Schools/Healthy Students Initiative

The Safe Schools/Healthy Students (SS/HS) Initiative funded by the U. S. Department of Education, the U. S. Department of Justice, and the U. S. Department of Health & Human Services supports the interagency collaboration necessary to prevent and reduce youth violence in schools and school communities as mentioned above and in other sections of this book. Local education agencies have found good results in partnership with their community law enforcement, mental health agencies, and juvenile justice systems in getting early and intensive intervention services in place for youth at risk (Tellen, Kim, Stewart-Nava, Pesce, & Maher, 2006). Schools and communities may be able to find support for additional services in the wraparound model and access to Functional Family Therapy through the planning and collaborative services encouraged by this grant initiative.

SUMMARY

Suicidal ideation or attempts, depression, self-injury, substance abuse, and threats to harm others or the school are some of the risk behaviors students exhibit that require intensive or individualized intervention. Through awareness and early identification of these risk behaviors, intervention can be given before a crisis occurs. All members of the school community must be taught to identify warning signs of risk behaviors and mental illness for the physical and psychological safety of the school, the students, and the staff. The needs of the small percentage of students who exhibit these patterns of high-risk internalizing and externalizing behavior are best met by schools in cooperation and partnership with their community agencies. School safety issues must be considered community safety issues for the safety and well-being of our youth.

Nine

Recovery Efforts and Management of Crises in Schools

The previous chapters in this section focused on multi-tiered interventions and supports for all students to help establish and maintain a safe learning environment. This final chapter of the book focuses on the Recovery Phase of the multi-phase model and specific multi-tiered crisis management efforts and interventions that may be needed when a crisis event occurs. As stated in Chapter 1, the purpose of care and recovery efforts is to determine the psychological impact of the event, identify the response and intervention services needed, assist with the coping and understanding of reactions to help stabilize students and staff, and restore psychological safety and learning. As discussed in Chapter 5, response efforts include those immediate, first actions that take place when an event occurs to ensure physical safety. Recovery then begins immediately in the aftermath of an event, once safety and security are restored, and includes repairing the building and other infrastructure for the return to use after a crisis as well as the care of students and staff that may be in need of psychological safety interventions. These efforts are necessary to "return to the business of learning" and implementation of specific efforts will depend on the level of physical and psychological need for particular crises (Brock, 2002a; OSDFS, 2007). Following a traumatic event at school, one of the decisions to be made includes what type of crisis recovery intervention to provide, as school crisis management efforts may include several levels of psychological service (Brock, 2002a). Physical and psychological recovery and crisis management after an event needs to be included within both the comprehensive safe school/district plan and the school/district crisis response plan. As emphasized earlier, staff development and training to implement these efforts need to occur *prior* to an event as part of the planning and preparation phases.

PHYSICAL RECOVERY EFFORTS

In physical recovery, the damage to the school building or other critical infrastructure of the school needs to be assessed. For instance, can the school continue operation that day or in the following days? What impact does the crisis have on any ability to return students and staff to the classrooms or school? What kind of assistance will be needed to manage the repair and clean-up? These basic decisions will need to be made, and any repair, restoration, or clean-up will need to be completed before students and staff return for learning. In some cases, school may be cancelled for the rest of the day, for instance, when off-site evacuation is needed for a water or gas leak, power outage, or minor fire. In other situations, perhaps in a natural disaster such as a tornado, repair to the structure may take days or weeks. School crisis plans need to have preparedness for this type of recovery effort. The school district facilities and risk management and insurance company will most likely assist a school building in some way with those repairs.

If school cannot be reopened immediately, communication with parents and the community will be essential. Preparedness plans should have considered those communications needs. The media can be used to reach the larger community, and in some cases, schools or communities have used a reverse 911 system or calling tree to parents for those types of communication. If the structure of the building cannot be used in the short term or long term, significant planning will need to occur about when and where to assemble staff and students. Depending on the nature of the crisis, personal communication may be needed or recommended to reassure families and students and encourage students to return. A return to school as soon as possible is recommended for the psychological recovery to begin (Brock, Nickerson, Reeves, Jimerson, Lieberman, & Feinberg, 2009; Brock, 2006a). After a crisis or trauma involving a physical threat of some kind, the visible presence of adults, staff, and police may be reassuring to both students and staff.

PSYCHOLOGICAL RECOVERY EFFORTS

Children's mental health services are a critical component to comprehensive crisis intervention planning (Health, Ryan, Dean, & Bingham, 2007) as they can help to mitigate the negative impact of trauma exposure and facilitate recovery. If significant traumatization occurs, lower academic achievement can result (Saigh, Mroueh, & Bremner, 1997; Saltzman, Pynoos, Layne, Steinberg, & Aisenberg, 2001) due to increased irritability, aggression, withdrawal, and difficulties with concentration and sustaining attention. In addition, violent events such as suicide or homicide are associated with contagion, which occurs when others copy that event in a similar fashion, resulting in a cluster of similar events (Brock, 2002d; Cherry Creek School District, 2008). High-quality psychological recovery and crisis management efforts are paramount not only for decreasing contagion, but also for reestablishing and sustaining a safe schools climate. The options include a site response, a district supported response, or a mutual aid response in a multi-agency recovery effort (Brock et al., 2009; Brock, 2006a, 2002b; Reeves et al., in press). This next section provides an overview of (a) crisis variables that can impact recovery efforts, (b) vulnerability factors that predispose students and staff to psychological trauma, (c) common crisis reactions, and (d) specific psychological crisis recovery interventions (each of which support the universal, targeted, and intensive interventions already being implemented prior to a crisis event occurring).

ASSESSMENT OF INDIVIDUAL PHYSICAL SAFETY AND PSYCHOLOGICAL IMPACT

A severe traumatic stressor is defined as an event that threatens life or physical integrity and overwhelms an individual's capacity to cope (American Psychiatric Association [APA], 2000; National Child Traumatic Stress Network, n.d.[b]). Physical trauma includes the body's response to the injury or threatened injury. Emotional trauma includes the mind's response to the injury or threatened injury, which then contributes to feelings and potential behavioral and emotional signs of trauma (NIMH, 2008a). It is important to acknowledge that some crisis events are more traumatic than others and will impact individuals differently. Before appropriate recovery efforts can be implemented, it is imperative to understand the type of crisis including the presence of injury or death, the duration and intensity of the event, and the number of individuals involved (Brock et al., 2009; Brock, 2006a, 2002b). Next it is important to assess the physical and psychological impact of trauma on individuals and the system as a whole. Psychological triage calls for school professionals to observe students and staff for certain psychological traumatization risk factors and warning signs and then to implement specific interventions as they are needed and appropriate (Brock, 2002c, 2006a; U. S. Department of Education, REMS, 2008b). Providing the appropriate level of psychological intervention is critical, as providing crisis intervention assistance to those who do not need it can cause undue harm (Brock, 2006a). For example, if a student is participating in a group crisis intervention when he or she does not need to be, he or she can unintentionally be exposed to traumatic details or reactions from others, which can then lead to unintended consequences such as increased anxiety and excessive worry about his or her own safety or vulnerability. In addition, if the student is coping relatively well and inappropriately placed in a more intensive intervention, it can send the message that he or she is unable to cope with the trauma, which then in turn decreases the likelihood that the student will utilize his or her own naturally occurring support systems or existing coping skills, and/or the student may be hesitant to ask for help as he/she feels they are "failing at coping." To the contrary, under-responding can lead to students and/or staff not having their needs met, which can then potentially lead to more serious mental health issues. Therefore, it is important to distinguish normal stress and reactions that do not typically exceed an individual's coping capacity from the crisis state and traumatic stress reactions, which are the result of an individual's coping capacity and are "outside" normal life experience for most (Brock, Sandoval, & Lewis, 2001; U. S. Department of Education, REMS, 2008b). In some cases, traumatic stress may develop into post-traumatic stress disorder (PTSD). PTSD is an anxiety disorder characterized by symptoms of reexperiencing the traumatic event (e.g., by having nightmares or intrusive thoughts), avoiding trauma-related stimuli (including places, people, and situations), and hyperarousal (e.g., by having sleep problems and hypervigilance; APA, 2000; Brymer, Jacobs, Layne, Pynoos, Ruzek, Steinberg, Vernberg, & Watson, 2006). By conducting appropriate psychological triage and crisis interventions, schools can help to mitigate the sometimes severe effects of traumatic stressors. To understand the level of impact of a traumatic event on individuals, and thus the school population, crisis variables need to be understood.

TRAUMA ASSESSMENT VARIABLES

Trauma assessment variables are those factors that affect the potential for an event to be psychologically traumatic and includes crisis exposure, personal vulnerability factors, threat perceptions, and crisis reactions (Brock et al., 2009; Brock, 2002c, 2002d; NIMH, 2008a). These variables increase risk of traumatic stress. However, they are not perfect predictors of such, as not all individuals who have crisis exposure, personal vulnerabilities, and/or crisis reactions will need the same level of crisis intervention assistance (Brymer et al., 2006; NIMH, 2002).

Crisis Exposure

Crisis exposure is comprised of both physical and emotional proximity to the crisis event. Physical exposure is where the individual was at the time of the event and is the single most important predictor of psychological trauma (Brock, 2002b, 2006a, 2006b; Brock, Nickerson, Reeves, & Jimerson, 2008; Pynoos, Fredrick, Nadar, Arroyo, Steinberg, Eth, Nunez, & Fairbanks, 1987; Reeves et al., 2006). The closer an individual is in physical proximity to the event (i.e., witnessed the event directly), the higher the likelihood of traumatic exposure and subsequent reactions by the individual (Brock, 2002c, 2006a; Brymer et al., 2006). Emotional proximity is the next most powerful predictor of traumatic reactions (Brock et al., 2009; Brock, 2006a; Brock et al., 2008; Pynoos et al., 1987; Reeves et al., 2006) and involves how close of an emotional relationship the person had with the victim(s). For example, if a student loses his or her best friend in a car accident, he/she is at higher risk for psychological trauma versus if a classmate he or she had only spoken to once was killed in the car accident. It is important to remember that proximity can also include the person's *perception* of how close of a relationship they had with the victim(s).

Personal Vulnerability

There are key vulnerability factors that will differ from individual to individual. These include the presence of risk factors (discussed in Chapter 7), warning signs (discussed in Chapter

8), and internal and external vulnerabilities. Again, the presence of risk factors for an individual increases the odds that an event(s) will generate psychological injury, whereas evidence of warning signs can signal that an individual may already be experiencing psychological trauma. Internal and external vulnerability factors are the "flip side" of resiliency variables and therefore *increase* the odds of students exhibiting symptoms of trauma exposure. The most common internal vulnerability factors include poor coping style or skills (avoidance coping), preexisting mental illness, poor self-regulation of emotion, low developmental level and poor problem solving, history of prior psychological trauma, a lack of self-efficacy (internalized appraisal of what one is capable to doing), and an external locus of control (Brock et al., 2009; Brock 2006a; Nickerson et al., 2009). Sometimes these factors are not known before a trauma occurs. It is also important to remember that some of these factors may exist in the adult staff also (i.e., previous trauma), and not just the students. External vulnerability factors include poor parent-child relationships, family dysfunction, parental traumatic stress, and a lack of social resources or social support systems (Brock, 2002a; Brock et al., 2008; Brymer et al., 2006; Nickerson et al., 2009). Lack of parent support, family conflict, and overprotectiveness after an event has also been found to predict levels of PTSD (Bokszczanin, 2008).

Threat Perceptions

An individual's perception of the threat (i.e., how negative he/she perceives the event or their perception of the event as having been capable of causing them physical or emotional pain) is a powerful predictor of psychological trauma (Brock, 2002c; Brock et al., 2008; Nickerson et al., 2009; Shaw, 2003). For example, if the student perceived the intruder to be coming specifically for him or her to cause harm (even though the intruder was randomly seeking students out), there is a higher likelihood of stronger traumatic reactions being exhibited.

Crisis Reactions

Children who are exposed to the same event can demonstrate different reactions. These reactions are influenced by all of the factors discussed above, in addition to the severity and durability of the crisis reactions. These reactions can occur in the immediate aftermath of an event or much later (Kanan & Plog, submitted for publication; NIMH, 2008a; U. S. Department of

Education, REMS, 2008b) and help to define the risk for and/or the presence of traumatic stress. How close the child was to the event, their relationship with the victims, and their own perceived threat and initial reactions are all based on the child's experience. Personal factors include child's age and developmental level, previous trauma history, current emotional health, support systems, previous coping skills, self-esteem, and cultural norms. Figure 9.1 provides a graphic representation of how crisis event variables and risk factors then impact the development of initial and durable crisis reactions.

Most students and staff will experience some level of crisis reactions and this is to be expected. These reactions are "concrete indicators that a student *may* be a psychological trauma victim" (Brock et al., 2008, p. 1497). If after four or more weeks the reactions do not seem to lessen and/or maladaptive coping skills (i.e., high risk-taking behavior, excessive illegal

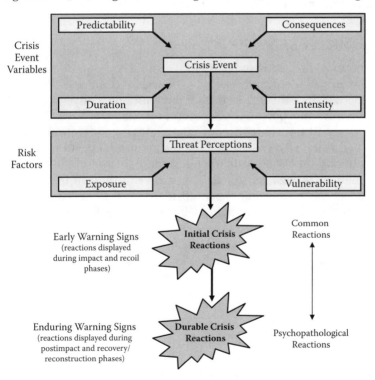

Figure 9.1   Factors impacting the level of psychological trauma to be considered when evaluating level of traumatic impact. (Copyright 2009 by the National Association of School Psychologists, Bethesda, MD. Reprinted with permission of the publisher.)

substance usage, suicidal/homicidal thoughts, extreme emotional output, excessive withdrawal) are evident, then more intensive crisis intervention services may be needed (Brymer et al., 2006). Below are the most common reactions to crises, but cultural differences in how grief and emotion are expressed need to be kept in mind and taken into consideration (Brymer et al., 2006; see Lipson & Dibble [2005] and Workgroup on Adapting Latino Services [2008] for further discussion regarding cultural differences and adaptations necessary pertaining to grief and trauma reactions). One might assume the person is having strong reactions that need immediate mental health intervention when the reaction is culturally appropriate and acceptable or assume the person is having no reactions when their culture does not permit expression of feelings or symptoms, such as crying. The cultural liaison or broker who is part of the ICS is a valuable resource in understanding these cultural implications.

COMMON REACTIONS

Common reactions to trauma fall into four general categories that are evident across all developmental stages. These are outlined in Table 9.1 and include emotional, physical, cognitive, and interpersonal/behavioral effects.

In addition, there are developmental considerations in crisis reactions (Brymer et al.; 2006 Kanan & Plog, submitted for publication; National Institute of Mental Health, 2008; Pfohl, Jimerson & Lazarus, 2002). These are outlined in more detail in Table 9.2. Preschool-aged children tend to express trauma reactions through nonverbal behavior due to minimal language skills to describe their feelings in words.

Elementary school-aged children may communicate trauma reactions verbally but behavioral expression continues to be common and the focus is more on event-specific fears or concerns. Adolescents are more self-conscious about their responses, fears, and feelings and have higher cognitive and verbal skills than younger children. They may express reactions directly, but this age level also tends to include an increase in risk-taking behaviors (Kanan & Plog, submitted for publication; Nickerson et al., 2009; Poland & McCormick, 1999). It is important to note that the younger the children (especially preschool and elementary-aged children), the more their reactions are strongly affected by adult caretakers' preexisting mental health conditions and reactions, prior victimization,

Table 9.1 Common Reactions to Crises

Emotional

Shock	Sadness	Hypersensitivity
Anger	Loss of pleasure	Helplessness
Terror/fear	Despair	Hopelessness
Irritability	Emotional numbing	Loss of pleasure from activities
Grief	Depression	Phobias
Guilt	Dissociation	

Cognitive

Difficulty with:	Intrusive thoughts,	Distortion
• Concentration	memories, or	Self-blame
• Decision making	nightmares	Intrusive thoughts or memories
• Memory	Decreased self-esteem	Reenactment through play
• Confusion	Decreased self-efficacy	(especially for younger children)
Worry	Disbelief	

Physical

Fatigue	Gastrointestinal	Decreased appetite
Sleep disturbance	problems	Decreased libido
Physical/somatic	Insomnia	Startle response
complaints	Hyperarousal	Increased activity level
Headaches	Impaired immune	
	response	

Interpersonal/Behavioral

Social withdrawal	Avoidance of reminders	Increased risk-taking
Relationship conflicts	Crying easily	Alienation
or aggression	Tantrums	Social withdrawal/isolation
School refusal	Regression to previous	Vocational impairment
School difficulties	developmental level	Change in eating patterns

Sources: Brock, S. E., Nickerson, A. B., Reeves, M. A., Jimerson, S. R., Lieberman, R. A., & Feinberg, T. A. (2009). *School crisis prevention and intervention. The PREPaRE model.* Bethesda, MD: National Association of School Psychologists; Brymer, M., Jacobs, A., Layne, C., Pynoos, R., Ruzek, J., Steinberg, A., Vernberg, E., & Watson, P. (2006, July). *Psychological first aid: Field operations guide,* 2nd Edition [Electronic version]. National Child Traumatic Stress Network and National Center for PTSD. www.ncptsd.va.gov; National Institute of Mental Health. (2008). *Helping children and adolescents cope with violence and disasters, what parents can do.* Publication No. 08-3518 [Electronic version]. http://www.nimh.nih.gov/health/publications/helping-children-and-adoles-cents-cope-with-violence-and-disasters-what-parents-can-do.pdf; Speier, A. H. (2000). *Psychosocial issues for children and adolescents in disasters,* 2nd Edition. Washington, DC: U.S. Department of Health & Human Services; and Young, B. H., Ford, J. D., Ruzek, J. I., Friedman, M., & Gusman, F. D. (1998). *Disaster mental health services: A guide for clinicians and administrators.* Palo Alto, CA: National Center for Post Traumatic Stress Disorder.

Table 9.2   Developmental Reactions to Trauma

Preschool Age
- Difficulty separating from caregivers
- Difficulty being alone
- Increase in anxious behaviors (clinging, immobility/aimless motion)
- Tantrums
- Crying easily or screaming
- Generalized fear
- Whimpering or trembling
- Moving aimlessly or becoming immobile
- Loss of developmental milestones (e.g., decreased verbalization, may begin wetting bed again, reoccurrence of thumb sucking)
- Re-creation of traumatic event though repetitive plan (may or may not be directly related to the event)
- Interrupted sleep (fear of going to sleep, nightmares)

Elementary School Age
- Worry about recurrence of event
- Worry about own safety or the safety of others
- Generalized worrying and/or developing unfounded fears
- Fear of being alone or can isolate him/herself
- More clingy or anxious
- Irritable or disruptive
- Outbursts of anger
- Overreaction to startling noises
- Obsessively retell the event
- Overwhelming emotions or apparent lack of feelings about event (emotional numbing)
- Preoccupation with their own behavior during the event (e.g., guilt or shame over something done/not done)
- Difficulty learning and concentrating in school; decrease in grades
- Refusal to go to school
- Difficulty with authority/increase in acting-out behaviors/aggression
- Physical symptoms or psychosomatic complaints (e.g., headaches/stomachaches)
- Avoidance of activities
- Loss of previously acquired developmental milestones (e.g., speech, toileting, school skills)
- Re-creation of the traumatic event through talk, writing, drawing, or play
- Interrupted sleep (fear of going to sleep, nightmares)

Adolescents
- Worry about recurrence or consequences of the event
- Worry about own safety or the safety of others

Table 9.2   (Continued) Developmental Reactions to Trauma

- Self-consciousness about fears or worries, shame, or guilt
- Repeated discussion about the event or avoidance of discussion
- Avoidance of reminders of the event
- Reactions to loud or startling cues
- Flashbacks to the event (this is the mind reliving the event)
- Difficulty expressing feelings or worries due to concerns about being different from peers
- Withdrawal from others
- Depression
- School refusal
- Attendance difficulties
- Revenge or retribution fantasies
- Decreased attention/concentration in school; decreased academic achievement
- Increased activity level (may include risk-taking or self-destructive behavior such as alcohol, drug use, sexual risk-taking, self-injury, suicidal ideation/behavior)
- Irritability
- Anger/aggression
- Difficulty with authority (increase in oppositional behaviors)
- Sleep disturbance, nightmares (may also re-experience event in day-dreams)
- Physical complaints (e.g., headaches, stomachaches)
- Repetitive thoughts, comments about death and dying; suicidal thoughts
- Sense of a foreshortened future or changed identity (e.g., life isn't worth it anyway)
- Increased conflict/difficulty with peers

Sources: Kanan L., & Plog A. (submitted for publication). Developmental issues and trauma reactions in children: Suggestions for parents and educators. In A. Caner, L. Paige, & S. Shaw (Eds.), *Helping children at home and school* (3rd Ed.). Bethesda, MD: National Association of School Psychologists; National Institute of Mental Health. (2008). *Helping children and adolescents cope with violence and disasters, what parents can do*. Publication No. 08-3518 [Electronic version]. http://www.nimh.nih.gov/health/publications/helping-children-and-adolescents-cope-with-violence-and-disasters-what-parents-can-do.pdf; Pfohl, W., Jimerson, S. R., & Lazarus, P. J. (2002). Developmental aspects of psychological trauma and grief. In S. E. Brock, P. J. Lazarus, & S. R. Jimerson (Eds.), *Best practices in school crisis prevention and intervention* (pp. 309–331). Bethesda, MD: National Association of School Psychologists.

and/or past traumatic experiences. These variables can exacerbate crisis responses (Bokszczanin, 2008; NIMH, 2008a; Pfohl, Jimerson, & Lazarus, 2002). While beyond the scope of this book to describe specific adult reactions, it is imperative that school staff effectively cope with the stressful event, as adult reactions have a direct impact on how students will cope (Brock, 2006a; U. S. Department of Education, REMS, 2008b). Also, the social support of adults is very powerful in students' recovery (U. S. Department of Education, REMS, 2008b). This is not to say that adults cannot express reactions or grief; however, this needs to be conveyed in a way that provides calmness, positive hope, security, and support for students. If the adult is having strong emotional reactions, he/she may need additional support services him/herself before resuming direct work with students. It is also the role of the school crisis recovery team to be attuned to the impact on staff.

PSYCHOLOGICAL TRIAGE

Psychological triage is the process of evaluating and sorting victims by immediacy of treatment needed and directing them to immediate or delayed treatment. The goal of triage is to "do the greatest good for the greatest number victims" (NIMH, 2002, p. 27). It helps educators identify student needs (U. S. Department of Education, REMS, 2008b), with immediate intervention provided to identified high-risk students (NIMH, 2002). Triage is a dynamic process, not a discrete event. An overview of the factors important to psychological triage has been described above and information regarding the levels of psychological triage is presented below based on the work of Brock (2002a, 2002b, 2006a).

Primary Level

This psychological triage level begins as soon as possible (once physical safety and security is secured and medical needs are addressed) but before any psychological crisis intervention takes place. It is primarily based upon the crisis facts and risk factors such as who witnessed the accident, who knew the victim(s), and who was injured; in essence, the crisis team members assess the proximity/exposure, relationship, personal vulnerabilities, and initial reactions to identify those in need of immediate crisis intervention. If reactions are within typical limits, natural coping strategies, supports, and resources are all that is needed. If further support is warranted, the secondary level of triage begins.

Secondary Level

This level of psychological triage begins when primary or universal interventions (e.g., class meetings, caregiver trainings, and naturally occurring support systems) are being offered. Reactions are observed in students identified in the primary level of triage and also those who have recently shown signs of impact. School professionals assess the combination of risk factors and warning signs (i.e., the concrete signs) of traumatic impact evident in students such as intense anger, acting out behaviors, not being able to get out of bed, attendance problems, or threatening behaviors. The Listen, Protect, Connect model (Schreiber, Gurwitch, & Wong, 2006; U. S. Department of Education, REMS, 2008b), which is recommended for use in schools, helps to train teachers to assist psychological helping staff in this triage process. For students whose symptoms are elevated, secondary level (targeted) interventions such as individual or group/classroom-based psychological first aid are provided. It is while these interventions are provided that the tertiary level of triage begins.

Tertiary Level

At this level, school professionals look for those concrete psychological trauma reactions such as flashbacks, severe depression, and anxiety that are more consistent with posttraumatic responses. If these are evident, more intensive mental health treatment (e.g., psychotherapy) is needed, as these services are typically not expected to be provided by schools.

At all levels of triage, parent input and feedback is critical. Good parent and school communication in the recovery phase facilitates the appropriate identification and acquisition of needed services to help foster recovery. Parents should be informed of the warning signs so that they may refer their child for services as needed. Lastly, it is important to remain flexible in the identification of students in the psychological triage process as those students initially deemed at high risk might actually have their risk factor status lowered due to good support systems, whereas those initially deemed as low risk may be elevated due to a lack of intended support systems or healthy coping skills or delayed onset of traumatic reactions.

PSYCHOLOGICAL RECOVERY INTERVENTIONS

Psychological recovery interventions span the entire multi-tiered service delivery system from reestablishing social support systems at the universal level to more targeted individualized and group crisis interventions or intensive psychotherapy. All of these interventions are complementary to each other and students can be involved in more than one type of intervention. A student does not have to begin with universal crisis interventions and then complete a targeted crisis intervention before he/she can access intensive supports. The "Student Care and Recovery Coordinator" (see Chapters 4 and 5 regarding ICS structure and crisis plans) will be critical in regards to these efforts as their primary role is to help coordinate the response and recovery services needed. It is also important to note that when an event impacts a large number of students or staff, has high traumatic impact, and/or the interventions needed are beyond the expertise of school professionals, a unified response may be needed and a community team (i.e., local mental health center) may need to be called upon to help the school and district provide interventions. These community team individuals need to be qualified, pre-screened, have specialized training, and understand the developmental needs of children and youth, including those with disabilities. This prescreening should have been done as part of the preparedness phase. Good collaboration with other support agencies is critical in regards to multi-tiered psychological recovery interventions. Schools may not be able to provide or may not have the expertise to provide (i.e., psychotherapy) all the necessary interventions, and other agencies can help to provide these multi-tiered services.

Psychological First Aid

Psychological first aid should not be confused with "psychological debriefing" or "critical incident stress debriefing" (CISD), which is a crisis intervention model that was initially developed to occur after a catastrophic event for first responders or primary victims of trauma. Debriefing interventions include discussing the traumatic event in detail (ventilation), with the facilitator providing normalization of the event and responses, and then providing education about psychological reactions. Debriefing is most often done as a single intervention either individually or in a group (Everly, Phillips, Kane, & Feldman, 2006; Inter-Agency Standing Committee [IASC],

2008; Kaplan, Iancu, & Bodner, 2001; The British Psychological Society, 2002). While there are some overlapping similarities between psychological first aid and psychological debriefing, psychological first aid is more general in scope and can be conducted as part of a continuum of services offered by schools in the recovery phase and is not just for first responders or direct victims of the event (Brock, 2006a; Brymer et al., 2006; U. S. Department of Education, REMS, 2008a).

The Inter-Agency Standing Committee (IASC, 2008) has developed guidelines on mental health and psychosocial support in the event of an emergency. The IASC guidelines define components of psychological first aid to include the following: (a) protect survivors from further physical or psychological harm; (b) identify and provide support for those most distressed; (c) reestablish social supports; (d) provide information and links to local resources; (e) return to school and familiar routines; (f) facilitate communication among students, families, and agencies; (g) educate about the expected psychological responses, basic coping tools; (h) listen in an accepting and nonjudgmental manner, convey compassion; (i) ask for and address concerns; (j) encourage participation in normal daily routines (if possible) and positive means of coping; and (k) refer to available resources.

The next section will highlight the continuum of psychological first aid and crisis recovery interventions (see Figure 9.2). One final distinction that should be understood is that crisis recovery interventions and psychotherapy are not synonymous; crisis interventions seek to restore immediate coping skills, while many forms of psychotherapy focus instead on in-depth processing and healing of trauma. Therefore, psychological first aid in a school setting typically encompasses those crisis interventions at the universal and targeted levels.

Reestablishing Social Support Systems

Most students and staff will recover from a crisis with minimal or no formalized intervention needed (Brymer et al., 2006; NIMH, 2002). Thus, they use their existing social support systems (e.g., friends, family, church) to help in the recovery process. Therefore, facilitating the reestablishment of naturally occurring support systems at the universal school level should become the focus of primary school crisis intervention (i.e., classroom and peer connections). All other school crisis interventions should complement the naturally occurring support systems (Brock et al, 2009, 2008) or be provided subsequent to

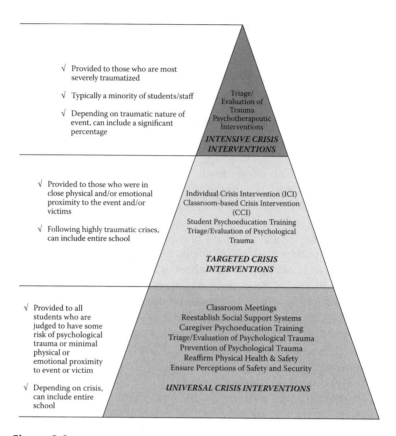

Figure 9.2 Multi-tiered levels of crisis interventions. *Source*: Adapted from Brock, S. E., Nickerson, A. B., Reeves, M. A., Jimerson, S. R., Lieberman, R. A., & Feinberg, T. A. (2009). *School crisis prevention and intervention: The PREPaRE model*. Bethesda, MD: National Association of School Psychologists. (Copyright 2009 by the National Association of School Psychologists. Bethesda, MD. Adapted with permission of publisher.)

or during the reestablishment of those support systems. Social support is directly linked to resiliency variables, risk factors, and traumatic stress; high levels of risk factors are related to minimal social support systems, which in turn are strong predictors of traumatic stress (Bokszczanin, 2008; Caffo & Belaise, 2003; Ozxer, Best, Lipsey, & Weiss, 2003). In contrast, students who tend to have more resiliency variables have stronger social support systems in place to help facilitate recovery from trauma. School professionals can help reestablish naturally occurring support systems by reuniting students with their parents, friends, and family (thus the importance of a good reunification plan), helping to reestablish routines and procedures as soon as possible (this also helps improve safety and security), facilitating community connections, and empowering with recovery knowledge (Brock, 2006a; Brock, et al., 2009, 2008). However, there are limitations to social support, as it may not be enough support or may be ineffective if the social support systems themselves have also been impacted. For example, in Hurricane Katrina, one of the worst natural disasters to strike the southern region of the United States in history, the entire community, including parents, education professionals, and community helping professionals, was impacted. As a result of the storm's impact, hundreds of programs were closed or operating at reduced capacity, thousands of families were displaced, and public agencies were unprepared and over-whelmed in regards to response and resources (Shores, 2006). Social support systems were greatly impacted and caregivers struggled with how to meet the extreme physical and psycho-logical needs of children and parents, in addition to meeting logistical needs such as where to enroll or transfer displaced children so parents could search for work, housing, medical care, or lost relatives. It is not surprising, then, that preva-lence rates of PTSD since Hurricane Katrina are estimated to be between 22% and 60% in the impacted areas (Galea, Tracy, Norris, & Coffey, 2008; Scherringa & Zeanah, 2008). In addition to the potential negative impact of an event on existing support systems, if the social support persons (e.g., parent or caregiver) have preexisting mental health conditions, typical recovery will be complicated (Gil Rivas, Holman, & Silver, 2004; Qouta, Punamäki, & El Sarraj, 2005).

Classroom Meetings

In the authors' first-hand experience in providing crisis inter-vention in schools, brief classroom meetings have been held to share the facts, answer questions, and dispel rumors, especially when this information needs to be disseminated in an expedi-ent manner with a large number of classes. In other school-based crisis intervention models, a class meeting as a brief intervention option is not specifically included, yet this com-ponent of crisis recovery intervention is likely to be an impor-tant part of the multi-tiered crisis intervention continuum. A class meeting only lasts about 5 to 10 minutes and is typically led by classroom teachers who have been provided a fact sheet and guidelines for how to answer the most anticipated ques-tions. If multiple classrooms need to have a class meeting, these are most often held simultaneously (e.g., first period of the day) so all students receive the same information at the same time. Class meetings can be critical to implement when intervention needs to begin, but there is not the time or resources immediately available to conduct more time-intensive interventions. Therefore, a class meeting can occur first, followed by more targeted or intensive interventions at a later time, if necessary. For example, there is a car accident on the way to school and with the arrival of students at school, rumors are already starting to multiply. The school administrator or school resource officer immediately contacts the Incident Commander of the local police department and obtains preliminary facts. A fact sheet is developed for teachers with the facts of the incident (as we know at the time); guidelines for how they can answer anticipated questions that may arise; where students can go to receive additional support, if needed; and how students and staff will be updated throughout the day of new information. The fact sheet is distributed to teachers (in a preplanned way) and they are instructed to read at the beginning of their first hour class while monitoring for crisis reactions. This format allows the dispelling of potentially disruptive or traumatizing rumors but also allows the school crisis recovery team the time to gather complete and accurate information and begin the primary level of psychological triage before implementing other crisis interventions. Any teacher who may not be able to complete the steps of a classroom meeting, due to physical or emotional proximity to the event or person or other personal variables, should be offered assistance from the crisis team in the facilitation of a classroom meeting. Table 9.3 reviews the general structure of conducting a classroom meeting.

Psychoeducation as Crisis Recovery Intervention

Psychological education (also referred to as psychoeducation) is used when students and caregivers (teachers and parents) can benefit from information on how they can help themselves and each other cope with the impact of the event (Brock et al., 2009; Brock 2006a). This intervention is also appropriate when information, coping skills, and resources need to be provided. Psychoeducation groups can be provided to students or caregivers, or psychoeducation principles can be used in individualized intervention when one student or family is impacted by a crisis event. For example, a teacher, who was very involved in sponsoring student activity groups, dies suddenly. A psychoeducation group is then held with that teacher's individual classes and various student activity groups to

Table 9.3   General Structure of a Classroom Meeting

1. *Introduction*—Validate the many rumors and emotions surrounding the event, but clarify that the purpose of the class meeting is to share facts and dispel the rumors. State that the meeting will last about 5 to 10 minutes and specify if there will be a time later to share emotions and get additional assistance for those who need it (if appropriate to offer). Review classroom rules for large group discussions (if necessary). For example, raise hands before speaking and one person speaks at a time.

2. *Share facts of event*—Provided on a fact sheet to the teacher, the teacher reads aloud.

3. *Open discussion for questions*—Teachers need to be provided with explicit parameters of what information they can share (especially if a police investigation is being conducted) and also understand that it is okay to say, "I don't know the answer to that question," or "I cannot share that information." If students are perseverating on inappropriate details or strong emotions surrounding event, teachers need to redirect students (i.e., "I understand there are a lot of emotions around this event, but the purpose of what we are doing right now is to share facts, dispel rumors, and answer questions. We need to keep that focus right now and if you would like to discuss further, please see me and we can arrange that.")

4. *Teacher referrals (if indicated)*—Teachers watch for students who may have additional information about the event (i.e., witnessed the accident on the way to school) or whose reactions indicate that individualized crisis intervention is needed. The names of students with information or intense reactions are given to the crisis team as soon as possible.

help them understand the event and identify coping strategies. In this example, psychoeducation most likely would *not* be conducted with all classes in the school, as some students may not have known the teacher. The circle of impact should be considered for each type of crisis. In a community-wide event such as a tornado, psychoeducation groups may be conducted with all classes in the school (which would most likely require the need for additional support staff from the district team or community crisis team). In an individualized psychoeducation intervention, a student might have a friend from another school that died. The student may be in need of psychoeducation to help understand the event, manage emotions, and identify coping skills and resources.

Brock et al. (2009) and Brock (2006a) also provide a structured process for conducting a caregiver training. This process is very similar to student psychoeducation training but the focus is on caregivers helping their children or students. Again, the process may be used in an individualized way with one family in crisis (i.e., a neighbor, grandparent, or other family member is in an accident or dies). The process follows the basic sequence above but provides the participants with fact sheets and information to help them dispel rumors when working with students and to understand the normal crisis reactions they may see in children or adolescents. In addition, psychoeducation for caregivers helps them to recognize possible reactions that may indicate a child is reacting outside the norm and is in need of a referral for further evaluation and intervention from a school-based helper. In the example provided above, parents of students who had known the teacher may be invited to attend a caregiver psychoeducation session (i.e., "Parent Meeting") or the meeting could be announced to all parents via a letter home, e-mail, or phone call, and all parents are invited to attend. Table 9.4 summarizes the student and caregiver psychoeducation process according to Brock et al. (2009) and Brock (2006a), but the reader is referred to these sources for further discussion of psychoeducation. Tables 9.5 and 9.6 discuss how adults and parents can further help children and adolescents.

INDIVIDUAL AND GROUP PSYCHOLOGICAL CRISIS INTERVENTIONS

In this section, Tier 2 (targeted/selected) crisis interventions will be discussed and are most commonly referred to as individual and group psychological crisis interventions involving more formalized psychological first aid (Brock, 2006a; Brymer et al., 2006; Everly et al., 2006; NIMH, 2002; U. S. Department of Education, REMS, 2008b). This level of intervention is for those students who had closer physical and emotional proximity to the event and/or who may be demonstrating risk factors or warning signs. Psychological first aid is an evidence-informed approach to help children in the immediate aftermath of a crisis to reduce initial distress and foster short-term and long-term coping skills (Brymer et al., 2006). According to the U.S. Department of Education, REMS (2008b), psychological first aid has two main goals: (a) to stabilize the emotions and behaviors of students, and (b) to return students to an improved mental and emotional state after a crisis or disaster so they are ready to attend school and re-engage in classroom learning. These interventions are usually provided by trained mental health professionals or crisis response personnel. It should be noted that knowledge of these specific forms of crisis intervention do not equate to the ability to appropriately conduct these

Table 9.4 General Process for Student Psychoeducation and Caregiver Psychoeducation Groups

Student Psychoeducation Process

1. Introduce the lesson: Introduce facilitators and present purpose of the meeting; set set parameters for the session, including the need for respectful participation confidentiality limits.

2. Answer questions/dispel rumors: Facts are clarified and questions are answered.

3. Prepare for crisis reactions: Common crisis reactions are outlined and normalized.

4. Teach how to manage and cope with crisis: Positive coping strategies (stress and relaxation strategies) are encouraged, including the use of existing support systems.

5. Close the lesson: Empowering participants to help each other and reassurance of a safe school climate.

Caregiver Psychoeducation Process

1. Introduce the training and facilitators: Introduce facilitators and present purpose of the meeting; set parameters for the session, including the need for respectful participation (this meeting is not to place blame or critique response); review confidentiality limits.

2. Provide crisis facts: Facts are clarified and rumors dispelled; emphasize current interventions to ensure physical and psychological safety of students.

3. Prepare caregivers for crisis reactions they may see: Explain common crisis reactions they may see in their children (or students); review risk factors and warning signs; identify referral procedures.

4. Review techniques for responding to crisis reactions: Describe stress management and relaxation technique; identify supports and referral sources (provide resource handout); emphasize threat perceptions are influenced by adult reactions.

Sources: Brock, S. E., Nickerson, A. B., Reeves, M. A., Jimerson, S. R., Lieberman, R. A., & Feinberg, T. A. (2009). *School crisis prevention and intervention. The PREPaRE model.* Bethesda, MD: National Association of School Psychologists; and Brock, S. E. (2006). *PREPaRE workshop #2: Crisis intervention and recovery. The roles of school-based mental health professionals.* Bethesda, MD: National Association of School Psychologists.

interventions. The reader is referred to the National Association of School Psychologists Web site (http://www.nasponline.org/prepare/index.aspx) for workshop information on the PREPaRE Crisis Prevention and Intervention Curriculum, which can train school personnel to conduct the various crisis interventions highlighted in this chapter. Although individual and group psychological crisis interventions have minimal systematic empirical support due to the challenges of doing true experimental design with students impacted by a trauma, the components have been guided by research. There is consensus among experts that these interventions help manage stress and

Table 9.5 How Adults Can Help

Attend to children:

- Listen to them
- Accept/do not argue about their feelings
- Help them cope with the reality of their experiences

Reduce effects of other sources of stress including:

- Frequent moving or changes in place of residence
- Long periods away from family and friends
- Pressures at school
- Transportation problems
- Fighting within the family
- Being hungry

Monitor healing:

- It takes time
- Do not ignore severe reactions
- Attend to sudden changes in behaviors, speech, language use, or in emotional/feeling states

Remind children that adults:

- Love them
- Support them
- Will be with them when possible

Source: National Institute of Mental Health. (2008). *Helping children and adolescents cope with violence and disasters, what parents can do.* Publication No. 08-3518. [Electronic version]. http://www.nimh.nih.gov/health/publications/helping-children-and-adolescents-cope-with-violence-and-disasters-what-parents-can-do. pdf (public domain).

adversities following a traumatic event while helping to identify those who need additional support (Brock, 2006b; Brymer et al., 2006; Everly et al., 2006). Objectives of psychological first aid integrated into individual and group crisis intervention protocols include providing physical and emotional comfort, calming and orienting emotionally distraught persons, helping survivors to share their stories and express their needs, offering practical assistance and information to help them begin the coping process, supporting adaptive coping through empowerment, emphasizing strengths, facilitating naturally occurring support systems, and providing referral information if needed while also being sensitive to the cultural, ethnic, racial, language, and religious diversity (Brock, 2006a; Brymer et al., 2006; NIMH, 2002).

Table 9.6 How Parents Can Help

After violence or a disaster parents and family should:
- Identify and address their own feelings—this will allow them to help others
- Explain to children what happened

Let children know:
- You love them
- The event was not their fault
- You will take care of them, be honest regarding limitations
- It's okay for them to feel upset

Do:
- Allow children to cry
- Allow sadness
- Let children talk about feelings
- Let them write about feelings
- Let them draw pictures

Don't:
- Expect children to be brave or tough
- Make children discuss the event before they are ready
- Get angry if children show strong emotions

Get upset if they begin:
- Bed-wetting
- Acting out
- Thumb-sucking

If children have trouble sleeping:
- Give them extra attention
- Let them sleep with a light on
- Let them sleep in your room or you sleep in their room (for a short time)

Try to keep normal routines (such routines may not be normal for some children):
- Bedtime stories
- Eating dinner together
- Watching TV together
- Reading books, exercising, playing games
- If you can't keep normal routines, make new ones together

—continued

Table 9.6   (continued) How Parents Can Help

Help children feel in control:
- Let them choose meals, if possible
- Let them pick out clothes, if possible
- Let them make some decisions for themselves, when possible

Source: National Institute of Mental Health. (2008). *Helping children and adolescents cope with violence and disasters, what parents can do.* Publication No. 08-3518. [Electronic version]. http://www.nimh.nih.gov/health/publications/helping-children-and-adolescents-cope-with-violence-and-disasters-what-parents-can-do.pdf (public domain).

Individual, group, and classroom-based psychological crisis intervention processes are highly directive and active attempts on the part of the crisis intervener to help facilitate the adaptive coping strategies of the student(s). They are distinct from the class meeting or psychoeducational intervention as this level of intervention involves students who were more impacted. In addition, these students actively explore their specific crisis experiences and reactions, while also identifying specific crisis problems and interventions to help cope. For many, these interventions will be sufficient, but for others with higher impact, it may only be the first step in the treatment process (Brock, 2006a) and they will benefit from additional crisis interventions being offered on the multi-tiered continuum. These are usually conducted at least 48 hours after the initial event but can also be utilized at a later time (e.g., anniversary dates).

Individual Crisis Interventions (ICI)

The goal of individual psychological first aid as described by Brock (2006a), or as newly referred to as individual crisis intervention (ICI) (Brock et al., 2009), is to help the individual reestablish immediate coping (Brock, 2006a; Brock et al., 2009; Brymer et al., 2006). Secondary goals are to ensure safety, provide support to reduce crisis distress, identify crisis-related problems, and support adaptive coping skills so the individual can begin the process of coping with and adapting to the changes and challenges that occur as a result of the event. Individual crisis intervention (ICI) is most often facilitated by a school-based mental health or counseling professional and typically occurs when a student is referred to a school mental health professional due to exhibiting risk factors or warning signs, but it can also happen spontaneously (you see a student crying in the hallway) for which then a school staff member may facilitate. While conducting ICI, the crisis intervener is assessing the trauma risk, prioritizing the crisis-related problems, and helping the student to problem solve and identify appropriate resources. The individual crisis intervention process can be used for almost any event that has had a physical or emotional impact on the student, for example, death of a family member or friend, witnessing or being in an accident, witnessing a violent or traumatizing event, or being affected by natural disaster. Table 9.7 summarizes the ICI process but the readers are referred to Brock et al. (2009) and Brock (2006a) for further discussion.

Table 9.7   Key Phases and Components for Individual Crisis Intervention (ICI)

1. *Establish rapport*—This is done by introducing yourself, inquiring about basic needs, and showing empathy, respect, and warmth. Confidentiality limitations also need to be reviewed, especially in regards to mandatory reporting statutes and medical and mental health privacy laws.

2. *Identify and prioritize the most immediate concerns*—The facilitator guides the student in sharing his or her crisis story and through this, the facilitator helps the individual identify the most immediate crisis-related concerns and needs. In addition, common reactions are emphasized and normalized so the individual does not feel alone in what he/she is experiencing. Individuals should not be forced to share details he/she is not ready to disclose; therefore, the child takes the lead.

3. *Address crisis problems*—During this phase, the primary goal is to identify practical adaptive coping strategies by asking about coping attempts already made, facilitating exploration of additional coping strategies, and proposing alternatives, if necessary. The crisis intervener needs to be prepared to take a more directive stance if the lethality is high or student is not capable of implementing positive coping strategies.

4. *Review progress*—In this final stage the intervener reviews progress and ensures the individual is moving towards adaptive coping responses and he/she has developed an action plan. Connections with social support systems should be clearly identified, a time for follow-up should be scheduled, and collaborative community services may need to be contacted to help foster the use of coping skills.

Sources: Brock, S. E., Nickerson, A. B., Reeves, M. A., Jimerson, S. R., Lieberman, R. A., & Feinberg, T. A. (2009). *School crisis prevention and intervention. The PREPaRE model.* Bethesda, MD: National Association of School Psychologists; Brock, 2006a; and Brymer, M., Jacobs, A., Layne, C., Pynoos, R., Ruzek, J., Steinberg, A., Vernberg, E., & Watson, P. (2006, July). *Psychological first aid: Field operations guide,* 2nd Edition [Electronic version]. National Child Traumatic Stress Network and National Center for PTSD. www.ncptsd.va.gov.

Group and Classroom-Based Crisis Interventions (CCI)

This process has been previously referred to as group psychological first aid (Brock, 2006a) and is most recently referred to as classroom-based crisis interventions (CCI) (Brock et al., 2009). This process is used when a group has had similar exposure to the crisis event (physical or emotional) and shares other similar crisis variables as discussed earlier in the chapter. However, it should be noted that this process is not designed for acute or physically injured victims (Brock et al., 2009; Brock, 2006a). Good psychological triage is critical as the crucial variable in selecting students for this type of intervention is the group must be homogeneous in respect to their crisis experiences, otherwise harm can be done by unintended exposure to trauma stories (Brock, 2006a). Due to the direct nature of this intervention and the skills needed in conducting group crisis intervention processes, the primary facilitator is a trained mental health professional; however, the co-facilitator can be a teacher who helps monitor student reactions. Two facilitators are necessary for this process, as if a student leaves the room during the intervention, the secondary facilitator follows that student to provide support. The goal of this process is to ensure the crisis event, experiences, and reactions are understood and normalized; adaptive coping and crisis problems are facilitated; and crisis survivors are beginning to look forward. Contraindications to the effectiveness of this process are if it is done as the only crisis intervention without a continuum of other interventions offered as follow-up; if a student is an acute trauma victim (physically injured); if the group has previous history of being hurtful, divisive, or not supportive; or if the process will generate polarized needs (Devilly, Varker, Hansen & Gist, 2007; Jacobs, Horne-Moyer, & Jones, 2004; Johnson, 1993). Participation should be voluntary, with parent notification occurring, and flexibility in class schedule is needed so that the intervention can last up to 2 hours, if needed. Table 9.8 summarizes the group/classroom-based crisis intervention (CCI) process, but the readers are referred to Brock et al. (2009) and Brock (2006) for further discussion.

Group crisis intervention can be used with a typical size classroom of up to approximately 30 students or as a selected small group of students who have had similar experience or similar level of trauma (see indications and contraindications above). In the authors' experience, if the event is highly emotionally charged, no more than six to eight participants

Table 9.8   Group and Classroom-Based Crisis Intervention Process (CCI)

1. *Introduction to the session*—Purpose, process, and steps of the session are outlined; facilitators are introduced; group rules and confidentiality limits are reviewed or established.

2. *Provide facts and dispel rumors*—Students will gain cognitive mastery over the event through dispelling rumors due to facts being provided and having the opportunity to ask questions. Don't provide unnecessary detail.

3. *Sharing of stories*—Students will share their crisis experiences and the facilitator identifies commonalities so the experiences can be normalized. Not all students have to talk so don't force.

4. *Sharing of reactions*—Facilitators ask about what reactions the student had to the event. Do not ask about their *feelings* but instead ask about reactions to the event (for which feelings will emerge). Ask, "What are the reactions you are experiencing right now as a result of this event?" For example, a typical response is often "fear" or "sadness," for which you can then assess anxiety and potential depressive symptomatology. Commonalities are identified while direct instruction of common reactions is conducted. Emotional release can take place so be prepared to deal with intense emotion. However, if a student's reaction begins to hinder group process, then the co-facilitator will remove the student from the group process and possibly take them to another location to begin the individual psychological first-aid process, thus the critical importance of two facilitators for this process. Student self-referral procedures also need to be highlighted in case students need to seek additional support once CCI process is completed.

5. *Empowerment*—Identify coping strategies and/or take action; identification and instruction of healthy stress management techniques is key.

6. *Closing*—Identify next steps and begin to prepare for the memorial (if appropriate). If appropriate, conduct an activity to express condolences (i.e., writing cards for the family). Before the session concludes, remind students they are experiencing common reactions to abnormal situations and that although grieving can take time, it can get better if they use support systems and strategies they just identified.

Sources: Brock, S. E., Nickerson, A. B., Reeves, M. A., Jimerson, S. R., Lieberman, R. A., & Feinberg, T. A. (2009). *School crisis prevention and intervention. The PREPaRE model.* Bethesda, MD: National Association of School Psychologists; and Brock, S. E. (2006). *PREPaRE workshop #2: Crisis intervention and recovery. The roles of school-based mental health professionals.* Bethesda, MD: National Association of School Psychologists.

are recommended. For example, one of the authors used the CCI crisis intervention process with a small group of six close friends in which their 6th grade friend died of an accidental gunshot wound over the weekend. These friends were a close group and all had been exposed to the event over the weekend by way of the victim's parents and family sharing the story when these peers were at the victim's house after the event, and were engaged in constant discussion of the event since it had occurred. They came to school Monday morning and needed a structure within which they could continue to share their stories and experiences, process the event, and receive support; however, due to their emotional and physical proximity to the event that was closer than other peers and classmates, it was most appropriate to conduct the CCI process with this small group of students. Classroom meetings were conducted with 7th and 8th grade classes (due to story being on local news), and the student psychoeducation group was facilitated with the other 6th grade classes. Table 9.9 provides an overview of the various types and levels of school crisis interventions that have just been described.

Research Regarding Group Crisis Interventions

There have been criticisms of group psychological crisis interventions or group psychological first-aid interventions, specifically that these interventions unnecessarily reexpose children to details of the event (Berkowitz, 2003). Even so, others have presented growing evidence of the effectiveness of group-based therapeutic approaches (Saltzman et al., 2001). Although the limited data do not indicate these interventions necessarily prevent psychological distress or PTSD, they may reduce trauma-related symptomatology (Stallard & Salter, 2003) as long as the group is homogenous in regards to trauma exposure and group members do not have physical injuries as a result of the event (Brock, 2006a). For instance, close friends traveling together in a car who all witnessed a car accident where a student was killed would constitute a homogenous group with no physical injuries. Group interventions in general have been found to have the following benefits: catharsis, ventilation and validation of feelings, universality (one's reactions were shared by others), increased sense of belonging and group cohesion, learning about self from others, decreasing isolation, fostering symptom management, and guidance regarding constructive behavior and symptom management (Berzon, Pious, & Parson, 1963; Everly et al., 2006; Ulman, 2004; Yalom, 1970).

Listen, Protect, Connect—Model and Teach

In addition to the various types of crisis interventions described above, the U.S. Department of Homeland Security, with guidance from experts in school crisis intervention and response, have also developed a model for school-based psychological

Table 9.9 Types and Levels of School Psychological Crisis Interventions

Type of Intervention	Purpose/Goal	Facilitator(s)	Time Needed	Group Size
• Classroom meeting	• Share facts • Answer questions	Teacher	5–10 min.	Typical class size
• Student psychoeducation group	• Share facts • Answer questions • Discuss coping skills and strategies	Teacher Crisis Team member Mental health professional Administrator	30–45 min.	Typical class size or smaller impacted group
• Caregiver psychoeducation group	• Share facts • Answer questions • Discuss how parents and caregivers can help their child/student cope • Discuss how parents and caregivers can help themselves	Teacher Crisis Team member Mental health professional Administrator	45–60 min.	Could be held in an auditorium
• Individual crisis intervention (ICI)	• Share facts • Answer questions • Share stories and reactions • Identify and prioritize most immediate concern(s) • Address the crisis problem and identify coping strategies	Mental health professional Crisis Team member Teacher Administrator	30–60 min.	1:1
• Group or classroom-based crisis intervention (CCI)	• Share facts • Answer questions • Share stories and reactions • Discuss how students can help themselves and each other	Primary facilitator: mental health professional Co-facilitator: Crisis Team member, mental health professional, or teacher	1–2 hours depending on age level	Typical class size or smaller impacted group *Homogenous group in regards to impact

Table 9.10   An Overview of the Listen, Protect, and Connect Model of Crisis Intervention

---

Step 1: Listen—Students are provided opportunity to share experiences and express feelings or concerns about safety. The teacher acknowledges what has happened and allows students to share experiences in a safe environment while listening to what they say and observing how they act, noting changes in behavior/mood, school performance, interactions, involvement, and/or behaviors reported by parents. Teachers typically ask the following questions, "Where were you when this crisis happened? What do you remember about this day?" Self-expression is encouraged, and the teacher shows interest and empathy in a nonjudgmental manner while also encouraging students to stay at school rather than be at home. The goal is for students to feel that school is a safe place where adults care and listen.

Step 2: Protect—This step is to reestablish feelings of physical and emotional safety for students. Emphasis is on ensuring physical and psychological safety and in maintaining structure, stability, and predictability by reestablishing routines, expectations, and rules. Facts are shared with students in a developmentally appropriate manner to eliminate confusion while students are monitored for negative or trauma-related behaviors. Questions at this stage are, "What is the most difficult thing to deal with right now? Are you worried about how you are reacting? Are you worried about your safety? Around other students? Around adults at school or outside of school?" Teachers let students know they are not alone in reactions to the event and provide opportunities for expression (talk, draw, play).

Step 3: Connect—This stage is to help students reestablish normal social relationships and stay connected to others for social support. Classrooms begin restoring normalcy and school staff help identify other "systems of care" that can help support students. Teachers check in with students and encourage students to interact, share activities, and be involved in team projects. Sample questions to be asked at this stage are "What can I do to help you right now? What can your teachers do to help? What can your friends do to help? What can your family do to help?" Encouragement of sharing concerns with school staff and building on student strengths is also emphasized.

Step 4: Model Calm and Optimistic Behavior—This is also based on the premise that students watch adult reactions and receive cues on how to respond to and confront adversity. Adults can acknowledge distress but demonstrate a positive and optimistic approach by maintaining level emotions and reactions, taking constructive actions to assure safety, expressing positive thoughts for the future, and help students cope while challenging them to think aloud about ways to solve their problems.

Step 5: Teach—This stage helps students understand the range of normal stress reactions and that school-based psychologists, counselors, or social workers can help to facilitate these discussions. School personnel serve as a resource for helping students help themselves and each other through activities to help cope and foster understanding of cultural differences. Specific ways of coping can also be taught that includes relaxation techniques and different ways to express feelings and experiences.

Sources: Schreiber, M., Gurwitch, R. & Wong, M. (2006). *Listen, Protect, and Connect: Model and teach*. Retrieved February 15, 2009, from http://www.ready.gov/kids/_downloads/PFA_SchoolCrisis.pdf; and U. S. Department of Education, Readiness and Emergency Management for Schools. (2008). [Electronic version.] *Helpful hints for school emergency management: Psychological first aid (PFA) for students and teachers: Listen, Protect, Connect—Model and teach.* http://www.ready.gov/kids/_downloads/PFA_SchoolCrisis.pdf.

first aid titled *Listen, Protect, Connect—Model and Teach* (Schreiber et al., 2006; U. S. Department of Education, REMS, 2008b). This model was designed for teachers to help in the psychological first-aid process and can be conducted with an individual or in small formal or informal groups, facilitated by teachers. This five-step program (see Table 9.10) was developed for educators to provide guidance on how to speak to students who have experienced a crisis or disaster in order to help reduce distress and facilitate a return to learning. It can be used as a psychoeducation intervention, as it provides information to teachers about how best to respond to children. There is also a built-in triage component to help identify risk factors and activate a referral to school or other mental health professional, if necessary.

It is important to remember that while teachers are critical in the psychological first aid process, they need guidance and training in how to do this, will need the support of the trained crisis team and school mental health team members, and if the teachers were impacted themselves by the crisis, they may not be in a position to help students. Psychological first aid may also need to occur for the school staff. In addition, it is important to remember the various variables discussed at the beginning of this chapter, and the impact on the school staff will need to be considered when determining which levels of crisis interventions are most appropriate. This speaks to the critical importance of having a well-developed preparedness and crisis response plan to have staff trained and able to delivery a continuum of crisis recovery interventions.

PSYCHOTHERAPEUTIC INTERVENTIONS

The most intensive level of intervention services (Tier 3—Intensive) may be needed for students who are demonstrating severe reactions that are impacting daily functioning (NIMH, 2008b). Many of these students may be exhibiting signs consistent with the diagnosis of acute or posttraumatic stress disorder (PTSD). If this is the case, psychotherapeutic interventions delivered by a mental health professional that has specialized training should be sought, especially if the child is not able to return to normal routines within approximately a month of the event or if new symptoms are developing instead of decreasing over time (NIMH, 2008b). These services may be offered in the school setting or the student may receive these services through a local community mental health center or private practice therapist. Schools are typically not expected to provide this type of intensive support, but recent models have been developed that show promise when implemented in a school setting.

Research currently supports cognitive behavioral interventions to be one of the most effective and supported treatments for students with PTSD symptomatology (American Academy of Child and Adolescent Psychiatry, 1998; Feeny, Foa, Treadwell, & March, 2004; Salloum & Overstreet, 2008). A study conducted by Stein, Jaycox, Kataoka, Wong, Tu, Elliott, & Fink (2003) analyzed a group cognitive-behavior therapy approach delivered in a school setting by school personnel. The intervention included psychoeducation, relaxation training, imaginal and in vivo exposure, strategies to combat negative thoughts, and problem-solving training. The 10-session intervention was found to lead to fewer PTSD and depression symptoms and fewer parent reports of psychosocial dysfunction. Another school-based intervention, CBITS (Cognitive Behavioral Intervention for Trauma in the Schools), was collaboratively developed by the Los Angeles Unified School District, UCLA, and the RAND Corporation. The CBITS is a structured group cognitive-therapy approach that was designed for implementation in the school setting for students exposed to trauma in order to relieve symptoms of PTSD, depression, and anxiety. It is not an immediate crisis intervention, but is designed to be implemented no sooner than 4 weeks after the event. Children learn relaxation strategies and social problem solving skills while challenging upsetting thoughts and processing the traumatic memories. It is primarily used with children ages 10–15, but also has been used with children as young as 8 years old. Preliminary research has demonstrated effectiveness in decreasing PTSD and depression symptoms while increasing functioning, and it has been listed as a proven program through the Promising Practices Network (National Child Traumatic Stress Network, n.d.[a]; Promising Practices Network [PPN], 2005; Stein et al., 2003).

Further replication of these results and types of interventions are needed to further support the effectiveness of school-based cognitive-behavioral interventions for trauma, but the emerging data are promising in that school-based cognitive-behavioral interventions can lower the signs and symptoms associated with trauma exposure, which in turn can help students be more available for learning.

CARE FOR THE CAREGIVERS

Providing crisis recovery interventions on a multi-tiered continuum can be both physically and emotionally exhausting for the caregivers, which include school staff and parents. Therefore, this component of a school's comprehensive safe schools plan and crisis plan is critical for ensuring that school staff have their own needs met so they in turn can help meet student needs. Care for the caregiver involves ensuring the crisis responders and staff themselves are being taken care of and are not experiencing negative effects from crisis response involvement. Table 9.11 lists common stress reactions and extreme stress reactions that can be seen in crisis responders and may signal additional support is needed.

Administrators are encouraged to support establishment of a culture in which it is okay for adults to ask for help or to

Table 9.11 Stress Reactions in Crisis Responders

Common Stress Reactions

- Increase or decrease in physical and social activity levels
- Substance use/abuse
- Difficulties sleeping
- Numbing, anger, irritability, frustration
- Vicarious traumatization in form of shock, fear, helplessness, horror
- Confusion, difficulties concentrating or making decisions
- Depressive or anxiety symptoms

Extreme Stress Reactions

- Compassion stress: helplessness, confusion, isolation
- Compassion fatigue: demoralization, resignation, alienation
- Reexperiencing trauma
- Withdrawal and isolations
- Attempts to be overly controlling
- Over reliance on substances (alcohol or drugs)
- Drastic changes in sleep (avoidance of sleep or not wanting to get out of bed)
- Depression and hopelessness
- Risk-taking behaviors

Sources: Brock, S. E., Nickerson, A. B., Reeves, M. A., Jimerson, S. R., Lieberman, R. A., & Feinberg, T. A. (2009). *School crisis prevention and intervention. The PREPaRE model.* Bethesda, MD: National Association of School Psychologists; Brock (2006a); and Brymer, M., Jacobs, A., Layne, C., Pynoos, R., Ruzek, J., Steinberg, A., Vernberg, E., & Watson, P. (2006, July). *Psychological first aid: Field operations guide,* 2nd Edition [Electronic version]. National Child Traumatic Stress Network and National Center for PTSD. www.ncptsd.va.gov.

ask for a break. In no way should this reflect a person cannot do their job. Quite the contrary, a responsible crisis responder and staff member knows his/her limits and is willing to seek help or support from others. There are many important ways schools can facilitate caring for the caregiver including ensuring there are enough responders and support staff to implement the needed interventions; limiting a work shift to 12 hours and then providing a break; providing a substitute teacher (if necessary); rotating crisis team members in regards to more intense versus less intense exposure or developing a yearly rotation schedule; providing additional professionals to help cover responders' day-to-day duties while they are responding; encouraging mentoring, staff development, and opportunities to seek professional help (if needed); encouraging and allowing staff time to access their own coping resources such as family, exercise, religious faith, and hobbies; and providing food to ensure they are maintaining a healthy diet during response (Brock, 2006a; Brock et al., 2009; Brymer et al., 2006; Figley, 2002; Schreiber et al., 2006).

GUIDELINES FOR DEALING WITH A DEATH AND MEMORIALS

Lastly, a large component of effective crisis recovery intervention is helping students understand death. A child's understanding of death is mostly determined by their age and cognitive development. As outlined by Poland and McCormick (1999), children under the age of 5 or 6 typically do not understand the permanence of death and have difficulty differentiating between a long-term absence and death. They may also exhibit magical thinking in that they can bring the person back. They are also very literal so if it is said that someone died in their sleep, the child may be afraid to go to sleep. Around 6 or 7 years old, children begin to understand that death has permanence but think it only happens to the elderly. Around 8–11 years old, children begin to see death as a natural part of life and that it could happen to them. Their cognitive developmental level allows them to see the permanence and they begin asking many questions about the science behind death. As they transition into adolescence, they typically understand the finality of death (around age 13), but yet due to exposure to media and video game characters, the understanding of permanence may not always be grounded in fact (Levine, 1998; Poland & McCormick, 1999). The CD contains a folder titled "Helping Handouts," which contains various handouts for helping students cope from preschool though adolescence, including special needs children.

The National Child Traumatic Stress Network publication by Brymer et al. (2006) has in-depth information on the do's and don'ts of handling a variety of death situations, and Poland and McCormick (1999) describe more in-depth guidelines around memorials. In the planning and preparedness stage, the school crisis team should discuss and outline the district and school parameters surrounding memorials. For example, in a suicide or death by high-risk behavior (e.g., drug overdose, driving drunk) there should be no memorial at school (Poland & McCormick, 1999; NASP, 2002a) due to possible contagion effects. This should be explicitly stated in the school crisis plan. Students see the attention the deceased is receiving in death and may want to receive the same sort of attention, leading to contagion risk (as discussed in Chapter 8).

When determining the appropriateness of a memorial, consider the cause of death and historically what the school has done. Remember, if the school holds a large memorial for one student because he/she was popular but does not for another student, this may lead to contention and the assumption of discrimination. General guidelines suggest that a "consumable" gesture (i.e., scholarship or donation) is preferred over a permanent memorial, such as a plaque or tree, to prevent the school from assuming the appearance of a shrine or cemetery (Poland & McCormick, 1999). Also, for example, if a living tree is planted and then dies, this can be traumatic for some survivors. Encouragement should be for positive actions that can lead to positive outcomes (i.e., in a natural disaster, collecting food and clothing; in a suicide, collecting funds for a suicide prevention program; with death following a long-term illness, making donations to the local cancer society or volunteering on the cancer floor of the children's hospital).

In regards to funerals or memorial services, schools are discouraged from providing busing to a memorial unless there are plenty of adults who can also attend to monitor the behavior and reactions of students. It is strongly encouraged that parents attend memorial services with their children and parents determine if their child should or should not attend. The school should also assign someone to talk with the family to ensure their wishes and belief systems are being honored and also have staff present at the service in case students show up without parent support. The CD also contains a folder labeled "Memorials," which contains handouts regarding appropriate use of and guidelines around memorials.

CONCLUSION

In conclusion, it is critical that planning for appropriate crisis interventions and recovery efforts be an integral part of the multi-phase, multi-hazards, multi-agency, multi-tiered (M-PHAT) approach to establishing a comprehensive safe learning environment. As stated earlier, crisis recovery interventions are actually prevention efforts for future negative events, as they can build additional coping skills and resiliency variables to protect students from the emotional impact of any future event. In addition, they help to restore the safe and positive learning environment so teachers can teach and students can learn.

Concluding Comments

Comprehensive planning for a safe learning environment takes leadership, commitment, direction, and planning. Working to ensure the physical and psychological safety of students is a vitally important task that can also positively impact academic achievement and success. It may be said that establishing and maintaining a safe learning environment "is a marathon, not a sprint"; but it remains one of the most valuable efforts that schools undertake in today's world, as it provides for the basic safety, security, and well-being of students and staff. It is important to realize that schools can often build upon those effective initiatives and interventions they already have in place, while also identifying short- and long-term goals to establish those components that are still needed. It is also important to seek engagement of positive leaders within your building, district, and community, as successful efforts are dependent on a team of committed individuals. At the same time, the relationships among and between students, staff, parents, and community stakeholders are essential as these positive relationships are your best form of prevention. Effective prevention and preparedness activities and good response and recovery plans and procedures are interconnected. They also serve as proactive efforts on the part of the school, and work together to mitigate any negative impact and potential future implications of crisis events that may occur.

We hope this book provides you with a framework for viewing efforts to create a safe learning environment through a comprehensive multi-phase, multi-hazard, multi-agency, and multi-tiered approach. We also hope it serves as a valuable tool to all of you who are involved in one of the most important jobs our society has to offer: ensuring the safety, security, and success of the youth of today.

Web Site Resources

U.S. DEPARTMENT OF EDUCATION RESOURCES

- Emergency Planning – Office of Safe and Drug Free Schools
  - http://www.ed.gov/admins/lead/safety/emergency-plan/index.html

- Readiness and Emergency Management for Schools (REMS) Technical Assistance Center — http://rems.ed.gov/
  - Publications — http://rems.ed.gov/index.cfm?event=publications
  - REMS Express Newsletters — http://rems.ed.gov/index.cfm?event=express
  - REMS Helpful Hints — http://rems.ed.gov/index.cfm?event=hints
  - Lessons Learned — http://rems.ed.gov/index.cfm?event=lessons

- United States Department of Homeland Security – School Preparedness
  - http://www.dhs.gov/xprevprot/programs/gc_1183486267373.shtm

NATIONAL INCIDENT MANAGEMENT SYSTEM WEB SITES

- National Integration Center (NIC) Incident Management Systems Integration Division
  - http://www.fema.gov/emergency/nims/index.shtm

- NIMS On-Line Training Courses
  - http://www.fema.gov/emergency/nims/nims_training.shtm#3

- NIMS Implementation Activities for schools and Higher Education Institutions
  - http://rems.ed.gov/index.cfm?event=NIMS

- Resources Supporting Schools' and Higher Education Institutions' (HEIs) Implementation of NIMS
  - http://rems.ed.gov/index.cfm?event=NIMS_resources

FEDERAL AGENCY WEB SITES

- Department of Health & Human Services
  - http://www.hhs.gov/

- Department of Justice
  - http://www.usdoj.gov/

- Federal Emergency Management Agency (FEMA)
  - http://fema.gov/

- National Institute of Mental Health
  - http://www.nimh.nih.gov/

- Substance Abuse and Mental Health Services Administration (SAMHSA)
  - http://www.samhsa.gov/

RESOURCE AND PROFESSIONAL ORGANIZATION WEB SITES

- American Association of School Administrators
  - http://www.aasa.org/

- American Psychiatric Association
  - http://www.psych.org/

- American Psychological Association
  - http://www.apa.org/

- American School Counselor Association
  - http://www.schoolcounselor.org/

- American Red Cross
  - http://www.redcross.org/

- International Critical Incident Stress Foundation
  - http://www.icisf.org/

- National Association of Elementary School Principles
  - http://www.naesp.org/

- National Association of School Psychologists
  - http://www.nasponline.org/

- National Association of Secondary School Principals
  - http://www.nassp.org/s_nassp/index.asp?CID =1138&DID=54609

- National Association of Social Workers
  - http://www.naswdc.org/

- National Association of State Directors of Special Education
  - http://www.nasdse.org/

- National Center for Post-Traumatic Stress Disorder
  - http://www.ncptsd.va.gov/ncmain/index.jsp

- National Organization for Victim's Assistance
  - http://www.trynova.org/

- National School Boards Association
  - http://www.nsba.org/

- National Voluntary Organizations Active in Disaster (NVOAD)
  - http://www.nvoad.org/

References

Aber, J. L., Brown, J. L., & Jones, S. M. (2003). Developmental trajectories toward violence in middle childhood: Course, demographic differences, and response to school-based intervention. *Developmental Psychology, 39*, 324–348.

Adamson, A. D., & Peacock, G. G. (2007). Crisis response in the public schools: A survey of school psychologists' experiences and perceptions. *Psychology in the Schools, 44*, 749–764.

Airaksinen, E., Larsson, M., & Forsell, Y. (2005). Neuropsychological functions in anxiety disorders in population-based samples: Evidence of episodic memory dysfunction. *Journal of Psychiatric Research, 39*(2), 207–214.

Alderman, T. A. (1997). *The scarred soul: Understanding and ending self-inflicted violence.* Oakland, CA: New Harbinger Publications.

American Academy of Child and Adolescent Psychiatry (1998). Practice parameters for the assessment and treatment of children and adolescents with posttraumatic stress disorder. *Journal of the American Academy of Child and Adolescent Psychiatry, 37*, 4–26.

American Psychiatric Association (APA). (2000). *Diagnostic and statistical manual of mental disorders (DSM-V-TR).* Washington, DC: American Psychological Association.

American Psychological Association Zero Tolerance Task Force. (2008, December). Are zero tolerance policies effective in the schools? *American Psychologist, 63*(9), 852–862.

Armstrong, K. H., Massey, O. T., & Boroughs, M. (2006). Implementing comprehensive safe school plans in Pinellas County Schools, Florida: Planning, implementation, operation, sustainability, and lessons learned. In S. R. Jimerson & M. Furlong (Eds.), *Handbook of school violence and school safety: From research to practice* (pp. 525–536). Mahwah, NJ: Lawrence Erlbaum.

Arnold, M. E., & Huges, J. N. (1999). First do no harm: Adverse effects of grouping deviant youth for training. *Journal of School Psychology, 37*, 99–115.

Arthur, M. W., Hawkins, J. D., Pollard, J. A., Catalano, R.F., & Baglioni, A. J. (2002). Measuring risk and protective factors for substance use, delinquency, and other adolescent behavior problems: The Communities That Care Youth Survey. *Evaluation Review, 26,* 575–601.

Aseltine. R. H., & DeMartino, R. (2004). An outcome evaluation of the SOS suicide prevention. *American Journal of Public Health, 94,* 446–451. Retrieved February 7, 2009, from http://www.mentalhealthscreening.org/downloads/sites/docs/sos/AJPHarticle.pdf.

Bailey, K. A. (2002). *Guide 2: School policies and legal issues supporting safe schools.* Guides to Creating Safer Schools. Portland, OR: Northwest Regional Educational Laboratory.

Bailey, K. A. (2006). Legal knowledge related to school violence and school safety. In S. R. Jimerson & M. Furlong (Eds.), *Handbook of school violence and school safety: From research to practice* (pp. 31–49). Mahwah, NJ: Lawrence Erlbaum.

Bailey, L. (2008). Bullying (verb). *State Legislatures: The National Magazine of Policy and politics.* Retrieved January 5, 2009, from http://www.ncsl.org/magazine/articles/2008/08sloctnov08_bullying.htm.

Batsche, G. M., & Knoff, H. M. (1994). Bullies and their victims: Understanding a pervasive problem in the schools. *School Psychology Review, 23*(2), 165–174.

Benson, P. L., Scales, P. C., Hamilton, S. F., Sesma, A., Hong, K. L., & Roehlkepartain, E. C. (2006). Positive youth development so far: Core hypotheses and their implications for policy and practice. *Insights & Evidence, 3*(1), 1–13.

Benson, P. L., Scales, P. C., Leffert, N., & Roehlkepartain, E. C. (1999). *A fragile foundation: The state of developmental assets among American Youth.* Minneapolis, MN: Search Institute.

Beran, T. N., & Tutty, L. (2002). *An evaluation of the Dare to Care Bully-Proofing Your School program.* Unpublished. Calgary, Alberta. RESOLVE Alberta.

Berkowitz, S. J. (2003). Children exposed to community violence: The rationale for early intervention. *Clinical Child and Family Psychology Review, 6,* 293–302.

Berzon, B., Pious, C., & Parson, R. (1963). The therapeutic event in group psychotherapy: A study of subjective reports of group members. *Journal of Individual Psychology, 19,* 204–212.

Björkqvist, K., Österman, K., & Kaukiainen, A. (2000). Social intelligence—Empathy=aggression? *Aggression and Violent Behavior, 5,* 191–200.

Blasé, K. A., & Fixsen, D. L. (2006, March). *Fidelity—Why it matters and what research tells us.* Presentation at the Blueprints Conference, Denver, Colorado.

Bokszczanin, A. (2008). Parental support, family conflict, and overprotectiveness: Predicting PTSD symptom levels of adolescents 28 months after a natural disaster. *Anxiety Stress Coping, 21*(4), 325–335.

Brock, S. E. (2002a). Crisis theory: A foundation for the comprehensive school crisis response team. In S. E. Brock, P. J. Lazarus, & S. R. Jimerson (Eds.), *Best practices in school crisis prevention and intervention* (pp. 5–17). Bethesda, MD: National Association of School Psychologists.

Brock, S. E. (2002b). Estimating the appropriate crisis response. In S. E. Brock, P. J. Lazarus, & S. R. Jimerson (Eds.), *Best practices in school crisis prevention and intervention* (pp. 355–365). Bethesda, MD: National Association of School Psychologists.

Brock, S. E. (2002c). Identifying individuals at risk for psychological trauma. In S. E. Brock, P. J. Lazarus, & S. R. Jimerson (Eds.), *Best practices in school crisis prevention and intervention* (pp. 367–383). Bethesda, MD: National Association of School Psychologists.

Brock, S. E. (2002d). School suicide postvention. In S. E. Brock, P. J. Lazarus, & S. R. Jimerson (Eds.), *Best practices in school crisis prevention and intervention* (pp. 553–575). Bethesda, MD: National Association of School Psychologists.

Brock, S. E. (2006a). *PREPaRE workshop #2. Crisis intervention and recovery: The roles of school-based mental health professionals.* Bethesda, MD: National Association of School Psychologists.

Brock, S. E. (2006b). *Trainer's handbook workshop #2. Crisis intervention and recovery: The roles of school-based mental health professionals.* Bethesda, MD: National Association of School Psychologists.

Brock, S. E., Jimerson, S. R., & Hart, S. R. (2006). Preventing, preparing for, and responding to school violence with the national incident management system. In S. R. Jimerson & M. Furlong (Eds.), *Handbook of school violence and school safety: From research to practice* (pp. 443–458). Mahwah: NJ: Lawrence Erlbaum.

Brock, S. E., Nickerson, A. B., Reeves, M. A., & Jimerson, S. R. (2008). Best practices for school psychologists as members of crisis teams: The PREPaRE model. In A. Thomas & J. Grimes (Eds.), *Best practices in school psychology V* (pp. 1487–1504). Bethesda, MD: National Association of School Psychologists.

Brock, S. E., Nickerson A. B., Reeves, M. A., Jimerson, S. R., Lieberman, R. A., & Feinberg, T. A. (2009). *School crisis prevention and intervention: The PREPaRE model.* Bethesda, MD: National Association of School Psychologists.

Brock, S. E., Sandoval, J., & Hart, S. (2006). Suicidal ideation and behaviors. In G. G. Bear & K. M. Minke (Eds.), *Children's needs III: Development, prevention, and intervention* (pp. 225–238). Bethesda, MD: National Association of School Psychologists.

Brock, S. E., Sandoval, J., & Lewis, S. (2001). *Preparing for crisis in the schools: A manual for building school crisis response teams* (2nd ed.). New York: Wiley.

Brown, J. L., Roderick, T., Lantieri, L., & Aber, L. (2004). The resolving conflict creatively program: A school-based social and emotional learning program. In J. E. Zins, R. R. Weissberg, M. C. Wang, & H. J. Walber (Eds.), *Building academic success on social and emotional learning: What does research say?* (pp. 151–169). New York: Teachers College Press.

Browning, C., Cohen, R., & Warman, D. M. (2003). Peer social competence and the stability of victimization. *Child Study Journal, 33*, 73–90.

Bryk, A.S., & Schneider, B. L. (2002). *Trust in schools: A core resource for improvement.* New York: Russell Sage Foundation.

Brymer, M., Jacobs, A., Layne, C., Pynoos, R., Ruzek, J., Steinberg, A., Vernberg, E., & Watson, P. (2006, July). *Psychological first aid: Field operations guide* (2nd ed.). [Electronic version]. National Child Traumatic Stress Network and National Center for PTSD. www.ncptsd.va.gov.

Buckley, M. A., Storino, M., & Sebastiani, A. M. (2003). *The impact of school climate: Variation by ethnicity and gender.* Poster presented at the annual meeting of the American Psychological Association, Toronto, Canada.

Burns, M. K., & Gibbons, K. A. (2008). *Implementing Response-to-Intervention in elementary and secondary schools: Procedures to assure scientific-based practices.* New York: Routledge.

California Governor's Office of Emergency Services. (1998, June). *School emergency response: Using SEMS at districts and sites. Guidelines for planning and training in compliance with the standardized emergency management system.* Sacramento, CA: Author.

Caffo, E., & Belaise, C. (2003). Psychological aspects of traumatic injury in children and adolescents. *Child & Adolescent Psychiatric Clinics of North America, 12,* 493–535.

Carlson, E. B. (1997). *Trauma assessments: A clinician's guide.* New York: Guilford Press.

Carnegie Council Task Force, Carnegie Council on Adolescent Development. (1989). *Turning points: Preparing American youth for the 21st century.* New York: Carnegie Corporation.

Catalano, R. F., Berglund, M. L., Ryan, J. A. M., Lonczak, H. S., & Hawkins, D. (2002). *Positive youth development in the United States: Research findings on evaluations of positive youth development programs. Prevention & Treatment, 5, Article 15.* Retrieved from http://psycnet.apa.org/journals/pre/5/1/15a.pdf.

Catalano, R. F., Mazza, J. J., Harachi, T. W., Abbott, R. D., Haggerty, K. P., & Fleming, C.B. (2003). Raising healthy children through enhancing social development in elementary school: Results after 1.5 years. Journal of School Psychology, 41, 143–164.

Center for Mental Health in Schools. (2006). Systemic change and empirically supported practices: The implementation problem. Retrieved April 27, 2009, from p://smhp.psych.ucla.edu/pdfdocs/Empirically-supported.pdf.

Center for Mental Health in Schools. (2008a). *Mental health in schools and school improvement: Current status, concerns, and new directions.* Los Angeles, CA: Author.

Center for Mental Health in Schools. (2008b). *Moving toward a comprehensive system of learning supports. The next revolutionary stage in school improvement policy and practice.* Los Angeles, CA: Author.

Center for Mental Health in Schools. (2008c). *A technical assistance sampler on protective factors (resiliency).* Los Angeles, CA: Author. http://smhp.psych.ucla.edu/.

Center for the Study and Prevention of Violence. (n.d.). *Blueprints for violence prevention: Functional family therapy.* Retrieved February 13, 2009, from http://www.colorado.edu/cspv/blueprints/modelprograms/FFT.html.

Centers for Disease Control and Prevention (CDC). (1990). *Youth Risk Behavior Survey.* Retrieved September 2008 from www.cdc.gov/yrbs.

Centers for Disease Control and Prevention (CDC). (2004). Methodology of the Youth Risk Behavior Surveillance System. *Morbidity and Mortality Weekly Report, 53*(RR-12), 1–14.

Centers for Disease Control and Prevention (CDC). (2008a). *Healthy youth! Coordinated school health program (CSHP).* Retrieved on January 9, 2009, from http://www.cdc.gov/HealthyYouth/CSHP/.

Centers for Disease Control and Prevention (CDC). (2008b). *Healthy youth! Student health and academic achievement.* Retrieved on January 9, 2009, from http://www.cdc.gov/HealthyYouth/health_and_academics/pdf/alcohol_other_drug.pdf.

Centers for Disease Control and Prevention (CDC). (2008c). *Using environmental design to prevent school violence.* Retrieved October 3, 2008, from http://www.cdc.gov/ncipc/dvp/CPTED.htm.

Centers for Disease Control and Prevention (CDC). (2008d, June 6). Youth Risk Behavior Surveillance—United States, 2007. *Morbidity and Mortality Weekly Report, 57*(SS-4). Retrieved December 31, 2008, from http://www.cdc.gov/healthyyouth/yrbs/pdf/yrbss07_mmwr.pdf.

Centers for Disease Control and Prevention (CDC). (2009). *Youth violence prevention scientific information: Risk and protective factors.* Retrieved on February 9, 2009, from http://www.cdc.gov/ncipc/dvp/YVP/YVP-risk-p-factors.htm.

Cherry Creek School District. (2007). *Getting to know us.* Retrieved January 9, 2009, from http://www.ccsd.k12.co.us/documents/provider/571GTKU2008.pdf.

Cherry Creek School District. (2008). *Emergency response and crisis management guide.* Greenwood Village, CO: Author.

Christensen, L., Young, K. R., & Marchant, M. (2004). The effects of a peer-mediated positive behavior support program on socially appropriate classroom behavior. *Education and Treatment of Children, 27,* 199–234.

Coggeshall, M. B., & Kingery, P. M. (2001). Cross survey analysis of school violence and disorder. *Psychology in the Schools, 38,* 107–116.

Collaborative for Academic, Social, and Emotional Learning (CASEL). (2007a). *Benefits of SEL—SEL & academics.* Retrieved on November, 29, 2008, from http://www.casel. org/sel/academics.php.

Collaborative for Academic, Social, and Emotional Learning (CASEL). (2007b). *Benefits of SEL—SEL & prevention.* Retrieved on November, 29, 2008, from http://www.casel. org/sel/prevention.php.

Collaborative for Academic, Social, and Emotional Learning (CASEL). (2007c). *The benefits of school-based social emotional learning programs: Highlights from a forthcoming CASEL report.* Retrieved on November, 29, 2008, from http://www.casel.org/downloads/metaanalysissum.pdf.

Collaborative for Academic, Social, and Emotional Learning (CASEL) & U.S. Department of Education Office of Safe and Drug Free Schools' National Center for Mental Health Promotion and Youth Violence Prevention. (2008). The social and emotional learning (SEL) and student benefits: Research implications for the safe schools/healthy students core elements. Retrieved September 22, 2008, from http:// www.promoteprevent.org/Publications/SELbenefits.pdf.

Colorado Safe Schools Act, *C.R.S. 22-32-109.1* (2000, amended 2008).

Colorado School District Self-Insurance Pool, Colorado Association of School Boards, Colorado Department of Public Safety, Colorado Department of Education, Colorado Department of Local Affairs. (2008, September). *The National Incident Management System and Colorado School District Compliance.* Denver, CO: Authors.

Colorado Senate Bill 08-181. (2008). Statute #C.R.S. 22-32-109. Concerning measures to improve coordination among agencies when responding to school incidents. Amendment to Safe Schools Act 2000. Retrieved on December 2, 2008, from http://cdpsweb.state.co.us/docs/POSITIONPAPER_ SB181%20final.pdf.

Committee for Children. (n.d.). *Second step overview.* Retrieved August 2005 from http://www.cfchildren.org/programs/ ssp/overview/.

Commonwealth of Virginia. (2007). *Mass shootings at Virginia Tech: A report of the review panel. A summary of findings.* Retrieved on February 15, 2009, from http://www. governor.virginia.gov/TempContent/techPanelReport-docs/4%20SUMMARY%20OF%20KEY%20FINDINGS. pdf

Constenbader, V., & Markson, S. (1998). School suspension: A study with secondary school students. *Journal of School Psychology, 36,* 59–82.

Conterio, K., Lader, W., & Kingston Bloom, J. (1998). *Bodily harm: The breakthrough healing program for self-injurers.* New York: Hyperion Press.

Copeland, W. E., Keeler, G., Angold, A., & Costello, E. J. (2007). Traumatic events and posttraumatic stress in childhood. *Archives of General Psychiatry, 64,* 577–584.

Cornell, D., & Sheras, P. (2006). *Guidelines for responding to student threats of violence.* Longmont, CO: Sopris West.

Cornell, D., Sheras, P., Kaplan, S., McConville, D., Posey, J., Levy-Elkon, A., McKnight, L., Branson, C., & Cole, J. (2004). Guidelines for student threat assessment: Field test findings. *School Psychology Review, 33,* 527–546.

Cornell, D., & Williams, F. (2006). Student threat assessment as a strategy to reduce school violence. In S. R. Jimerson & M. J. Furlong (Eds.), *Handbook of school violence and school safety: From research to practice.* Englewood Cliffs, NJ: Earlbaum.

Coyle, J. P. (2005). Preventing and reducing violence by at-risk adolescents: Common elements of empirically researched programs. *Journal of Evidence-Based Social Work, 2,* 125–139.

Craig, W. M., & Pepler, D. J. (1997). Observations of bullying and victimization in the schoolyard. *Canadian Journal of School Psychology, 13(2),* 41–60.

Crawford, D., & Bodine, R. (1996). *Conflict resolution education: A guide to implementing programs in schools, youth-serving organizations, and community and juvenile justice settings.* Program Report OJJDP—US DOE. Retrieved December 2008 from http://www.ncjrs.gov/pdf-files/conflic.pdf.

D'Andrea, M. (2004). Comprehensive school-based violence prevention training: A developmental ecological training model. *Journal of Counseling & Development, 82,* 277–286.

Davis, J. M., & Brock, S. E. (2002). *Suicide.* In J. Sandoval (Ed.), *Handbook of crisis counseling, intervention, and prevention in the schools* (2nd ed., pp. 273–300). Mahwah, NJ: Erlbaum.

DeMary, J. L., Owens, M., & Ramnarain, A. K. V. (2000). *School safety audit protocol*. Virginia Department of Education. Retrieved October 2008 from http://www.doe.virginia.gov/VDOE/Instruction/schoolsafety/safetyaudit.pdf.

Devilly, G. J., Varker, T., Hansen, K., & Gist, R. (2007). An analogue study of the effects of psychological debriefing on eyewitness memory. *Behavior Research and Therapy, 45,* 1245–1254.

DeVoe, J. F., Peter, K., Kaufman, P., Miller, A., Noonon, M., Snyder, T. D., & Baum, K. (2004). *Indicators of school crime and safety: 2004* (U.S. Departments of Education and Justice, NCES 2005-002/NJC205290). Washington, DC: Government Printing Office.

Dinkes, R., Cataldi, E. F., & Lin-Kelly, W. (2007). *Indicators of school crime and safety: 2007* (NCES 2008-021/NCJ 219553). National Center for Education Statistics, Institute of Education Sciences, U.S. Department of Education, and Bureau of Justice. Statistics, Office of Justice Programs, U.S. Department of Justice. Washington, DC. http://nces.ed.gov/programs/crimeindicators/crimeindicators2007/.

Dunkle, M. C., & Nash, M. A. (1991). *Beyond the health room*. Washington, DC: Council of Chief State School Officers, Resource Center on Educational Equity.

Dupper, D. R., & Meyer-Adams, N. (2002). Low-level violence. *Urban Education, 37,* 350–364.

Dusenbury, L., Falco, M., Lake, A., Brannigan, R., & Bosworth, K. (1997). Nine critical elements of promising violence prevention programs. *The Journal of School Health, 67,* 409–414.

Dwyer, K., Osher, D., & Warger, C. (1998). *Early warning, timely response: A guide to safe schools*. Washington, DC: U.S. Department of Education.

Dwyer, K. P., & Jimerson, S. R. (2002). Enabling prevention through planning. In S. E. Brock, P. L. Lazarus, & S. R. Jimerson (Eds.), *Best practices in school crisis prevention and intervention* (pp. 23–46). Bethesda, MD: National Association of School Psychologists.

Elias, M. J., Zins, J. E., Graczyk, P. A., & Weissberg, R. P. (2003). Implementation, sustainability, and scaling up of social emotional and academic innovations in public schools. *School Psychology Review, 32,* 303–319.

Elliott, D. S. (2006, March). *Improving the effectiveness of delinquency, drug and violence prevention efforts: Promise and practice.* Presentation at the Blueprints Conference, Denver, Colorado.

Elliott, D. S. (2008, March). *The future of violence prevention research and practice.* Keynote address presented at the 2008 Blueprints Conference, Denver, Colorado.

Elliott, D. S., Grady, J. M., Shaw, T. E., Aultman-Bettridge, T., & Beaulieu, M. T. (2000). *Safe communities-safe schools planning guide: A tool for community violence prevention.* Boulder, CO: Institute of Behavioral Science, University of Colorado. Retrieved October 2008 from http://www.colorado.edu/cspv/publications/safeschools/SCSS-001.pdf.

Elliott, S. N., Kratochwill, T. R., & Roach, A. T. (2003). Commentary: Implementing social-emotional and academic innovations: Reflections, reactions, and research. *School Psychology Review, 32*, 320–326.

Elliott, S. N., Roach, A. T., & Beddow, P. A. (2008). Best practices in preschool social skills training. In A. Thomas & J. Grimes (Eds.), *Best practices in school psychology V* (pp. 1531–1546). Bethesda, MD: National Association of School Psychologists.

Epstein, L., Plog, A. E., & Porter, W. (2002). Bully-proofing your school: Results of a four-year intervention. *The Report on Emotional and Behavioral Disorders in Youth, 2*(3), 55–56, 73–77.

Everly, G. S., Phillips, S. B., Kane, D., & Feldman, D. (2006). Introduction to and overview of group psychological first aid. *Brief Treatment and Crisis Intervention, 6*(2), 130–136.

Family Education Rights and Privacy Act of 1974 (FERPA). 20 U.S.C. 1 1232g; 34 CFR Part 99.

Federal Emergency Management Agency (FEMA). (2004a). *Developing and promoting mitigation best practices and case studies.* Retrieved November 2008 from http://www.fema.gov/library/viewRecord.do?id=1774.

Federal Emergency Management Agency (FEMA). (2004b). *IS-362 Multi-hazard emergency planning for schools. Lesson 1: Course overview.* Retrieved October 29, 2008, from http://training.fema.gov.

Federal Emergency Management Agency (FEMA). (2006, March). *NIMS basic: Introduction and overview.* Washington, DC. Retrieved December 2, 2008, from http://www.fema.gov/pdf/nims/NIMS_basic_introduction_and_overview.pdf.

Federal Emergency Management Agency (FEMA). (2007, June). *IS-100.SC Introduction to the Incident Command System.* Washington, DC. Retrieved April 28, 2009, from http://rems.ed.gov/views/documents/emigram_ics_100sc_2007.doc.

Federal Emergency Management Agency (FEMA). (2008a). *Frequently asked questions: School districts, colleges, and universities.* Retrieved October 2008 from http://www.nimscompliance.com/nims_faq.htm#14b.

Federal Emergency Management Agency (FEMA). (2008b). *Government resources.* http://www.fema.gov/government/index.shtm.

Federal Emergency Management Agency (FEMA). (2008c, February). *National Incident Management System: Five-year training plan.* Washington, DC. Retrieved December 2, 2008, from http://www.fema.gov/library/viewRecord.do?id=3192.

Federal Emergency Management Agency (FEMA). (2008d, March). *NIMS compliance objectives and metrics for local governments.* Retrieved December 2, 2008, from http://www.fema.gov/library/viewRecord.do?id=3242.

Feeny, N. C., Foa, E. B., Treadwell, K. R. H., & March, J. (2004). Posttraumatic stress disorder in youth: A critical review of the cognitive and behavioral treatment outcome literature. *Professional Psychology: Research and Practice, 35*(5), 466–476.

Fein, R., Vossekuil, F., Pollack, W., Borum, R., Modzeleski, W., & Reddy, M. (2002; revised, 2004). *Threat assessment in schools: A guide to managing threatening situations and to creating safe school climates.* Washington, DC: U.S. Secret Service and Department of Education.

Feindler, E. L., & Weisner, S. (2006). Youth anger management for school violence prevention. In S. R. Jimerson & M. Furlong (Eds.), *Handbook of school violence and school safety* (pp. 353–363). Mahwah, NJ: Lawrence Earlbaum Associates.

Figley, C. R. (2002). *Treating compassion fatigue.* New York: Brunner-Routledge.

Fixsen, D. L., Naoom, S. F., Blase, K. A., Friedman, R. M., & Wallace, F. (2005). *Implementation research: A synthesis of the literature.* Tampa, FL: University of South Florida, Louis de la Parte, Florida Mental Health Institute, The National Implementation Research Network (FMHI Publication # 231).

Fong, R. S., Vogel, B. L., & Vogel, R. E. (2008). The correlates of school violence: An examination of factors linked to assaultive behavior in a rural middle school with a large migrant population. *Journal of School Violence, 7*, 24–47.

Forman, S. G., & Burke, C. R. (2008). Best practices in implementing evidence-based school interventions. In A. Thomas & J. Grimes (Eds.), *Best practices in school psychology V* (pp. 799–811). Bethesda, MD: National Association of School Psychologists.

Frey, K. S., Hirschsttein, M. K., & Guzzo, B. (2000). Second step: Preventing aggression by promoting social competence. *Journal of Emotional & Behavioral Disorders, 8*(2), 102–112.

Furlong, M. J., Felix, E. D., Sharkey, J. D., & Larson, J. (2005). Preventing school violence: A plan for safe and engaging schools. *Principal Leadership, 6*(1), 11–15.

Furlong, M. J., Greif, J. L., Bates, M. P., Whipple, A. D., Jimenez, T. C., & Morrison, R. (2005). Development of the California School Climate and Safety Survey—Short Form. *Psychology in the Schools, 42*, 137–149.

Furlong, M. J., Sharkey, J. D., Bates, M. P., & Smith, D. C. (2004). An examination of the reliability, data screening procedures, and extreme response patterns for the Youth Risk Behavior Surveillance Survey. *Journal of School Violence, 3*, 109–130.

Galea, S., Tracy, M., Norris, S., & Coffey, S. F. (2008). Financial and social circumstances and the incidence and course of PTSD in Mississippi during the first two years after Hurricane Katrina. *Journal of Traumatic Stress, 21*(4), 357–368.

Gallay, L., & Pong, S. (2004, May) *School climate and students' intervention strategies.* Paper presented at the annual meeting of the Society for Prevention Research, Quebec City.

Garrity, C., Jens, K., Porter, W., Sager, N., & Short-Camilli, C. (2004). *Bully proofing your school* (3rd ed.). Longmont, CO: Sopris West.

Gil Rivas, V., Holman, E. A., & Silver, R. C. (2004). Adolescent vulnerability following the September 11th terrorist attacks. A study of parents and their children. *Applied Developmental Science, 8*, 130–142.

Glassman, L. H., Weierich, M. R., Hooley, J. M., Deliberto, T. L., & Nock. M. K. (2007). Child maltreatment, non-suicidal self-injury, and the mediating role of self-criticism. *Behaviour Research & Therapy, 45*, 2483–2490.

Glew, G., Rivara, F., & Feudtner, C. (2000). Bullying: Children hurting children. *Pediatrics in Review, 21*(6), 183–189.

Goldstein, A. P. (1999). *Low level aggression: First steps on the ladder to violence.* Champaign, IL: Research Press.

Gottfredson, D. C., & Gottfredson, G. D. (2002). Quality of school-based prevention programs: Results from a national survey. *Journal of Research in Crime & Delinquency, 39*(1), 3–35.

Gottfredson, D. C., Gottfredson, G. D., & Hybl, L. G. (1993). Managing adolescent behavior: A multiyear, multischool study. *American Educational Research Journal, 30,* 179–215.

Gottfredson, D. C., Wilson, D. B., & Najaka, S. S. (2002). School-based crime prevention. In L. W. Sherman, D. P. Farrington, B. C. Welsh, & D. L. Mackenzie (Eds.), *Evidence-based crime prevention* (pp. 56–164). London: Routledge.

GovTrack.us. H.R. 3132—110th Congress. (2007a). S*afe Schools Improvement Act of 2007,* GovTrack.us (database of federal legislation). Retrieved September 8, 2008, from .govtrack. us/congress/bill.xpd?bill=h110-3132&tab=summary.

GovTrack.us. H.R. 3407—110th Congress. (2007b). *Positive Behavior for Effective Schools Act.* Retrieved September 8, 2008, from http://www.govtrack.us/congress/bill. xpd?bill=s110-2111.

GovTrack.us. S. 2111—110th Congress. (2007c). *Positive Behavior for Effective Schools Act.* Retrieved September 8, 2008, from http://www.govtrack.us/congress/bill. xpd?bill=s110-2111.

Graves, K. N., Frabutt, J. M., & Vigliano, D. (2007). Teaching conflict resolution skills to middle and high school students through interactive drama and role play. *Journal of School Violence, 6,* 57–79.

Green, M. W. (1999). The appropriate and effective use of security technologies in U.S. schools. U.S. Department of Justice Research Report. Retrieved November 23, 2008, from http://www.ncjrs.gov/school/178265.pdf.

Greenberg, M., Weissberg, R. P., O'Brien, M. U., Zins, J. E., Fredricks, L., Resnik, H., & Elias, M. J. (2003). Enhancing school-based prevention and youth development through coordinated social, emotional, and academic learning, *American Psychologist, 58,* 466–474.

Greene, M. B. (2005). Reducing violence and aggression in schools. *Trauma, Violence, & Abuse, 6,* 236–253.

Greene, S. M., Anderson, E. R., Doyle, E. A., & Riedelbach, H. (2006). Divorce. In G. G. Bear & K. M. Minke (Eds.), *Children's needs III: Development, prevention, and intervention* (pp. 745–757). Bethesda, MD: National Association of School Psychologists.

Griffiths, A., Sharkey, J. D., and Furlong, M. J. (2008, Winter). Targeted threat assessment: Ethical considerations for school psychologists. *National Association of School Psychologists: School Psychology Forum, 2*(2), 30–48. Retrieved September 15, 2008, from http://www.nasponline.org/publications/spf/issue2_2/griffiths.pdf.

Grossman, D. C., Neckerman, H. J., Koepsell, T. D., Liu, P. Y., Asher, K. N., Beland, K., Frey, K., & Rivara, F. P. (1997). Effectiveness of a violence prevention curriculum among children in elementary school: A randomized controlled trial. *Journal of the American Medical Association, 277,* 1605–1611.

Guerra, N., & Williams, K. (2002). Youth development and violence prevention: Core competencies. Southern California Center of Excellence on Youth Violence Prevention Fact Sheet. Retrieved December 2008 from http://www.stopyouthviolence.ucr.edu/publications/violenceprevention.pdf.

Han, S. S., & Weiss, B. (2005). Sustainability of teacher implementation of school-based mental health programs. *Journal of Abnormal Child Psychology, 33,* 665–679.

Hanson, T. L., Austin, G., & Lee-Bayha, J. (2004). *Ensuring that no child is left behind: How are student health risks and resilience related to the academic progress of schools?* San Francisco: WestEd.

Hawken, L. S., & Horner, R. H. (2003). Evaluation of a targeted intervention within a school-wide system of behavior support. *Journal of Behavioral Education, 12*(3), 225–240.

Hawkins, J. D., Farrington, D. P., & Catalano, R. F. (1998). Reducing violence through the schools. In D. S. Elliott, B. A. Hamburg, & K. R. Williams (Eds.), *Violence in American schools* (pp. 188–216). New York: Cambridge University Press.

Hawkins, J. D., Smith, B. H., & Catalano, R. F. (2004). Social development and social and emotional learning. In J. E. Zins, R. P. Weissberg, M. C. Wang, & H. J. Walberg. (Eds.), *Building academic success on social and emotional learning. What does the research say?* (pp. 135–150). New York: Teachers College Press.

Heath, N. L., & Beettam, E. (2005, April). *Self-injury in the community: Implications for treatment.* Psychiatric Rounds, Royal Victoria Hospital. Retrieved June 25, 2007, from http://www.education.mcgill.ca/heathresearchteam/conferences.htm.

Heath, N. L., Beettam, E., & DeStefano, J. (2005, November). *Adolescent self-injury: What every high school teacher needs to know.* Workshop presented to the Quebec Provincial Association of Teachers annual convention, QPAT, Montreal, QC. Retrieved June 25, 2007, from http://www.education.mcgill.ca/heathresearchteam/images/QPAT2005SelfInjury.pdf.

Health, M., Ryan, K., Dean, B., & Bingham, R. (2007). History of school safety and psychological first aid for children. *Brief Treatment and Crisis Intervention, 7*(3), 206–233.

Hetherington, E. M., & Kelly, J. (2002). *For better or for worse: Divorce reconsidered.* New York: Norton.

Huberty, T. J. (2008). Best practices in school-based interventions for anxiety and depression. In A. Thomas & J. Grimes (Eds.), *Best practices in school psychology V* (pp. 1473–1486). Bethesda, MD: National Association of School Psychologists.

Hunter, L., Elias, M., & Noms, J. (2001). School-based violence prevention: Challenges and lessons learned form an action research project. *Journal of School Psychology, 39,* 161–175.

Individuals with Disabilities Education Improvement Act of 2004. 20 USC 1400 [Electronic version]. http://idea.ed.gov/explore/view/p/,root,statute.

Institute of Education Sciences (IES), U. S. Department of Education—National Center for Education Statistics. (2008). *The condition of education: School violence and safety.* Retrieved July 25, 2008, from http://nces.ed.gov/surveys/AnnualReports/.

Institute for Education Sciences (IES), United Sates Department of Education—National Center for Education Statistics. (n.d.). *Fast facts: How many students with disabilities receive services?* Retrieved February 17, 2009, from http://nces.ed.gov/fastfacts/display.asp?id=64.

Inter-Agency Standing Committee (IASC). (2007; updated 2008). *IASC guidance on mental health and psychosocial support in emergency settings.* Geneva:

IASC. Retrieved February 14, 2008, from http://www.who.
int/hac/network/interagency/news/iasc_guidelines_men-
tal_health_psychososial_upd2008.pdf.

Jacobs, J., Horne-Moyer, H. L., & Jones, R. (2004). The effectiveness of critical incident stress debriefing with primary
and secondary trauma victims. *International Journal of
Emergency Mental Health, 6,* 5–14.

Jagers, R. J., Morgan-Lopez, A. A., Howard, T.-L., Browns, D. C.,
Flay, B. R., & Aya, A. (2007). Mediators of the development
and prevention of violent behavior. *Prevention Science, 8,*
171–179.

Jimerson, S. R., & Brock, S. E. (2004). Threat assessment,
school crisis preparation, and school crisis response. In
M. J. Furlong, M. P. Bates, D. C. Smith, & P. Kingery (Eds.),
*Appraisal and prediction of school violence: Methods,
issues, and contexts* (pp. 193–214). Hauppauge, NY: Nova
Science.

Johns, S. K., Patrick, J. A., & Rutherford, K. J. (2008). Best practices in district-wide positive behavior support implementation. In A. Thomas & J. Grimes (Eds.), *Best practices in
school psychology V* (pp. 721–733). Bethesda, MD: National
Association of School Psychologists.

Johnson, D. W., Johnson, R. T., & Stanne, M. B. (2000). *Cooperative
learning methods: A meta-analysis.* [Electronic version].
http://www.co-operation.org/pages/cl-methods.html.

Johnson, K. (1993). *School crisis management: A hands-on
guide to training crisis management teams.* Alameda. CA:
Hunter House.

Johnston, L. D., O'Malley, P. M., Bachman, J. G., & Schulenberg, J.
E. (2006). *Monitoring the future national results on adoles-
cent drug use: Overview of key findings.* (NIH Publication
No. 06-5882). Bethesda, MD: National Institute on Drug
Abuse.

Jones, T. S. (2004). Conflict resolution in education: The field,
the findings, the future. *Conflict Resolution Quarterly, 22,*
233–267.

Juvonen, J. (2001). *School violence: Prevalence, fears, and
prevention.* Issue paper: Rand Education. Retrieved
November 2008 from http://www.rand.org/pubs/issue_
papers/2006/IP219.pdf.

Juvonen, J., Graham, S., & Schuster, M. A. (2003). Bullying
among young adolescents: The strong, the weak, and the
troubled. *Pediatrics, 112,* 1231–1237.

Juvonen, J., Nishina, A., & Graham, S. (2000). Peer harassment, psychological adjustment, and school functioning in early adolescence. *Journal of Educational Psychology, 92,* 349–359.

Kam, C.-M., Greenberg, M. T., & Walls, C. T. (2003). Examining the role of implementation quality in school-based prevention using the PATHS curriculum. *Prevention Science, 4,* 55–63.

Kanan, L. M. (2008a). *Threat/danger assessment: Safe solutions for threatening behavior.* Workshop presented at the annual meeting of the National Association of School Psychologists, New Orleans, LA.

Kanan, L. M. (2008b). *Danger assessment: Planning for safety step by step.* Workshop presented to the Cherry Creek School District Mental Health Team, Greenwood Village, CO.

Kanan, L. M., & Finger, J. (2006, March). *Self-injury and youth: Best practices for school mental health providers.* Workshop presented at the annual meeting of the National Association of School Psychologists, Anaheim, CA.

Kanan, L. M., & Lee, R. W. (2004, October). *Danger assessment: Threatening behaviors, safe solutions.* Workshop presented at the annual meeting of the South Carolina Association of School Psychologists.

Kanan, L., & Plog, A. (submitted for publication). Developmental issues and trauma reactions in children: Suggestions for parents and educators. In A. Canter, L. Paige, & S. Shaw. *Helping children at home and school* (3rd ed). Bethesda. MD: National Association of School Psychologists.

Kaplan, Z., Iancu, I., & Bodner, E. (2001). A review of psychological debriefing after extreme stress. *Psychiatric Services, 52*(6), 824–827.

Karcher, M. J. (2002). The cycle of violence and disconnection among rural middle school students: Teacher disconnection as a consequence of violence. *Journal of School Violence, 1,* 35–51.

Kneese, C., Fullwood, H., Schroth, G., & Pankake, A. (2003). Decreasing school violence: A research synthesis. In M. S. Fishbaugh, T. R. Berkeley, & G. Schroth (Eds.), *Ensuring safe school environments: Exploring issues, seeking solutions* (pp. 39–48). Mahwah, NJ: Lawrence Erlbaum Associates.

Knoff, H. M. (2002). The stop and think social skills program: Teaching children interpersonal, problem solving, and conflict resolution skills, *Communiqué, 30*(6).

Kratochwill, T. R., & Shernoff, E. S. (2004). Evidence-based practice: Promoting evidence-based interventions in school psychology. *School Psychology Review, 33*, 34–48.

Larson, J. (2008). Best practices in school violence prevention. In A. Thomas & J. Grimes (Eds.), *Best practices in school psychology V* (pp. 1291–1307). Bethesda, MD: National Association of School Psychologists.

Lassiter, B., & McEvoy, P. (2008). *Prevention-mitigation: Emergency management for schools.* Retrieved November 2008 from http://rems.ed.gov/views/documents/Training_SFCA08_PreventionMitigation.pdf.

Lavoie, R. (1989). *How difficult can this be?* The F.A.T. City Workshop Video. www.ricklavoie.com.

Leadbeater, B., Hoglund, W., & Woods, T. (2003). Changing context? The effects of a primary prevention program on classroom levels of peer relational and physical victimization. *Journal of Community Psychology, 31,* 397–418.

Leahy, S. K. & Judge Nearing, K. (2003). The Evaluation of the Assets for Colorado Youth Initiative. Presented at a research forum sponsored by the Colorado Trust. Denver, CO.

Levine, K. (1998, June). How children grieve. *Parents,* 133–137.

Lewis, S., Brock, S. E., & Lazarus, P. J. (2002). Identifying troubled youth. In S. E. Brock, P. J. Lazarus, & S. R. Jimerson (Eds.), *Best practices in school crisis prevention and intervention* (pp. 249–271). Bethesda, MD: National Association of School Psychologists.

Lewis, T. J., & Sugai, G. (1999). Effective behavior support: A systems approach to proactive school-wide management. *Effective School Practices, 17*(4), 47–53.

Lewis, T. J., Sugai, G., & Colvin, G. (1998). Reducing problem behavior through a school-side system of effective behavioral support: Investigation of a school-wide social skills training program and contextual interventions. *School Psychology Review, 27,* 446–459.

Lichtenstein, R. (2008). Best practices in identification of learning disabilities. In A. Thomas & J. Grimes (Eds.), *Best practices in school psychology V* (pp. 295–317). Bethesda, MD: National Association of School Psychologists.

Lieberman, R. (2004,March). Understanding and responding to students who self mutilate. *Principal Leadership Magazine, 4*(7). Retrieved June 25, 2007 from http://www.nasponline.org/resources/principals/nassp_cutting.aspx

Lieberman, R., & Davis, J. (2002). Suicide intervention. In S. E. Brock, P. J. Lazarus, & S. R. Jimerson (Eds.), *Best practices in school crisis prevention and intervention* (pp. 531–551). Bethesda, MD: National Association of School Psychologists.

Lieberman, R., Poland, S., & Cassel, R. (2008). Best practices in suicide intervention. In A. Thomas & J. Grimes (Eds.), *Best practices in school psychology V* (pp. 1457–1472). Bethesda, MD: National Association of School Psychologists.

Limber, S. P. (2006). The Olweus bullying prevention program: An overview of its implementation and research basis. In S. R. Jimerson & M. Furlong (Eds.), *Handbook of school violence and school safety: From research to practice* (pp. 293–307). Mahwah, NJ: Lawrence Erlbaum.

Limber, S., & Small, M. A. (2003). State laws and policies to address bullying in schools. *School Psychology Review, 23*, 445–455.

Lipson, J. G., & Dibble, S. L. (Eds.). (2005). *Culture & clinical care.* San Francisco: UCSF Nursing Press.

Lloyd, E. E. (1997). Self-mutilation in a community sample of adolescents (doctoral dissertation, Louisiana State University, 1998). *Dissertation Abstracts International, 58*, 5127.

Lochman, J. E., Powell, N. R., Clanton, N., & McElroy, H. K. (2006). Anger and aggression. In G. G. Bear & K. M. Minke (Eds.), *Children's needs III: Development, prevention, and intervention* (pp. 115–133). Bethesda: MD: National Association of School Psychologists.

Lohrmann, S., Forman, S., Martin, S., & Palmieri, M. (2008). Understanding school personnel's resistance to adopting school wide positive behavior support at a universal level of intervention. *Journal of Positive Behavior Intervention, 10*, 256–269.

Luiselli, J. K., Putnam, R. F., Handler, M. W., & Feinberg, A. B. (2005). Whole-school positive behaviour support: Effects on student discipline problems and academic performance. *Educational Psychology, 25*(2-3), 183–198.

Ma, X. & Willms, J. D. (2004). School disciplinary climate: Characteristics and effects on eighth grade achievement. *The Alberta Journal of Educational Research, 50,* 169–188.

Mandell, D. J, Hill S. L., Carter L., & Brandon R. N. (2002). *The impact of substance use and violence/delinquency on academic achievement for groups of middle and high school students in Washington.* Seattle, WA: Washington Kids Count, Human Services Policy Center, Evans School of Public Affairs, University of Washington.

Martin, G., & Pear, J. (2007). *Behavior modification: what it is and how to do it.* New Jersey: Pearson.

Mauk, G. W., & Sharpnack, J. D. (2006). Grief. In G. G. Bear & K. M. Minke (Eds.), *Children's needs III: Development, prevention, and intervention* (pp. 239–254). Bethesda: MD: National Association of School Psychologists.

May, S., Ard, W., Todd, A., Horner, R., Glasgow, A., Sugai, G., & Sprague, J. (2000). *School-wide Information System (SWIS©).* University of Oregon, Educational and Community Supports.

McKevitt, B. C., & Braaksma, A. D. (2008). Best practices in developing a positive behavior support system at the school level. In A. Thomas & J. Grimes (Eds.), *Best practices in school psychology V* (pp. 735–747). Bethesda, MD: National Association of School Psychologists.

McMahon, S. D., & Washburn, J. J. (2003). Violence prevention: An evaluation of program effects with urban African American student. *Journal of Primary Prevention, 24,* 43–62.

Menard, S., Grotpeter, J., Gianola, D., & O'Neal, M. (2007). *Evaluation of bullyproofing your school: Final report.* Retrieved June 2008 from http://www.ncjrs.gov/App/Publications/abstract.aspx?ID=242926.

Mental Health Parity Act of 2007. S. 558—110th Congress [Electronic version]. http://www.govtrack.us/congress/bill.xpd?bill=s110-558.

Metzler, C. W., Biglan, A., Rusby, J. C., & Sprague, J. R. (2001). Evaluation of a comprehensive behavior management program to improve school-wide positive behavior support. *Education and Treatment of Children, 24,* 448–479.

Miesner, M., & Maki, R. H. (2007). The role of test anxiety in absolute and relative metacomprehension accuracy. *European Journal of Cognitive Psychology, 19*(4/5), 650–670.

Miller, C., Swearer, S., & Siebecker, A. B. (2003). *Bullying and school climate: Examining student and teacher perceptions.* Poster presented at the annual meeting of the American Psychological Association, Toronto.

Minke, K. M., & Anderson, K. A. (2005). Family school collaboration: Relationship building and positive behavior support. *Journal of Positive Behavior Interventions, 7*(3), 181–185.

Minnesota Department of Education. (2008). *Safe and healthy learners: An overview of pandemic influenza planning for schools.* Retrieved November 5, 2008, from http:// togeventsco.web135.discountasp.net/rr/handouts/3F.doc.

Morrison, G. M., Cosden, M. A., O'Farrell, S. L., & Campos, E. (2003). Changes in Latino students' perceptions of school bonding over time: Impact of language proficiency, self-perceptions and teacher evaluations. *The California School Psychologist, 8,* 87–98.

Muehlenkamp, J. L. (2006). Empirically supported treatments and general therapy guidelines for non-suicidal self-injury. *Journal of Mental Health Counseling, 28,* 166–185.

Munro, S., O'Brien, M. U., Payton, J., & Weissberg, R. P. (2006). Cooperative learning helps crease the essential skill of working (and compromising) within a group. *Edutopia, 2*(6), 53–58.

Nansel, T. R., Overpeck, M., Pilla, R. S., Ruan, W. J., Simons-Morton, B., & Scheidt, P. (2001). Bullying behaviors among U.S. youth: Prevalence and association with psychosocial adjustment. *Journal of the American Medical Association, 285,* 2094–2100.

Nation, M., Crusto, C., Wandersman, A., Kumpfer, K. L., Seybolt, D., Morrissey-Kane, E., & Davino, K. (2003). What works in prevention: Principles of effective prevention programs. *American Psychologist, 58,* 449–456.

National Association of School Psychologists (NASP). (2002a). *Memorials/activities/rituals following traumatic events.* Retrieved on December 15, 2008, from http://www.nasponline.org/resources/crisis_safety/memorials_general.aspx.

National Association of School Psychologists (NASP). (2002b*). Social skills: Promoting positive behavior, academic success, and school safety.* [Electronic version]. http://www.naspweb.org/resources/factsheets/socialskills_fs.aspx.

National Association of School Psychologists. (2006). Responsible media coverage of crisis events impacting children. Retrieved August 9, 2009 from http://www.nasponline.org/resources/crisis_safety/Media%20Guidelines.pdf.

National Center for Education Statistics. (2004). *Crime and safety in America's public schools: Selected findings from the school survey on crime and safety.* Retrieved August 1, 2008, from http://nces.ed.gov/pubs2004/2004370.pdf.

National Center for Educational Statistics. (2006). *Indicators of school crime and safety, 2006.* Washington, DC: U.S. Department of Justice, Bureau of Justice Statistics.

National Center for Mental Health Promotion and Youth Violence Prevention. (2008). *Social and emotional learning (SEL) and student benefits: Research implications for the Safe Schools/Healthy Students core elements.* Retrived September 16, 2008, from http://www.promoteprevent.org/Publications/SEL/SELbenefits.pdf.

National Child Traumatic Stress Network. (n.d.[a]). *Cognitive Behavior Intervention for Trauma in the Schools (CBITS).* [Electronic version]. http://www.nctsnet.org/nctsn_assets/pdfs/CBITSfactsheet.pdf.

National Child Traumatic Stress Network. (n.d.[b]). *Defining trauma and child traumatic stress.* Retrieved on February 16, 2009, from http://www.nctsnet.org/nccts/nav.do?pid=faq_def.

National Child Traumatic Stress Network. (n.d.[c]). *The effects of trauma on schools and learning.* (www.NCTSNet.org). Retrieved September 10, 2008, from http://www.nctsnet.org/nccts/nav.do?pid=ctr_aud_schl_effects.

National Clearinghouse for Educational Facilities (NCEF). (2008). *Mitigating hazards in school facilities.* Retrieved October 29, 2008, from http://www.ncef.org/pubs/mitigating_hazards.pdf.

National Conference of State Legislatures. (2000). Who's responsible for school safety. *State Legislature Magazine.* Retrieved September 7, 2008, from http://www.ncsl.org/programs/pubs/1200scl.htm.

National Institute of Mental Health (NIMH). (2002). *Mental health and mass violence: Evidence-based early psychological intervention for victims/survivors of mass violence. A workshop to reach consensus on best practices.* NIH Publication No. 02-5138, Washington, DC: U.S. Government Printing Office.

National Institute of Mental Health (NIMH). (2007, February). *Half of adults with anxiety disorders had psychiatric diagnoses in youth.* Retrieved November 25, 2008, from http://www.nimh.nih.gov/science-news/2007/half-of-adults-with-anxiety-disorders-had-psychiatric-diagnoses-in-youth.shtml.

National Institute of Mental Health (NIMH). (2008a). *Helping children and adolescents cope with violence and disasters, what parents can do.* Publication No. 08-3518. [Electronic version]. http://www.nimh.nih.gov/health/publications/helping-children-and-adolescents-cope-with-violence-and-disasters-what-parents-can-do.pdf.

National Institute of Mental Health (NIMH). (2008b). *Suicide in the U.S.: Statistics and preventions.* [Electronic version]. http://www.nimh.nih.gov/health/publications/suicide-in-the-us-statistics-and-prevention.shtml.

National School Safety and Security Services. (2008). *U.S. Department of Education endorses crisis drills, plans.* Retrieved on October 30, 2008, from http://www.schoolsecurity.org/resources/DOEcrisisplanletter.pdf.

National Weather Service. (2008). *Public alert radios for schools.* Retrieved onNovember 29, 2008, from http://public-alert-radio.nws.noaa.gov/faq.htm#1.

Neel, R. (n.d.). A presentation given to the Colorado Society of School Psychologists.

Neiman. S., & DeVoe, J. F. (2009). *Crime, violence, discipline, and safety in U.S. public schools: Findings from the school survey on crime and safety: 2007–2008 (NCES 2009-326).* National Center for Education Statistics, Institute of Education Sciences, U.S. Department of Education. Washington, DC. [Electronic version]. http://nces.ed.gov/pubsearch/pubsinfo.asp?pubid=2009326.

Nickerson, A., & Martens, M. (2008). School violence: Associations with control, security/enforcement, educational/therapeutic approaches, and demographic factors. *School Psychology Review, 37*(2), 228–243.

Nickerson, A. B., Reeves, M. A., Brock, S. E., & Jimerson, S. R. (2009). *Identifying, assessing, and treating posttraumatic stress disorder at school.* Developmental Psychopathology at School Series. New York: Springer.

Nickerson, A. B., & Zhe, E. J. (2007). Effects of an intruder crisis drill on children's knowledge, anxiety, and perceptions of school safety. *School Psychology Review, 36*(3), 501–508.

Nicoletti, J. (2007, September 27). *Managing threats in schools.* A workshop presented to the Cherry Creek Schools.

No Child Left Behind Act of 2001, Pub. L. No. 107-110, § 9532, . *Unsafe School Choice Option,* Part E—Uniform Provisions-Subpart 2: Other Provisions. Retrieved on August 13, 2008 from http://www.ed.gov/policy/elsec/leg/esea02/pg112. html#sec9532.

No Child Left Behind Act of 2001, Public Law 107–110 (2002, January 8) 115 Stat. 1425 http://www.ed.gov/policy/elsec/ leg/esea02/index.html.

Nock, M. K., & Prinstein, M. J. (2004). A functional approach to the assessment of self-mutilative behavior. *Journal of Counseling and Clinical Psychology, 72,* 885–890.

Noguera, P. A. (1995). Preventing and producing violence: A critical analysis of responses to school violence. *Harvard Educational Review, 65,* 189–212.

Office of Safe and Drug Free Schools (OSDFS), U. S. Department of Education. (2006). *The challenge: Safe schools. Academic success depends on it. 14*(2). Retrieved on April 20, 2009, from http://www.thechallenge.org/safe.html.

Office of Safe and Drug-Free Schools (OSDFS), U. S. Department of Education. (2007). *Practical information on crisis planning: A guide for schools and communities.* Washington, DC.

Office of Safe and Drug Free Schools (OSDFS), U. S. Department of Education. (2008a, July). *Checklist: NIMS implementation activities for schools and higher education institutions (HEIs).* Retrieved on December 2, 2008, from http://rems.ed.gov/views/documents/NIMS_ ImplementationActivitiesChecklist.pdf.

Office of Safe and Drug Free Schools (OSDFS), U. S. Department of Education. (2008b, July). *Frequently asked questions about NIMS implementation activities for schools and higher education institutions (HEIs).* Retrieved on December 2, 2008, from http://rems.ed.gov/index. cfm?event=FAQNIMS.

Office of Safe and Drug Free Schools (OSDFS), U. S. Department of Education. (2008c). *A guide to school vulnerability assessment: Key principles for safe schools.* Washington, DC.

Office of Safe and Drug Free Schools (OSDFS), U. S. Department of Education. (2008d, July). *Key personnel and NIMS training for schools and high education institutions.* http://rems. ed.gov/views/documents/NIMS_KeyPersonnelTraining. pdf.

Office of Safe and Drug Free Schools (OSDFS), U. S. Department of Education. (2008e, July). *NIMS implementation activities for schools and higher education institutions.* Retrieved on December 2, 2008, from http://rems.ed.gov/views/documents/NIMS_Comprehensive GuidanceActivities.pdf.

Office of Special Education Programs (OSEP). (2009). *Response to intervention and PBS.* Retrieved on April 11, 2009, from http://www.pbis.org/rti/default.aspx.

Office of Special Education Programs (OSEP), Center on Positive Behavioral Interventions and Supports. (2004). *School-wide positive behavior support implementers' blueprint and self-assessment.* Retrieved on April 25, 2009, from http://www.osepideasthatwork.org/toolkit/pdf/SchoolwideBehaviorSupport.pdf.

OMNI. (2005). *Colorado Healthy Kids Survey.* Retrieved June 2008 from http://www.omni.org/survey.aspx.

Onacki, M. (2005). Kids who cut: A protocol for public schools. *Journal of School Health, 75,* 400–401.

Orpinas, P., Horne, A. M., & Staniszewski, D. (2003). School bullying: Changing the problem by changing the school. *School Psychology Review, 23,* 431–444.

Osher, D., Sprague, J., Weissberg, R. P., Axelrod, J., Keenan, S., Kendziora, K., & Zins, J. (2008). A comprehensive approach to promoting social, emotional, and academic growth in contemporary schools. In A. Thomas & J. Grimes (Eds.), *Best practices in school psychology V* (pp. 735–747). Bethesda, MD: National Association of School Psychologists.

Osterman, K. E. (2000). Students' need for belonging in the school community. *Review of Educational Research, 70,* 323–367.

Oswald, K., Safran, S., & Johanson, G. (2005). Preventing trouble: Making schools safer places using Positive Behavior Supports. *Education and Treatment of Children, 28,* 265–278.

O'Toole, M. E. (2000). *The school shooter: A threat-assessment perspective.* Quantico, VA: National Center for the Analysis of Violent Crime, Federal Bureau of Investigation.

Ozxer, E. J., Best. S. R., Lipsey, T. L., & Weiss, D. S. (2003). Predictors of post-traumatic stress disorder and symptoms in adults: A meta-analysis. *Psychological Bulletin, 129,* 52–73.

Pagliocca, P. M., & Nickerson, A. B. (2001). Legislating school crisis response: Good policy or just good politics? *Law and Policy, 23,* 373–407.

Patton, G. C., Hamphill, S. A., Bond, L., Toumbourou, J. W., McMorris, B. J., & Catalano, R. F. (2007). Pubertal stage and deliberate self-harm in adolescents. *Journal of the American Academy of Child and Adolescent Psychiatry, 46,* 508–514.

Payton, J. W., Wardlaw, D. M., Graczyk, P. A., Bloodworth, M. R., Tompsett, C. J., & Weissberg, R. P. (2000). Social and emotional learning: A framework for promoting mental health and reducing risk behavior in children and youth, *Journal of School Health, 70,* 179–185.

Pellegrini, A. D., & Bartini, M. (2000). An empirical comparison of methods of sampling aggression and victimization in school settings. *Journal of Educational Psychology, 92,* 360–366.

Perkins, D. F., & Borden, L. M. (2003). Positive behaviors, problem behaviors, and resiliency in adolescence. In R. M. Lerner, M. A. Easterbrooks, & J. Mistry (Vol. Eds.), and I. B. Weiner (Series Ed.), *Handbook of Psychology, Vol. 6: Developmental Psychology* (pp. 373–394). Hoboken, NJ: John Wiley and Sons.

Peterson, R. L. (n.d.). *Ten alternatives to suspension.* Impact. Retrieved on November 29, 2008, from http://www.ici.umn.edu/products/impact/182/over5.html.

Peterson, R. L., Larson, J., & Skiba, R. (2001). School violence prevention: Current status and policy recommendations. *Law & Policy, 23,* 345–371.

Peterson, R. L., & Skiba, R. J. (2002). *Safe and responsive schools strategic planning outline.* Retrieved September 2008 from http://www.unl.edu/srs/pdfs/strplnotln.pdf.

Pfohl, W. (2006, February). President's Message, National Association of School Psychologists. *Communiqué, 34*(5).

Pfohl, W., Jimerson, S. R., & Lazarus, P. J. (2002). Developmental aspects of psychological trauma and grief. In S. E. Brock, P. J. Lazarus, & S. R. Jimerson (Eds.), *Best practices in school crisis prevention and intervention* (pp. 309–331). Bethesda, MD: National Association of School Psychologists.

Pitcher, G., & Poland, S. (1992). *Crisis intervention in the schools*. New York: Guilford Press.

Poland, S. (1994). The role of school crisis intervention teams to prevent and reduce school violence and trauma. *School Psychology Review, 23*(2), 175–189.

Poland, S., & Lieberman, R. (2002). Best practices in suicide intervention. In A. Thomas & J. Grimes (Eds.), *Best practices in school psychology IV* (pp. 1151–1165). Bethesda, MD: National Association of School Psychologists.

Poland, S., & McCormick, J. (1999). *Coping with crisis: Lessons learned*. Longmont, CO: Sopris West.

Pollack, W. S., Modzeleski, W., & Rooney, G. (2008). *Prior knowledge of potential school based violence: Information students learn may prevent a targeted attack*. Washington, DC: U.S. Secret Service and U.S. Department of Education. Retrieved February 4, 2009, from http://www.ustreas.gov/usss/ntac/bystander_study.pdf.

Porter, W., Jens, K., Epstein, L., & Plog, A. (2000). Colorado School Climate Survey. In C. Garrity, K. Jens, W. Porter, N. Sager, & C. Short-Camilli (Eds.), *Bully proofing your school* (2nd ed., pp. 51–61). Longmont, CO: Sopris West.

Porter, W., Plog, A., Jens, K., Garrity, C., & Sager, N. (in press). Bully-proofing your elementary school: Creating a caring community. In S. R. Jimerson, S. M. Swearer, & D. L. Espelage (Eds.), *The handbook of bullying in schools: An international perspective*. Mahwah, NJ: Lawrence Erlbaum Associates.

Prevention Tools. (n.d.). *All hazards approach: School crisis management guide for timely response to school emergencies*. www.preventiontools.net.

Promising Practices Network (PPN). (2005). *Programs that work: Cognitive behavioral intervention for trauma in schools*. Retrieved on April 24, 2009, from http://www.promising-practices.net/program.asp?programid=145.

Purington, A., & Whitlock, J. (2004, August). *ACT for Youth Upstate Center for Excellence: Research facts and findings—Self-injury fact sheet*. Retrieved on June 25, 2007, from http://www.actforyouth.net/documents/fACTS_Aug04.pdf.

Pynoos, R. S., Fredrick, C., Nadar, K., Arroyo, W., Steinberg, A., Eth, S., Nunez, F., & Fairbanks, L. (1987). Life threat and posttraumatic stress in school-age children. *Archives of General Psychiatry, 44*, 1057–1063.

Qouta, S., Punamäki, R. L., & El Sarraj, E. (2005). Mother-child expression of psychological distress in war trauma. *Clinical Child Psychology & Psychiatry, 10,* 135–156.

Quinn, K. P., & Lee, V. (2007). The wraparound approach for students with emotional and behavioral disorders: Opportunities for school psychologists. *Psychology in the Schools, 44*(1), 101–111.

Ratner, H. H., Chiodo, L., Covington, C., Sokol, R. J., Ager, J., & Delaney-Black, V. (2006). Violence exposure, IQ, academic performance, and children's perception of safety: Evidence of protective effects. *Merrill-Palmer Quarterly, 52,* 264–287.

Reddy Ranzano, M., Borum, R., Vossekuil, B., Fein, R., Modzeleski, W., & Pollack, W. (2006). Threat assessment in schools: Comparison with other approaches. In S. R. Jimerson & M. J. Furlong. (Eds.), *Handbook of school violence and school safety: From research to practice* (pp. 147–156). Englewood Cliffs, NJ: Earlbaum.

Reid, R., Peterson. A., Hughey, J., & Garcia-Reid, P. (2006). School climate and adolescent drug use: Mediating effects of violence victimization in the urban high school context. *Journal of Primary Prevention, 27,* 281–292.

Reeves, M. A., Nickerson, A. B., & Brock, S. E. (in press). *Preventing and intervening in crisis situations.* In E. Snyder & R. W. Christner (Eds.), *A practical guide to developing competencies in school psychology.* New York: Springer.

Reeves, M., Nickerson A., & Jimerson, S. (2006). *PREPaRE workshop #1. Prevention and preparedness: The comprehensive school crisis team.* Bethesda, MD: National Association of School Psychologists.

Rigby, K. (2007). *Bullying in schools and what to do about it* (Rev. ed.). Melbourne: Australian Council for Educational Research.

Risi, S., Gerhardstein, R., & Kistner, J. (2003). Children's classroom peer relationships and subsequent educational outcomes. *Journal of Clinical Child and Adolescent Psychiatry, 32,* 351–361.

Robinson, J. H., & Clay, D. L. (2005). Potential school violence: Relationship between teacher anxiety and warning sign identification. *Psychology in the Schools, 42*(6).

Rose, L. C., & Gallop, A. M. (2006). The thirty-eighth annual PDK/Gallup poll of the public's attitudes toward the public schools. *Phi Delta Kappan, 88,* 41–53.

Rozalski, M. E., & Yell, M. L. (2004). Law and school safety. In J. C. Conoley and A. P. Goldstein (Eds.), *School violence intervention: A practical handbook* (2nd ed., pp. 507–523). New York: Guilford Press.

Ryan, A. M., & Patrick, H. (2001). The classroom social environment and changes in adolescents' motivation and engagement during middle school. *American Educational Research Journal, 38*(2), 437–460.

Safe2Tell. http://www.safe2tell.org.

Safran, S. P., & Oswald, K. (2003). Positive behavior supports: Can schools reshape disciplinary practices? *Exceptional Children,* 69, 361–373.

Saigh, P. A., Mroueh, M., & Bremner, J. D. (1997). Scholastic impairments among traumatized adolescents. *Behaviour Research and Therapy, 35,* 429–436.

Salloum, A., & Overstreet, S. (2008). Evaluation of individual and group grief and trauma interventions for children post disaster. *Journal of Clinical Child Adolescent Psychology, 37*(3), 495–507.

Saltzman, W. R., Pynoos, R. S., Layne, C. M., Steinberg, A. M., & Aisenberg E. (2001). Trauma- and grief-focused intervention for adolescents exposed to community violence: Results of a school-based screening and group treatment protocol. *Group Dynamics: Theory, Research and Practice,* 5, 291–303.

Sams, D. P., & Truscott, S. D. (2004). Empathy, exposure to community violence, and use of violence among urban, at-risk adolescents. *Child & Youth Care Forum,* 33, 33–50.

Sandhu, D. S., Arora, M. & Sandhu, V. S. (2001). School violence: Risk factors, psychological correlates, prevention and intervention strategies. In D. S. Snadhu (ed.) *Faces of violence: Psychological correlates, concepts, and intervention strategies.* Huntington, NU: Nova Science Publishers (pp. 45–71).

Sandoval, J., & Zadeh, S. (2008, Winter). Principles for intervening with suicide. *School Psychology Forum: Research in Practice, 2*(2), 67–79. Retrieved on December 31, 2008, from http://www.nasponline.org/publications/spf/issue2_2/sandoval.pdf.

Scales, P. C., & Roehlkepartain, E. C. (2003, October). Boosting student achievement: New research on the power of developmental assets. *Search Institute Insights & Evidence, 1*(1), 1–10.

Schaeffer, C. M., Bruns, E., Weist, M., Stephan, S. H., Goldstein, J., & Simpson, Y. (2005). Overcoming challenges to using evidence-based interventions in schools. *Journal of Youth and Adolescence, 34,* 15–22.

Schaughency, E., & Ervin, R. (2006). Building capacity to implement and sustain effective practices to better serve children. *School Psychology Review, 35,* 155–166.

Scheeringa, M. S., & Zeanah, C. H. (2008). Reconsideration of harm's way: Onsets and comorbidity patterns of disorders in preschool children and their caregivers following Hurricane Katrina. *Journal of Clinical Child Adolescent Psychology, 37*(3), 508–518.

Schneider, T., Walker, H., & Sprague, J. (2000). *Safe school design: A handbook for educational leaders.* Eugene, OR: ERIC Clearinghouse on Educational Management.

Schonfeld, D., & Newgrass, S. (2003, September). School crisis response initiative. *OVC Bulletin.* Washington, DC: U.S. Department of Justice, Office of Victims of Crime.

School Health Policy and Programs Study (SHPPS). (2007). Crisis preparedness, response and recovery. *Journal of School Health, 77,* 385–397.

Schreiber, M., Gurwitch, R., & Wong, M (2006). *Listen, Protect, and Connect: Model and teach.* Retrieved on February 15, 2009, from http://www.ready.gov/kids/_downloads/PFA_SchoolCrisis.pdf.

Schwartz, D., & Gorman, A. H. (2003). Community violence exposure and children's academic functioning. *Journal of Educational Psychology, 95,* 163–173.

Scott, T. M., & Barrett, S. B. (2004). Using staff and student time engaged in disciplinary procedures to evaluate the impact of school-wide PBS. *Journal of Positive Behavior Interventions, 6(1),* 21–27.

Scott, T. M., & Eber, L. (2003). Functional assessment and wrap-around as systemic school processes: Primary, secondary, and tertiary systems as examples. *Journal of Positive Behavior Interventions, 5,* 131–143. (NCJ 18473).

Search Institute. (1996). *Search Institute profiles of student life: Attitudes and behaviors assessment.* Minneapolis, MN: Search Institute.

Sexton, T. L., & Alexander, J. F. (2000, December). Functional family therapy. *Juvenile Justice Bulletin.* Washington, DC: U.S. Department of Justice, Office of Juvenile Justice and Delinquency Prevention.

Shaw, J. A. (2003). Children exposed to war/terrorism. *Clinical Child and Family Psychology Review, 6,* 237–246.

Shores, E. (2006). Proceedings of the rural early childhood forum on hurricane recovery and emergency preparedness (Mobile, AL, December 5, 2005). Rural Early Childhood Report No. 4. National Center for Rural Early Childhood Learning Initiatives—Mississippi State University Early Childhood Institute, The Rural Early Childhood Forum on Hurricane Recovery and Emergency Preparedness. *Psychology Review, 6,* 237–246.

Simeon, D., & Favazza, A. R. (2001). Self-injurious behaviors: Phenomenology and assessment. In D. Simeon & E. Hollander (Eds.), *Self-injurious behaviors: Assessment and treatment.* (pp. 1–28). Washington, DC: American Psychiatric Publishing.

Skiba, R. (1999). *Creating a positive climate: Violence prevention and conflict resolution curricula.* Retrieved February 2008 from http://www.indiana.edu/~safeschl/ViolencePrevention.pdf.

Skiba, R. (2000). *Zero tolerance, zero evidence* (Policy Research Report SRS2). Bloomington, IN: Indiana Education Policy Center.

Skiba, R. (2004). Zero tolerance: The assumptions and the facts. *Indiana Youth Services, Education Policy Briefs, 2*(1).

Skiba, R. J., & Peterson, R. L. (2000). School discipline at a crossroads: From zero tolerance to early response. *Exceptional Children, 66,* 335–347.

Skiba, R. J., Peterson, R. L., & Williams, T. (1997). Office referrals and suspension: Disciplinary intervention in middle schools. *Education and Treatment of Children, 20,* 295–315.

Skiba, R., & Rausch, K. (2006). School disciplinary systems: Alternatives to suspension and expulsion. In G. G. Bear & K. M. Minke (Eds.), *Children's needs III: Development, prevention, and intervention.* Bethesda, MD: National Association of School Psychologists.

Smith, D. C., Adelman, H. S., Nelson, P., Taylor, L., & Phares, V. (1987). Perceived control at school and problem behavior and attitudes. *Journal of School Psychology, 25,* 167–176.

Smith, D. C., Larson, J., DeBaryshe, B., & Salzman, M. (2000). Anger management for youth: What works and for whom? In S. D. Sandhu, & C. Aspy (Eds.), *Violence in American schools: A practical guide for counselors* (pp. 217–230). Reston, VA: American Counseling Association.

Smith, D. C., Larson, J., & Nuckles, D. R. (2006). A critical analysis of school-based anger management programs for youth. In S. R. Jimerson & M. Furlong (Eds.), *Handbook of school violence and school safety* (pp. 365–382). Mahwah, NJ: Lawrence Earlbaum Associates.

Smith, D. C., & Sandhu, D. S. (2004). Toward a positive perspective on violence prevention in schools: Building connections. *Journal of Counseling and Development, 82,* 287–293.

Smith, P. K., & Sharp, S. (1994) *School bullying: Insights and perspectives.* London: Routledge.

Sprague, J. (2007). *Creating school-wide prevention and intervention strategies: Effective strategies for creating safer schools and communities.* Washington, DC: Hamilton Fish Institute on School and Community Violence.

Sprague, J., & Walker, H. (2002). *Creating school-wide prevention and intervention strategies.* Portland, OR: Northwest Regional Educational Laboratory. http://www.safetyzone. org/pdfs/ta_guides/packet_1.pdf.

Sprague, J., Walker, H., Golly, A., White, K., Meyers, D., & Shannon, T. (2001). Translating research into effective practice: The effects of a universal staff and student intervention on indicators of discipline and school safety. *Education and Treatment of Children, 24*(4), 495–512.

Stallard, P., & Salter, E. (2003). Psychological debriefing with children and young people following traumatic events. *Clinical Child Psychology and Psychiatry, 8,* 445–457.

State of Colorado. (2001). *The report of Governor Bill Owens' Columbine Review Commission.* [Electronic version]. Denver, CO: Author. http://www.state.co.us/columbine/ Columbine_20Report_WEB.pdf.

Stein, B. D., Jaycox, L. H., Kataoka, S. H., Wong, M., Tu, W., Elliott, M. N., & Fink, A. (2003). A mental health intervention for school children exposed to trauma. *Journal of the American Medical Association, 290,* 603–611.

Stiegler, K., & Lever, N. (2008). *Summary of recognized evidenced-based programs implemented by expanded school mental health programs.* Center for School Mental Health. University of Maryland School of Medicine. Retrieved on November 29, 2008, from http://csmh.umaryland. edu/resources.html/Summary%20of%20Recognized%20 Evidence%20Based%20Programs6.14.08.doc.

Stollar, S. A., Schaeffer, K. R., Skelton, S. M., Stine, K. C., Lateer-Huhn, A., & Poth, R. L. (2008). Best practices in professional development: An integrated, three-tier model of academic and behavior supports. In A. Thomas & J. Grimes (Eds.), *Best practices in school psychology V* (pp. 875–886). Bethesda, MD: National Association of School Psychologists.

Stone, G., & Dover, A. (2007). An exploration of violent attitudes in adolescent males: Personal, family, and environmental factors. *Journal of Aggression, Maltreatment, & Trauma, 15*, 59–77.

Substance Abuse and Mental Health Services Administration (SAMHSA). (1996). *Prevalence of serious emotional disturbance in children and adolescents.* Washington, DC: U.S. Department of Health & Human Services.

Substance Abuse and Mental Health Services Administration (SAMHSA). (2005). *Overview of findings from the 2004 National Survey on Drug Use and Health.* Rockville, MD: Author, Office of Applied Studies, NSDUH Series H-27, DHHS Publication No. SMA 05-4061.

Substance Abuse and Mental Health Services Administration (SAMHSA). Office of Applied Studies. (2008, September 25). *Mental health service use among youths Aged 12 to 17: 2005 and 2006.* Rockville, MD. Retrieved on November 25, 2008, from http://www.oas.samhsa.gov/2k8/MHyouthTX/MHyouthTX.pdf.

Substance Abuse and Mental Health Services Administration (SAMHSA). (n.d.[a]). *Children's mental health facts: Children and adolescents with mental, emotional and behavioral disorders.* Retrieved on February 13, 2008, from http://mentalhealth.samhsa.gov/publications/all-pubs/CA-0006/default.asp.

Substance Abuse and Mental Health Services Administration (SAMHSA). (n.d.[b]) *Systems of care.* Retrieved on February 13, 2008, from http://mentalhealth.samhsa.gov/publications/allpubs/Ca-0014/default.asp.

Substance Abuse and Mental Health Services Administration (SAMSHA). National Mental Health Information Center (n.d.[c]). *Child and adolescent mental health.* Retrieved on November 25, 2008, from http://mentalhealth.samhsa.gov/publications/allpubs/CA-0004/default.asp.

Sugai G., & Horner, R. R. (2006). A promising approach for expanding and sustaining school-wide positive behavior support. *School Psychology Review, 35*, 245–259.

Sugai, G., Horner, R. H., Dunlap, G., Hieneman, M., Lewis, T. J., Turnbull, A. P., Turnbull, H. R., III, Wickham, D., Wilcox, B., & Ruef, M. (2000). Applying positive behavior support and functional behavioral assessment in schools. *Journal of Positive Behavior Interventions, 2*(3), 131–143.

Sugai, G., Horner, R. H., & McIntosh, K. (2008). Best practices in developing a broad scale system of support for school-wide positive behavior support. In A. Thomas & J. P. Grimes (Eds.), *Best practices in school psychology V.* Bethesda, MD: National Association of School Psychologists.

Suldo, S. M., & Shaffer, E. J. (2008). Looking beyond psychopathology: The dual-factor model of mental health in youth. *School Psychology Review, 37*(1), 52–68.

Taub, J. (2002). Evaluation of the Second Step violence prevention program at a rural elementary school. *School Psychology Review, 31*, 186–200.

Taylor-Greene, S., Brown, D., Nelson, L., Longton, J., Gassman, T., Cohen, J., Swartz, J. Horner, R. H., Sugai, G., & Hall, S. (1997). School-wide behavioral support: Starting the year off right. *Journal of Behavioral Education, 7*, 99–112.

Tellen, S., Kim, Y. O., Stewart-Nava, H., Pesce, R.C., & Maher, S. (2006). Implementing Comprehensive Safe Schools Plans: Effective school and community mental health collaborations to reduce youth violence. In S. R. Jimerson & M. J. Furlong. (Eds.), *Handbook of school violence and school safety: From research to practice* (pp. 567–586). Englewood Cliffs, NJ: Earlbaum.

Texas School Safety Center. (2008). *Campus Safety and Security Audit Toolkit.* Retrieved on October 29, 2008, from http://cscs.txstate.edu/txssc/downloads/TxSSC/Audit/Campus%20Safety%20and%20Security%20Audit%20Toolkit%202008.pdf.

The British Psychological Society (2002). *Psychological debriefing: Professional practice board working party.* [Electronic copy]. Leicester: Author. http://www.bps.org.uk/downloadfile.cfm?file_uuid=1B299392-7E96-C67F-D4A092C173979F33&ext=pdf.

Thornton, T. N., Craft, C. A., Dahlberg, L. L., Lynch, B. S., Baer, K., Potter, L., Mercy, J. A., & Flowers, E. A. (2002). *Best practices of youth violence prevention: A sourcebook for community action.* Retrieved December 2008 from http://www.cdc.gov/ncipc/dvp/bestpractices/Introduction.pdf.

Tobin, T., & Sugai, G. (1996). Patterns in middle school discipline records. *Journal of Emotional and Behavioral Disorders, 4,* 82–95.

Ulman, K. H. (2004). Group interventions for treatment of trauma in adults. In B. J. Buchele & H. I. Spitz (Eds.), *Group interventions for treatment of psychological trauma.* New York: AGPA.

U. S. Department of Education. (2006a). All hazards network radio now available. *ERCM Express, 2*(4). Retrieved on October 3, 2008, from http://rems.ed.gov/views/documents/NOAA_NewsletterV2I4.pdf.

U. S. Department of Education. (2006b). Emergency "Go-Kits". *Helpful Hints for School Emergency Management, 2*(2). Retrieved on October 3, 2008, from http://rems.ed.gov/views/documents/HH_GoKits.pdf.

U. S. Department of Education. (2006c). The national incident management system (NIMS). Emergency Response and Crisis Management (ERCM) Technical Assistance Center. *ERCM Express, 2*(6), 1–12. Retrieved on September 13, 2008, from http://rems.ed.gov/views/documents/NIMS.pdf.

U. S. Department of Education. (2006d). The national incident management system and schools. *Helpful Hints for School Emergency Management, 1*(1). Retrieved on December 2, 2008, from http://rems.ed.gov/views/documents/HH_NIMS.pdf.

U. S. Department of Education. (2007a). *Balancing student privacy and school safety: A guide to the Family Educational Rights and Privacy Act (FERPA) for elementary and secondary schools.* Retrieved on April 20, 2009, from http://www.ed.gov/policy/gen/guid/fpco/brochures/elsec.html.

U. S. Department of Education. (2007b). *Family educational rights and privacy act (FERPA).* Retrieved on May 24, 2008, from http://www.ed.gov/policy/gen/guid/fpco/ferpa/index.html.

U. S. Department of Education. (2007c). *Practical information on crisis planning brochure.* Retrieved on August 13, 2008, from http://www.ed.gov/admins/lead/safety/crisisplanning.html.

U. S. Department of Education. (2007d). Steps for developing a school emergency management plan. *Helpful Hints for School Emergency Management, 2*(1). Retrieved on

October 3, 2008, from http://rems.ed.gov/views/documents/Steps4DevelopingSchoolEmergencyMgmtPlans.pdf.

U. S. Department of Education. (2007e). Tapping into nontraditional community partners for emergency management. *Emergency Response and Crisis Management Express, 3*(1), 1–8.

U. S. Department of Education (n.d.). Elementary and secondary education, subpart I—state grants (Sect. 4115). Retrieved August 10, 2009 from http://www.ed.gov/policy/elsec/leg/esea02/pg52.html#sec4115

U. S. Department of Education. (2007f). *Why No Child Left Behind will make schools safer and drug free.* Retrieved on September 7, 2008, from http://www.ed.gov/nclb/freedom/safety/keepingkids.html.

U. S. Department of Education. (2008). *REMS newsletter: Barriers to collaboration.* Retrieved on December 21, 2008, from http://rems.ed.gov/views/documents/REMSNews_Barriers_to_Collaboration.pdf.

U. S. Department of Education, Emergency Response and Crisis Management (ERCM) Technical Assistance Center. (2006). Creating emergency management plans. *ERCM Express, 2*(8). Retrieved on September 13, 2008, from http://rems.ed.gov/views/documents/CreatingPlans.pdf.

U. S. Department of Education, Emergency Response and Crisis Management (ERCM) Technical Assistance Center. (2007a). Beyond the school walls: Community events and their impact on schools. *ERCM Express, 3*(6), 1–12. Retrieved on September 13, 2008, from http://rems.ed.gov/views/documents/ERCMX_Vol3Issue6.pdf.

U. S. Department of Education, Emergency Response and Crisis Management (ERCM) Technical Assistance Center. (2007b). Coping with the death of a student or staff member. *ERCM Express, 3*(2). Retrieved on September 13, 2008, from http://rems.ed.gov/views/documents/CopingW_Death_StudentOrStaff.pdf.

U. S. Department of Education, Emergency Response and Crisis Management (ERCM), Technical Assistance Center. (2007c). Establishing and developing strategic partnerships with media representatives. *Helpful Hints for School Emergency Management, 2*(8). Retrieved August 10, 2009 from http://rems.ed.gov/views/documents/HH_Vol2Issue8.pdf.

U. S. Department of Education, Readiness and Emergency Management for Schools (REMS). (2008a). *School emergency supplies and "Go-Kits."* Retrieved on November 12, 2008, from http://rems.ed/gov/views/documents/EmergencySupplies_n_GoKit101705.doc.

U. S. Department of Education, Readiness and Emergency Management for Schools (REMS) Technical Assistance Center. (2008b). [Electronic version]. *Helpful hints for school emergency management: Psychological first aid (PFA) for students and teachers: Listen, Protect, Connect— Model and teach.* http://www.ready.gov/kids/_downloads/PFA_SchoolCrisis.pdf.

United States Department of Health & Human Services (DHHS). (2001). *Youth violence: A report of the Surgeon General.* Rockville, MD: U.S. Department of Health & Human Services, Substance Abuse and Mental Health Administration, Center for Mental Health Services, National Institute of Health, National Institute of Mental Health. http://www.ncbi.nlm.nih.gov/books/bv.fcgi?rid=hstat5.chapter.12080.

United States Department of Health & Human Services (DHHS), Health Resources and Services Administration, Maternal and Child Health Bureau. (n.d.). *Misdirections in bullying prevention and intervention.* Retrieved on April 20, 2009, from http://stopbullyingnow.hrsa.gov/HHS_PSA/pdfs/SBN_Tip_5.pdf.

United States Departments of Health & Human Services, Justice and Education. (2007). *Report to the president on issues raised by the Virginia Tech tragedy.* Retrieved on February 15, 2009, from http://www.hhs.gov/vtreport.pdf.

United States Department of Homeland Security. (2007). *Homeland security exercise and evaluation program (HSEEP).* Washington, DC. Retrieved on August 14, 2008, from https://hseep.dhs.gov/pages/1001_HSEEP7.aspx.

United States Department of Homeland Security. (2008, January). *National Response Framework.* Washington, DC. http://www.fema.gov/emergency/nrf/.

United States Department of Justice, Bureau of Justice Statistics. (2003). *School crime supplement to the national crime victimization survey.* Washington DC: Author.

United States Government Accountability Office (U.S. GAO). (2007, June). *Emergency management: Most school districts have developed emergency management plans, but would benefit from additional federal guidance.* Washington, DC: Author: (GAO-07-609). Retrieved on August 15, 2008, from http://www.gao.gov/new.items/d07609.pdf.

United States Office of Special Education Programs (OSEP), National Technical Assistance Center on Positive Behavior Interventions and Supports. (n.d.). *What is school-wide PBS?* Retrieved on November 25, 2008, from http://www.pbis.org/schoolwide.htm.

United States Secret Service and U. S. Department of Education. (2008). *Prior knowledge of potential school-based violence: Information students learn may prevent a targeted attack.* Washington DC: Author.

Vam Schoiack-Edstrom, L., Frey, K. S., & Beland, K. (2002). Changing adolescents attitudes about relational and physical aggression: An early evaluation of a school-based intevention. *School Psychology Review*, 31, 210–216.

Veenman, M. V. J., Kerseboom, L., & Imthorn, C. (2000). Test anxiety and metacognitive skillfulness: Availability versus production deficiencies. *Anxiety, Stress, and Coping, 13,* 391–412.

Vossekuil, B., Reddy, M., Fein., R., Borum, R., & Modzeleski, W. (2000). *U.S.S.S. Safe Schools Initiative. An interim report on the prevention of targeted violence in schools.* Washington, DC: U.S. Secret Service, Threat Assessment Center.

Vossekuil, B., Reddy, M., Fein., R., Borum, R., & Modzeleski, W. (2002). *The final report and findings of the safe schools initiative: Implications for the prevention of school attacks in the United States.* Washington, DC: U.S. Department of Education, Office of Elementary and Secondary Education, Safe and Drug Free Schools Program, and U.S. Secret Service, National Threat Assessment Center.

Walker, H. M. (2001). *School safety issues and prevention strategies: The changing landscape of what we know.* Retrieved December 2008 from http://www.cde.state.co.us/cdesped/download/pdf/brm_SchoolSafetyPreventionStrategies.pdf.

Walker, H. M. (2004). Use of evidence-based interventions in schools: Where we've been, where we are, and where we need to go. *School Psychology Review, 33,* 398–407.

Walsh, B. (2006). *Treating self-injury: A practical guide.* New York: Guilford Press.

Warner, B. S., Weist, M. D., & Krulak, A. (1999). Risk factors for school violence. *Urban Education, 34,* 52–68.

Warren, J., Edmonson, H., Griggs, P., Lassen, S., McCart, A., Turnbull, A., & Sailor, W. (2003). Urban applications of school-wide positive behavior support: Critical issues and lessons learned. *Journal of Positive Behavior Interventions*, 5(2), 80–92.

Webster Dictionary. (2008). Retrieved on July 25, 2008, from http://www.merriam-webster.com/dictionary/crisis.

Weissberg, R. P. (2004). *U.S. Senate committee on health, education, labor and pensions*. Statement before the subcommittee on substance abuse and mental health services. Retrieved March 2006 from www.k12coordinator.org/testimony.pdf.

WestEd. (1997). *California Healthy Kids Survey*. Retrieved June 2008 from http://www.wested.org/cs/we/view/pj/245.

WestEd. (2003). Student well-being. Essential to academic success. *R&D Alert, 5*(1), 8–9.

WestEd. (2004). *What does the HKS offer you?* Retrieved on January 9, 2009, from http://www.wested.org/chks/pdf/hks_flyer_04.pdf.

Wester, K. L., & Trepal, H. C. (2005). Working with clients who self-injure: Providing alternatives. *Journal of College Counseling, 8*, 180–198.

White Kreiss, V. E., Gibson, D. M., & Reynolds, C. A. (2004). Adolescents who self-injure: Implications and strategies for school counselors. *Professional School Counseling, 7*, 195–201.

Whitlock, J., & Knox, K. L. (2007). The relationship between self-injurious behavior and suicide in a young adult population. *Archives of Pediatric and Adolescent Medicine, 161*, 634–640.

Whitlock, J. L., Powers, J. L., & Eckenrode, J. (2006). The virtual cutting edge: The Internet and adolescent self-injury. *Developmental Psychology, 42*, 401–417.

Wittmann, M., Estibaliz, A., & Santisteban, C. (2008). How impulsiveness, trait anger, and extracurricular activities might affect aggression in school children. *Personality and Individual Differences, 45*, 618–623.

Workgroup on Adapting Latino Services. (2008). *Adaptation guidelines for serving Latino children and families affected by trauma* (1st ed.). San Diego, CA: Chadwick Center for Children and Families.

Wyles, P. (2007). Success with wraparound: A collaborative, individualized, integrated and strengths based model. *Youth Studies Australia, 25*(6), 45–53.

Yalom, I. D. (1970). *Theory and practice of group psychother-apy.* New York: Basic Books.

Yates, T. M. (2004). The developmental psychopathology of self-injurious behavior: Compensatory regulation in posttrau-matic adaptation. *Clinical Psychology Review, 24,* 35–74.

Zins, J. E., Weissberg, R. P., Wang, M. C., & Walberg, H. J. (Eds.). (2004). *Building academic success on social and emo-tional learning: What does the research say?* New York: Teachers College Press.

Index

A

Adequate Yearly Progress, 20
Anger management, 210

B

Bully-Proofing Your School, 65
Bullying, 65, 224. *See also*
    Violence in schools

C

CARES model, 65, 66f
    asset-building, 164–165
    communities are connected,
      164
    components, 164
    creation, 161, 164
    expectations, clear, 164,
      165–166
    large suburban school, real-
      world example of use
      in, 173, 181
    research-based model,
      183–188t
    responsive decision making,
      164, 165
    social-emotional-behavioral
      skills, 164, 166
Cherry Creek School District
    Comprehensive Safe
    Schools Plan, 28–30,
    63, 66f
    CARES model (*see* CARES
      model)
    NIMS model, use of, 111–113
    resources created by, 73–74
    Safe Schools Design Team,
      72–75
    threat assessment, 244–245
Child abuse, 234

Classroom-based crisis
    interventions (CCI),
    274–276
Code of silence. *See also*
    Violence in schools
    breaking, 216–217, 222–224
    real-world example, 224–225
    staff identification of
      students, 222–223
    tip lines (*see* Tip lines)
    warning signs, 223–224
Columbine High School
    shooting, 63–64
Crime Stoppers, 217
Crisis
    characteristics of, 9
    defining, 8
    impacts of, 99
    M-PHAT approach (*see*
      M-PHAT)
    preparedness (*see*
      Preparedness, crisis)
    prevention (*see* Crisis
      prevention)
    response planning (*see*
      Response planning)
    response teams (*see* Crisis
      teams; Safety teams)
Crisis go-kits, 93, 94t
Crisis prevention, 7
    planning, 28–30
    prevention-mitigation, 12–13
Crisis responders, stress
    reactions of, 281–282.
    See also Crisis teams
Crisis teams
    District Crisis Teams, 107,
      108
    importance, 99–100
    large schools, 112f

NIMS Incident Command
    System (*see* NIMS
    Incident Command
    System)
response planning, 132, 133f,
    134
roles and responsibilities,
    114–118t
small schools, 113f
stress reactions, 281–282

D

Debriefing, 262–263
Department of Homeland
    Security school-based
    psychological first aid,
    276, 279
Drills and exercises, safety
anxiety caused by, 139
elements of, 138
learning objectives, 136–138t
procedures, 140–141t
usage, 134–135
Dropout rates, 219
Drugs and alcohol. *See*
    Substance abuse
    prevention

E

Emergency response kits, 93, 94t

F

Family Educational Rights and
    Privacy Act, 26–27,
    221–222
Federal Emergency Management
    Agency
multi-hazard emergency
    planning for schools,
    36–38
Risk Index Worksheet, 54–55t
Functional Family Therapy
    (FFT), 247–248

G

Grief counseling, 211–213
Group and classroom-based
    crisis interventions
    (CCI), 274–276

I

Incident Command System,
    NIMS. *See* NIMS
    Incident Command
    System
Individual crisis interventions
    (ICI), 272–273
Interventions, crisis
early and targeted (*see*
    Targeted interventions)
evidence-based, 166–168,
    174–181t
group and classroom-based
    crisis interventions,
    274–276
individual crisis
    interventions, 272–273
intensive/indicated/tier 3,
    18–20, 219, 279–280 (*see
    also* Risk behaviors)
overview, 16
school psychological
    interventions, 277t
targeted/selected/tier 2, 18,
    268–270
universal level/tier 1, 16, 18,
    157–158t, 160t, 161f

L

Listen, Protect, Connect—Model
    and Teach, 276, 278t,
    279
Lockdown, 91–92

M

M-PHAT, 8. *See also* Specific
    elements of
comprehensive safe learning
    environment model, 32f

multi-agency elements, 16
multi-hazards plan, 15–16
multi-tiered intervention
    elements, 16, 18–20
overview, 11
preparedness, 13
prevention-mitigation, 12–13
recovery, 14–15
response, 14, 123 (*see also*
    Response planning)
Media, working with, 143–144,
    250
Medical emergencies, 92–93,
    110t
Memorials, guidelines for,
    282–284
Mental health issues, student
    collaborative care, 246
    community agency
        involvement, 246–248
    Functional Family Therapy
        (FFT), 247–248
    prevalence, 193–194, 245
    wraparound services,
        246–247
Mental Health Parity Act, 192
Multi-hazards safety planning
    accidents and medical
        emergencies, 92–93
    building and system control
        and procedures, 86,
        89–90t, 90–92
    categories, 98
    communications, 85–86,
        90–91
    FEMA plan (*see under*
        Federal Emergency
        Management Agency)
    first responders, 84–85
    framework, 82
    hazard-specific building
        response, 96
    lockdown, 91–92
    M-PHAT model, 15–16
    modifications for schools,
        83–84
    multi-agency collaboration,
        84–86

natural disasters/weather,
    94–96
overview, 81–82, 86
parental reunification, 92
perimeter security, 91
preparedness plan, 10-step,
    87–88t
protocols, 82–83
psychological safety
    response, 96–97
staff preparation, 83, 84–85
types of hazards, 82, 84

N

National Incident Management
    System. *See* NIMS
    Incident Command
    System
Natural disasters, 3
    NOAA Weather All Hazards
        Alert radios, 94–95
    preparedness, 21, 94–96
NIMS Incident Command
    System, 100
    command and management,
        103, 106–107, 108–109
    communication and
        information
        management, 103
    compliance, 102–103
    coordinators, 110–111
    development of, 103–104
    district crisis team, 107
    flow chart of command, 107f
    government
        recommendations, 101
    medical triage, 110t
    ongoing management and
        maintenance, 103
    overview, 101
    personnel training, school,
        101–102
    preparedness, 103
    resource management, 103
    roles, assigning, 119–121t
    specific personnel positions,
        104–106
    supporting technologies, 103

No Child Left Behind Act, 16, 20
  Unsafe School Choice Policy,
    24–25
  zero-tolerance policy, 25–26
NOAA Weather All Hazards
    Alert radios, 94–95

P

Parents
  crisis and trauma recovery,
    role in, 271–272t
  involvement in prevention
    efforts, 159
  reunification following crisis
    (*see* Reunification
    planning)
Perimeter security, 91
Physical safety, 4
  audit, 39–41, 42–53t
  characteristics of, 9–10
  data assessment, 63–64
  defining, 9
  planning, 31t
  prevention strategies,
    148–151
Positive Behavior for Effective
    Schools Act, 27–28
Positive Behavior Interventions
    and Supports (PBIS), 4,
    153f, 154f
Positive Behavior Supports
    (PBS), 4, 153f, 154f
Preparedness, crisis, 7
  natural disasters (*see* Natural
    disasters)
  overview, 13
  planning, 28–30, 87–88t (*see
    also* Multi-hazards
    safety planning)
Prevention, crisis
  coordination, 159–161
  evidence-based interventions,
    166–168, 174–181t
  overview, 147–148
  physical safety precautions,
    148–151
  psychological (*see*
    Psychological safety)

resources for, 168–169,
    170–173t
  universal prevention and
    precaution programs,
    157–158t, 160t, 161f
Privacy issues
  Family Educational Rights
    and Privacy Act, 26–27,
    221–222
Psychoeducation, 266–268, 269t
Psychological first aid, 262–263
Psychological safety, 4
  anxiety issues, 151
  assessment, 41, 53, 56, 57–59t,
    61, 62–63t
  assessment data, 41
  behavior recognition and
    reinforcement, 152–153,
    154f, 155
  characteristics of, 11
  climate/culture, overall, 156
  data assessment, 64–65,
    67–68
  interventions, school-wide,
    151–152
  models for prevention efforts,
    162–163t
  overview, 10–11
  parental involvement, 159
  planning, 31t
  positive youth development,
    156, 159
  psychological triage (*see*
    Triage, psychological)
  recovery issues, 251
  response planning, 96–97
  social-emotional skill
    building, 155–156, 166

R

Recovery, crisis
  adult help, 270t
  Cherry Creek model, 75
  classroom meetings, 265–266
  media communications, 250
  overview, 14–15, 249–250
  parent help, 271–272t
  physical cleanup, 250

physical safety assessment, 251–253

psychoeducation, 266–268, 269t

psychological recovery, 251, 262

reactions, crisis, 254–256, 257t, 260

reopening, 250

threat perception, 254

Response planning

components of plan, 126–131t, 135f

comprehensiveness, 124–125

district level, 124–125

drills (see Drills and exercises, safety)

media component, 143–144

overview, 123–124

school crisis team response (see Crisis teams)

school level, 124–125

school/building level plans, 125, 132

staff response plan, 134

Reunification planning, 92, 141, 142–143t

Risk behaviors

abuse victims, prevalence among, 234

legal issues, 221–222

overview, 220

policy issues, 221–222

preventive measures, 220

self-injury, 233–234, 235–236t

suicide (see Suicide prevention)

zero-tolerance policy (see Zero-tolerance policy)

S

Safe schools

barriers to establishing, 7–8

characteristics of, 5–7

comprehensive assessment example, 61, 63–65, 67–68

comprehensive planning, 28–30, 31t

data establishment, 63

hostile learning environments, 219

overview, 5–6

physical safety (see Physical safety)

psychological safety (see Psychological safety)

response planning (see Response planning)

safety teams (see Safety teams)

stakeholders (see Stakeholders)

Safe Schools/Health Students Initiative, 248

Safety teams

crisis teams, overlap with, 70–71

establishing, 68, 70–72

evaluative role, 71–72

school district-level, 68

Sexual abuse, 234

Sexual assault, 234

Shelters, weather-related, 95–96

Social support systems, 263–265

Social-emotional interventions

anger management, 210

divorce coping skills, 213

effective, components of, 212t

emotional regulations, teaching, 209–210

grief and loss coping skills, 211–213

overview, 204, 205–209t

social skills training and problem solving, 210–211

substance abuse prevention (see Substance abuse prevention)

suicide prevention (see Suicide prevention)

Social-Emotional Learning (SEL), 4

Stakeholders

barriers to collaboration,
35–36
community agencies, 75–77
data analysis, 69t
data gathering, 38–39
data summary worksheet, 60f
identifying, 34–35
importance of, 33–34
physical safety audit data,
39–41, 42–53t
psychological safety
assessment data, 41, 53,
56, 57–59t, 61, 62–63t
safety teams (*see* Safety
teams)
Substance abuse prevention, 3,
4, 213
awareness of, 237
statistics on prevalence, 234,
236
Suicide prevention, 213
assessment by trained staff,
227
best practices, 227–229
documentation of risk, 233
gatekeeper training, 225–226
intervention, 228f
safety issue, 225–227
threat response, 228t,
230–232t
warning signs, 226t
Suspension, alternatives to, 202,
203–204t

T

Targeted interventions
academic outcomes, 195, 202
benefits of, 194–196
code of silence, breaking (*see*
Code of silence)
defining, 190–192
educational outcomes, 195
evidence-based, 196–197
instructional gaps, 200f
necessity for, 192–194
overview, 189
risk factors, 214, 215–216t

school demands versus
student functioning,
199–201
selecting the intervention,
197–198
selecting the participants,
198
social-emotional (*see*
Social-emotional
interventions)
staff resources, 199
staff training, 198, 214
types of, 201–202
warning signs, 214, 216
Threat response
assessment, 237, 239–240,
241t
categorizing, 242
documentation, 244
evaluation, 242
interventions, matching
to level of concern,
243–244
planning and intervention,
238–239t
real-life example, 244–245
Tip lines, 217–218, 222
Trauma
assessment, 251–253
crisis exposure as assessment
variable, 253
impact on learning, 3–4
reactions to, 256, 258–259t
stressors, defining, 251
vulnerability assessment,
253–254
Triage, medical, 110t
Triage, psychological
overview of process, 260
primary level, 260–261
secondary level, 261
tertiary level, 261
Truancy, 202

V

Violence in schools
code of silence, breaking (*see*
Code of silence)

Columbine High School
     shooting (*see*
     Columbine High
     School shooting)
crime statistics, 20–21,
     22–23t
disciplinary infractions,
     20–21
increase in, 3
legislation, 24
No Child Left Behind Act
     (*see* No Child Left
     Behind Act)
perceptions of crime, 21

prevention programs,
     ineffective, 166–167
threats (*see* Threat response)
tip lines, 217–218
warning signs in attackers,
     7–8, 214, 216, 223–224

W

Wraparound services, 246–247

Z

Zero-tolerance policy, 25–26,
     220

CD Contents

CHAPTER 2

Brief School Climate Survey—Summary Report
Psychological Safety Progress Review—Revised
Sample: Emergency Response and Crisis Management
(ERCM) Preparedness Template

CHAPTER 4

Colorado Senate Bill 08-181 Position Paper

CHAPTER 5

Media:
　　Helpful Hints: Establishing and Developing Strategic
　　　　Partnerships With Media Representatives
　　NASP: Responsible Media Coverage of Crisis Events
　　　　Impacting Children
　　NASP: Suggestions for Dealing with Media

Comprehensive Safe School Plan Checklist
Checklist: Evaluating the Crisis Response
Sample School Staff Crisis Response Plan
Specific Guidelines for Conducting Crisis Drills and
　　Exercises

CHAPTER 8

Sample Documentation of Suicide Risk Intervention
Sample Danger Assessment and Intervention Plan
(DAIP)
Trees and Other Interventions for Aggressive or Dangerous
　　Behavior
Parent Tips: Keeping Your Child Safe

CHAPTER 9

NASP: Memorials/Rituals/Activities Following Traumatic
   Events
Tips for Helping Children:
   Tips for Adults
   Tips for Parent With Infants and Toddlers
   Tips for Parent With Preschool Children
   Tips for Parent With School-Age Children
   Tips for Parent With Adolescents